CULTURE LEARNING: THE FIFTH DIMENSION IN THE LANGUAGE CLASSROOM

CULTURE LEARNING: THE FIFTH DIMENSION IN THE LANGUAGE CLASSROOM

LOUISE DAMEN

SANDRA J. SAVIGNON
Consulting Editor

ADDISON-WESLEY PUBLISHING COMPANY

Reading, Massachusetts • Menlo Park, California
Don Mills, Ontario • Wokingham, England • Amsterdam • Sydney • Bonn
Singapore • Tokyo • Madrid • Bogota • Santiago • San Juan

THE ADDISON-WESLEY SECOND LANGUAGE PROFESSIONAL LIBRARY SERIES

Sandra J. Savignon
Consulting Editor

CANTONI-HARVEY, Gina
Content-Area Language Instruction

CONNOR, Ulla and KAPLAN, Robert
Writing Across Languages: Analysis of L2 Text

DUBIN, Fraida, ESKEY, David and GRABE, William
Teaching Second Language Reading for Academic Purposes

HIGGINS, John and JOHNS, Tim
Computers in Language Learning

MOHAN, Bernard A.
Language and Content

PENFIELD, Joyce
The Media: Catalysts for Communicative Language Learning

SAVIGNON, Sandra J.
Communicative Competence: Theory and Classroom Practice

SAVIGNON, Sandra J. and BERNS, Margie S.
Initiatives in Communicative Language Teaching Volumes I and II

SMITH, Stephen M.
The Theater Arts and the Teaching of Second Languages

VENTRIGLIA, Linda
Conversations of Miguel and Maria

WALLERSTEIN, Nina
Language and Culture in Conflict

Library of Congress Cataloging-in-Publication Data

Damen, Louise.
  Culture learning.

  Bibliography: p.
  Includes index.
    1. Language and languages—Study and teaching. 2. Intercultural communication. 3. Intercultural education. 4. Language and culture. I. Title.
  P53.45.D36 1986   418'.007   86-3630
  ISBN 0-201-11478-X

ISBN: 0-201-11478-X
ABCDEFGHIJ-AL-8987

To Cheryl

Contents

List of Tables, Figures, Exercises, and Examples

Tables

Figures

Exercises

Examples

Preface

Research and practice in the fields of intercultural communication and second or foreign language learning and teaching have generally followed similar paths of inquiry and application. Both have examined the nature of culture, language, and communication, but have approached them from different perspectives.

In the case of the former, major concerns have been communicative styles and goals, training for intercultural communication, and the role of language and cultural patterns in communicative effectiveness. The focus of the latter has been upon the variables affecting second language learning and methods to facilitate the acquisition of a new linguistic system. Few professionals have dared to bridge the gap between the two fields.

Yet, today several circumstances bring into question a continuation of this separate but equal pursuit of common professional concerns. First, the current dedication to the development of the communicative competence of language learners mandates the development of intercultural communicative skills and an understanding of the processes of culture learning on the part of students and teachers alike. Thus, knowledge of major research questions, theory, training methods, and practice in the field of intercultural communication must be incorporated as a part of the professional preparation of present-day language teachers. Second, there is a need for professionals in the field of intercultural communication to understand the particular circumstances, problems, and variables at work in the multicultural language classroom so that those who do bridge the gap between the two fields receive the maximum benefits from the exchange. Professionals in both fields have much to share.

Finally, the complexities of any multicultural context in which intercultural contact and communication must take place are so great that the building of bridges, theoretical and practical, seems the better part of wisdom for all concerned. In so doing, professionals in intercultural communication will discover that verbal language and nonverbal behavior as major channels of human communication are also important variables in the processes of intercultural communication and cross-cultural miscommunication. Language practitioners, on the other hand, will learn that they can no longer limit their efforts to the strictly verbal and pretend that they are teaching communicative skills. They can no longer confine their instruction to "culture-free, out-of-context" practice in "meaning-free" linguistic patterns.

It is time to build two-way, multi-lane bridges of interchange so that professionals in intercultural communication and in second or foreign language learning may combine forces to their mutual benefit and to the ultimate advantage of their students. Together they may profitably explore the multifaceted concepts of language and culture and their roles in human interaction. Their combined efforts should enhance research and practice in both fields.

About This Book

Although this book has been specifically designed for the training and guiding of classroom teachers of English as a second or as a foreign language practicing in the United States, its approach to culture and language learning need not be so restricted. Because culture and language learning are part of the human condition, the theory and insights contained in this book are valid in and generalizable to many other contexts.

This book represents syntheses of salient findings, theories, conclusions, and practice that shed light upon the relationship of language and culture learning. Care has been taken to support observation and suggested activities with appropriate documentation from research and practice in the academic disciplines of anthropology, sociology, psychology, and communication. To the many researchers and eminent scholars whose works have been cited, this author expresses gratitude for the permission to do so. Any interpretive or translation errors are hers alone.

This book has been divided into two sections. Part I is concerned with the development of the field of intercultural communication, definitions of the major concepts of *communication* and *culture*, and discussion of the processes of language and culture learning in general, as well as the major variables affecting these processes, including nonverbal behavior, values and beliefs, and cultural themes and patterns.

Each chapter contains a list of suggested readings, discussion questions, and learning exercises. The readers who follow the suggested exercises will practice the major processes of culture learning through personal exploration and experience. Some culture-specific information is supplied by means of the examples provided to illustrate major points or concepts. Readers are expected to become "expert" in culture-specific points through the choice of a "target culture" to study. The results of individual study, when shared in the study group or class, will not only provide interesting and pertinent information about given cultural groups but will also shed light upon the perils and pitfalls as well as the joys of culture learning.

This approach has been named "pragmatic ethnography" to distinguish it from professional anthropological practice. This is not an attempt to impose a neologism; it is intended to alert the readers to the fact that they are undergoing a simulation in culture learning—but culture learning undertaken with open eyes and for the purpose of learning how to learn a culture.

The second portion of the book is devoted to theory in practice. It outlines the theoretical and practical elements to be considered in the planning, implementation, and evaluation of culturally sensitive curricula and projects in second or foreign language classrooms. The readers are asked to plan, implement, and evaluate teaching projects or modules. If practice does make perfect, then these lessons, activities, and evaluations in the language classroom should, at the very least, make familiar the ways and bring the means to make culture learning the fifth dimension in the language classroom.

To the Teacher

This book may serve as a learning guide for both students and teachers. Each chapter contains a list of suggested readings, discussion questions, and learning activities. Answers to the questions are interspersed throughout the text. Additional insights are contained in the recommended readings.

Students are requested to follow an eclectic model of cognitive cultural training and actual practice. This model introduces basic theory and concepts related to language and culture learning by means of secondary materials and personal experience. Both knowledge sources are important; to limit training to one or the other is to restrict the possible benefits of the approach.

The Glossary at the end of this book contains brief definitions of key terms. The contents of this book have been presented in a manner that affords maximum opportunities for student participation. The book is organized in a spiral format so that key concepts and perspectives are examined in ever greater depth as the knowledge and the expertise of the students grow.

Additional information concerning the development of the communicative competence of students is contained in other volumes in this series: *Communicative Competence: Theory and Classroom Practice* by Sandra J. Savignon (1983) and *Initiatives in Communicative Language Teaching. A Book of Readings* (*Vols. I and II*) by Sandra J. Savignon and Margie S. Berns (eds.) (1984 and 1987).

To the Student

This is first and foremost a practical guide to the understanding of the processes of intercultural communication, and to the relationships of these processes to second/foreign language learning and teaching.

The reader is asked—indeed strongly urged—to embark upon a personal adventure in culture learning. It is hoped that this active learning and understanding-by-doing may well serve as the first vital step in learning to "walk in another's shoes"—that is, to develop empathy or the ability to transcend one's own cultural world.

It is the conviction of the author that each individual life span is a continuing journey in culture learning, repeatedly punctuated by cross-cultural adventures. These experiences provide the impetus for personal growth and development over a lifetime. It is hoped that the lessons learned herein will be good for use in life as well as in the classroom, and, further, that they will be good for life. *Bon voyage!*

Acknowledgments

This book has been made possible through the support of those students and friends who have been so eager to accompany me on a journey of culture learning. Their desire to learn has been the source of the energy and will needed to complete this volume and share our adventures. No one has been more rewarded by the experience of completing this volume than its author.

My unending gratitude goes to my husband, my son and daughter-in-law, my friends and colleagues, and my elderly cat, who have supported my efforts even through periods of benign neglect and outright panic. Their contributions are not documented in the bibliographic entries, yet without them this book would have remained an unfulfilled dream.

Finally, I would be remiss if I did not express my gratitude to my friend and colleague, Barbara Sinnott. Her sharp editorial pencil unraveled many a convoluted phrase and erased more than one grammatical sin. Her unrelenting insistence on putting the right word in the right place was invaluable. Furthermore, she read the whole thing!

To all, *merci, mille fois!*

Part I

Theory, Research, and Practice in the Fields of Intercultural Communication and Second Language Learning/Teaching

Chapter 1

Culture Learning: The Fifth Dimension in the Language Classroom

1.1 A TRUE STORY

"How many of you come from families of more than five children?" asked the North American teacher one dreary Friday afternoon, in a desperate effort to unglaze the eyes of her student charges during a discussion of a story about a family with a dozen children.

She looked around the classroom. She saw Phung, Abdullah, Chulala, Ahmad, a sweet young thing from Venezuela, a passel of boys from Surinam, and three seemingly impassive Japanese faces.

A soft voice from the back of the room said, "Eleven." That was Phung from Vietnam; only part of her family was in the States with her. She was always depressed by discussions of family.

Ahmad from Saudi Arabia replied, "I come from a family of eleven, too." Heads whirled as Abdullah from Jordan offered, "Thirty."

"Thirty!" all countered as one, except for the Japanese, who maintained a monolithic silence.

Leo from Surinam turned toward the Middle Eastern enclave in the room, and asked, "Say, how many wives can you have?" To the teacher's dismay, he added, "I hear you can have seven wives—one for every day of the week. . . ."

Abdullah quickly countered with, "And I have been wondering about you Christians. Why can't nuns and priests get married? It is everyone's duty to get married!"

As a chorus of voices rose in a Tower-of-Babelian response, the teacher wondered why she had ever asked such a question. This class had been meeting for more than a month, five hours a day. Finally, she thought, they're beginning to ask some good questions, but somewhat less explosive issues might have launched a more meaningful cultural exchange. What should she do—(a) change the subject; (b) let them argue; (c) join the discussion and present her point of view; (d) none of the above; (e) all of the above?

Although some type of intercultural contact was taking place in that classroom, an untrained observer might have had a hard time deciding whether communication or miscommunication was being effected. In the short space of a few minutes, cultural values and beliefs, misunderstandings, and culture shock had become unexpected parts of that day's lesson. The issues were important, but was the context appropriate?

The teacher's reactions are of more importance than any subsequent action she may have taken. All too often teachers are reluctant to allow such confrontational cultural probing. When it does happen, they are prone to calm troubled waters by choosing option (a). Yet it may well be that such episodes are made to order for opening our classroom doors to culture learning. They provide insight into the complexities of intercultural communication in multicultural contexts, uncover cross-cultural differences, and provide a first step toward real understanding. Perhaps we as teachers should elect to choose option (e) and search for acceptable and appropriate responses. If culture is to have a respected role in the language classroom, we must become more comfortable with all that it implies than we are now.

1.2 MAKING THE CULTURAL CONNECTION

It is generally accepted that specialized training is required in order to provide guidance in the acquisition of a new linguistic system. Although largely unrecognized, there is an equally compelling need to train our teachers as cultural guides.

While cultural guidance is seldom part of the stated curriculum of the ESL (English as a Second Language), EFL (English as a Foreign Language), or any language classroom, [1] [2] it is nonetheless often a part of the hidden agenda, a pervasive but unrecognized dimension, coloring expectations, perceptions, reactions, teaching and learning strategies, and is, more often than not, a contributing factor in the success or failure of second or foreign language learning and acquisition.

Thus, language learning implies and embraces culture learning.[3] In what manner and to what degree may be questioned by experts in the fields of language learning and linguistics, but the connection cannot be denied. A seemingly unstructured or even cavalier approach to culture learning in the second or foreign language classroom speaks to the inherent risks and difficulties involved in tinkering with someone else's rules for living. Yet the teaching of another language to someone who has already acquired competence in both the language and the culture of another portion of our common world makes this tinkering inevitable. To become bilingual means to become bicultural to some degree.

Indeed, success in learning a second or even third language is partially related to the acquisition of the cultural baggage that is carried along with any linguistic system.

It may be assumed that most language teachers, second or foreign, are culturally sensitive to an extent; some of us have had extensive experience in cross-cultural communication. Rarely are we cross-culturally sophisticated in more than one or two cultures, or in any depth, except in our native cultures. We do have some clues. We may notice the averted eyes of the Latin American student who is being chastised. We may understand the purpose of the embarrassed giggle of the Asian who has lost "face." We may know how to encourage the silent and out-shout the reciters. We realize that such student behavior has its roots in cross-cultural differences. But is it enough just to know about different patterns of social response? How should we feel when we discover, after years of teaching, that the check mark we have been using to indicate satisfactory work has been interpreted as failure by our students from Japan? Who would not feel a sense of shame and frustration when a student, who had accumulated enough cultural *savoir faire* to do so, finally reveals that he thought he had failed all previous levels of language study, or, at least, had merely received social promotions?

1.3 LIMITATIONS AND CHALLENGES

Why are we not more competent and self-assured in guiding our students toward the attainment of linguistic and cultural competence? Must we continue to send them out into the "real" world so ill-prepared to know what is happening? Often the student request for more "conversation" is simply a plea to explain the rules—rules of the game we are all playing as native users of shared linguistic and cultural systems.

We, of course, are not deliberately holding out. There are several reasons for the limitations of our efficiency as cultural guides. First, we do not know what "culture" to teach, and, if we did, we might be uncomfortable about the ethics of doing so. It appears to be acceptable to assist in the change of a student's linguistic code, but somewhat less desirable to delve into the touchier subject of cross-cultural *do's* and *don'ts*, except on a fairly superficial level.

Second, until recently only a few textbooks of methodologies have been available to aid us in the direction of culture learning. The insertion into lesson plans of inventories of cultural tidbits, which can be gleaned from a wide variety of sources including anthropological studies, guides for business men and women going overseas, counseling studies, and the uncle who has just returned from a two-week trip to Riyadh, is often counterproductive.

However, the recognition of cultural and linguistic variations in performance need not preclude the acceptance of universals or generalizations; indeed, the differences noted are but reflections of universal themes of human experience.

Therefore, if we are to give full due to the role of cultural training and culture learning in language acquisition, we must deal with both similarities and differences. We must not continue resting on our universals. To remain in the deep-structured grip of the social scientists to whom cross-cultural generalizations are primary research goals is more likely to result in a continuation of an off-hand approach to culture learning than in the implementation of a real commitment to forging the cultural connection in our language classrooms.

In order to make this link, adequate and appropriate skills must be acquired by teachers. This task—to assist and enhance the development of the cultural and linguistic competence of students—should not be undertaken by untrained, albeit well-intentioned, "natives." To succeed in the goal of assisting cultural travelers to adjust to their new worlds to the degree and to the level they desire, we, as trainers, must first be trained. We can begin with an examination of the relationship of language learning and intercultural communication. For the moment, intercultural communication will be defined as communication between two persons or groups not sharing similar cultural patterns.

1.4 THE LANGUAGE AND CULTURE EQUATION IN THE CLASSROOM

As stated in the Preface of this book, the fields of intercultural communication and second language learning/teaching[4] have evolved separately. Yet professionals in both fields are being drawn together by renewed interest in common concerns. These include the relationship of language and culture in human communication, the understanding of the communicative functions of language, and the development of the communicative competence of their clients, be they language students, business executives, diplomats, or tourists. All these persons are involved in some form of intercultural communication when they venture outside their own cultural nests.

First and Second Language and Culture Acquisition

It is necessary to recognize at the outset that the acquisition of a first or native language and that of an additional language or languages differ in terms of the characteristics of the physical, cognitive, affective, and linguistic processes by which they are effected (Brown 1980a:46). In the same way, the acquisition of a first culture (enculturation) and that of a second or additional culture (acculturation) exhibit unique variations. This is to say that although language learning and culture learning are interdependent and mutually reinforcing, the processes differ from each other in first as well as in subsequent acquisitions. It is the nature of all these differences that the language teacher must understand. Findings relative to given strategies, attitudes, motivation, language ego, and other significant variables identified in research in first and second language and culture acquisition are contained in the work of Ausubel (1964), Dulay and Burt (1972, 1974a, 1974b), Guiora *et al.* (1972), Krashen (1976, 1982), Lenneberg (1967), Scovel (1969), and others. Some of the answers to the Language 1 (L1) + Culture 1 (C1)/ Language 2 (L2) + Culture (C2) equation that every language teacher must solve may be found in the interplay of these variables.

Thus, "inhabitants" of second or foreign language classrooms are engaged in culture learning and attempting intercultural communication just as surely as those who embark upon packaged tours to parts unknown. Although some may see the classroom context as more conducive to language learning than language acquisition (Krashen 1976, 1982), it may still provide a specialized environment for intercultural communication and learning. In some cases, this is the only way in which cultural contact can be made. Therefore, the environment of the classroom should be made as open as possible to meaningful culture learning.

The Classroom as a Specialized Context

The language classroom, as a specialized context for language and culture learning, has both disadvantages and advantages. One disadvantage is that the classroom is a substitute for the "real" world. The practice of intercultural communication and experiential culture learning projects is just that—practice or simulation. Furthermore, classroom organization is generally designed to encourage deductive presentations and cognitive, rule-ordered pedagogy. The institutional context, as Krashen notes (1982), has apparently little to recommend it as a site for language or culture learning, providing as it does, little "natural input" and being traditionally dedicated to language learning, not acquisition.[4] Yet, as Krashen (37) comments, "language teaching certainly *can* help." He explains:

> Its primary function is to supply comprehensible input for those who cannot get it elsewhere, those constrained by their situation (i.e., foreign language students who do not have input sources outside the class) or by their competence (those unable to understand the language of the outside world). While it is less useful for those who have other sources of input, there still are things the competent classroom can contribute to the intermediate student.

Thus, this imperfect locus can provide a specialized environment for intercultural communication and learning. In some cases, this is the only location in which cultural contact can be made.

If the classroom context is envisioned as an "artificial or administered community" in the sense used in the anthropological studies of refugee camps in Israel[5] (Kushner 1973; Weingrod 1962, 1966), then it may present unanticipated advantages as the site of culture training. That is to say, the members of a language class may be regarded as forming a transient, *ad hoc* group composed of a teacher and students whose communal existence is limited in time and space.

This community will develop a group culture and at the same time engage in explorations of the culture "outside." As such, the classroom context may serve as a practice stage for intercultural communication as well as language learning. This specialized context provides some distinct advantages:

1. As an artificial community, it draws a culturally protective wall around those within, bestowing less severe punishment for the commission of linguistic and cultural errors than might be met outside its walls.

2. The classroom community is managed, unreal, forgiving, and protective, but it is also an environment that offers unique opportunities for experimental intercultural communication. If administered well, this community can provide the first step on a long voyage of cultural discovery that will end in the world outside the classroom.

The nature of the administered cultural classroom community will be discussed at greater length in a later chapter. In the following section of this chapter, you will be asked to revisit the multicultural language classroom described previously and to consider the implications of the vignette presented. You will be invited to examine the cultural clash that appears to have taken place and consider suggested counter strategies for the teacher to employ. Finally, you will be urged to test your own intercultural communicative know-how in preparation for the discussion in Chapter 2 of the historical development of the field of intercultural communication.

1.5 THE MULTICULTURAL CLASSROOM REVISITED: LESSONS TO BE LEARNED

Let us return to the classroom scene sketched at the beginning of this chapter. What should the teacher have done? What can we observe from this particular exchange? In point of fact, the answer to the first question lies in the second; it is in the observation of the realities of the exchange that the solutions are hidden.

First, just as children wanting to uncover some particularly intriguing bit of sexual lore unfailingly pick the wrong time and place to ask the right questions, so our culture learners seldom accommodate us by asking only polite questions, masking their cultural prejudices, or showing interest in learning about the North American political system or Halloween just because these subjects are described in their textbooks or reading assignments. The teachable moment, or the moment when learning is most likely to be optimal, is rarely the given or convenient moment.

Second, more than half of the students in this particular class were refugees, either by chance or by choice, so that the subject of families was a delicate one. Culture shock and culture loss were painful realities in that multicultural[6] classroom.

Third, it was clear that the culture learning game was hard ball and did not include all members of the class. Who knew what the Japanese students were thinking? Were they suffering from culture shock, disinterested, or just being Japanese? Or all three?

Fourth, the discomfort of the teacher lay in her cultural value system, which ordained that religion and politics should not be discussed on a personal basis and especially not in the classroom. Hers was a problem of ethnocentrism or cultural bias.

Finally, just as the questions appeared at the wrong time, the manner of questioning had that distinctly confrontational aura many teachers are reluctant to encourage. Yet it may be that such directness must occur in order for learning to take place. The teacher may also have been reacting to a cultural bias that avoids confrontation as an effective communicative strategy. Even if the teacher had not shared such a conviction, surely those of her students from the Far East did.

In the vignette described, the heart of the discussion lay in divergent belief systems underlying marriage customs and religious values. Explanation might have served better than justification. In any case, the fight-or-flight choices appear woefully inadequate.

1.6 WHAT DO YOU THINK?

Before further consideration of the classroom drama recounted above, read the following statements to assess what you already "know" or believe about the general subject of intercultural communication and cross-cultural awareness. Because this text is addressed to you who are teachers and practitioners, it is expected that you will have experienced a variety of instances of such communication or miscommunication and will bring your knowledge, insights, and convictions to bear upon the following statements.

As we all know, the first step in any learning process is self-assessment. Thus, the following pre-test is designed to help you begin an inventory of your own store of intercultural facts, assumptions, beliefs, and, perhaps, myths. Complete the test and then read the ensuing discussion. The "answers" are meant to encourage comment; indeed, they are designed to lead the way to dispute, disagreement, agreement, and ultimately, enlightenment.

What Do You Really Think?

Following is a list of thirteen statements concerning concepts, theories, facts, opinions, or myths about intercultural communication and cross-cultural awareness. Mark each statement True or False, according to your own opinion. Be prepared to justify your position.

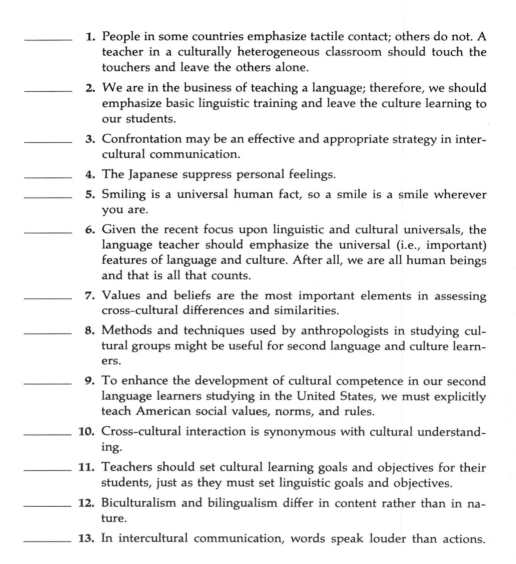

_____ 1. People in some countries emphasize tactile contact; others do not. A teacher in a culturally heterogeneous classroom should touch the touchers and leave the others alone.

_____ 2. We are in the business of teaching a language; therefore, we should emphasize basic linguistic training and leave the culture learning to our students.

_____ 3. Confrontation may be an effective and appropriate strategy in intercultural communication.

_____ 4. The Japanese suppress personal feelings.

_____ 5. Smiling is a universal human fact, so a smile is a smile wherever you are.

_____ 6. Given the recent focus upon linguistic and cultural universals, the language teacher should emphasize the universal (i.e., important) features of language and culture. After all, we are all human beings and that is all that counts.

_____ 7. Values and beliefs are the most important elements in assessing cross-cultural differences and similarities.

_____ 8. Methods and techniques used by anthropologists in studying cultural groups might be useful for second language and culture learners.

_____ 9. To enhance the development of cultural competence in our second language learners studying in the United States, we must explicitly teach American social values, norms, and rules.

_____ 10. Cross-cultural interaction is synonymous with cultural understanding.

_____ 11. Teachers should set cultural learning goals and objectives for their students, just as they must set linguistic goals and objectives.

_____ 12. Biculturalism and bilingualism differ in content rather than in nature.

_____ 13. In intercultural communication, words speak louder than actions.

Yes, No, and Maybe

First, was there anything particularly strange about the test? Did it seem somewhat untidy? Shouldn't there have been one or two more statements? Or some fewer?

If you answered "yes" to the above questions, you are probably wedded to the Western decimal system honoring the neatness of "even" numbers as well as to the Western superstition that thirteen is an unlucky number. These matters are relatively trivial except as illustrations of the continual, unconscious force of our personal cultural givens.

What then about the statements? Which are true and which are false? If you found yourself scratching your head and saying, "Yes, but . . .", then you are well on your way to developing cross-cultural sophistication. Indeed, almost all of these questions are answerable only within the context of given intercultural communicative episodes. Each statement is partially true, but different cultural patterns preclude acceptance or rejection as cross-cultural universals except in very broad terms.

For example, Statement 1 involves decisions that can only be made in context. The restrictions and appropriate use of tactile contact are culture-specific (Frank, 1957). Rules for tactile contact exist in every culture, but these rules vary cross-culturally. The top of the head should not be touched in certain Far Eastern cultures, as, for example, in Vietnam. The experienced intercultural communicator must be aware of these patterns. A generalization, such as is contained in Statement 1, is not only useless but also dangerous.

Statement 2 must be labeled False, for one cannot teach a language without teaching culture. What we teach and how are questions to be discussed later.

Statement 3 takes us back to the classroom drama described at the beginning of this chapter. In some cultures, confrontation is an acceptable mode of discussion. Loud voices do not always signal anger. However, in others confrontation may seem disruptive and unsettling, as it appeared to be for our poor, beleaguered teacher. Cross-cultural episodes are often perceived as exercises in rudeness and callousness.

Statement 4 represents a cultural generalization that must be qualified. The term "suppress" should be defined in Japanese terms, for much of the affective communication that takes place among those using the Japanese nonverbal communicative system is overlooked by Westerners. Statement 5 is also culturally loaded. The first part of the statement is true; the second is not. That is to say while smiling is a universal human act, this behavior does not carry the same meaning in all cultures (Ekman *et al.* 1969, 1971; Ekman 1975)

Statement 6 links theoretical approaches to the relationship of language and culture; it implies that language and culture are similar to each other as human systems of adaptation. It also implies that the similarities shared in all cultures and languages are more important than their differences. The reality is less simple than this statement would suggest. While we all share common features as human beings, we are also all members of various cultural groups. Our commonalities as human beings provide the rationale and bases for intercultural communication; our differences provide the framework within which this communication must take place. Thus, neither similarities nor differences can be ignored in intercultural contexts.

Statement 7 appears to be true, but the discerning reader should be warned that "assessing" similarities and differences may not lead to an understanding of these elements as parts of highly complex cultural systems. Values and beliefs appear to be highly resistant to change; they form the core of cultural identity. Thus, the simple recognition of similarities and differences will not lead to automatic intercultural understanding.

Statements 8 and 9 speak to the methods and techniques appropriate for culture learning and guidance. Both might be true in given contexts. The former is concerned with the manner in which anthropological field techniques, such as ethnography and participant observation, can be used in the process of cultural discovery. Writers and researchers in the field of language learning have urged teachers to assist their students in mastering these methods and employing them as they scout about a new culture (McLeod 1976, 1981; Paulston 1974, 1978). Many current student textbooks follow the suggestion in Statement 9 by providing specific content about a given culture. Yet one should be very cautious in accepting both Statements 8 and 9 as foundations for lesson planning. The use of both anthropological methods and direct cultural instruction must be approached with deep understanding of the nature of cultural discovery and the interplay of cultural values and beliefs. Statement 10 is the myth upon which many of the suggested methods and techniques involved in the implementation of Statements 8 and 9 are based. Although intercultural contact is a necessary first step in cross-cultural understanding, more often than not misunderstanding precedes understanding.

Statement 11 calls for False with a capital F for it implies that learning a language is a process similar in nature and degree to that of learning a culture. As we shall find later, such a statement calls for much qualification. In any case, the acquisition of a second language and a second culture may occur simultaneously, and yet be similar neither in nature nor degree. Thus, Statement 12 must also be rejected unless qualified.

Finally, Statement 13 defies the conventional wisdom among intercultural communication experts that nonverbal communication carries a greater load of social meaning in the communicative act than does the verbal. Indeed, some say it carries as much as 65 percent of the social content of a message (Birdwhistell 1970:158).

1.7 CONCLUSION

Thus, we must conclude that the statements listed on the pre-test focused upon important elements in intercultural communication, including nonverbal communication, universals of human behavior, methods of cultural discovery, and the strengths of various cultural patterns. There were few statements that did not call for qualification, and thus, in our true/false Western tradition, which disdains ambiguity, must be labeled false. However, let us widen our cultural horizons and admit that, at least in instances of intercultural communication, ambiguity is the name of the game, and proceed to explore in more depth the interesting implications gleaned from consideration of the statements in the pre-test.

As for our uncertain and somewhat unnerved teacher, she would have been well advised to have remembered that an emphasis upon discovery and explanation rather than on justification of cultural patterns and beliefs might have guided such confrontations as occurred in her classroom toward communication rather than catastrophe. A teacher in charge of such a classroom must be informed about the cultural patterns of her students. The teacher in the instance described needed to be reminded that religion and religious beliefs do have a place in a multicultural classroom in spite of her North American[7] bias. Indeed, any teacher who invites culture into the classroom must be prepared to make its various manifestations equally welcome. Ethnocentrism, or the belief in the inherent and unassailable validity of one's own cultural values, ways, and beliefs, has no place in such a classroom. There were many cultural barriers in that classroom, including cultural evaluations, preconceptions, stereotypes, and anxiety. These are many of those identified by Barna (1982:322–330) as "stumbling blocks" to intercultural communication. These must all be confronted and understood if communication is to take place. In the following chapters we shall investigate the nature of the field of intercultural communication, the concepts of culture, language, and communication, and practical methods to deal with all of these in the multicultural classroom context. Approached in this manner, culture learning, along with the four traditional skills—reading, writing, listening, and speaking—can be accorded its rightful place as a fifth skill, adding its particular dimension to each of the other four.

In the meantime, it is suggested that each reader review the pre-test and classroom drama. All the observations made about them are open to discussion. Indeed, the pre-test will be revisited in the last chapter of this book. It is hoped that when this is done, your answers will be appropriately ambiguous, clearly culturally sophisticated, and far more satisfying than the present "Well, maybe . . . but . . . ."

FOR STUDY AND DISCUSSION

1. Identify these terms:

   administered community

   learning

   teaching

   ethnocentrism

   language acquisition/language learning

ESL/EFL

culture learning

acculturation/enculturation

2. Discuss possible responses the teacher might have made to the incident related at the beginning of this chapter. Should the teacher have asked the question about families in the first place? Were the students wrong to ask the questions they did?

3. Apparently, the teacher was uncomfortable about allowing a religious discussion in the classroom. Was she correct? What other type of ethnocentric behavior did she reveal?

4. Can you identify other types of cultural bias that might have been at work in the participants of this classroom drama?

5. Devise a short scenario for the conversion of this potentially explosive situation into a positive culture learning experience.

6. Why does intercultural interaction not necessarily lead to intercultural tolerance?

7. List some "stumbling blocks" to intercultural communication in classrooms that you have observed.

8. We all exhibit cultural differences in attitudes and behavior. List three instances which you have observed in intercultural contexts.

9. What features of an administered or artificial community might be found in a language classroom?

10. Describe several examples of ethnocentric behavior that you have observed. Be specific!

11. Recall a culturally explosive situation that you have experienced or observed in a classroom. How was it handled?

12. How might culture learning differ from language learning? Which is more difficult in your opinion?

CULTURE LEARNING EXERCISE

Each chapter of this book presents suggested learning exercises, experiential in nature and designed to guide you along a personal voyage of cultural discovery. Each set of exercises emphasizes activities, procedures, or foci and constitutes an important step in the process of culture learning.

Observation

The first step in the process of learning about a new culture involves the undertaking of conscious observation of given events, behavior, or situations. Because communicative acts are often carried out at an unconscious level, it is helpful to bring the observation of familiar sights and sounds to a conscious level of awareness. Often that which is most familiar is also that of which we are least aware.

Self-awareness precedes understanding the unfamiliar. The process of culture learning begins at home.

A. Observe and record the daily greeting patterns you employ in meeting three different groups. For example, how do you greet your family members, your colleagues, and strangers? Record both verbal and nonverbal behavior.

B. Observe the greeting patterns between North Americans and persons from another cultural area (Far East, Middle East, Latin America). What differences did you observe between the patterns used and those you use?

Go out and observe! Don't just sit there and write down what you think would happen. If you observe carefully, you may be very surprised at what you discover. Remember, if you wish to ask questions of those you are observing, please explain why you are asking these questions. If you do not, you may be considered at best nosy and at worst dangerous.

C. Ask persons from the three areas mentioned how they would interpret the following:

1. The American hand signal for "Come here!"
2. The smiling and stylized face of the Have A Nice Day! logo.
3. The American hand signal for "Goodbye."

Report what responses, both verbal and nonverbal, you received. You should explain the purpose of your questions and be prepared for unexpected interpretations. If your respondents indicate a different gesture or sign for any of these "messages," find out how they would convey this information.

FOR FURTHER READING

L. Barna. 1982. "Stumbling Blocks in Intercultural Communication" (322–330). This article lists several barriers to effective intercultural communication in the context of the classroom. The author lists such blocks as language problems, misinterpretation of nonverbal behavior, preconceptions and stereotyping, evaluations, and stress or anxiety. Recognition and understanding of these barriers are the first steps toward overcoming them.

H. Brown. 1980a. *Principles of Language Learning and Teaching* (1–63). Brown provides an excellent review of the theoretical foundations of foreign language teaching, with special emphasis on second language acquisition and the many variables affecting this process. Readers unfamiliar with theory and research concerning language learning and teaching as well as first and second language acquisition will find the first three chapters of this book particularly helpful.

E. Condon. 1982. "Cross-cultural Interferences Affecting Teacher–Pupil Communication in American Schools" (340–347). Proceeding from the premise that good communication is the "keystone" of successful teaching–learning, the author lists several vital factors to be assessed in situations of cross-cultural communication in the American school context. These include use of language and language auxiliaries, norms of classroom interaction, and the context of human interaction. This article provides a useful introduction to cross-cultural variables affecting communication.

S. Krashen. 1982. *Principles and Practice in Second Language Acquisition*. Chapter 2, "Second Language Acquisition Theory" (9–56), and Chapter 3, "Providing Input for Acquisition" (57–82), contain background information on theory and practice in second language acquisition. Chapter 2 reviews current theory, including Krashen's own input hypothesis, the affective filter hypothesis, and Schumann's acculturation hypothesis. Chapter 3 brings the reader from theory to practice in discussions of various means of encouraging input for acquisition.

NOTES

1. The terms *ESL* and *EFL* indicate either the different contexts in which language learning may take place or the purposes for which the language is learned. The "E" refers to English in these acronyms. In general *second language* instruction refers to programs taking place in a context in which the language studied is spoken or used. The term second language carries with it the assumption that the language is accorded some status in the context in which it is being studied. For example, English is a second language in many parts of India. Foreign language instruction refers to instruction in a language used outside the territory in which the instruction takes place. Thus, *ESL* refers to the situation in which foreign students study English in a country in which it is the native language, such as in the United States. On the other hand, *EFL* would be used to refer to English language classes in a country, such as Spain, for example, in which English is not a native or second language. Another term, *EIL* (English as an International Language), is coming into use. This refers to the employment of English as a type of *lingua franca* among non-native speakers.

   The cover terms *second language learning* and *second language teaching* are used in this book to refer to the learning and instruction of any language and culture in any context to non-native speakers of the target language. It should be clearly understood that this term is used for convenience; the use of the generalized term underscores this author's belief that the approach to culture learning advocated in this book is applicable in any context and for any language and can be used by any teacher. Needless to say, many of our so-called "second" language learners are already studying their third or fourth language when they enter our classrooms so the term in no way is descriptive of student proficiency.

2. The term *classroom* includes any type of instructional environment, formal or informal, one-to-one or group, in native or foreign, linguistic and cultural habitats.

3. The terms *culture* and *cultural* used as modifiers may carry different meanings. *Culture learning* is often used to refer to processes directed toward a given target culture or group, while *cultural learning* serves to delineate the general processes of learning any unknown cultural system. The first is limited to a specific culture; the second to universal processes associated both with *enculturation* (learning a primary culture) and *acculturation* (learning a supplementary culture). The *culture/cultural learning* distinction is generally maintained in the field of intercultural communication as culture-specific and culture-general approaches. In this book, the general term *culture learning*

will be used for the sake of simplicity. Distinctions between the culture-specific and culture-general designations will be made when necessary. Culture learning will be defined as encompassing both learning appropriate to the development of intercultural communicative skills and of cross-cultural awareness. As such, it may be defined as intrapersonal changes in conjunction with interpersonal and intercultural contact.

4. The uses of the terms, *learning, teaching,* and *acquisition* in relation to language may cause some question. Krashen's Monitor Theory of Second Language Acquisition (SLA) (1976, 1982) posits two types of processes in relation to attaining proficiency in another language—*language acquisition* and *language learning.* The former is a less formal process, closely related to the circumstances involved in the development of first language skills, while the latter is associated with deductive, rule-learning, and conscious correction or monitoring by the learner. In this book, the term *language learning* is used in a broader sense than that used by Krashen. It covers both language learning and language acquisition and refers to the association of new or previously unknown information with the known as applied to a language system. *Teaching* is defined as the "facilitation" of these processes, as Brown suggests (1980a:1). Language learning, then, may include intake and input from both formal and informal contexts, that is, the classroom and the "real" world. The same distinctions may be applied to culture learning and cultural training or instruction.

5. The terms *artificial* or *administered community* as employed in the studies of refugee camps in Israel and elsewhere refer to communities established to promote acculturation in a protected environment. Their purpose was to support, protect, and educate their residents in a pattern of planned social change. The designation *administered* indicates the limitations placed upon the group within the community; the designation *artificial,* the transient nature and the directed formation of the group forming the community. This concept has been applied to descriptions of mobile home communities and congregate meals programs for older adults in the United States (Angrosino 1976). The term is used in this book to suggest that many of the features of the language classroom are similar to those of artificial or administered communities. The value of this analogy is that it leads the observer to assign a special purpose to the classroom in terms of cultural change and to the class as a very special transient community. The comparison is particularly appropriate in relation to programs in which instruction is intensive and lengthy. For additional information on the subject, consult the works of Kushner (1973) and Weingrod (1962, 1966), as listed in the bibliography.

6. The term *multicultural* as used in this book refers to groups or situations in which persons from various cultural backgrounds interact. It is not meant to describe a type of content.

7. The terms *American* or *North American* refer to persons inhabiting the geographical area of the continental United States; *Latin American* identifies those of Central and South America who share patterns of Hispanic culture. These terms are used for ease of identification and are in no way meant to be derogatory, either to these people or to those of subcultures within those areas.

In addition, comparisons will be made between persons from the Far East, Middle East, Latin America, and North America. Although these areal divisions, of course, are clumsy, they may serve as general points for contrast and comparison. Peoples from these general areas do share some cultural characteristics. The observations made concerning these areas can only be very general and in no way should serve to mask the very real cultural differences that do separate them.

Chapter 2

The New Perspectives of Intercultural Communication

Although intercultural communication as a field of research and practice has had only a brief history and is, as yet, ill-defined, it is today enjoying unprecedented attention from second language teachers and researchers as well as from others concerned with cross-cultural contact and interaction (Althen *et al.* 1981; Baxter 1983; Pusch 1979; Savignon 1983; Saville-Troike 1978, 1982; Seelye 1984). The principles, concepts, and findings that guide those identified with the field of intercultural communication are seen by other professionals outside the field as the means by which the problems and pitfalls encountered in contact between members of diverse cultural groups may be met and overcome.

2.1 SOME WORDS OF WARNING

Yet two aspects of the field as it is practiced today in the United States should warn the novice to proceed with caution. The first concerns the theoretical bases upon which the field rests; the second has to do with the lack of agreement in the definition of basic concepts. The major theoretical foundations for the field of intercultural communication were formulated and borrowed from Western scientific social disciplines. Techniques, methodologies, and training models seem to carry the stamp of Western logic, rhetoric, and explanation. It has been suggested that the scientific precepts and approaches used to investigate, explain, and understand cross-cultural differences and intercultural communicative processes have reflected cultural bias and might be inappropriate in some cultural contexts. Smart's 1983 discussion of the use of role play in an Asian setting should give pause for thought to any teacher planning to use such a method in a multicultural classroom.

In addition, because most of the major concepts and the definitions associated with the field of intercultural communication were developed in sister social sciences, the field itself has been identifiable more in practice than in theory, more in "borrowed" than in field-specific concepts. Although this situation is being slowly remedied, the uninitiated seeking to delve into current literature may be confounded by the use of contradictory definitions of basic terms and seemingly incompatible theoretical positions.[1]

Examples of the problems that these characteristics of the field present to the novice abound. Consider the difficulty of discussing "American" culture. Whose culture? What culture? What rules? What patterns? Any teacher who has tried, and probably failed, to spark a lively discussion on almost any subject with students from the Far East is well aware that "communicating" doesn't seem to be an international skill. At least, it doesn't seem to involve that lively give-and-take, opinion-expressing, up-fronting style so characteristic of American rhetorical interaction. Undertaking role play or other active, participatory activities often seems to call for more explanation than participation. Many of our students simply don't seem to know how to play our pedagogical games.

A reader has only to leaf through one of the several anthologies or collections of readings on the subject of intercultural communication to become painfully aware of the various definitions given to such key concepts as *culture, communication,* or *acculturation* (Condon and Yousef 1975; Samovar and Porter 1982; Smith and Luce 1979). Contributors to such volumes define basic concepts according to their own personal or professional persuasion. Thus, the term *culture* may be regarded by an anthropologist as a major unifying force, by a communication professional as a major variable, or by a psychologist as an individual mental set. Each of these definitions is associated with a particular perspective; each attests to the complexity of the phenomenon involved. However, inexperienced intercultural communicators searching for definitional nooks into which to tuck their newly acquired knowledge, experiences, and insights may find it difficult to tolerate such apparent confusion or lack of precision.

Yet there is strength in diversity, so that while problems relating to methodologies and definitions persist, a field of research and practice known as intercultural communication is now fully recognized and supported by professional organizations such as *SIETAR* (Society for Intercultural Education, Training, and Research) and its official publication, *International Journal of Intercultural Relations,* as well as by related research and publications in the fields of linguistics, language learning, cross-cultural psychology, and communication. The problems its professionals address are universal in nature and human in origin. The strength of the field lies in its eclecticism, a result of the willingness of its professionals to draw upon many diverse points of view and theoretical positions. The resulting perspective is unique. Hoopes and Pusch (1979a:2), in an article defining terms used in intercultural and multicultural education, comment:

> Nothing about intercultural or multicultural human relations is really new, but by putting certain ideas about communication, culture, society, education and human psychology together, a different way of looking at and learning about interaction among cultures has emerged.

This uniqueness of perspective is achieved through a refining and redefining of "borrowed" concepts and their interrelationships. Such familiar terms as *culture, language, communication, perception,* or *world view* reflect unexpected dimensions and cast unfamiliar shadows when viewed from intercultural perspectives.

For example, this unique perspective can be found in the intercultural approach to the often posed but as yet unanswered question of the relationship of language and culture. Inquiry on this subject originated in the field of anthropology as early field work at the end of the nineteenth and beginning of the twentieth century uncovered exotic, heretofore undreamed-of, languages and cultures. The attempt at an explanation and reconciliation of the very different linguistic and cultural patterns being described has become known as the Sapir-Whorf hypothesis. This so-called hypothesis in its strong form presumably posited a causal relationship between language and culture with language as the dominant force controlling the very minds, actions, and world views of its speakers. In recent years, the strong version of this hypothesis has been largely rejected by linguists and anthropologists. Yet it remains a viable concept in the field of intercultural communication, albeit in its weakened form, which postulates a strong, two-way relationship between language and culture, and with some fundamental alterations of terminology.

The addition of variables attendant upon human communication to the language and culture puzzle and the substitution of a hypothesis that proposes a relationship between language, culture, and perceptual patterns have turned the attention of those in the field of intercultural communication to a continuing pursuit of the interlocking relationships of language, culture, communication, and thought. The intercultural approach to the unanswered questions these relationships generate is based on a redefinition of "thought" as perception and culture as an inclusive term covering a wide range of behavior (Singer 1982). Thus, the amalgam of concepts drawn from anthropology, but enriched by insights from linguistics and psychology, represents the new perspectives to old puzzles the field of intercultural communication offers. These distinctions are discussed in greater detail in Chapter 7.

2.2 OF MESSAGES AND MEANING

What then are these intercultural perspectives that appear to hold such promise? How can we define intercultural communication and snare all the important nuances of its complexities? We may begin by identifying some of the components or themes that must be included in a working definition of the term.

The five statements listed below refer to aspects of culture and communication. Each contains a clue—carries a message, so to speak—contributing to the meaning of the term *intercultural communication.*

1. ". . . if we truly are to understand communication, we must also understand culture" (Samovar, Porter and Jain 1981:18).

2. *Deru kugiwa utareru,* but God helps those who help themselves.

3. "The world each person creates for himself is a distinctive world. . . . Every communication, interpersonal or intercultural, is a transaction between these private worlds." (Barnlund 1975:11–12)

4. "Nonverbal sources of information represent an expressive network that reveals and informs." (Galloway 1979:197)

5. "Intercultural communication can best be understood as cultural variance in the perception of social objects and events." (Porter and Samovar 1982:37)

What are these clues?

Statement 1 raises the fundamental question concerning the relationship of culture and communication. Edward T. Hall, the eminent anthropologist and diligent recorder of cultural variations, especially nonverbal behavior, placed culture and communication in the same basket. In Hall's theory of culture and its processes, which he developed with George L. Trager, culture was defined as being "concerned more with messages than it is with networks and control systems" (1959:169). Yet those in communication often accord culture as the shaper of human perception a respected but not so powerful or pervasive a role as did Hall and Trager. In general, communication professionals have focused upon specific cross-cultural variations attendant on the communication process (E. Condon 1982).

Statement 2 represents divergent cultural evaluations concerning the role of the individual in human society. The first part of the statement is a well-known Japanese aphorism, which warns that the "nail that sticks up is hammered down." It emphasizes the consequences of not striving for group harmony. The second expresses the well-known American belief in the great rewards of independence and individuality. Taken together, these statements suggest that there are alternative solutions to a common human problem, getting along with others.

Statement 3 highlights the dichotomies—the public and the private, the individual and the group, the shared and the unshared—that characterize most human interaction.

Statement 4 warns the unsophisticated observer that communicating consists of more than just sending verbal messages. The nonverbal channels carry heavy communicative loads, although often unconsciously sent and received.

The final statement is a reminder that communication, even among those who share basic cultural patterns, is highly colored by personal perception so that what each person perceives (intrapersonally) affects what occurs between that person and another (interpersonally). Because no two persons are alike, all acts of human communication are in some manner intercultural.

Yet even though the ambiguities of the cross-cultural messages and the complexities of the act of communication are staggering, the effort to understand is in itself often ample reward. Indeed, inhabitants of the modern world have little choice but to communicate interculturally, linked as they are by satellites and bombarded by a deluge of information instantaneously transmitted. None should be more aware of this fact of modern life than the second/foreign language teacher to whom intercultural communication or miscommunication is the name of the game.

In the following portion of this chapter a working definition of the term *intercultural communication* is presented. This definition will be refined as different facets of the processes of such communication and the parameters of the field it has spawned are considered in subsequent chapters.

2.3 INTERCULTURAL COMMUNICATION: A WORKING DEFINITION

The phenomenon of intercultural communication is as old as human society. The process occurs when "a message producer is a member of one culture and a message receiver is a member of another" (Porter and Samovar 1982:27). In this context, let us for the moment define culture as learned and shared human patterns and models for living.

In the following discussion and throughout this book, the term *intercultural communication* will be defined as acts of communication undertaken by individuals identified with groups exhibiting intergroup variation in shared social and cultural patterns. These shared patterns, individually expressed, are the major variables in the purpose, the manner, the mode, and the means by which the communicative process is effected.

In the past the field of intercultural communication has been identified by many names: *cross-cultural communication, transcultural communication, interracial communication, international communication,* or even *contracultural communication* (Rich and Ogawa 1982:43). Each name has served to designate a particular focus or interest.

A basic assumption reflected by most writers on the subject is that instances of intercultural communication are more likely to result in miscommunication than in meaningful communication. This need not be so although it often is the case. Intercultural communication can entail "error in social perception brought about by cultural variations that affect the perceptual process" (Porter and Samovar 1982:42). Thus, the perception or interpretation of the communicative act by any and all of those involved is of major importance. Communication may indeed be taking place, but unless it is "perceived correctly," problems will arise and the communicative chain will be broken.

For example, an English-speaking American teacher was addressed as "Miss" by a student whose native language was Dutch. The teacher reacted coldly because she perceived the use of the term "Miss" with no surname as an inappropriate mode of address, usually reserved for waitresses or clerks with whom such impersonal terms could be used. In point of fact, the student had merely translated the traditional Dutch term for female teachers, *Juffrouw*, to the English *Miss*. The student was confounded by the teacher's instant disapproval—a clear case of misperception colored by not a little cultural snobbery on the part of the teacher.

Thus, intercultural communication as a process involving an attempt to bridge cultural chasms is often marked more by pain than by pleasure and less by success than by failure. The interplay of the varied cultural patterns, beliefs, and values each communicator brings to the intercultural communicative process is to be reckoned with in every act of communication; the greater the variation in these patterns, the stronger the divisive force of these variables and the more likely the instances of miscommunication.

Different cultural patterns, translated into rules for living, artifacts, values, beliefs, naming, social relations, and all elements of human social life, have evolved to meet universal human problems. The problems are universal; the solutions are culture-specific. In addition, while these patterns are shared to some degree by members of the same cultural group, individual perception and transactions between the public and private worlds of senders and receivers provide a unique frame of reference for every intercultural or intracultural communicative act.

2.4 THE FIELD OF INTERCULTURAL COMMUNICATION: A BRIEF HISTORY

While the field of intercultural communication as an academic discipline is of recent origin, the processes involved are not. Indeed, the first human beings who wandered from their caves, met others of their kind exhibiting strange behavior and making strange sounds—and were curious—were also the first intercultural communicators. The foundation of the field of intercultural communication today lies in this primary and primitive human need to communicate.

In an article titled "Intercultural Communication Concepts and the Psychology of Intercultural Experience" (9–38) in *Multicultural Education: A Cross Cultural Training Approach* (1979a), David S. Hoopes briefly reviews the development of the field of intercultural communication. He dates the emergence of the academic discipline of intercultural communication from the 1959 publication of Edward T. Hall's *The Silent Language*, which gave "the first comprehensive analysis of the relationship between communication and culture" (10). Prior to this time the definitions of the concepts of *communication* and *culture* had already been redefined in the respective fields of communication and anthropology. *Communication* had been distinguished from *speech; culture* broadened to include the study of modern as well as traditional societies.

However, the driving force behind these redefinitions came from outside academia. World War II and its aftermath made the need for communication between diverse cultural groups no longer a matter of personal choice. Americans, who had previously enjoyed the privileges of isolationism, had to assume world leadership if the promises of global peace and cooperation were to be fulfilled. Linguists, anthropologists, and communicators were summoned to the national headquarters to translate and to explain the cultural differences being manifested by friend and foe alike.

Anthropologists such as Margaret Mead, Ruth Benedict, Geoffrey Gorer, Weston La Barre, and others, sought to explain the "odd" behavior of the mysterious American enemies (Japan and Germany) and the equally mysterious allies (Russia and China). Their work focused on cultural patterns and themes and the concept of modal or characteristic cultural personalities. They were concerned with the relationship of various cultural patterns and characteristic behavior. Thus, Margaret Mead (1954), Gorer and Rickman (1949), and others found much that "explained" the Russian modal personality in the practice of child swaddling. Ruth Benedict, in *The Chrysanthemum and the Sword* (1946), posited a relationship between the strictness of Japanese toilet training and the national passion for order and personal cleanliness. Others (Gorer 1943; La Barre 1945), searching for psychocultural relationships, linked behavior in war, regarded by Americans as brutal, to this same strict toilet training. Although these hypothetical relationships were never to be supported by hard evidence (M. Harris 1968, 443–448), their articulation did serve to alert heretofore generally insulated American observers to the diversity of human culture.

At the same time, linguists, also called to battle, grappled with uncommon languages and left their mark in the field of second language learning and teaching by the development of immersion techniques in language instruction at the Army Language School at Monterey, California. Their work only made it clearer that culture learning was an important ingredient in language learning.

Needless to say, all these efforts at understanding the new and the different had an air of desperation and *ad hoc*-ism about them. More often than not these observations, buttressed more by intuition than by fact, merely served to encourage stereotypic or unwarranted generalizations in application. What did become very clear was that Americans in general were sadly inept in the fine art of intercultural communication. They were willing to communicate, but were soon proved to be unable, being painfully ill-prepared, both linguistically and culturally, to do so.

After World War II, the development of aid programs and the dispatch of technical experts and Peace Corps volunteers abroad spurred interest in changes in the field. Techniques to provide information concerning unfamiliar cultures were devised and refined. The early training programs were usually of relatively short duration and largely confined to the processing of information concerning given target groups. Snippets of cultural information were drawn together and assembled into hastily prepared manuals. As Hoopes (1979a:11) notes, the first cross-cultural training manual only appeared in 1970 in the United States.

Peace Corps volunteers who had been sent abroad as worldwide ambassadors returned with stories of frustration, miscommunication, and often mission failure. The efforts to draw trainees out of their ethnocentric wombs proved to be woefully inadequate. In some ways, the volunteers were scarcely better prepared than tourists with their traditional guidebooks. This circumstance ultimately led to changes in training methods and a new focus on the development of intercultural communicative skills rather than simple information processing.

These early efforts to understand culturally different groups and to prepare Americans to undertake global missions fostered development of academic interest in the field. Because so many different sources of information and expertise had been tapped in the sister fields of anthropology, communication, and psychology, and because so many professionals had been consulted, the field of intercultural communication was from the beginning characterized by eclecticism and a propensity to "borrow" fundamental concepts from allied fields of study.

Hoopes notes that as training methods changed, the works of Maslow (1954) and Rogers (1951) in human relations were consulted. Value orientations (Kluckhohn and Strodtbeck 1961) became a major interest as trainers began to realize the power of value and belief systems in cross-cultural contexts. This brought an interest in the characteristics of the successful intercultural communicator and in the processes of cross-cultural communication.[2]

In addition, the demands for training were augmented as groups of foreign students, technicians, and business personnel flocked to the United States seeking information and instruction (Hoopes 1979a:10–11). Thus, Americans needed to be trained to communicate with much of the rest of the world—at home and abroad. Many foreigners were coming to the United States for purposes other than permanent residence. The traditional melting pot approach to cultural differences was suddenly outmoded, speeded to its demise by the sweep of the civil rights movement, and made obsolete by the foreign sojourners who wished to understand Americans but not necessarily join them. Teachers and trainers found themselves called to "explain" the culture of the United States, parts of which they certainly did not share or even understand.

As professionalism grew, so did its accoutrements. The first basic textbook, *An Introduction to Intercultural Communication* by John C. Condon and Fathi Yousef, appeared in 1975. The founding of the professional organization SIETAR (See Appendix C) provided a common meeting ground for professionals in the various contributing disciplines to come together to discuss mutual interests and concerns.

Thus, the field of intercultural communication came into being in the heat of a bitter and encompassing war; it grew from the wartime need to understand both allied and enemy strangers. It was developed by means of contributions plucked from academic disciplines treating human relationships and conditions. Its unique history has provided the field with a rich analytical and theoretical base; its philosophical base reflects these varied sources of knowledge. Those who examine these perspectives closely will be rewarded by a deepened understanding of the complex interrelationships of culture and communication, language and culture, language and thought, and second language learning/teaching.

Eclecticism has enriched the field of intercultural communication immeasurably, for this borrowing has given new meaning to many old and familiar concepts. The field of intercultural communication, in turn, also has much to offer those who have freely provided its theoretical foundations. In research and practice, the development of the field of intercultural communication has shed new light on old questions.

2.5 THEORY, FIELD, AND PRACTICE IN INTERCULTURAL COMMUNICATION

Many of the contributions from various academic disciplines to the field of intercultural communication were chosen as much by serendipity as by foresight, as much by the dictates of theoretical fashion as by rigorous choice. An understanding of these theoretical threads and the tracing of their passage from the source disciplines into the field of intercultural communication is essential for those who would translate the insights afforded by the intercultural perspective into practice. The remaining portion of this chapter is devoted to the sorting out of some salient strands now so deftly woven into the theoretical tapestry of the field of intercultural communication.

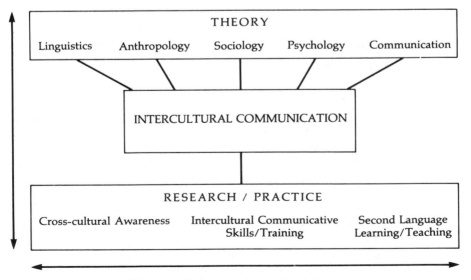

Figure 2.1. Theory and Research/Practice in Intercultural Communication

Figure 2.1 presents a schematic view of the relationships of theory and practice in the field or discipline known as intercultural communication. The field covers both cross-cultural practice, theory, and research, as well as that of intercultural communication. The two-way arrows indicate that the flow of information and knowledge moves both horizontally and vertically, within and without the "field" of intercultural communication, and between both individuals and groups. Thus, theoretical contributions, for example, may be traced from outside the field of intercultural communication into the practice of second language teaching and learning. "Borrowed" concepts, such as culture and perception, when filtered through the field of intercultural communication into practice, are altered as are the pieces of glass when shifted by the turn of a kaleidoscope. The same pieces are there but their relationships, one to another, have been altered; new patterns are formed. What was familiar now seems unfamiliar. In like manner, theoretical positions developed in the field of communication have come under closer scrutiny and have been questioned more rigorously when viewed in an intercultural frame. The addition of the intercultural filter through which theoretical concepts and theories from a variety of academic disciplines and professional practice pass brings added dimension to both theory and practice.

Although field-specific theory is developing in the field of intercultural communication, major theoretical support continues to come from sister disciplines. The main threads of theory forming the warp and woof of intercultural communication as an academic discipline today have been drawn from the social sciences. Some of their major contributions are discussed in the following paragraphs.

Linguistics

Because language is a major tool of cultural interaction, changing theories of language have been influential in forming the approaches taken to the same relationship in the field of intercultural communication. Modern linguistic theories have evolved from the structuralism espoused by American descriptive linguists to the generative/transformational school of Chomsky and his disciples to the modern functionalism of Halliday, Hymes, and others. The movement has been from concern with surface or manifested linguistic forms, their distribution and processes, to studies of "deep structure" and the arrangement of these forms (syntax), to the relationship of language and meaning, or semantics.

Each of these theoretical positions has found its way into the discussions in the professional literature in intercultural communication. These positions have been revised and reformulated to fit the field. Today, remnants or wisps of each of these linguistic theoretical positions remain firmly embedded in the web of intercultural communication theory in a remarkably functional symbiosis.

Let us examine some of these wisps. From American structural linguistics have come discovery methods still so valuable to the cultural explorer in the pursuit of either professional or personal insights. These include the methods and techniques of the ethnographer and the field researcher. A continued interest in the relationship of language and culture led to the suggestion by K. L. Pike (1954), anthropologist and linguist, that field methods used in the analysis of linguistic forms and systems could be applied to the analysis of cultural data. Pike sought to identify relevant cultural categories for given cultural groups. This approach emphasized the systematic nature of cultural data and the role of the cultural informant, the unconscious but, according to Pike, the unquestioned source of culturally meaningful knowledge. In intercultural communication this has placed the communicator in the position of being an important variable in the communicative process as well as a source of knowledge and evaluation.

Today, renewed interest by linguists such as Halliday (1978), Hymes (1972a, 1972b, 1974) and Searle (1969), in language use, linguistic and social variations, semantics, and the functions of language has been transmitted to the "borrowers." In intercultural communication this revival has brought the communicative act front and center, linking again those disparate parts of the puzzle: language–culture–thought–perception. The questions being asked about these relationships are but echoes of those being pursued in the academic groves of anthropology and other social sciences, including sociology, linguistics, psychology, and communication sciences.

Current interest in the functions of language and language in use has not only had a major impact on second language teaching but has also brought the attention of language teachers to the influence of cultural differences in the processes attendant upon language use and functions.

Thus, each of the major changes in linguistic theory in this century is still reflected in the perspectives and approaches taken in the field of intercultural communication today.

Anthropology

In addition to the legacy of cultural discovery methods, a gift from linguistically oriented anthropologists, the discipline of anthropology has contributed its unifying concept—culture. Culture, as a major human adaptive mechanism, in all its world-wide diversity colors all of the major variables that must be taken into account in investigating and understanding the processes of intercultural communication.

The anthropological gospel of cultural relativity, or the value of a non-evaluative approach to cultural diversity, forms a major tenet in the practice of cross-cultural research and intercultural contact. Research and observation viewed across cultures has, in turn, shed new light on the understanding of the relationship between language and culture, culture and personality, and the processes of social change and acculturation (Bochner 1982; Brislin 1977, 1981; Brislin et al. 1975; Gudykunst and Kim 1984; Hall 1959, 1969, 1977; Osgood et al. 1975; Shweder and LeVine 1984). Indeed, the work of the anthropologist Edward Hall appears to have had far greater effect on the theory, research, and practice in the field of intercultural communication than it has had in his own discipline.

In addition, changes wrought in the field of anthropology as a result of the Chomskyan revolution in linguistics have also been filtered through the field of intercultural communication. Orientations in regard to field work and theory building were greatly altered as a result of linguistic interest in the production of generalizations about the nature of human language and universal linguistic properties. This focus on similarities was carried into anthropology, psychology, and intercultural communication on a wave of enthusiasm for the promise of discovering general laws and formulating elegantly stated rules to account for these data. This search for cross-cultural universals continues today in anthropology as well as in other social sciences. It is also reflected in the questions that researchers in intercultural communication pose in relation to the generalizable aspects of the processes of communication, intercultural contact, and acculturation, as well as in the training methods based upon universal characteristics of human social interaction and accommodation (Abe and Wiseman 1983; Casse 1981; Rohrlich 1983).

Sociology

From sociology has come concern with individual sociocultural variables, such as age, sex, attitude, and motivation, and with theories of social organization, descriptions of social groups, and social psychology. Viewed cross-culturally, these variables have provided the bases for numerous studies with the added dimension of an intercultural context. In turn, the addition of cross-cultural factors has called for the reassessment of the use of instruments, definitions, methods of sociological and psychological measurements, and conclusions developed and tested in monocultural (and usually Western) contexts (Asante and Vora 1983; Berry 1969; Gudykunst 1983b; Hui 1982).

In some cases an entire approach to intercultural communication has been based upon a set of "borrowed" concepts. For example, Gudykunst and Kim (1984) build their discussion of intercultural communication around a revised version of German sociologist Georg Simmel's *The Stranger*, contending that meeting the culturally different is best viewed in the context of "strangerhood."

In addition, the development of the field now known as sociolinguistics, or the study of language in context and in the crucible of human interaction, has joined the forces of the linguists and anthropologists to those of the sociologists in a shift of interest from the linguistic competence of the ideal speaker/listener, the primary concern of the generative grammarians under the leadership of Chomsky, to an interest in the communicative competence/performance of the real speaker interacting in a real world ordered by rules of communicative appropriateness and variability. The work of Dell Hymes, John Gumperz, and others in the early 1970s forced a shift in the theoretical positions of anthropologists and linguists in relation to such basic concepts as language, culture, and communica-tion, and brought about revised interpretations of the analyses of sociological variables relating to community, social class, and social norms (Bernstein 1966; Labov 1966, 1972).

Psychology

In many ways the field of intercultural communication can be said to have been forged in the somewhat unexpected relationship of professionals in the field of communication and in psychology and social psychology. Psychologists, in both Europe and North America, have long been interested in cross-cultural differ-ences in perception, evaluation, personality, and cognition. In addition, cultural training methods have been strongly influenced by behavioral psychology (Skin-ner 1957) and Jungian psychology. The latter constitutes the rationale for case training models and exercises designed to draw upon the force of the assumed underlying psychological unity of mankind (Casse 1981).

The impact of the individual communicator's personality as well as psycho-cultural variations in perception, attitudes, and motivation represent major vari-ables in the outcome of any communicative act, including language learning (Gardner and Lambert 1972; Guiora et al. 1972; Sapir 1964). In the past, research in the fields of psychology and anthropology established cross-cultural variations, some of which have been identified with given cultural and communicative themes and patterns as noted previously (Benedict 1934, 1946; Gorer 1943; Mead 1928). These studies take on new meaning and call for reconsideration when filtered through the field of intercultural communication.

As was the case in the borrowing of sociological concepts, the borrowing of psychological constructs, methods, instruments, and generalizations has fostered their reappraisal. Shweder and Bourne (1984) in an article titled "Does the Con-cept of the Person Vary Cross-culturally?", give a resounding "yes." Again, the cross-cultural perspective has shed new light on old concepts.

Communication

Developments in the field of intercultural communication came most directly from those in communication who first were asked to grapple with the problems of understanding those who sought to communicate. Interest in communication as more than mere speech acts arose as writers in the field, such as Edward Stewart, John Condon, Fathi Yousef, David Hoopes, and others, insisted that communica-tion involved perception, a physical and social context, interaction, and feedback, but, above all, showed cross-cultural variations.

The early tillers in the field of intercultural communication were communica-tion professionals. From their discipline they brought some basic assumptions concerning the nature of communication. Gudykunst and Kim (1984) list several such assumptions about the nature of human communication now widely accepted. It is safe for us to assume that these givens, originating in the field of communication, were refined and altered as they passed through the intercultural filter. Communication is assumed to be symbolic, processual, transactional, attributional, and sometimes nonintentional. It involves the coding and decoding of messages, and takes places at varying levels of awareness (Gudykunst and Kim 1984:6–10). These characteristics, as we shall see later, are of vital interest to all intercultural communicators; they should be understood in theory and practice by every language teacher.

In addition, knowledge and understanding of differences in the uses and modes of communication, including the nonverbal, communicative styles, and other cross-cultural variables have been made available to us through the efforts of those in communication who were among the first to recognize the force of the culture and communication connection. Porter and Samovar (1982:31) state:

> . . . communication is an intricate matrix of interacting social acts that occur in a complex social environment. . . . This social environment is culture, and if we truly are to understand communication, we also must understand culture.

Practice

The field of intercultural communication has served to filter concepts and perspectives from many allied disciplines and in so doing has provided its own unique perspectives. In practice, then, these perspectives have been applied to research into cross-cultural differences and similarities in perception, communicative styles, socialization, evaluation, cognition, culture change, and many other sociocultural phenomena. The pitfalls of translation, equivalence, and information transmission have been examined (Gumpert and Cathcart 1982; Osgood et al. 1957; Sechrest et al. 1972). In addition, problems of prejudice, acculturation, culture shock, and second language learning viewed from the intercultural aspect have taken on new dimensions. Finally, "borrowed" concepts have been redefined and selectively honed in the new field and are now emerging with greater force and potential as explanatory devices.

In practice, the development of cross-cultural awareness as the first step in cross-cultural understanding and communication has been the focus of study and training. The communicative act itself in all its many individual and cultural guises is now recognized as a major analytical unit. In practice, this has meant that success or failure to communicate rests to a great extent upon the combination of personal, social, and cultural characteristics each communicator brings to the communicative act. Techniques to develop cross-cultural awareness and intercultural communicative skills are now being used in the field of second language learning. Many of our student textbooks reflect the concepts, assumptions, and principles listed above; they have been filtered from the social sciences through the field of intercultural communication to us.

Consideration of the relationships indicated in Figure 2.1 should sensitize the reader to the implications of the eclecticism of the theoretical foundations of research and practice in the field of intercultural communication. These are the sources of those confusing and often contradictory definitions of key concepts found in the literature and research in the field. The fluid nature of theory in the field of intercultural communication has proved to be both a welcome asset and a burdensome liability. The flexibility inherent in fluidity has permitted the continued borrowing from allied disciplines and the subsequent enrichment of the new field. On the other hand, this constant borrowing has set intercultural communication researchers, theorists, and practitioners adrift upon a sea of paradoxes and contradictions with a boatload of ill-defined terms and many theoretical stars to follow.

Yet for anyone willing to ignore Polonius' warning neither to borrow nor to lend, but to accept some equivocation, the enrichment that comes from the filtering effect will be rewarded with greater understanding of the very complex phenomena under study in the field of intercultural communication. Given the current focus on communicative competence and culture learning in conjunction with second language study, to fail to understand these theoretical sources may mean that teachers will find themselves plying their trade with textbooks whose contents and objectives are very "foreign" indeed.

FOR STUDY AND DISCUSSION

1. Identify these terms:

   intercultural communication

   cross-cultural training

   intercultural communicative skills

   intracultural communication

2. In the preceding chapter several unanswered questions were posed concerning the basic approaches taken in intercultural communication research and practice. These included the question of the relative importance of similarities and differences. Which are more important in your opinion? Should this be an "either/or" question?

3. Discuss the major contributions made to intercultural communication theory by the contributing disciplines of sociology, linguistics, communication, psychology, and anthropology. Relate these contributions to research and practice in the field of second language learning.

4. It has been observed in this chapter that those who do not have an understanding of the theoretical foundations of the present communicative ap-

proach to second language teaching and learning may find themselves uncomfortable with modern student textbooks. What type of problems might they have in using such texts? How could these problems be overcome? What is meant by the statement that the contents and objectives of some textbooks might be very "foreign" to some teachers?

5. The problem of dealing with intracultural variations has plagued those responsible for intercultural and cross-cultural communication and training. Should cultural descriptions be confined to the so-called "mainstream" culture or should minority cultures also be represented? Discuss this question in relation to the situation in the United States. What has been the traditional approach to this problem?

6. What is the role of perception in intercultural communication?

7. If every communicative act is in some degree intercultural because no two persons are alike, is there any reason to regard intracultural variation as different from intercultural variation? If there are differences, what might they be?

8. Describe a personal intercultural communicative encounter that was somewhat less than satisfactory. What happened? What were the causes of the unsatisfactory result? If you could reenact the encounter, how would you change your behavior?

9. What are some of the new perspectives that a knowledge of the processes and problems of intercultural communication might bring to the practice of second language learning/teaching?

CULTURE LEARNING EXERCISE

Discovery

Learning about a new culture involves seeking out information, asking questions, and making observations. It also involves bringing the characteristics of the cultural patterns and ways of behaving of both oneself and of others to a conscious level so that these patterns may be examined and understood in a nonevaluative manner. The following activities have been chosen as a means of helping you plan your own voyage of cultural discovery.

Select several communicatively oriented student language textbooks currently used in second language learning. Choose textbooks whose stated objectives include the teaching of culture and/or the development of the communicative competence of the student. Examine these books and answer the following questions. Then make a brief report to the class about your findings.

1. What has been included in these textbooks that might have been "missing" from standard texts? Are the changes a matter of content, organization, or both?

2. How has culture learning been approached? Is the cultural content related to a specific culture or to culture in general?

3. How is communicative competence defined and how is it encouraged by the format of the textbooks you have examined?

4. Do you feel you would need any special training to use this textbook? Are you familiar with all the cultural patterns shown? Are you comfortable with the cultural materials presented?

FOR FURTHER READING

M. Asante, E. Newmark, and C. Blake (eds.). 1979a. *Handbook of Intercultural Communication*. This volume contains a series of state-of-the-art essays on the field of intercultural communication in 1979. General topics covered include: theory, conceptual framework, issues, data handling, research, and practice. Because it provides a historical dimension, this is a useful reference for those new to the field.

J. Condon and F. Yousef. 1975. *An Introduction to Intercultural Communication*. This was the first textbook in the field. It is written in an informal style and covers issues of general interest, including values, language and culture, culture and thought, and nonverbal communication. It is recommended to the novice in the field although its emphasis is more on communication than on culture. Its major focus is upon the influence of value and belief systems in cross-cultural contexts.

W. Gudykunst and Y. Kim. 1984 *Communicating with Strangers: An Approach to Intercultural Communication*. The approach taken in this book reflects a model of intercultural communication "based on the premise that communication between people from different cultures is essentially the same as communication between people from different subcultures." The authors conceptualize the "process of communication with people who are unknown and unfamiliar as communication with strangers" (v). This book contains theoretically sensitive yet clearly stated discussions of the major influences affecting the processes of intercultural communication. It is concerned with personal interaction, but in the context of cross-cultural variation and the processes of intercultural interaction.

D. Hoopes. 1979a. "Intercultural Communication Concepts and the Psychology of Intercultural Experience" (10–38). This is a concise and very enlightening discussion of the development of the field of intercultural communication and some of the problems that have been encountered in research and practice.

M. Prosser. 1978. *The Cultural Dialogue: An Introduction to Intercultural Communication*. The focus of this introductory textbook is on interpersonal relations. The author examines major components of communication and culture. The final section of the book is devoted to practical examination of interactive processes in a cross-cultural perspective.

L. Samovar and R. Porter. 1982. *Intercultural Communication: A Reader*. First published in 1972, this anthology of readings in intercultural communication has proved a perennial favorite. Its major sections cover approaches to intercultural communication, the sociocultural variables affecting such communication, intercultural interaction, and means of overcoming communication problems. This book, along with the book of readings edited by Smith and Luce (see below), provides a general overview of the field with enough theory, culture-specific information, and variety to satisfy most readers. It offers an ample spread to those who would take the buffet approach to intercultural communication. There is something for everyone. It contains excellent bibliographic entries so that any one of the tidbits offered can become the main course. In the first chapter, the article, "Approaching Intercultural Communication," by Porter and Samovar (26–42) presents a general definition of intercultural communication, a model, and a discussion of major variables affecting interaction.

E. Smith and L. Luce (eds.) 1979. *Toward Internationalism: Readings in Cross-Cultural Communication.* As noted above, this is one of the two most widely used books of readings. It contains an introduction and overview of the field of intercultural communication. Its fourteen articles were written by leading authorities in the field. As stated in the Introduction (ix), the articles included were "selected with the view to help the nonspecialist reader gain an understanding of culturally conditioned behavior as it relates to intercultural relations between people of different nations." Thus, cross-cultural differences are emphasized.

E. Stewart. 1978. "Outline of Intercultural Communication." In F. Casmir (ed.). *Intercultural and International Communication* (265–344). This is an exhaustive account of the roots and fundamental concepts incorporated in the field of intercultural communication and their sources in the disciplines of communication, linguistics, and anthropology.

NOTES

1. Readers may find it surprising that a textbook devoted to culture learning in language classrooms does not present a series of definitions of key concepts in an opening chapter. It might be argued that such definitions are essential in order to understand the arguments set forth.

    Yet it may also be said that the early imposition of definitions of key concepts, such as language, culture, and communication, will lock the reader/learner into a formalistic approach to culture learning. Because various perspectives on these concepts emphasize different features, it is the basic premise of this book that multiple perspectives are right and proper when approaching matters intercultural and cross-cultural.

    Readers are assured that acceptance of the stricture of delayed definitions will facilitate their understanding of these complex phenomena. Those who find this restriction intolerable, may turn to Chapter 5. There they will find a discussion of the various definitions of culture, communication, and language. Those who can wait, but would like to lower their ambiguity anxiety level, may consult the Glossary provided at the end of the book. To those who are willing to postpone, for a short time, the question of definitions, may your rewards be all that the author hopes they will be.

2. The terms *cross-cultural* and *intercultural* are, in a sense, synonymous. In this book, however, the designation *intercultural* is used to indicate interaction between persons or groups from different cultural areas. The emphasis is on interaction. The term *cross-cultural* focuses on the differences to be found between interacting individuals and groups who do not share common cultural patterns and orientation. Thus, employing the common usage in the field of intercultural communication, we will speak of "intercultural interaction" and "intercultural communication" on the one hand, but, on the other hand, will refer to "cross-cultural awareness" and "cross-cultural contexts."

Chapter 3

Queries and Theories in Intercultural Communication

Although, as is clear from the previous discussion, theory, research, and practice in the field of intercultural communication are still evolving, it is worthwhile to consider briefly some of the analytical models and research questions associated with the field and to assess their implications for language learning theory, research, and practice.

3.1 SOME PARADIGMS

One of the major theoretical questions concerns the most useful model, or paradigm, to employ in examining instances of intercultural interaction and/or communication. Several models have been suggested; they are not necessarily mutually exclusive, but rather focus on different aspects of intercultural events. None has proved completely satisfactory.

Some observers feel it is too early to construct formal theory, opting for continued emphasis upon discovery. Although some see the field as "preparadigmatic," a state in which there are conflicting paradigms, this does not necessarily mean that there is no room for theorizing. Gudykunst (1983b:15) writes, "It is my contention that theorizing is necessary in intercultural communication if we are to *understand* the process of communication between people from different cultures and have guides for our future research efforts." It is for the first reason that we must take a brief look at the several means by which the processes and components of intercultural communication have been viewed and the major research questions raised.

Rohrlich (1983), in a discussion of intercultural paradigms describes two levels of theorizing—the interpersonal process level and the personal psychological level. He traces these differences to a division between theorists who view the problems experienced in intercultural communication "as a dysfunction of symbolic communication, stressing the need for a better communicative vehicle, and theorists who view it as a dysfunction of the interpretive translation, emphasizing the need for enhanced interpretive mechanisms" (192).

Rohrlich finds that, in general, communication professionals have been associated with the "vehicle school" and psychologists with the "interpretive school." From the sidelines, anthropologists and sociologists have seen themselves as "mediating influences on either end" (192).

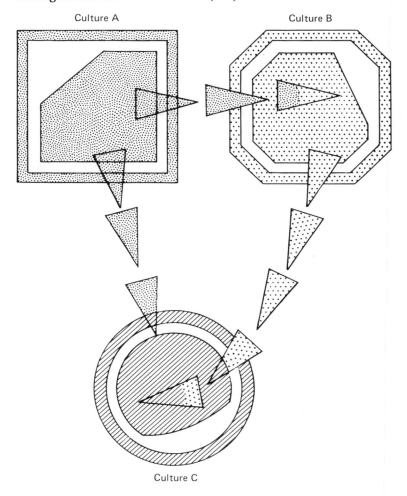

Model of Intercultural Communication

Figure 3.1. The Porter and Samovar Model

from *Intercultural Communication: A Reader*, Third Edition, by Larry A. Samovar and Richard E. Porter © 1982 by Wadsworth, Inc. Reprinted by permission of the authors and the publisher.

Some paradigms or models of the phenomenon of intercultural communication that have been suggested are shown in Figures 3.1 and 3.2. The Porter and Samovar model (Figure 3.1) is concerned with the dysfunction of symbolic communication. It represents three cultures. The various shapes indicate the degrees of difference and similarity. In the model the squares and octagons are more similar to one another in form than either are to circles. The distance between the forms indicates the degree of cultural distance—A and B being closer to each other than they are to C. Individuals are represented by forms within the culture which show differences from the general pattern. The authors (1982:34) comment:

> The shape of the individual is slightly different from that of the influencing culture. This suggests two things. First, there are other affecting influences besides culture that help shape the individual. And, second, although culture is a dominant shaping force on an individual, people vary to some extent from each other within any culture.

An Organizing Model for Studying Communication with Strangers

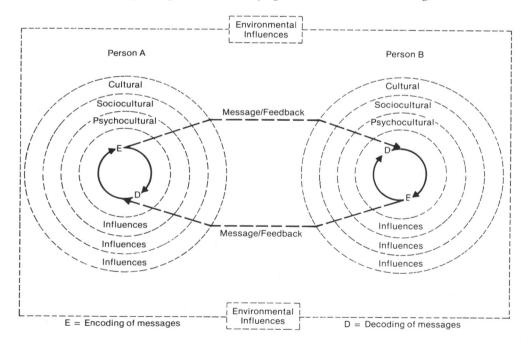

Figure 3.2. The Gudykunst and Kim Model

W. Gudykunst and Y. Kim, *Communicating with Strangers: An Approach to Intercultural Communication.* (Reading, MA.: Addison-Wesley; 1984), p. 30.

The Gudykunst and Kim model (Figure 3.2) focuses upon the act of communication, bringing the communicative act to the individual level. It concentrates on the ways in which cultural, sociocultural, and psychocultural influences affect the communication process. In this model, the circles represent individuals. The box of environmental influences is drawn with dashed lines "because the immediate environment in which the communication takes place is not an isolated or 'closed system' " (1984:29). The authors point out that most communication takes place in a social environment in which other people and other influences may be present. The cultural, sociocultural, and psychocultural or personal influences serve as conceptual filters, which limit what is attended to and how messages are perceived and evaluated (31). Psychocultural influences are cognitive and affective variables that affect communication, while sociocultural influences are those variables that relate to social organization. The latter include role, status, and other socially influenced relationships.

Both of these models focus upon the components in intercultural interaction and circumstances at work on the processes of communication within such contexts.

3.2 A UNIFIED APPROACH

Although these models are very useful, as we shall see, in the analysis of a given event and the behavior of individuals, they do not help us deal with the various levels at which observation, analysis, and theorizing may take place.

Rohrlich (1983) has suggested a systems theory approach to a unified conception of intercultural communication. He posits three levels of analysis: intrapersonal, interpersonal, and synthetic. A modified version of his table is shown in Table 3.1.

TABLE 3.1 UNIFIED CONCEPTUAL TABLE FOR INTERCULTURAL COMMUNICATION

Level	Characteristics	Processes
Intrapersonal	Cognitive/Perceptual	Psychological
Interpersonal	Interpretational	Communicative
Synthetic	Systemic	Adjustment

Source: Information contained in this table was drawn from an article and table by P. Rohrlich (1983), "Toward a Unified Conception of Intercultural Communication. An Integrated Systems Approach." *International Journal of Intercultural Relations* 7:191–209.

The Intrapersonal Level—The Private Perspective

At this level the individual stands alone. Personal perception molded by private experience in a cultural context colors communicative processes. This perception, centered as it is in the individual psyche, reflects some of the cultural values shared by fellow culture bearers but is expressed in unique and individual patterns due to the communicator's personal experience and social history.

Rohrlich (1983:199) comments: "It is at the level of the individual that the values and behaviors instructed by culture meet incoming human and environmental data, and the reconciliation that takes place yields perceptions" (199). Singer (1982:54), in proposing a perceptual model of culture, states that "man behaves as he does because of the ways in which he perceives the external world. . . . In terms of human behavior . . . there exists, for man, only subjective reality— i.e., the universe as individual men perceive it." A given communicator's formulation of his own subjective reality is a powerful force at the psychocultural level of intercultural communication.

It is at the intrapersonal level—the division between two individuals or groups of individuals—that culture shock is experienced, and, perhaps, overcome. Here the processes of language and culture learning or acquisition are carried out. Here ethnocentrism flourishes. It is also here that the forces of values and beliefs are so strongly felt and that "subjective culture"—"a group's characteristic way of perceiving its social environment" (Triandis *et al.* 1972:339)—meets each individual culture bearer's subjective reality. It is also here that the individual's view of the world, in part shared with others of his own group, collides with other views and other worlds. It is the level of personal perception.

Theory at this level has been drawn from research and practice in anthropology (culture and personality, the processes of enculturation and acculturation, or socialization); social psychology (universals of human perception, cognition, personality characteristics); communication (processes, barriers, styles, cross-cultural differences, cross-cultural awareness) and linguistics (the nature of language acquisition processes and the relationship of language and culture).

The Interpersonal Level—The Public Perspective

This level involves the act of communication and is concerned with interpretation. The communicative act brings into contact two or more individuals wrapped in their own psychocultural worlds of values, beliefs, ways of behaving, and evaluations. If one subscribes to the theory that because no two individuals can share the same personal, social, and cultural experiences, then one is also constrained to identify any and all acts of communication as intercultural to some degree. It is at the interpersonal level of communication or miscommunication that intercultural interaction takes place.

Research at this level has been concerned with finding ways and means of facilitating the processes of intercultural interaction as well as identifying cross-cultural variations of communicative style, the nature of the act of communication, and problems of cross-cultural interpretation and translation. Theory has been drawn from anthropology (cross-cultural studies, ethnographies), psychology (cross-cultural studies of motivation, attitudes, and perceptions), communication (communicative processes, facilitating methods, cross-cultural variations) and sociolinguistics (code rules, sociocultural variables).

The Synthetic Level—The Dynamic Perspective

Rohrlich (1983:200–201) proposes a third level of analysis—the synthetic level—which "captures the results of interpersonal interactions. . . . Behaviors explained by this plane are synthesized from these interactions, and are system structural in origin." It is a level of analysis directed at the dynamics of group interaction and communicative processes; it involves the effects of feedback (positive and negative) as well as the "unpredictability of cross-cultural contacts . . ."(201).

Synthesis may encourage the development of cross-cultural awareness, understanding, empathy, and intercultural communicative skills. It may also nurture what has been called a "third culture." This is a perspective springing from the effects of the melding of the subjective cultures of the communicants. Gudykunst, Wiseman, and Hammer (1977:424) describe persons who use the third-culture perspective as those who do not use their native perspectives in interpreting the actions of persons from other cultures. Those who do develop such insights may serve as communication links between persons of other cultures. (See Chapter 16.)

Finally, Rohrlich identifies the context of communication as the "environment," which includes both the physical environment and the cultural backgrounds of the actors. He explains (203):

> . . . our systemic view of intercultural communication sees a system as a set of interacting elements, actors, interacting in a physically and culturally compounded environment. While the environment exists apart from the system, its cultural relevance derives from cultural perception of it by the system's actors, and hence it can be studied as a systemically important variable without becoming part of the system.

This somewhat ingenuous way of dealing with the cultural context of any act of intercultural communication, both as an external variable (the environment) and as a variable of the system, leaves unclear which elements in the environment are culturally colored and which are not.

In any case, Rohrlich's description of the three analytical levels does sort out some puzzling relationships and allows the untutored observer to proceed with some degree of understanding of the various forces at work in intercultural communication. There are, of course, many other models or paradigms of intercultural communication that have not been discussed (Hall 1977; Sarbaugh 1979; Szalay 1981). Each provides a particular focus upon the phenomena under scrutiny. In the following chapters of this book, Rohrlich's trifocal approach will serve as a general framework in the discussion of the importance of personal characteristics of individual learners, salient variables at work in the communication process, and the effect of intercultural contact and interaction. It must be added that the use of this framework in no way should be construed as an attempt to test the analytical force of the model. That must be left to those more directly involved in providing a well-rounded and firm foundation for research and practice in the field of intercultural communication.

3.3 THE MIRROR OF CULTURE

The systems approach provides us with a means of integrating our examination of various contributions made to the field of intercultural communication by other disciplines, the processes of intercultural communication, and the types of training and discovery methods that enhance the development of intercultural communicative skills and cross-cultural awareness. Figure 3.3 presents yet another model of intercultural communication; one that has been devised not to guide research but to present a graphic reminder of all that must be considered in enhancing effective intercultural communication. Thus, the *Mirror of Culture* reflects an image of the patterns of the native culture, including artifacts, subjective orientations, and social/communicative patterns influencing intercultural communication. It makes clear that these patterns are filtered through the individuals' values, assumptions, beliefs, and perceptions. What each communicant brings to the intercultural encounter is partially public and shared with other members of his or her cultural group. But it is also private and personal. Thus, no one person represents a whole culture, and cultural patterns are not shared by all members of a cultural group in exactly the same way. To fail to recognize the public/private dichotomy is to provide fertile ground for the noisome seeds of stereotyping. The boxes to the left and right of the communication line in Figure 3.3 represent ways and means of facilitating understanding and enhancing communicative effectiveness.

This figure is not just another model of intercultural communication; it is meant to be a reference tool to hold up to our students, our culture, their culture, and ourselves. We cannot afford to let ourselves use only one-way mirrors. It is often as hard to know oneself as it is to know others.

3.4 SOME ISSUES AND QUESTIONS

In forging a connection between theory and practice in the fields of intercultural communication and language teaching and learning, it is important to give some consideration to issues vital to research and practice in both fields if only for the purposes of seeking safety in numbers and new ideas in alternative views.

What then are some of these issues to be considered and questions to be answered? Let us first examine them as intercultural communication issues and

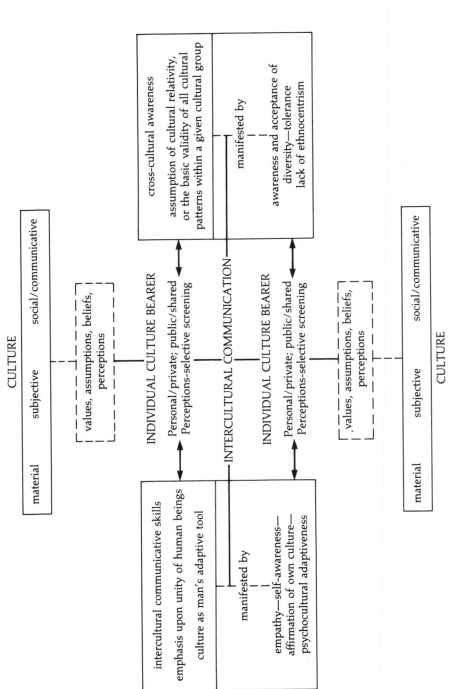

Figure 3.3. The Mirror of Culture

problems, and then rephrase or consider these questions in the language learning and teaching context. You are warned that, as the jury is still out, there are few resolutions or unequivocal answers.

Intercultural Communication Issues

One major issue relates to theorizing. What philosophical approach should be used? The traditional empirical-positivist models, being linear and causal, have been seen as ill-suited to intercultural or cross-cultural research. Blackman (1983:284) comments that as these models focus upon fragments of the world they are "inadequate to deal with the complex, processual nature of communication." He suggests that more holistic models are needed in which descriptive research forms a major methodology. He suggests the use of a grounded theory approach,[1] a method of theorizing more easily tailored to the complexities of intercultural communication than quantitative measures.

Other intercultural communication issues involve the variables to be considered in developing adequate theory, the measurement of cross-cultural validity, the relationship of language theory to communication theory, and the value of maintaining multiple philosophical approaches as suggested by Asante and Vora (1983:296):

> Theories of communication explaining an intercultural phenomenon should not be bound by Western philosophies and premises about human interactions and behaviors. Persons from each culture may develop their own theoretical frameworks based on their own perception of an intercultural experience.

Thus, although scientific methods, collection of data, and rigorous observations have their place in intercultural research, these authors conclude that the use of instruments, explanations, and conclusions must be approached from a multicultural rather than a global or noncultural perspective.

The complexity of such a theoretical stance boggles the mind. In a simple dyadic act of communication in an intercultural setting there are at least three perceptual versions of a culture, as Asante and Vora note (296): 1) one communicant's personal perception of his or her native culture; 2) the perception of that culture by the other or others; and 3) the communicant's perception of the culture of the other or others. Multiply each perspective by two and try to communicate.

In addition, Samovar, in an article entitled "Intercultural Communication Research: Some Myths, Some Questions" (1979), points out that there are still questions and debates concerning "parameters, prescription, description, boundaries, definitions, and subject matter" (22). One may well ask what issues are *not* under consideration. He continues by noting that some of the unresolved issues relate to the definition of key terms, the relationship of communication and culture, the influence of context, the best training methods to use, and the identification of the ingredients of successful intercultural communication. He also calls attention to the questions that have been raised and noted previously concerning the commonality of these variables cross-culturally, as well as the universality of generalizations about culture and communication formed in the Western context and using Western subjects and Western research methods.

Grounding the Theory

The theoretical problems of the researcher in intercultural and cross-cultural matters may seem far removed from the problems of the individual culture learner or the more practical matters of language and cultural guidance. Yet their implications provide clues as to the manner in which the individual culture learner should proceed and the means to facilitate the processes of culture learning in the classroom.

What does a grounded theory approach have to offer intercultural researchers and intercultural learners? The approach to theory-building and foundation suggested by Glaser and Strauss (1967) calls for the development of theory in the field and in practice. Hypotheses generation and testing, data collection, the integration of categories occur simultaneously and are guided "by the emerging theory" (Glaser 1978:2). Such "theory" or organization of data, in turn, provides the grounding for testable hypotheses and the discovery of generalizable statements pertaining to these hypotheses.

Blackman (1983) concludes that the characteristics of a grounded theory approach that make it attractive for practical use include its properties of theory development from data, natural processing, pragmatism, and flexibility. This approach makes use of the processes of natural culture learning as will be made clear in subsequent discussions of the nature of culture learning. Blackman explains (289):

> In the Grounded Theory method, the researcher reacts holistically to the research context and creates and organizes categories and a framework through the constant/comparative process. When the researcher begins to identify concepts and to make connections between them, he or she is "no longer a passive receiver of impressions, but is drawn naturally into actively generating and verifying his hypotheses through comparison" (Glaser and Strauss 1967:39). The process of perceiving and organizing and interpreting sensory data has been described as a likely focal point for intercultural communication research.

If the term *culture learner* is substituted for *researcher*, then it is clear that a grounded theory approach represents a useful culture learning perspective. In addition, teachers in the field are well-situated to gather some of these data for the grounding of theory—the generating of theory from data in the process of research—in intercultural communication and language learning. As Glaser and Strauss point out, ". . . theory can be developed only by professionally trained sociologists, but can be applied by either laymen or sociologists" (249). In any case, the flow of information need not always move from the researcher to the practitioner. Grounded theory methodology offers a means of gathering theoretically relevant data in the field and is available to all who would take advantage of its methodology.

Pedagogical Questions

Let us consider how these issues lie hidden in the practical and pedagogical questions we ask ourselves daily. In translating these theoretical and methodological issues into pedagogical questions, we may focus more directly on the areas in which an intercultural perspective is vital.

1. What constitutes the ability to function in a specific culture? In other words, what is communicative or intercultural competence?

2. What is the nature of learning, learning a language, learning a second language, and their relationships to culture learning in general and the acquisition of communicative skills in a specific culture?

3. Closely related to the questions above are those which have to do with the learning of a new language and its cultural notions and functions. What methods are most successful? Can we employ an approach that concentrates on the universal processes associated with culture learning, or must we take cross-cultural variations in learning styles and purposes into consideration? If so, to what extent?

4. How may current theoretical approaches to second language learning or acquisition be reconciled with the answers to the above questions?

5. What is biculturalism? What is bilingualism? How do these constructs relate to the twin levels of competence and performance as set forth in current linguistic theory and as general theoretical support for current practice in ESL/EFL?

6. What sociocultural variables, such as race, class, age, or sex, influence second language and culture learning? How?

7. What content is most appropriate for use in the classroom? What criteria should be used in selecting or creating culturally sensitive materials?

8. What principles and assumptions should guide the planning of culturally sensitive and informative curricula and the implementation of facilitating lesson plans?

9. How can culture learning be tested? What objectives and criteria should be set?

10. How may a multicultural language classroom become an effective locus for language *and* culture learning? What skills should the teacher develop in order to serve as an effective intercultural communicator and guide?

3.5 CONCLUSION

These are only some of the many issues to be met and questions to be answered if culture is to be accorded its rightful place in the language classroom. There is no longer any question of whether culture should be part of the language curricula. The questions to ask are *how* and *what* and *when*.

In several aspects, the answers to these questions are unclear. Experts in the field remain divided. There is the question of same or different. Should the similarities we share as human beings and natural communicators or miscommunicators receive attention, or should the great differences found in cultural and subcultural patterns demand the attention of researchers and trainers? How do we balance these extremes?

Then, there are questions of the importance of subcultural variations, the maintenance of cultural diversity, and the implications of a policy of cultural pluralism in a heterogeneous society such as that in the United States. These questions are rooted in divisiveness; the answers are often equally so.

Finally, there is the question of the dual nature of all intercultural communicative acts. Their nature is both personal and private as well as public and shared. Each individual is a representative of a given culture and a unique human being who internalizes these shared patterns in a distinctive manner and in varying degrees.

The issues and questions discussed above must be considered along with many other variables in the sorting out of the intricate jigsaw puzzle of intercultural communication. They are only answerable in an approach, such as offered by the grounded theory model, that permits the widest possible theoretical perspectives. The borrowing or accommodating of so many concepts from various sources has brought strength to the field of intercultural communication. At the same time, it has, as Rohrlich (1983:193) points out, "resulted in a diffuse theory base, leaving islands of insight with little connection between them to make their unrelated though often compatible approaches mutually useful."

In the following chapters, each of these "islands of insight" will be explored in relation to the topics being discussed. The relationships of these concepts to each other in the crucible of intercultural communication will be examined for the purpose of demonstrating their compatibility and utility in the processes of second language learning and teaching.

FOR STUDY AND DISCUSSION

1. Identify the following terms:

   grounded theory

   psychocultural variables

   subjective culture

   sociocultural variables

2. Consult Figure 3.3 *The Mirror of Culture* and then discuss the following statements or questions:

   a) What type of training might be useful in the development of intercultural communicative skills? Cross-cultural awareness? How would the two types of training differ in terms of goals, objectives, and content?

   b) "Culture" is shown in this figure as composed of three types of elements or patterns: material, subjective, and social/communicative. In general, material culture refers to physical objects or artifacts and ways of arranging cultural life; subjective culture refers to attitudes; and social/communicative elements are those concerned with human communication. Give examples of each type of element. How might the examples you choose vary cross-culturally?

   c) What is meant by the statement that each person brings elements that are personal and private (hidden and unique) and public and shared (open and exhibited by others) to all communicative events? How does this affect intercultural communication?

3. What does a grounded theory approach to cultural discovery have to offer the culture learner? Would it provide a means of reducing prejudice and stereotypic behavior in a cross-cultural context? How?

4. Several issues were discussed in this chapter relative to the importance of context and training methods as unresolved issues in the field of intercultural communication. What types of problems do you think might arise concerning these factors? Are there similar problems in ESL/EFL?

5. Review the questions listed on page 47 concerning pedagogical issues. Try to frame additional questions, provide examples of problems connected with these questions, and, if possible, suggest some solutions. Use your own experience, personal and professional, to think about these important questions.

CULTURE LEARNING EXERCISE

Self-Discovery

An important step in developing cross-cultural awareness and intercultural communicative skills is to know yourself. The following exercises are designed to help you begin to explore your own cultural identity.

1. It has been stated in this chapter that each person who tries to communicate with another brings elements that are private (hidden), personal (idiosyncratic), public (acknowledged), and shared (socially appropriate). Using the outline below as suggested in Seelye (1984:201) from Kraemer (1973), give personal examples of these elements. Then select a person from another culture and, using the same general outline, ask that person how he or she would complete the outline. Did you find any differences? Any similarities? Any surprises? Any disappointments?

Every person thinks and acts in *some* respects

	Examples	
	Yourself	Another
—like all other persons		
—like some other persons of the same age of the same sex of the same profession		
—like no other person		

Source: Alfred Kraemer, *Development of a Cultural Self-Awareness Approach to Instruction in Intercultural Communication.* In H. Ned Seelye. 1984: *Teaching Culture: Strategies for Intercultural Communication.* p. 202.

2. Recall some communicative episode in which you were a participant. This might be an exchange with a friend, a stranger, a student, or a family member. Consider what you might have brought to that event in terms of the public, the private, the shared, and the personal (as defined above). Note your recollections in the grid that follows. Did any of these features affect the outcome of the communicative event? If so, how?

If you cannot recall such an event, then consider the interaction between the teacher and the Dutch student described in Chapter 2.

Personal	Private
Shared	Public

FOR FURTHER READING

W. Davey (ed.). 1979. *Intercultural Theory and Practice: Perspectives on Education, Training and Research.* This volume contains abstracts of significant sessions, keynote presentations, and selected papers resulting from the SIETAR (Society for Intercultural Education, Training, and Research) meeting in Phoenix, Arizona, February 1978. Of particular interest are articles by Larry Samovar, "Intercultural Communication Research: Some Myths, Some Questions" (21–27) and by Edward Stewart, "Research in Intercultural Communication" (8–20).

W. Gudykunst (ed.). 1983a. *Intercultural Communication Theory: Current Perspectives.* This is the seventh volume of the *International and Intercultural Communication Annual* sponsored by the Speech Communication Association's Commission on International and Intercultural Communication. All of the previous annuals, which are cited in whole or in part in the bibliography, are valuable to those who would understand the history and development of the field of intercultural communication. This volume, unlike the others, is concerned not with various issues and problems in the field but is organized around a single theme—theorizing in intercultural communication. Although these discussions may be somewhat difficult for those not conversant with theory in this field and related disciplines, they merit the effort required. Of particular interest in connection with this chapter are the articles by Gudykunst, "Theorizing in Intercultural Communication: An Introduction" (13–20) and B. Blackman, "Toward a Grounded Theory" (283–292). The latter article presents an excellent description of the grounded theory approach and its value in intercultural communication research.

P. Rohrlich. 1983. "Toward a Unified Conception of Intercultural Communication" (191–209). This article presents the systems theory explained in this chapter. Rohrlich's systems approach describes a practical model for the examination of the various levels of analysis and theorizing in the field of intercultural communication.

NOTE

1. The grounded theory approach to research was defined and developed by Glaser and Strauss (1967:1) as a strategy for the "discovery" of theory from data "systematically obtained and analyzed". In their research design, the generation of theory and analytical categories are continuous processes carried out during the period of research as opposed to the verification of theory or the testing of hypotheses formulated before the research is undertaken. The theory developed by the Glaser and Strauss model is grounded in the sense that "most hypotheses and concepts not only come from the data, but are systematically worked out in relation to the data during the course of the research" (6). Theory generation is part of the process of research. The grounded theory approach is also characterized by the use of a constant comparative method of analysis by which data gathered and categories defined are constantly being revised as new data become available. This involves the comparison of slices of data.

   Because the methods of grounded theory involve the gathering of data about what is new and different and the formulation of hypotheses about their significance, the grounded theory approach parallels the processes of all learning. This approach to qualitative research is a strategy for gathering and analyzing data for purposes of description, explanation—and understanding.

Chapter 4

A Pragmatic Approach to Intercultural Inquiry

In spite of the many obstacles and pitfalls that may be expected, each of you, as an active learner, is encouraged to undertake a proposed personal journey of cultural discovery. Such a trip is the first step in the process of making culture learning a fifth skill to be nurtured in the language classroom. It is important to note that culture learning as a process, not simply learning about a culture, is the focus of this book. All recommendations, exercises, questions, discussions, and suggested readings contained in this book have been designed and selected with one simple assumption in mind—learning how to learn about a new culture is the primary skill needed for effective intercultural communication. If the culture learning processes are understood, then all other subsidiary skills can be developed.

Theoretically sensitive practitioners in search of the means to weave theory into practice and practice into theory must first thoroughly understand the ways in which cultures are explored and subsequently learned, or at least internalized. In turn, what they learn by doing may be transmitted to their language students.

The use of traditional training methods such as role play, cultural simulations, workshops, selected readings, lectures, visits, and other devices for enhancing cross-cultural awareness and encouraging intercultural communication are, of course, means to the same end. These methods and techniques have not been rejected, for they are the bases for many of the exercises and activities recommended in this book. They do not, however, form the primary method of training advocated in this book. A more practical approach is suggested.

4.1 PRAGMATIC ETHNOGRAPHY

This approach has been named "pragmatic ethnography" in order to clarify the limitations of the method as a scientific procedure and to allay any fears that the highly structured and complex organization of ethnographic research as practiced by professional anthropologists has been popularized, watered down, and rendered trivial. Quite to the contrary, the pragmatic ethnographic approach to culture learning involves simulating the processes of exploring, describing, and understanding an unknown culture by means of actual ethnographic inquiry, contrastive analysis of real cultural groups, and contact with real culture bearers. It is simulation and role play taken out of the classroom and practiced in the real world of the cultural traveller. It is a grounded theory approach in practice.

Although not carried out in a rigorous scientific mode, the adaptation of techniques used in cross-cultural research may lessen the amount of oversimplification and distortions risked in contrived simulations and traditional role play. In addition, such a practical approach approximates the "natural" ways of dealing with new cultures. The bringing of both cultural patterns and themes under scrutiny, and methods of learning and discovery to a conscious level should shed light on the nature of culture and the difficulties, hazards, and rewards of gaining knowledge of the cultural worlds of others.

Such experiences are necessary because culture, as a form of human adaptation, serves many functions. One of these functions, as Edward T. Hall points out in *Beyond Culture* (1977:85), is "to provide a highly selective screen between man and the outside world. . . . This screening function provides structure for the world and protects the nervous system from 'information overload'."

Readers are warned that they may suffer considerable anxiety, even annoyance, as they attempt to follow the proposed training model. They must be prepared to search out and organize considerable cultural data. They must also be prepared to let insights emerge as investigations continue, to understand processes by engaging in them, and to wait for definitions to be formed rather than to be served up at the beginning of each chapter. They will be asked to ground their own personal theories concerning intercultural communication and its place in their language classrooms.

Of course, the method suggested smacks of American cultural values that place such a premium upon doing. The author pleads guilty to the charge, but argues that each researcher may bring his or her own particular style of learning and doing to the tasks suggested. Indeed, the more cross-cultural variation, the better!

Although there is risk of bringing on a severe case of reader information overload, the remainder of this chapter is devoted to a discussion of the methods of cultural discovery and cross-cultural analytical techniques that have proved so useful as professional tools for anthropologists. This review should provide some understanding of the value of these methods as guidelines for those searching for the "how" of cultural inquiry.

4.2 WHY ANTHROPOLOGY?

In an article in the *TESOL Quarterly* (1976) titled "The Relevance of Anthro-pology to Language Teaching," Beverly McLeod suggests that "there are some basic tenets of anthropology which may be useful" to language teachers (211). Expanding upon a suggestion by Paulston (1974:356) that teachers become an-thropologists, she adds: "Not only should the teacher become an anthropologist, but he should also encourage his students to become anthropologists as well" (213).

Both McLeod and Paulston were responding to the need to bring culture as an active force into the language classroom—a recommendation brought about by the development of interest in student communicative competence, or the ability to communicate in a given speech community. McLeod envisioned the language classroom as a type of cultural learning laboratory in which both students and teachers were learners, fellow cultural travellers. Such a solution, she concluded, would obviate the teacher's need to know everything about each student's cul-tural patterns and communicative styles, an obviously overwhelming task in the usual multicultural classrooms in which teachers function in the United States and often elsewhere. In any case, the cultural patterns of teacher and students must contrast as a function of the use of different linguistic and cultural systems.

It was assumed that the protected learning context of the classroom could serve as a haven in which to test cultural hypotheses concerning appropriate behavior without risking severe reprisals for errors. The classroom then could become, if you will, a type of administered or protected community.

In the ensuing years this suggestion has been more discussed than practiced. There are several reasons this should be so. First, the logic of the suggestion seems irrefutable given the overwhelming evidence of the close connection be-tween language and social and cultural patterns as reported in sociological, psy-chological, and linguistic literature (Hymes 1972a,b; Labov 1966; Saville-Troike 1978). Yet there are clear and present dangers that the use of the specialized and sophisticated research tools of anthropological field work by well-meaning ama-teurs may turn these finely honed tools into bludgeons. Field work is difficult and time-consuming. It calls for a high degree of empathy for those under scrutiny and also demands acceptance of the new and the strange. Few of these conditions are easily met by simply wishing they were present.

Second, time must be taken to develop the necessary research skills; anthro-pologists are made, not born. Lengthy training and long-term commitments to developing and using these skills are demanded in professional field work if valid data are to be obtained. Thus, the proposal that teachers or students, as naïve intercultural learners, can undertake such work without careful preparation, is at best unrealistic and at worst doomed to less than satisfactory results.

Third, cultural searching and theory formulation can often be both painful and disturbing for all concerned. Does not the teacher often risk complete communication breakdown in a classroom dedicated to cross-cultural probing and soul searching? Remember the plight of the teacher in Chapter 1!

4.3 WHY TEACHERS?

One may well ask why teachers or others need to embark on a cross-cultural research project, pragmatic or not. Wouldn't it be better to read about a cultural group and adjust teaching methods to the needs of that group? McLeod (1976:213) provides an answer:

> There is no reason to assume that the teacher is any more skillful in learning the culture of his students through implicit means alone than the students are in learning the teacher's culture.

To designate the teacher as chief anthropologist is to subscribe to some assumptions concerning the competencies of individual teachers that may not be justified and certainly should be assessed. For example, it is often assumed that persons entering the field of second language teaching are psychologically and professionally prepared to deal with cultural differences with understanding and sensitivity. Although many teachers have had cross-cultural contacts, these may not have produced much culture learning. Teachers and students alike are subject to culture shock and indulge in stereotyping. Thus, teachers must accept their own cultural bonds as well as those of their students.

In addition, it is often assumed that any teacher as a bearer of a target culture can, by right of group membership, competently supply inventories and explanations of cultural patterns by simply drawing on personal explanation and text selections. In effect, much of our behavior is so culturally conditioned that it is mediated at an out-of-awareness level; therefore, much of what is perceived as right and natural and correct is merely a reflection of shared cultural values, patterns, and beliefs. Hoopes (1979a:16) comments: "One of the major sources of intercultural misunderstanding and conflict lies in the clash of these deeply rooted and culturally conditioned perceptions of reality."

Finally, it cannot be assumed that a warm, understanding, and encouraging attitude on the part of the teacher will suffice to open the door to culture learning. Such attitudes will contribute to the ease with which the learning process takes place; they cannot be taken as substitutes for other preparatory efforts.

4.4 CULTURE LEARNING, ANYONE?

Alas, native culture learning (enculturation) is complex and additional culture learning (acculturation) doubly so. Both, however, can be facilitated by using a combination of knowledge acquisition, experience, and practice (Albert and Triandis 1985:329). The following discussion seeks to open the way to all three methods. Any readers who are uncomfortable without the benefit of definitions of some basic terms should turn to the Glossary of this book. Remember, however, as suggested in Chapter 2, that most useful definitions are context-sensitive; each of the Glossary definitions appears in the text of this book. If you wait long enough, you will receive not only dictionary definitions but also pragmatic ones as well.

Finally, the following discussion of the anthropological perspective should prepare teachers to expand their roles in the language-culture learning game to that of experienced guide, trained observer, and fellow intercultural communicator. To do so, they need not attempt to become closet anthropologists, ill-prepared and uncertain of their exploratory skills, but rather amateur cultural explorers who understand the general purposes and forms of cross-cultural research as well as of the basic field methods that have proved so effective in the practice of anthropology. Specifically, the ethnographic methods suggested as appropriate are: *ethnography* (structured cultural inquiry), *contrastive analysis*, and *cultural hypothesis formulation*. The techniques employed in these methods, combined with information from secondary sources such as handbooks, ethnographic reports, and journals, should prepare teachers to respond effectively to the call to bring anthropology into the language classroom. In the following sections of this chapter, the general features of these methods will be presented, followed by a specific plan for their use.

4.5 ETHNOGRAPHY AS CULTURAL DESCRIPTION

In the past, the terms *ethnology* and *ethnography* have been applied respectively to the study and description of so-called "primitive societies." Indeed, dictionary definitions still reflect early ethnocentric biases. As late as 1969, the *American Heritage Dictionary of the English Language* defined *ethnology* as "the anthropological study of socio-economic systems and cultural heritage, especially of cultural origins and of factors influencing cultural growth and change, in technologically primitive societies" (450). This definition underscores the propensity of early cultural explorers to equate nonindustrialization with primitiveness and all that the latter implies. Today ethnology and ethnographies (written descriptions) are no longer concerned exclusively with the far–away and exotic but also examine the nearby, the more familiar, and the modern.

Guidelines and Principles

Spradley in his excellent book *The Ethnographic Interview* (1979) presents a clear and easily followed set of guidelines for the execution of some of the basic processes related to ethnographic work. The book, written for budding anthropologists, has much to offer the pragmatic ethnographer. This author defines ethnography (9) in its modern guise as a "body of knowledge that includes research techniques, ethnographic theory, and hundreds of cultural descriptions." These descriptions are seen as the central task of the ethnographer.

As Spradley states: "There are as many ways to do ethnography as there are ethnographers" (230). Generally, ethnography involves informant interviewing or, as Spradley suggests, "learning from people" (3). Most current procedures are guided by a set of assumptions concerning culture, cultural themes and patterns, and attendant research postures. These principles and their implications include the following:

1. Learned cultural patterns, themes, and postulates characterize given cultural groups and provide solutions to human problems and guidelines for action.

2. These cultural givens bind culture bearers together but may blind them to the existence and/or efficacy of alternative cultural solutions and guidelines.

3. Descriptions of these themes and patterns must include the viewpoints and meanings assigned by the group under study.

4. Cultures should be studied in so-called "thick" descriptions, which examine the complex relationships of cultural categories and assumptions.

5. An attitude of cultural relativity, or nonevaluation by arbitrary outside standards, is essential for scientific rigor and ethnographic validity.

In practice, adherence to these principles has meant that any efforts aimed at understanding another culture should be guided toward the identification of salient cultural patterns and themes, that all efforts should be made to overcome ethnocentric bondage and blindness, that the internal "logic" of given cultural systems provides a unique "world view" for their bearers, that this world view is best conveyed by reference to the perceptions of those who share these patterns, and that no cultural group should be judged as being inherently superior or inferior to another.

The View from Inside

Those who learn about unfamiliar cultures are often painfully aware that a rose is not a rose—or at least a friend is not always a *real* friend—when encountered outside one's own world of cultural givens. These dilemmas arise in the paradox of the human experience. Although all human beings find themselves faced with similar problems of survival, nurture, and protection, they do not apply similar solutions to these universal problems, nor do they even refer in the same terms to relationships and conditions that all human beings share.

These differences are manifested in the interweaving of cultural patterns and symbols and their meanings to those who espouse them. In brief, what acts, artifacts, customs, and beliefs "mean" is defined in the context of the culture in which they occur. Spradley (1979:99) notes:

The meaning of any symbol is its relationship to other symbols in a particular culture. . . . The task of ethnography is to decode cultural symbols and identify the underlying coding rules. This can be accomplished by discovering the relationships among cultural symbols.

These meanings are expressed through the use of categories or classifications of cultural items and acts. Because these classifications are context-specific, they may vary cross-culturally. Thus, a friend may have very different attributes, be expected to behave in a different manner, and be accorded different roles in Thailand and Venezuela. The concept of "friend" is probably culture-general; the definitions of a "friend" are culture-specific.

This approach to cultural meaning is based on the assumption that different cultures "create" different realities and that those interacting in these cultural "worlds" share a common or very similar world view. World views are based on given sets of cultural postulates or "truths," which guide daily living and sharing, and combine to produce recurrent themes. An example of such a postulate might be the American subscription to activity and competition as positive forces. The dedication to this postulate is marked in our judgments of others as "winners" or "losers" and in our proverbial reluctance to just sit around and do nothing. A contrastive postulate calls for the kinds of passivity and harmony evidenced in many of the cultures of the Far East, so baffling to the "movers and shakers" who dominate the American business world of today.

Indeed, in addition to postulates, there are cultural variations in classification and categorization reflected not only in the use of language but also in the names bestowed upon artifacts and concepts and the characteristics assigned to these "realities." Not even the parts of the human body are labeled in the same way in all cultures. Ardener (1983) points out that a hand may be classified as inclusive of all parts of the forearm to just below the shoulder or merely as inclusive of the palm and fingers. Thus, if a person from a just-below-the-shoulder culture, such as the Ibo of southeastern Nigeria, is asked to give a hand, an entire forearm may be offered. (See Chapter 7 for additional variations on the same theme.)

The -Emics and -Etics of Cultural Inquiry

The value of describing a culture in its own cultural terms and from the point of view of the insider dominated early ethnographic field studies in the United States. This has been called an -emic approach. Although still widely used in modern practice, it is often supplemented with other methods of analysis including participant observation and quantitative studies.

Because much of the literature and research in both intercultural communication and second language learning is cast in an -emic perspective, it is important to understand the source and implications of the use of this approach to cultural discovery. A general discussion follows. The implications of the distinction and the application of linguistic models to cultural data is discussed at greater length in Chapter 6.

The terms, -emic and -etic, are abbreviated versions of the terms, phonemic and phonetic. In the analysis of unknown languages, researchers, including Kenneth Pike and Eugene Nida, used the term phonemic in contrast to the term phonetic. In phonological analysis, or the study of the sounds used in human language, the term phonetics has been used to indicate the physical sounds and their descriptions, while phonemics was reserved to indicate the sound system and categories of distinctive, abstract sound units in a given language.

Thus, what was true for language, Pike and others concluded, was true for culture. Pike (1954: 8–10) wrote:

> In contrast to the Etic approach, an Emic one is in essence valid for only one language (or one culture) at a time. . . . An etic analytical standpoint . . . might be called "external" or "alien," since for etic purposes the analyst stands "far enough away" from or "outside" of a particular culture to see its separate events, primarily in relation to their similarities and their differences, as compared to the events of other cultures.

Trueba and Wright (1980–1981:31) point out that an -emic analysis of ethnographic data calls for "congruence between the ethnographer's interpretation of observed behavior and the social meaning attached to that behavior by the actors . . ."

The theoretical and explanatory values of the meticulous uncovering of native categories as demanded by the -emic/-etic distinction have been and remain sources of dispute and misinterpretation in the field of anthropology (Harris 1968). However, the description of native classifications and shared meanings, by whatever method of analysis used, remains a fundamental step in current ethnographic field work and serves well those who would understand the cultural world of others. The establishment of culture-specific data elicited either from native informants or from observation permits descriptions of given cultural groups on their own terms and furthers theory formulation in the field based upon hypotheses generated from culture-specific data. It has also rekindled research interest in the problems of the relationship of language categories, perception, and world view.

Although such methods and their resultant analyses have often proved to be cumbersome to anthropologists searching for cross-cultural generalizations, they hold promise for those who would observe different cultural behavior or understand their own. An -emic approach encourages closer listening to and rejection of foregone ethnocentric interpretations, classifications, and evaluations of different behavior, verbal and nonverbal. It is based on the assumption that some understanding of native categories of meaning must precede cross-cultural comparison if apple/orange types of errors are to be avoided.

4.6 CONTRASTING FRAMES
OF REFERENCE

Robert Lado, in *Linguistics Across Cultures* (1957:vii) suggests that a comparative approach to language and cultural differences would be a useful means to predict and describe patterns that "will cause difficulty in learning, and those that will not cause difficulty, by comparing systematically the language and culture to be learned with the native language and culture of the student." Using field methods developed in structural linguistics and tagmemics, Lado describes methods to compare and contrast languages on the bases of their sound systems, grammatical structures, and vocabulary. Meaning, forms, and distributional characteristics were analyzed. Thus, Lado proposes the application of an adapted form of the Pike model to contrastive cultural or *-emic* units or concepts.

Lado's assumptions of the efficacy of contrastive analysis as a means to predict and describe linguistic patterns that would prove troublesome to language learners were apparently either false, or at least unverifiable, as research indicated. A moderated approach posited that more difficulties would be encountered in areas of subtle rather than in more apparent differences (Oller and Ziahosseiny 1970). As interest in contrastive analysis dimmed, researchers began to investigate the promise of error analysis and the phenomenon of interlanguage in the search for a more productive approach to investigating language acquisition problems (Dulay and Burt 1972, 1974a, 1974b; Oller 1971; Richards 1971, 1974; Selinker 1971).

Although the *-emic* approach and the method Lado and others have suggested for cross-cultural contrast may not have proved wholly adequate for the purposes to which they were put in the fields of anthropology and language learning, they do provide two means to facilitate the process of learning a new culture: understanding the view from inside one's own culture and that of another's, and uncovering distinctive differences by means of contrastive frames of reference. Comparison and contrast are powerful means of recognizing cultural differences.

Analysis of the attributions (meanings), form, and distribution of cultural units of meaning must be based upon authentic cultural data supplied by those who share these patterns (informants) or by participant observation (direct or indirect). Data thus obtained can be used to formulate reasonably valid expectations of socially appropriate behavior in a given culture.

Intercultural learners must contrast and compare their own frames of reference or world views with and to those of the "stranger." To plaster new cultural patterns into old frames of references *unconsciously* is to court miscommunication. Thus, contrastive analysis in its *-emic* guise has a place in intercultural exploration, and, indeed, in language classrooms. Its power lies in the facilitation of the development of the skills needed to distinguish culturally appropriate behavior from culturally inappropriate behavior. Used correctly, it may prevent rather than predict embarrassing errors.

4.7 MAKING EDUCATED
CULTURAL GUESSES

The formation of cultural hypotheses or guesses about culturally appropriate behavior, attributions, or expectations, is a major goal in culture learning and should be the natural result of effective cultural analysis. Such analyses are only predictive in the sense that they permit the culture learners to test out their understanding of the cultural patterns they are analyzing.

The role of perception, or the way in which data derived from the senses are evaluated, stored, and assimilated in patterns of beliefs and behavior, is an important ingredient in social interaction and hypothesis formulation. (Adelman and Lustig 1981; Albert and Triandis 1985; Condon and Yousef 1975; Hall 1977; Singer 1982). In addition, it is assumed that those who become acculturated will have learned to understand and may even share the cultural perceptions of a given group; in the process of doing so, they become more and more adept at forming cultural hypotheses, or predictive statements of attributions or expectations, as well as appropriate responses in a given cultural setting. This, of course, sounds suspiciously like most of the objectives set forth for communicative language activities.

A simple example of the power of hypothesizing should illustrate the point. Suppose you, as a teacher, call a student from a Middle Eastern country into your office. This student is studying in an intensive language program in the United States, and his country has paid a considerable sum of money for him to do so. He is very conscientious, so when he handed in a library report, clearly not written in his hand, you were surprised and dismayed. When you asked him about the matter, he said he had asked a friend to copy the material for him because she wrote so neatly. Well, it was true; she did. You try to explain the horror with which most American teachers regard this type of behavior, and that, if unexplained, this might be considered a form of cheating. He explains that his friend wanted to help him and he let her. You dismiss him with a warning. The next day the friend rushes up to you, wringing her hands, and begs you not to believe her friend had done anything wrong. She was just "helping" him. Obviously, the perception of the act of helping was being looked at quite differently by the teacher and by the students. Some discussion was in order concerning the cultural limitations of assistance and the definitions of cheating. As the teacher reminded herself, one should ask questions first and then draw some conclusions. In any case, cultural rules surrounding the execution of homework certainly needed more clarification.

4.8 PREPARING TO ASK THE
RIGHT QUESTIONS

At this point, the readers, perhaps overwhelmed by the wealth of suggestions, hints, new viewpoints, and terminology, are prepared to stop right here, leave the traveling to others, and plead lack of practice, professional credentials, or energy. To take off, so seemingly ill-prepared, appears to court failure. Yet if we subscribe to the dogma that we learn by doing, then it is time to do something. It is good to remember that most intercultural explorers, such as tourists, visitors, students, or sojourners in foreign lands, generally start out far less well-prepared than will the readers of this book. It is the experience, rather than the results, that will bring the most reward.

As explained previously, developing an ethnographic report involves collecting and analyzing data, formulating testable hypotheses, and then actually testing them against data. These are tasks for trained anthropologists. Such field work is time-consuming, difficult, and complex. The exercises and procedures that follow in this book are based on a limited application of ethnographic methods in the process of culture learning. They are seen as a means of overcoming ethnocentric bias, dealing with cultural differences, some of which will prove "unacceptable," and looking at these differences through the referential mirror of those who find these differences the "right" way. All second/foreign language teachers and their students need such skills.

The suggestions made by McLeod and Paulston, as well as others, that teachers apply ethnographic research methods in the classroom are not new. The results of such research are often referred to as microethnographies. These are studies characterized by the use of ethnographic methods but with limited periods of inquiry, limited data collection, and limited scope. They have been generally focused on specific problems of intercultural contact in schools, hospitals, and other institutions and designed to investigate certain relationships and problems. Reviews of this type of research can be found in Trueba, Guthrie, and Au (1981) and Trueba and Wright (1980). These discussions should be of special interest to those concerned with bilingual/bicultural education.

As might be expected, anthropologists have not received the development of microtechniques altogether kindly, finding that the limited nature of the data collection may render suspect any possible generalizations. The procedures suggested in this book risk the same type of censure. Random and restricted sampling of cultural patterns and the collection of unrelated data can lead to distortion. However, the purposes of the exercises and activities to follow are designed to bring the processes of culture learning and the ways in which intercultural communication can be effected to a conscious level. Thus, systematic compilation of descriptive materials about a particular cultural group through the mediation of one or more of its members (hereafter called "informants"), in conjunction with the investigation of the frames of reference used by both those who question and those who answer, is one means to develop valid cross-cultural hypotheses and ultimately more effective intercultural communicative skills. This method is to be called *pragmatic ethnography*. This designation has been chosen in order to remind all of us that the procedures used are to serve personal and practical purposes and not to provide scientific data and theory. It should also remind us that any attempt at intercultural communication involves efforts to understand the views of the others.

4.9 STEPS IN
PRAGMATIC ETHNOGRAPHY

The following procedures, while subject to adjustment to specific situations and recursive in practice, have proved to be useful in cross-cultural inquiry. They combine two general approaches to skills development—cognitive training and experiential training—gained through both secondary sources and personal experience. The combination of these two methods serves to provide maximum learning opportunities in limited contact situations. The steps listed below are those you will be asked to follow in the cultural learning exercises in this and succeeding chapters. The steps are explained in some detail in order to guide you in your ethnographic inquiry.

Step 1: Choosing a Target Group

Choose a cultural or ethnic group about which you know very little, but would like to know more. This group might represent a subcultural group in your own native culture or one that is "foreign" to you. You do not need to speak the language of the group chosen, but you should have some knowledge of its linguistic system or systems.

Step 2: Choosing Informants

Choose an informant (or informants) who is a native of the culture in question and who is willing to serve as a source of an insider's, or -*emic*, view of the target culture. The designation "informant" carries no pejorative sense; the informant is in no way an informer or "tattletale," but simply a data source, an explainer.

Much caution should be exercised both in interviewing an informant and in using the information gained. The relationship between the informant and the investigator must be one of mutual respect and confidence. The information sought is often personal and might be, if divulged, embarrassing or even detrimental to the individual informant. Appendix A contains a set of principles to guide the ethnographic interviewing process in the university context. This statement should be read with great care and its provisions observed.

It is wise to choose an informant who has a sufficiently broad knowledge base about his or her culture and is willing to share this knowledge. The informant's command of the language in which the ethnographic interviews are to be conducted should be sufficient to permit the expression of personal views and the discussion of complex propositions. Informants who are recent arrivals in a foreign country are often in the beginning stages of acculturation or adjustment. They may either be enjoying an overly optimistic and euphoric period as new arrivals, or, if they have been in the new context for a longer period of time, have passed into a second stage of acculturation known as culture shock. If they are experiencing the latter stage, their points of view may be unduly gloomy.

Step 3: Providing a Foundation for Inquiry

This step involves searching and using secondary sources relative to the general features of the culture group under study. There are many handbooks, studies, journal articles, and training manuals that provide orientational information. It is important that the language teacher review information relative to language learning problems as well as culture-specific materials. Journals such as the *International Journal of Intercultural Relations, NABE Journal* (bilingual education), *TESOL Quarterly* (ESL), the *International and Intercultural Communication Annual*, papers from the East/West Learning Center, and many others will serve as excellent information sources. Also helpful are the materials contained in various anthologies of readings on intercultural communication. Two of these, *Intercultural Communication: A Reader* (Samovar and Porter) and *Toward Internationalism* (Smith and Luce), have already been listed as suggested readings. These sources and those listed in the bibliography at the end of this book should provide solid foundations for inquiry.

Culture-specific information can be obtained from area handbooks, special governmental reports, and background reports such as those prepared by the Brigham Young University Center for International and Area Studies. Additional resources are discussed in Appendix C.

Step 4: Informant Interviewing

Following a search of available secondary and ethnographic material, you will be asked to initiate contact and conduct interviews with your informant(s). Begin by searching out general information and establishing a feeling of rapport and confidence.

In conducting ethnographic inquiry, some of the most important points to remember are:

1. Do not identify any informant by name or by personal characteristics in reports, discussions, or in research materials unless you have received written permission to do so from the informant.

2. Do not make evaluative comment on differences, either to your informant or to others. Search for meanings, not ways to judge.

3. Decide in advance the type of information needed and how it might best be elicited. You should keep field notes, or some type of written or taped record of the questions asked and replies received. Permission should be requested to take notes or make recordings. For the purposes of pragmatic ethnography, journal entries noting dates, major questions asked, and replies received would be sufficient.

You should plan to conduct at least four or five hour-long interviews in order to establish confidence, to elicit information, and to explore implications of the information received during the course of the inquiry.

In general, first interviews should be used to establish basic data concerning the informant and to explain the purposes of the interviews, and different types of questions. Ethnographic interviews are not just "friendly conversation"; they should be structured to produce one-way exchanges of information from the informant to the interviewer. Thus, according to Spradley (1979:67) ethnographic interviewing is characterized by assymetrical question-asking, repetition, the seeking of explanations and the posing of different types of questions, including descriptive questions, structural questions, and contrast questions. Descriptive questions focus on setting and context, structural questions on basic units of cultural knowledge, and contrast questions on the relationship of culture-specific terms and categories.

Because descriptive questions provide the most fundamental information, the novice interviewer is encouraged to start with these. Spradley identifies five major types of descriptive questions: grand tour questions, mini-tour questions, example questions, experience questions, and native-language questions (85–91). Grand tour questions are very general and "encourage the informant to ramble on and on." Mini-tour questions are more restricted and deal with specific areas. Example questions, experience questions, and native-language questions focus on the specific knowledge of a given area an informant possesses. Native-language questions encourage the informant to use culturally relevant terms.

Descriptive questions should elicit specific types of responses and, it is hoped, culture-specific data elucidating cultural meanings, relationships, categories, and classes. In other words, skillful descriptive questions can open a window on the informant's view of the world, or the small portion under study.

For example, if the investigator is interested in assessing the differences in educational contexts and relationships, questions could include:

What is a typical day like in your school?   (grand tour)

What courses did you take last year?   (mini-tour)

Can you give me an example of a disruptive or troublesome student? What would such a student do?   (example)

How did you feel when the teacher called on you yesterday?   (experience)

What do you mean when you say no one "respects" a disruptive student? (native language)

Who is the informant? A teacher? A student? Can you suggest any further line of general inquiry?

In addition to the above, Spradley suggests (67–68) that the interviewer should express interest, admit cultural ignorance, and repeat important terms in order to achieve clarification.

As the interviewing process continues areas of interest will emerge. The interviewer should choose several specific areas to investigate in more detail. This focal area should relate to the processes of language and culture learning but in the context of the target group. For example, if Saudi Arabia is chosen as a target cultural area, then it would be useful to investigate the role of religion in education, both in its own terms and in contrast to other educational models, such as that of the United States. Such a focus of interest can lead to the development of structural questions about the Saudi system and to contrastive questions. This type of questioning would help clarify the role of religion in Saudi life, a role any teacher charged with the instruction of Saudi students, at home or abroad, must understand.

Step 5: Analyzing Data and Forming Cultural Hypotheses

This step is concerned with the analyses of the data received through secondary sources and by informant interviewing, and the formulation of cultural hypotheses reflecting patterns relative to expected and/or appropriate behavior.

At this stage the differences discovered may be explored, more data gathered, and hypothetical situations investigated. For example, if the focus of investigation has been student conduct and class discipline, the interviewer might elicit examples of punishable conduct and corrective measures. The resulting classification, or taxonomy, may serve as a useful guide for the interviewer who does not have this cultural ready reference at hand.

Step 6: Looking in the Mirror

In this step the interviewer's frame of reference is brought to a conscious level. In the spirit of "Know Thyself" and in preparation for the direction of the culture learning of others, investigators must scrutinize their own personal perception of the phenomena under study as well as that of fellow culture bearers. This involves self-questioning and understanding that no one individual represents all possible beliefs and values or views of a particular culture. Cultural patterns change. For example, perceptions concerning the role of religion in the United States in the 1980s vary considerably among its citizens, particularly in relation to its role in schools. Yet there are certain shared "givens," as, for example, the general belief that opportunities for the practice of all types of religion should be permitted. Thus, the fact that cultural patterns and constellations of beliefs and values change and provoke disagreement, especially in a multicultural society such as that of the United States, means that the foreign visitor, sojourner, immigrant, or refugee must deal with a wide range of conflicting opinions and subcultural variations. It behooves pragmatic ethnographers therefore to:

1. understand their own cultural perceptions and frames of reference; and

2. present descriptions and explanations of given behavior and meanings as simply one's person's view.

This commitment is crucial as the ethnographer enters the classroom and assumes the role of educated guide and cultural mediator—not arbiter.

Step 7: Putting Theory and Knowledge to Work

As the final step in the practice of pragmatic ethnography, you, the investigator as teacher, are asked to bring the insights gained about culture learning in general or about a specific cultural group into the realm of practice and weave them quite literally into the process of selecting teaching materials, developing lesson plans, and directing the protected or administered classroom.

In short, these directions to the practice of pragmatic ethnography are those you will be asked to follow in your own *practicum* in culture learning. In a very practical sense, you will become a very specialized type of anthropologist, prepared to guide your students along the enlightening path of focused cultural inquiry.

Figure 4.1 recapitulates the steps that have been discussed. The general sequence of activities is suggested by their designations as "steps." The term "steps" is somewhat misleading. They are rather stages of inquiry, recursive in nature and to be repeated as long as cultural inquiry continues. The progress should be from Steps 1 to 7 with frequent repetition of Steps 3 to 6. Questions, answers, hypotheses, or analyses should only lead to more questions, clearer answers, and more appropriate hypotheses.

Such an undertaking cannot be accomplished easily. You will be guided in your progress through these steps by the culture learning exercises at the end of each chapter. You are urged to sustain your contact with your informant and your examination of secondary sources even though you may not be asked to provide specific reports. Completion of the reports, exercises, and projects recommended will require hard work, considerable time commitment, and, perhaps some anguish. The experience will serve you, now and in the future, as you deal with culture change at home and abroad. It is time to get going—ready or not!

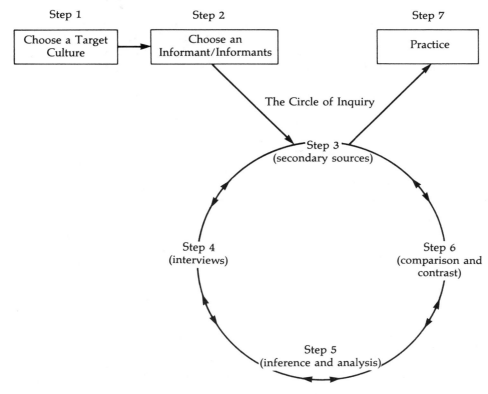

Figure 4.1. Steps in the Practice of Pragmatic Ethnography

FOR STUDY AND DISCUSSION

1. Identify the following terms:

   ethnography

   informant

   contrastive analysis

   microethnography

   frames of reference

   cultural hypotheses

   cultural relativity

   cultural meaning

2. What is meant by the statement that the use of ethnographic methods and contrastive analysis to investigate actual cultural groups is closer to the "natural" way of dealing with culture learning than structured simulations and role play? Can you describe a "natural" culture learning experience? How "natural" are most of the classroom experiences of language students?

3. What are some personal qualities associated with a "good" informant? Why is an informant needed in cultural exploration?

4. What is the value of describing a culture in and on its own terms?

5. Explain the origin and implications for cultural discovery of the terms -emic and -etic. What are some of the advantages of achieving an -emic perspective? Are there any disadvantages or dangers in using such an approach?

6. What types of questions are useful in the search for ethnographic information? Spradley lists five types of such questions. What are the purposes of these questions? What answers might be given and how might they be useful in cultural analysis? Give examples.

7. It has been said that more difficulties arise when there are minimal differences between the linguistic elements of the native language and the target language (Oller and Ziahosseiny 1970:186). Why should this be true? Have you noted any instances that would support this statement? Would such a statement be equally true in the case of cultural elements? Can you supply any examples in which minimal differences made the difference?

8. If you were serving as an informant about cultural patterns in the United States and were asked to define the term *teacher*, how would you respond? List the characteristics of a teacher and contrast these with the attributes you would assign to a student. How would you define *nerd, wimp* (or any other current term for a "loser")?

9. What is meant by the term *perception* as it is used in intercultural communication? What is its relationship to the formulation of cultural hypotheses?

10. Explain the North American cultural rules which might be appropriate in the following situation: A university professor has not yet arrived for an 11:00 a.m. class. It is now 11:11. What should the students do? Would the same behavior be expected if the students were in high school? in elementary school?

11. How would you explain to a foreigner the differences between a piece of cake, a hamburger bun, and a cookie? How are they alike and how do they differ? Do any of the terms carry other meanings? If so, what are they?

CULTURE LEARNING EXERCISE

Choose a target group with which you are unfamiliar but about which you would like to learn more. You are to gather information concerning this group both from people who are natives of the target culture (informants) and from secondary sources. Eventually, you will be asked to interview these people and present a report about your target group based on the information you have gained as a pragmatic ethnographer.

In general, the information you will present should focus upon data related to your group and issues or problems related to second language/culture learning. Bibliographic sources should provide you with general background information. Informant elicitation should be used to gain the perspective of the native culture bearer.

Your first assignment is to:

1. Choose your target culture.

2. Locate an informant (or informants). These should be persons willing to serve as informants and having time available.

3. Locate five bibliographic sources for general information on your target culture.

4. List five questions you intend to ask your informant. Focus these questions upon areas of interest you would like to explore.

5. Meet with your informant(s) as often as possible in order to obtain permission and establish rapport.

If you are unable to locate an informant from a target culture, then choose one representing a cultural or social group within your own culture with which you have had minimal contact.

FOR FURTHER READING

R. Lado. 1957. *Linguistics Across Cultures.* This book offers a lesson in applied linguistics that should be heeded by every language teacher. Even though the method of contrastive analysis did not provide the means of accurate error prediction that Lado had hoped, it is still a valid method of sorting out areas of incongruity. His application of the Pike model to cultural data, as illustrated in Chapter 6, provides a useful model for language teachers who wish to incorporate culture learning in their lesson plans.

B. McLeod. 1976. "The Relevance of Anthropology to Language Teaching" (211–220). The author recommends that language teachers and language students engage in anthropological inquiry and use anthropological discovery methods as means of bringing culture learning into the language classroom. This article was an early plea for the explicit teaching of culture in the language classroom. Its message is still timely.

J. Spradley. 1979. *The Ethnographic Interview.* This is a most readable book and quite comprehensible even for lay readers. It is a practical discussion of the techniques of ethnographic interviewing, and, as such, offers useful guidelines for getting the most out of any such episodes. For those readers who have the time, the whole book is recommended reading. For those who do not, the chapters dealing with asking descriptive questions, making componential analyses, and discovering cultural themes will be instructive.

H. Taylor (ed.). 1979. *English and Japanese in Contrast.* The articles contained in this book illustrate a modern day use for contrastive analysis and provide ample examples to prove the point. As Taylor points out in an introductory chapter: "A focus is possible through the lens of comparison that is not possible on the flat plane of a single language" (15). Of particular interest are Parts 2 and 3, "Semantics in Contrast" and "Culture in Contrast."

H. Trueba, G. Guthrie, and K. Au (eds.). 1981. *Culture and the Bilingual Classroom: Studies in Classroom Ethnography.* This is a book of readings on the general subject of the cultural diversity in the classrooms in the United States; its purpose, according to its editors, is to "emphasize the importance of cultural factors in influencing the outcomes of schooling for minority children" (1). It is an enlightening book for several reasons. It reviews major issues in bilingual education in the United States and reports of studies using ethnographic methods (microethnography) in analyzing classroom interaction or variables. These studies are helpful both for the information they contain and as examples of practicing ethnography in the classrooms.

In addition, the textbooks, articles, and other bibliographic references cited in this chapter bear closer scrutiny than was possible here. The reader is urged to examine them in greater depth.

Chapter 5

The Communication and Culture Riddle

It is reasonable to expect that a book devoted to the incorporation of culture and language learning in language classrooms would contain an early chapter of definitions of culture and language. (See Note, Chapter 2.) This has not been done because the teacher/student must undertake defining not as an exercise in memorizing a set of characteristics extrapolated by experts in the field, but as an active, personal learning exercise. Because the basic concepts of *communication* and *culture*, along with *language*, are the foundations upon which the modern practice of ESL/EFL must rest, it is important not to be limited by the arbitrary designation of *the* definitions for *this* text. Just as we are practicing pragmatic ethnography, we must also practice eclectic defining.

5.1 DEVELOPING DEFINITIONS

First, let us consider some general statements about culture and communication.

1. "Culture is that which binds men together" (Ruth Benedict, cited in Kluckhohn 1944:27).

2. "Culture or Civilization taken in its wide ethnographic sense, is that complex whole which includes knowledge, belief, art, morals, law, custom, and any other capabilities and habits acquired by man as a member of society" (Tylor 1871:1).

3. "Culture is communication and communication is culture" (Hall 1959:169).

4. "Culture refers to that relatively unified set of shared symbolic ideas associated with societal patterns of cultural ordering" (Gudykunst and Kim 1984:11).

5. "Communication is a symbolic process involving the attribution of meaning" (Gudykunst and Kim 1984:17).

73

6. "Cultural similarity in perception makes the sharing of meaning possible. . . . Communication is cultural" (Samovar, Porter, and Jain 1981:36).

7. "Communication is our primary means of utilizing the resources of the environment in the service of humanity" (Kim 1982:359).

8. "Culture is the unique life style of a particular group of people. . . . Culture is also communicable knowledge, learned behavioral traits that are shared by participants in a social group and manifested in their institutions and artifacts" (Harris and Moran 1979:57).

These eight statements all touch upon some aspects of the culture and communication conundrum. Each contains a message for those who would communicate with and teach those from other cultures. Each part is only one piece of the puzzle. But which ones would serve us best? The answer should be an equivocal *none* and *all*. Before investigating additional statements concerning both *communication* and *culture*, let us first explore what the eight listed above can tell us.

Definition 1 emphasizes the social nature of culture and its functions as a means of social cohesion. As Hall points out (1959:39), culture may also actually prevent the recognition of differences. It does link us to others of "our own kind."

Definition 2 is the classic anthropological definition of culture; it emphasizes the inclusive nature of the concept of culture as the major unifying concept under which all other variables must be subsumed, including forms of communication, artifacts, belief systems, and habits. This definition is still valid, but, as we shall see, culture, as used by anthropologists, has been defined and redefined as the field has developed and research foci have shifted.

Definition 3 joins the two concepts of communication and culture so that questions of primacy are avoided and definitions broadened. Thus, it may be said that if communication is culture, and *vice versa*, then human beings cannot *not* communicate (Watzlawick, Beavin, and Jackson, 1967:51).

Definition 4 focuses on the symbolic nature of cultural meaning and its relationship to the way societies are ordered as well as the role of culture in this ordering. This definition represents an interpretational approach to communication and culture.

Definition 5 extends the definition of communication and its role in the attribution or assignment of meaning by the communicators.

Definition 6 provides a very comprehensive definition of communication, adding the ingredient of perception as a process tied to the cultural dimension.

Definitions 7 and 8 present contrasting views of the primacy or importance of each concept; in 7, communication takes precedence, but, in 8, it is culture.

Which term then is most important? Are the terms synonymous? What did Hall really mean? Closer reading of the sources from which the above definitions have been somewhat unceremoniously plucked will serve to warn the reader that the use of these terms generally reflects the professional orientation of the author as an anthropologist or a communication theorist as well as a variety of approaches to these concepts. As must be clear, there are no simple neat definitions to tuck away and bring out for inspection when needed. We are locked into a state of permanent definitional ambiguity—a mixed blessing.

5.2 COMMUNICATION: COMPONENTS AND CHARACTERISTICS

The components and characteristics of the process known as communication are complex and interlocked as shown in Figure 5.1.

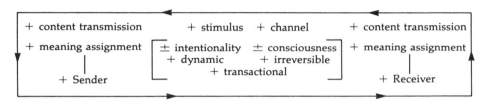

Figure 5.1. Communication Components and Characteristics

Communication viewed as a process involves content transmission and re-transmission or response. The twin components of stimulus/channel indicate that there must always be some form of stimulus and a channel or channels of trans-mission. These channels may be verbal, nonverbal (gestures, looks, expression), or contextual. In the last case the act of communication is embedded in the setting (external context) or in the intrapersonal component (internal context of cultural programming, experience, or innate ability of the communicator). According to Samovar, Porter, and Jain (1981:17):

> When we interact with someone, it is not in isolation but within a specific physical surrounding and under a set of specific social dynamics. . . . Many, many aspects of the physical environment can and do affect communication. . . . Social context defines the types of social relationships that exist between source and receiver.

As they point out, the influence of culture in communication is most evident in the social environment.

Finally, the assignment of meaning or attribution assumes that communica-tion is the kind of behavior that can be assigned meaning and defined in terms of its attributions or what the receiver and sender think it means. These meanings are also culturally colored so that each sender and receiver may be drawing upon different "meaning reservoirs." These various meanings are developed through-out the human lifetime as a result of cultural and personal experiences. Meanings are relative to some degree to each of us in that we are all unique human beings with singular histories and experiences. Attributions, or interpretations of the message, are then assigned by the observer or receiver. In turn, the receiver may become the sender and proceed in the same manner. Each of the components and characteristics of the communicative process is subject to cross-cultural variation.

There are, of course, the universal characteristics of communication, which include its dynamic, social, and transactional nature. Yet these universal characteristics are often manifested quite differently around the world.

The generally accepted assumptions that buttress modern definitions of communication and are important in cross-cultural communication are that the communication process is dynamic, transmitted verbally and nonverbally, irreversible, and contexted. This indicates that the message cannot be recalled although it can be amended, as Samovar *et al.* indicate (1981:16–17). This aspect of communication is often overlooked. It underscores the danger of those unconscious and/or unintentional messages we all send and receive. Human communication is structured and may be interpreted on both content (*what*) and relationship (*who, when, where, why*) levels (Watzlawick, Beavin, and Jackson 1967). Gudykunst and Kim point out that the content level is usually carried on the verbal channel, but the relationship on the nonverbal. They add that "cultures vary with respect to the emphasis they place on these two levels" (1984:9).

An example is in order. Let us imagine that a teacher of a multicultural class composed of students from various foreign areas has decided to read aloud a short essay written by one of her Japanese students. She has made it clear that this is a fine, well-executed essay and that she feels the students could profit from hearing it. As she begins to read she notes that the student-author has slumped forward in her seat, head hung low, and apparently is not enjoying the experience.

So the teacher thinks, "I shouldn't have done this, but then what can I do now? Is she crying? Is she embarrassed? Is she angry?"

The reading ended, the teacher turns to the rest of the members of the class, who have applauded politely, and says, "Wasn't that well done?" They agree, perhaps with more enthusiasm than conviction. The author remains silent. The teacher begins to feel somewhat uncomfortable and wishes the whole episode could be rescored.

This teacher began to gain some understanding of the communication that had been taking place only when she undertook the study of Japanese patterns of communication and group behavior. True enlightenment came when she read that Japanese patterns of group behavior often call for the avoidance of being singled out for praise or blame (Cathcart and Cathcart 1982). The Japanese group is not just a collection of individuals; it is a place in which to integrate the self. This teacher had learned the meaning of *deru kugiwa utareru* (the nail that sticks up is hit). The communicative process had been halted at the cultural chasm between the meaning assignment of the sender and the attributions of the receivers. If the teacher had questioned each member of that class, she might have been surprised at the attributional assignments given her actions. It is doubtful that all would have shared her simple desire to provide a good example and praise a worthy student. Perhaps, such singling out should not have been done at all in any class and was simply an example of bad pedagogy. Finally, the student's posture, which the teacher interpreted as despair, was merely the conventional manner of receiving either praise or blame—it hardly mattered which, as it involved being singled out.

Understanding the dynamics of group behavior in the cross-cultural context and in view of various cross-cultural variations is a fundamental skill for every language teacher to cultivate. One of the ways to acquire this skill is simply to be observant and—alas—make mistakes.

Context and Meaning

The importance of context in communication is very great. The term may be used in two ways. It may indicate the environment (surroundings) or settings in which communication takes place; it may also relate to the process of what has been called cultural "programming" or assignment of cultural meaning (Hall 1977:90). For our purposes the term *setting* will be used hereafter to indicate the environment or surroundings of the communicative act, and *context* or *contexting* the social, cultural, and personal elements or variables, internal and external, acting on the communication process.

Edward Hall is credited with providing a theoretical connection, or at least suggesting one, between context and meaning. In his book *Beyond Culture* (1977:85–103) he points out that the nature of culture is such that it serves to limit the number of stimuli to which a person must respond. Just as we do not have to listen to all the phonetic permutations of [p] and [b] to distinguish in English between a /p/ and a /b/—voicing or use of the vocal cords will do—neither do we have to attend to all stimuli connected with the process of communication or of the cultural environment. The selection of the salient or important stimuli in a given culture involves what Hall calls *contexting*, or cultural preprogramming. Much of such contexting occurs during the period of enculturation.

Gudykunst and Kim (1984:120) comment upon Hall's concept of contexting as follows:

> . . . . Hall uses the term contexting to describe the perceptual process of recognizing, giving significance to, and incorporating contextual cues in interpreting the total meaning of any stimulus in a particular communication transaction. Here contextual cues refer to all the messages implicit in a communication transaction, including the nature of the interpersonal relationship between the communicators, the nonverbal expressions of the communicators, the physical setting, and the social circumstances.

The programming acquired in one cultural context, however, may be carried over to another one, often with unexpected results. For example, a back-and-forth nod of the head may mean "yes" in one culture, but "no" in another. Slight inclinations of the body in the direction of the speaker may mean attention in one culture and have no significance in another.

Selection and attention, according to Hall, are characteristic of both language and culture so that ". . . in real life the code [language], the context, and the meaning can only be seen as different aspects of a single event" (1977:90 emphases deleted). This statement sheds light on Hall's definition of culture as communication and communication as culture.

Hall has stated (1977:95):

Contexting probably involves at least two entirely different but interrelated processes—one inside the organism and the other outside. The first takes place in the brain and is a function of either past experience (programmed, internalized contexting) or the structure of the nervous system (innate contexting), or both. External contexting comprises the situation and/or setting in which an event occurs (situational and/or environmental contexting).

Innate contexting refers to the ability of the human brain to supply details when they are not present—to fill in the blanks, so to speak. External contexting comprises what we have called the "setting."

Finally, Hall, in continuing discussion of the relationships of culture, context, and communication describes what he calls high-context and low-context messages and also high-context and low-context cultures. He explains (1977:91):

. . . high-context messages are placed at one end and low-context messages at the other end of a continuum. A high-context (HC) communication or message is one in which most of the information is either in the physical context or internalized in the person, while very little is in the coded, explicit, transmitted part of the message. A low-context (LC) communication is just the opposite; i.e., the mass of the information is vested in the explicit code. Twins who have grown up together can and do communicate more economically (HC) than two lawyers in a courtroom during a trial (LC), a mathematician programming a computer, two politicians drafting legislation, two administrators writing a regulation, or a child trying to explain to his mother why he got into a fight.

Restricted and Elaborated Codes

Hall also correlated high- and low-context messages with Basil Bernstein's restricted and elaborated codes of language. An elaborated code (low-context) was described as marked by more verbal differentiation than the restricted, which uses shortened words and sentences and which, to the uninitiated, may seem disjointed. Elaborated codes were associated with public speech, while restricted

codes were the means of communication among friends, family, cohorts, professional peers, and in contexts in which much is understood (Bernstein 1966). Anyone who has attended a professional conference in the role of a nonprofessional
knows the difference. Elaborated codes call for extensive use of both verbal and
nonverbal means of communication, while restricted codes are more closely associated with "hidden implicit cues of the social context (such as interpersonal
relationship, physical and psychological environment, and other contextual cues)
and thus the vocabulary and structure of the verbalized messages are drawn from
a narrow range" (Gudykunst and Kim 1984:138).

According to Bernstein (1966:433–434):

> . . . the speech is played out against a backdrop of assumptions common to
> the speakers, against a set of closely shared interests and identifications,
> against a system of shared expectations; in short, it presupposes a local cul-
> tural identity which reduces the need for the speakers to elaborate their intent
> verbally and to make it explicit.

High-Context and Low-Context Cultures

While Bernstein associated restricted and elaborated codes with social classes,
Hall applied the concepts cross-culturally. Although no cultures were exclusively
one or the other, North American culture was seen as LC and Far Eastern groups
as HC. High context groups were characterized as generally more traditional, slow
to change, and highly stable; while low context groups were associated with technological, fast-paced, and less stable groups. Hall noted that although high contexting demanded time for primary programming, high context communication
was "economical, fast, efficient, and satisfying" (101). He raised the question of
how much time should be associated with contexting (1977:92). This is a question
that must also be answered by language teachers who are in many ways dealing
with cultural programming or contexting, when they use language learning to
promote culture learning and intercultural interaction.

Hall also notes that although the type of context distinguishes given types of
communication, adjustments can be made. He concludes (1977:100–101):

> In summary, . . . a universal feature of information systems is that meaning
> (what the receiver is expected to do) is made up of: the communication, the
> background and preprogrammed responses of the recipient, and the situ-
> ation. (We call these last two the internal and external context.)
>
> Therefore, what the receiver actually perceives is important in under-
> standing the nature of context. Remember that what an organism perceives is
> influenced in four ways—by status, activity, setting, and experience. But in
> man one must add another crucial dimension: *culture.*

5.3 CULTURE: COMPONENTS
AND CHARACTERISTICS

What is culture? The reader has already been subjected to several *ad hoc* definitions of culture and a variety of hints, clues, and partial definitions. Now it is time
to investigate the nature of culture, its components and characteristics. In so
doing, an explanation is in order. There have been so many definitions of culture
that it would appear foolish to add yet another; the reader might be more at ease
if the most comprehensive definition possible is provided and the matter left at
that. This type of short cut, however, would not serve our purposes well. The
concept of culture and its relationship to intercultural communication and language learning is so complex that neither its definition nor any discussion of its
role in communication and language learning should be reduced to only a few
dimensions. On the contrary, the more inclusive the definitions and descriptions,
the more useful they will be.

The next portion of this chapter considers some theoretical principles relating
to culture. This is followed by the examination of several definitions of culture,
each valid and revealing one or more of the many facets of the concept. These
definitions are presented not in order of importance, but rather in the sequence in
which they were developed in the fields of anthropology, sociology, psychology,
and, most recently, in intercultural communication research and practice. The
contribution of each field in this kaleidoscopic approach to the understanding of
the concept of culture may promote a feeling of confusion in the face of such
complexity; it will *not* promote ethnocentrism.

The Anthropological View: Other Guiding Principles

Writers dealing with the definition of culture like to point out that the anthropologists Alfred Kroeber and Clyde Kluckhohn (1952) once reviewed several
hundred definitions and yet did not find the perfect one. Some of the general
characteristics they uncovered include its historical dimension, the interdepen-
dency of its components, and its highly complex nature (Kluckhohn 1944).

The interpretation of culture, its centrality and definition, have kept anthropologists occupied and often in dispute for many years. Changing positions on
the role and nature of culture as an explanatory and theoretical concept have
marked the course of the major theoretical stances which, in turn, have enjoyed
favor.

Understanding the changing and evolving view of the concept of culture as
developed in the field of anthropology can be facilitated by a consideration of the
theories and circumstances by which each type of definition was fashioned and
molded.

Anthropologists have "owned" the concept of culture for nearly a hundred
years. In their study of the science of human beings the defining of culture and

how it works have been central themes and unifying elements in a richly diverse field. Because nothing that is human is beyond the concern of anthropologists, a single concept, *culture*, has provided a means of gaining some common base upon which to build theory and hang the ever-increasing flow of detail that ethnographic studies have brought.

Definitions of culture have been changed, refined, redefined, and yet again defined as theories and purposes have changed. Each change has been in a sense an addition rather than a replacement and each reflects the increasing realization on the part of the definers that there are no simple ways to describe mankind's primary adaptive and evolutionary mechanism: culture. Its power lies in its diversity and resistance to definition. It never allows reductionism; it constantly challenges. Culture, as Kluckhohn states, is a "theory." He adds that "if a theory is not contradicted by any relevant fact and if it helps us to understand a mass of otherwise chaotic facts, it is useful" (1944:25).

Although there are many conflicting definitions of culture, there seems to be nearly universal agreement on some points. First, it is generally agreed that the study of human beings and their cultures should be approached holistically. This is to say that the human condition must be examined from all perspectives and in all its aspects, all elements of culture being parts of the whole and the whole greater than the sum of its parts. Second, cultural groups exhibit the principle of selectivity in the ways they serve their bearers. In turn, each culture bearer selects from the cultural cafeteria of choices. Thus, there are many cultural means to serve the same human needs. Finally, the inevitability of change is a fact of cultural life. Viewed in evolutionary terms, it is merely change over time.

The principles these commonalities represent still obtain in the field and its subfields of archaeology, cultural anthropology, physical anthropology, and linguistics, and are reflected in the various theoretical and definitional stances. It is, of course, risky to place all anthropologists in the same theoretical basket; many schools of theoretical thought, practice, and research exist. Yet the principles listed above would be found in one form or another tucked away in the ideological baggage of the anthropologists, psychologists, sociologists, or intercultural communication professionals who must deal with culture, define it, and try to understand it. These tenets form a set of fundamental assumptions about the processes of intercultural communication.

Separating the Social from the Cultural

Before considering the various definitions of culture, the theories that have supported them, and the insights which they have provided over the years, it is useful to draw a distinction between the social aspects of human life styles and their cultural aspects. Or, to put it simply, it is necessary to differentiate between the approach or perspective of the sociologist and that of the anthropologist. By so doing, we can understand the full meaning of the term *sociocultural*.

In general, *social* refers to the interactions of groups of people, with the group serving as a major focus of analysis, while *culture* refers to a set of behavioral, cognitive, and emotional patterns. In anthropological parlance, a society has a culture and represents an organized way of life. A given population also has a cultural inventory; this cultural inventory includes a language and a social organization. Thus, while culture and society are not the same, social and cultural phenomena or behavior may be. If society is approached from the sociological point of view, the group is more likely the main focus of inquiry and investigation is concerned with socially acquired knowledge.

Both social and cultural perspectives are important. Kluckhohn points out that neither anthropologists nor sociologists can claim to occupy the most advantageous point of view, adding: "Anthropologists have often failed to see the forest for the trees, whereas one sometimes wonders if sociologists recognize that such a thing as a tree exists" (1944:226). This wry comment underscores the penchant of sociologists to use quantitative methods of research, which rely heavily on statistics and hypotheses testing, while, in the past, anthropologists have been inclined to use qualitative methods of study and detailed data gathering. Each approach, used exclusively, presents problems in analyzing data and forming generalizations. Because in recent times professionals in both disciplines have borrowed from each other, it is difficult to separate the cultural anthropologists from the sociologists.

The use of the term *sociocultural* in reference to behavior and variables in the study of communicative acts and cultural diversity, then, is a recognition that the variables under scrutiny have both social and cultural dimensions. The traditional social categories of age, class, status, and role are accorded different meanings and behavioral ranges in different cultures. Thus the designation *sociocultural* bridges the gap between the cultural focus of anthropology and the social focus of sociology. Because culture and society exist together, those studying intercultural contact can ill afford to dismiss either point of view.

Culture: Variations on the Theme

Listed below are several definitions of culture. They each reveal some facet of this concept and offer insights to those who would understand its nature, function, components, and characteristics. They range from the earliest formulations to some of the most recent. The chronological arrangement provides a simplified way of reviewing the changing nature of theories of culture as they have evolved in the field of anthropology and related disciplines from the mid-nineteenth century to the present time. Each definition will be considered briefly in its historical perspective and for its value today to those who would understand its cross-cultural manifestations.

- "Culture . . . is coterminous with man himself . . ." (Sapir 1964:79).

- "God gave to every people a cup, a cup of clay, and from this cup they drank their life. . . . They all dipped in the water but their cups were different" (Benedict, 1934:21–22).

- "Culture is a *way* of thinking, feeling, believing. It is the group's knowledge stored up (in memories of men; in books and objects) for future use. . . . A culture constitutes a storehouse of the pooled learning of the group" (Kluckhohn, 1944:24–25).

These definitions reflect the early approaches to culture that dominated the field of anthropology for many decades, in both Europe and the United States. The field of anthropology had grown out of interest in primitive societies; its main practitioners in the mid-nineteenth century were often dilettantes, enamored of scientific research and with little more to do than travel to far-away places to observe strange people. Anthropology as an academic discipline began as the science of history. Its philosophical roots were in the eighteenth century European Enlightenment's dream of the compilation of a universal history of mankind.

The concept of culture, or patterned ways of living, was recognized early; the dogma of cultural relativism came much later. Most nineteenth-century theories of the sources of sociocultural patterns reflected the assumption that civilized human beings had thought themselves out of a natural state of savagery, the natural order being from barbarism to civilization—i.e., Western style. Many subscribed to the notion of geographical determinism, or the influence of geographical conditions on cultural life, and sallied forth buttressed by a belief in the psychic unity of mankind. The majority were engaged in the search for general laws of human behavior.

American anthropologists at the turn of the century, while influenced by European approaches to the riddle of language, thought, and culture, were less inclined to accept the application of the general laws of human behavior that placed those they were studying at the level of savages. Franz Boas, the father of American anthropology, a transplanted European who studied American Indians and Eskimos, urged his colleagues and students to defer theorizing and searching for general laws until sufficient data had been collected (1911). His insistence upon high standards of field work, accumulation of extensive data on each cultural group, and the use of an inductive approach to research not only formed the fundamental methods of ethnographic field work—which his students, such as Kroeber, Sapir, Benedict, and Mead were to follow so faithfully—but also influenced the work of generations of American anthropologists.

To these, culture was a uniquely human mode of adaptation, at work in every facet of human life. Its functions were to hold human groups together and to provide ways of behaving, believing, and evaluating for its human bearers. It was seen as learned and transmitted; it included knowledge, accepted manners of behaving, and was reflected in the artifacts and institutions of its given groups.

The above definitions were offered at a time when the emphasis was on anthropological field work, highly inductive research, and the discovery of the many variations that cultural patterns might take. The concept of culture so defined emphasized the observable, the material, and the shared.

Additional definitions touched on the close relationships of language and culture and on the individual culture bearer and a given cultural system.

- "Human culture without language is unthinkable" (Kluckhohn 1944:26).

- ". . . we may think of language as the *symbolic guide to culture*" (Sapir 1964:70).

- "Culture is like a map. . . . No participant in any culture knows all the details of the cultural map" (Kluckhohn 1944:29–30).

Several early leaders in American anthropology, including Boas, were deeply concerned with the relationship of language and culture. Their field work among American Indians fostered the realization that they were not dealing with primitive or ill-formed languages and cultures, as had been previously assumed, but with complex languages and cultural systems, which must be described through direct observation and the collection of masses of details rather than by means of general laws of behavior and principles.

Culture groups were to be studied in the light of their particular histories. Indeed, this approach has been named historical particularism for obvious reasons. Boas and his students concerned themselves with the accumulation of a vast pool of ethnographic information about each culture studied. They were driven by a pressing need to document the vanishing cultures of the American Indians, threatened by the white man's incursion into Indian territory. Boas emphasized study of native languages and was a moving force for the development of the school of descriptive linguistics in the United States. He insisted on the description of a culture in and on its own terms. His was a major influence on the work of Sapir and Whorf. (See Chapter 7.)

An additional facet of culture is highlighted by Kluckhohn's statement concerning the relationship of the individual culture bearers to their cultures (1944:29–31):

> Just as a map isn't the territory but an abstract representation of a particular area, so also a culture is an abstract description of trends toward uniformity in the words, deeds, and artifacts of a human group. If a map is accurate and you can read it, you won't get lost; if you know a culture you will know your way around in the life of a society. . . . No participant in any culture knows all the details of the cultural map. . . . Thus, part of a culture must be learned by everyone, part may be selected from alternative patterns, part applies only to those who perform the roles in the society for which these patterns are designed.

Yet, Frake (1981:375–376) warns us that people are not just "map readers" but are also "map makers."

> Culture does not provide a cognitive map, but rather a set of principles for map-making and navigation. Different cultures are like different schools of navigation designed to cope with different terrains and seas.

This statement points to the fact that while an individual is the culture bearer, cultural knowledge encompasses much more than the sum of the knowledge of any individual. No one person can know all the facets of a given culture or follow all the roads it provides. Just as cultural patterns reflect a selection of the possible ways of serving human needs, the culture bearer is also a selective learner of the cultural patterns offered by the native culture.

These early definitions of culture emphasized the magnitude of human diversity and variations in patterns of behavior. They stressed the importance of the insider's view and the role culture played in human perception.

Subsequent approaches to culture linked forms and patterns of culture to their ecological environment.

- "Culture is all those means whose forms are not under direct genetic control . . . which serve to adjust individuals and groups within their ecological communities" (Binford 1968:323).

Cultures were seen as systems of adaptation with the driving force of change derived from ecological and/or economic systems. Such pronouncements promulgated by cultural adaptationists represented in large part an attempt to move away from the former "mentalistic" theories that involved getting into the minds of the culture bearers. These cultural ecologists or materialists were said to be using an -etic rather than an -emic approach in the interest of more scientific research, -etic research being seen as more detached and hence more reliable.

Of most recent date, theories and definitions of culture have focused on cultures as systems of ideas or organizations of cognitive knowledge. Not surprisingly, those who have espoused these definitions and the resultant theories have been called cognitive anthropologists. In practice, the cognitive approach became known as ethnoscience, or the study of folk classifications and categories.

According to Goodenough (1964:36), one of its spokesmen:

> . . . a society's culture consists of whatever it is one has to know or believe in order to operate in a manner acceptable to its members. . . . By this definition . . . culture is not a material phenomenon; it does not consist of things, people, behavior, or emotions. It is rather an organization of these things. It is the forms of things that people have in mind, their models for perceiving, relating, and otherwise interpreting them.

This is what Keesing (1974:77) terms one of the ideational theories of culture. It places culture in the same epistemological basket as language, possessing both an observable level of performance and a less accessible one, competence. As we shall see later, such definitions grew out of the application of linguistic methods and models to the analysis of culture.

Another ideational definition and theory of culture can be gleaned from the writings of Claude Lévi-Strauss. This European sociologist/anthropologist adapted the European structural linguistic model to cultural analysis. Lévi-Strauss proposed that all cultures reflect fundamental and universal principles of the human mind. Researchers should seek then to uncover the principles of the fundamental relationships at work in all human minds. Cultures were shared creations of human minds.

Keesing (1974:78–79), commenting on the Lévi-Strauss formulation, explains:

> The mind imposes culturally patterned order, a logic of binary contrast, of relations and transformations, on a continuously changing and often random world. The gulf between the cultural realm, where man imposes his arbitrary order, and the realm of nature becomes a major axis of symbolic polarity: "nature vs. culture" is a fundamental conceptual opposition in many—perhaps all—times and places. Lévi-Strauss . . . is more concerned with "Culture" than with "a culture".

Lévi-Strauss found these principles most readily revealed in the myths and folklore of various cultures.

To the language teacher the approaches of both the ethnoscientists and the European structuralist/anthropologists are of interest, for they illustrate the relationship of language, linguistic models of analysis, and culture as discussed in Chapter 6.

Such definitions avoided concern with the problems of intensive field work and overstocked data banks; they diverted some anthropologists from the compilation of cultural grammars to the pursuit of more abstract pan-human cognitive patterns of organization. In contrast to earlier theories and definitions, the new formulations concentrated more on the universal patterns of human minds than on the mental images and perceptions of individual culture bearers. In the first instance, proposed universal principles were at work; in the second, variations were fundamental.

Other definitions were to follow—even more abstract formulations, concentrating not only on universal properties of the human mind but also on the process of symbol sharing and the relationships they engendered.

- "Culture takes man's position *vis à vis* the world rather than *a* man's position on how to get along in the world as it is given . . ." (Schneider 1972:38).

- "The culture of a people is an ensemble of texts, themselves ensembles, which the anthropologist strains to read over the shoulders of those to whom they properly belong" (Geertz 1972:29).

The locus of inquiry then moved from within the human mind to the relationships in which the mental representations were joined. The study of cultures meant the study of shared codes of symbolic meanings. As Keesing (1974:84) points out, these cultural codes were seen as existing more between than in the minds of men.

As the complexity of the concept of culture became more evident, the similes became more exotic. Cultures were likened to old cities full of winding streets, dead ends, and small alleys or, oddly enough, to octopi (Geertz 1966:66).

An even more abstract approach to culture as an ideational phenomenon is represented in Schneider's definition. To Schneider (1972), culture floats on a higher plane than observable behavior. Thus, culture is defined as a system of symbols and meaning. It is comprised of categories, or units and rules about relationships and modes of behavior, that are no less epistemologically true for being unobservable. He differentiated between what he called the normative system of action and the cultural system. The latter was "the stage setting and the cast of characters." The normative system was seen to contain stage directions for the actors and rules for actions on the prearranged stage. According to Schneider (1972:38):

> . . . it [culture] asks "Of what does this world consist?" where the normative level asks, "Given the world to be made up in the way it is, how does a man proceed to act in it?"

All this has taken us from the concrete to the abstract, from the familiar to the esoteric, and into territory best left to other professionals. Let us now look at the concept of culture from a less lofty position and with an eye to its practical use. A final definition, taken from Keesing's excellent review of the evolution of theories of culture (1974), on which the previous discussion was generally based, may serve well as an end point and afford a soft landing for the itinerant culture learner. This definition addresses the recurrent problem that faces all those who would study culture. Cultural symbols and meanings are shared through interactions between individuals, and yet the full range of meaning is never fully understood by any one culture bearer. In addition, if a person acquires cultural patterns as an individual, then the locus of culture must be in the individual. Goodenough (1971:20) wrote: ". . . cultural theory must explain in what sense we can speak of culture as being shared or as the property of groups . . . We must go on to try to explain how this analytically useful construct relates to human phenomena. . . ."

Keesing (1974:89) offers a definition that holds some promise of clarification:

> Culture, conceived as a system of competence shared in its broad design and deeper principles, and varying between individuals in its specificities, is then not all of what an individual knows and thinks and feels about his world. It is his *theory of what his fellows know, believe, and mean*, his theory of the code being followed, the game being played, in the society into which he was born.

According to Keesing, then, it is this theory that a native actor uses in strange settings. He explains (*ibid.*):

> . . . the actor's "theory" of his culture, like his theory of his language, may be in large measure unconscious. Actors follow rules of which they are not consciously aware, and assume a world to be "out there" that they have in fact created with culturally shaped and shaded patterns of mind.

These cultural theories vary from actor to actor. Keesing's definition represents a theory of culture as an idealized body of competence realized in individual manners in the minds of individuals. He also posited a level of performance—sociocultural performance—in the real world in terms of social relationships, economic organization, and other types of human interaction.

For the time being, we shall leave the more fundamental question concerning the means whereby human beings are guided by a general conceptual code (competence). It may be that an individual's cultural competence rests more on a vast array of general knowledge than on a set of ideal schemes and codes. This may also be true of linguistic competence. The questions are still unanswered.

In like manner we must leave open the question concerning the interplay between individual behavior and group norms. Individuals are socialized to group norms, but by their selection and adherence to or rejection of these rules bring about change and adjustment over time.

These questions remain. We must place the onus of response on those more qualified than we to reply. For the moment, we must be content with the insights and clues we may glean from the efforts of those to whom the concept of culture has for so long been the major focus of inquiry.

Characteristics of Culture

There are several notable characteristics of culture that have been woven and rewoven into the definitions and the theories upon which they are built. These, in addition to the general principles guiding anthropologists as noted above, can provide a set of guiding principles suitable for the pragmatic ethnographer and should give the foregoing discussion a practical focus.

1. *Culture is learned.* If it can be learned, it can also be taught or acquired.
2. *Cultures and cultural patterns change.* It is more important to learn how to learn a culture or adapt to these changes than to learn the "facts" and "truths" of the moment.
3. *Culture is a universal fact of human life.* There is no human group or society without culture. Cultural patterns and themes are related to universal human needs and life conditions.
4. *Cultures provide sets of unique and interrelated, selected blueprints for living and accompanying sets of values and beliefs to support these blueprints.* Strong net-

works of relationships and meaning link these blueprints and values systems. These networks provide life support systems for those who interact within them.

5. *Language and culture are closely related and interactive.* Culture is transmitted in great part through language; cultural patterns in turn are reflected in language.

6. *Culture functions as a filtering device between its bearers and the great range of stimuli presented by the environment.* This filtering device is both protective and limiting. Intercultural communicators must traverse the boundaries of their own filtering systems or screens and enter the systems of others.

Components of Culture

Just as we have examined the definitions and features of the components of communication and their characteristics, we must also look at the components of culture. We have mentioned artifacts, material objects, beliefs, values, and a host of features which are either part and parcel of cultural patterns or affected by cultural patterns.

We may examine culture from the point of view of its individual components or parts or from the more social point of view of its systems. The list of components of culture is dishearteningly lengthy. Variations of human life styles may be found in:

• dress	or societal systems such as:
• systems of rewards and punishments	• kinship
• uses of time and space	• education
• fashions of eating	• economy
• means of communication	• government
• family relationships	• association
• beliefs and values	• health

Edward Hall (1959), in an attempt to bring some order into such seemingly interminable lists, has suggested that there are ten primary message systems or ten kinds of human activity. The systems are universal, but their manifestations are not. His two-dimensional grid of the PMS (primary message systems) is duplicated in Figure 5.2. The PMS are combined with types of activities to produce a "map of culture."

The Hall grid provides a handy reference to consider major areas of cross-cultural variation, including such social categories as role, status, class, and hierarchy, as well as the physical and psychological environment. Other variations

Primary Message Systems	Interactional 0	Organizational 1	Economic 2	Sexual 3
Interaction 0	Communication Vocal qualifiers Kinesics Language 00	Status and Role 01	Exchange 02	How the sexes interact 03
Association 1	Community 10	Society Class Caste Government 11	Economic roles 12	Sexual roles 13
Subsistence 2	Ecological community 20	Occupational groupings 21	Work Formal work Maintenance Occupations 22	Sexual division of labor 23
Bisexuality 3	Sex Community (clans, sibs) 30	Marriage groupings 31	Family 32	The Sexes Masc. vs. Fem. Sex (biological) Sex (technical) 33
Territoriality 4	Community territory 40	Group territory 41	Economic areas 42	Men's and women's territories 43
Temporality 5	Community cycles 50	Group cycles 51	Economic cycles 52	Men's and women's cyclical activities 53
Learning 6	Community lore—what gets taught and learned 60	Learning groups— educational institutions 61	Reward for teaching and learning 62	What the sexes are taught 63
Play 7	Community play—the arts and sports 70	Play groups— teams and troupes 71	Professional sports and entertainment 72	Men's and women's play, fun, and games 73
Defense 8	Community defenses— structured defense systems 80	Defense groups —armies, police, public health, organ-ized religion 81	Economic patterns of defense 82	What the sexes defend (home, honor, etc.) 83
Exploitation 9	Communica-tion networks 90	Organizational networks (cities, build-ing groups, etc.) 91	Food, resources, and industrial equipment 92	What men and women are concerned with and own 93

Territorial		Temporal		Instructional		Recreational		Protective		Exploitational	
Territorial 4		**Temporal** 5		**Instructional** 6		**Recreational** 7		**Protective** 8		**Exploitational** 9	
Places of interaction	04	Times of interaction	05	Teaching and learning	06	Participation in the arts and sports (active and passive)	07	Protecting and being protected	08	Use telephones, signals, writing, etc.	09
Local group roles	14	Age groups roles	15	Teachers and learners	16	Entertainers and athletes	17	Protectors (doctors, clergy, soldiers, police, etc.)	18	Use of group property	19
Where the individual eats, cooks, etc.	24	When the individual eats, cooks, etc.	25	Learning from working	26	Pleasure from working	27	Care of health, protection of livelihood	28	Use of foods, resources, and equipment	29
Areas assigned to individuals by virtue of sex	34	Periods assigned to individuals by virtue of sex	35	Teaching and learning sex roles	36	Participation in recreation by sex	37	Protection of sex and fertility	38	Use of sex-differentiating decoration and adornment	39
Space Formal space Informal space Boundaries	44	Scheduling of space	45	Teaching and learning individual space assignments	46	Fun, playing games, etc., in terms of space	47	Privacy	48	Use of fences and markers	49
Territorially determined cycles	54	Time Sequence Cycles Calendar	55	When the individual learns	56	When the individual plays	57	Rest, vacations, holidays	58	Use of time-telling devices, etc.	59
Places for learning	64	Scheduling of learning (group)	65	Enculturation Rearing Informal learning Education	66	Making learning fun	67	Learning self-defense and to stay healthy	68	Use of training aids	69
Recreational areas	74	Play seasons	75	Instructional play	76	Recreation Fun Playing Games	77	Exercise	78	Use of recreational materials (playthings)	79
What places are defended	84	The When of defense	85	Scientific, religious, and military training	86	Mass exercises and military games	87	Protection Formal defenses Informal defenses Technical defenses	88	Use of materials for protection	89
Property— what is enclosed, counted, and measured	94	What periods are measured and recorded	95	School buildings, training aids, etc.	96	Amusement and sporting goods and their industries	97	Fortifications, armaments, medical equipment, safety devices	98	Material Systems Contact w/ environment Motor habits Technology	99

Figure 5.2. A MAP OF CULTURE

Source: Edward T. Hall, *The Silent Language,* (Garden City, NY: Doubleday & Co., Inc., 1959), pp. 174–175.

can be found in perception, patterns of thinking, relationships of individuals, functions of language, and nonverbal communication, including uses of space, time, gestures, and body movement. There is a place for each of those in the Hall grid.

5.4 CULTURE AND COMMUNICATION

Thus, we may conclude that the concepts of culture and communication are not so much synonymous as inextricably linked in the process of communication and in the minds and perceptions of the communicators. If we expand the definitional boundaries of communication to include all forms of human interaction, verbal and nonverbal, and culture to include both explicit and implicit features, then we may draw yet an even more revealing schema of their relationships, in which the dynamic interactional, irreversible process of communication is constantly influenced and molded by the ever-changing rules of the public game each individual privately plays.

The schema shown in Figure 5.3 may remind the readers of a set of Chinese boxes or a latter-day tagmemic analysis. Such resemblances are no accident. Communication is all too often approached in the linear fashion of Western logic, and culture is compartmentalized into unrelated tiny boxes labeled "religion," "child rearing," "marriage patterns," or the like. Of the many ways the complex relationships of communication and culture can be shown, the linear is the least useful.

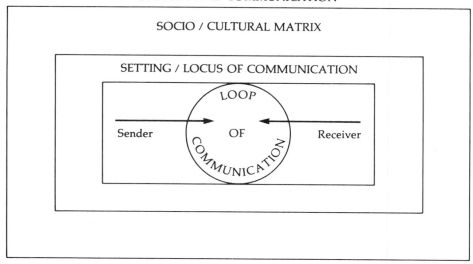

CULTURE AND COMMUNICATION

SOCIO / CULTURAL MATRIX

SETTING / LOCUS OF COMMUNICATION

LOOP

OF

COMMUNICATION

Sender

Receiver

Figure 5.3. Culture and Communication

In Figure 5.3 a communicative act takes place within the context of a socio-cultural matrix whose boundaries are drawn by the identification of a number of individuals as sharing given cultural assumptions, behaviors, and patterns. The setting, which operates within the general matrix, provides the locus of communication; it is also culturally conditioned, for example, in terms of the uses of communication, manner of speech, or styles of communication. The communicative act itself is nestled within this setting and takes place in a circular manner so that sender and receiver roles can be assigned interchangeably.

An example of the cultural influence upon communication is illustrated by a study carried out by Naoki Nomura and Dean Barnlund and reported in an article titled "Patterns of Interpersonal Criticism in Japan and the United States" (1983:1–18). In this study the researchers found that modes of giving criticism varied between a group of Japanese and a group of Americans. The Japanese favored a more passive form of criticism and often engaged in banter, while their American counterparts were more active and angry in their patterns. In expressing criticism, the Japanese took into account the status of their communicative partners, the Americans, the type of provocation. Yet each group favored expression of dissatisfaction. The authors conclude (17) that each group "not only possesses a somewhat different hierarchy of ways of expressing dissatisfaction, but each perceives different features of social settings as relevant in mediating the particular form of criticism they employ."

To apply this to the classroom situation, then, what kinds of communication problems might Japanese students have in expressing criticism in a North American setting? You should be able to make some incisive observations based upon the information provided in this chapter.

In another study Abe and Wiseman (1983:53–67) examined perceptions of the elements of intercultural effectiveness of a Japanese group and an American group. The Americans were concerned with their own performances in relation to intercultural communication and with explicit communication, while the Japanese emphasized the continuity of the communication and emotional communication. (65) Yet both groups shared the feeling that the establishment of personal relationships facilitated interpersonal communication and, hence, intercultural effectiveness.

For those with limited understanding or experience of the cultural underpinnings of the peoples of the Middle East, Yousef's article (1982) "North Americans in the Middle East: Aspects of the Roles of Friendliness, Religion, and Women in Cross-Cultural Relations," contrasts low-context North American and high-context Middle Eastern orientations on these sensitive subjects and their effects upon communicative expectations. In contrasting these cultural frames of reference, Yousef (99) points out the dangers of ignoring the unwritten rules and expectations that operate in the high-context societies of the Middle East.

The articles discussed above are only a few of the many illustrating the interrelationships of communication and culture. The reader is urged to study these and others like them with care. However, even this present cursory discussion should provide a glimpse of the intertwining of things communicative and cultural.

5.5 CONCLUSION

A multitude of sociocultural variables must be taken into account in every intercultural communicative event. Fortunately, most of us are blissfully unaware of the dancing molecules of meaning that cavort around our attempts to communicate. The amount of actual communication and understanding that *does* take place is far greater than even the most optimistic communicator has any right to expect. Indeed, let us end this lengthy tour of all the winding streets, dead ends, and alleys of our "cities" of culture with a note of encouragement. We do manage to keep communication lines open more often than not. Given the complexities of the processes, such success can only be attributed to the overpowering desire of most human beings to "communicate."

In the following chapter we shall investigate the changing theories and definitions of language and the use of linguistic analogies in cultural exploration. In subsequent chapters we shall discuss in greater detail some of the types of cultural variations found in value orientations, message decoding, and verbal and nonverbal aspects of communication. We shall concentrate on differences as a method of highlighting our own individual theories of our own cultures and those of others. This is done with the clear admonition that, while there are great differences, there also are many similarities. It is what we share that makes it possible for us to learn another culture; this is the most fundamental insight this chapter has to offer.

As Gudykunst and Kim (1984:172) advise, "We must strive to maintain an optimal balance between the two [the fundamental duality of similarities and differences] by recognizing and appreciating cultural uniqueness, while at the same time embracing the shared human conditions and characteristics." And so be it!

FOR STUDY AND DISCUSSION

1. Explain the meaning of the following quotation: "If communication is process, different persons are likely to impose different structures on the 'same process' based on different backgrounds, assumptions, and purposes" (Condon and Yousef, 1975:11).

2. What are the components and characteristics of the concept of communication of particular importance in intercultural communication?

3. How are the various definitions of culture presented in this chapter related to changing theories of the nature of culture? Which definitions do you think are most applicable to the classroom context?

4. What is meant by the terms setting/context and contexting as defined in this chapter? What are high-context and low-context cultures? How do they differ?

5. Relate the conclusions drawn by Hall as to the existence of high-context and low-context cultures to your target culture. Is your research area high- or low-context? What features in the culture led to your conclusions?

6. In the example given in the chapter, the teacher in reading the essay of one of her students made some assumptions about group behavior. Should she have read the essay to the class in the first place? How might she have handled the matter more effectively?

7. What aspects of group behavior, other than the relationship of the individual to the group, present pitfalls for the cross-culturally unaware?

8. What are some implications of the guiding principles of anthropology listed in this chapter? How are they reflected in the approach taken in this book and in the assigned readings?

9. What is meant by an ideational approach to culture? How does it contrast with other approaches?

CULTURE LEARNING EXERCISE

Make an oral report about your target group. This report should be based on

Make an oral report about your target group. This report should be based on information gathered from secondary sources and from your informant. It will be a preliminary report. You are expected to continue your study of the target culture as you investigate other aspects of intercultural communication and second language learning/teaching.

Organize your report in order to provide the following information:

1. Name and location of target group
2. Information sources
   a) Informant (do not name)—age, sex, any salient personal characteristics
   b) Secondary sources
3. Important general information
   a) Demographic data
   b) Language
   c) Sociocultural variables
4. Historical data of interest
5. Salient cultural themes or patterns
6. Major features of educational system, if appropriate
7. Identification of a problem or area of research interest for the target group in relation to second language or second culture learning
8. Cross-cultural training areas to be emphasized for students from the target group and for teachers from those target areas

Make a brief written report of your experience in interviewing your informant.

FOR FURTHER READING

D. Cathcart and R. Cathcart. 1982. "Japanese Social Experience and Concept of Groups" (120–127). As noted in the previous chapter this article discusses the contrastive concepts of self and group as manifested by Japanese and Americans. This essay is of particular moment for the teacher who perforce must deal with multicultural group behavior in the classroom.

J. Clifton (ed.). 1968. *Introduction to Cultural Anthropology: Essays in the Scope and Methods of the Science of Man*. This book is intended as an introduction to the field of cultural anthropology. Chapter 14 titled "Ethnography: Method and Product" by G. Berreman analyzes the processes of ethnography and the ethnographic experience. It contains a useful bibliographic listing for those who would delve into classic ethnographic reports. Indeed, the bibliography for the volume is a fine introduction to classic anthropological literature.

R. Keesing. 1974. "Theories of Culture" (73–97). This review of the changing theories of culture, while perhaps hard going for the uninitiated, presents a coherent and systematic discussion of the various theoretical twists and turns taken by professionals in the fields of anthropology and sociology. The discussion in Chapter 5 was supported by the insights contained in Keesing's discussion. Although literature in the field of intercultural communication contains references to each of these theoretical stances, Keesing's article brings these permutations into focus for those whose interests lie in reading between the lines and understanding where certain theorists are "coming from."

C. Kluckhohn. 1944. *Mirror for Man*. Although somewhat dated, this volume still provides a readable and fundamentally sound introduction to the foundations of the present-day practice of anthropology.

R. Manners and D. Kaplan (eds.). 1968. *Theory in Anthropology*. This is a collection of classic writings on culture theory. The collection reflects the "*current* theoretical interests of anthropology (ix)" at the time of its publication. Lévi-Strauss, Geertz, Frake, Goodenough, and others number among the contributors. The volume is recommended to those interested in delving deeper into the mysteries of culture theory.

H. Nostrand. 1978. "The 'Emergent Model' (Structured inventory of a sociocultural system) Applied to Contemporary France" (277–294). In this article, Professor Nostrand, long an advocate of cultural instruction in the foreign language classroom, describes a structured inventory of sociocultural elements (an "emergent model") for guidance in the development of cultural instructional units. The inventory, suggested as an alternative to the "ambiguities" of the Hall grid, organizes 32 main features of a sociocultural system into four component (sub-) systems. Nostrand applies the inventory to contemporary France. Readers will profit from a perusal of this model.

A. Smith (ed.). 1966. *Communication and Culture: Readings in the Codes of Human Interaction*. The readings in this book deal with the various types of communication and their cultural implications. Articles by Bernstein, Hymes, and others, found herein, relate directly to the topics discussed in Chapter 5.

Chapter 6

On the Road to Communicative Competence

In the previous chapters we looked at the concepts of *communication* and *culture*. Each was seen to possess distinctive components and characteristics. At the same time the concepts, each in a very special way, are bound together through social interaction.

The following chapter will examine the nature of human language and its relationship to culture. Language is one mode of communication; culture may mediate the manner in which this mode is used. Because aspects of communication reflect cultural differences, Hymes (1962, 1972a, 1972b, 1974) suggested that an ethnography of communication was needed. Such research would investigate the ways in which communication takes place among interacting cultural groups.

The present pedagogical focus on the development of the communicative competence of second language learners is but one facet of the language and culture connection. This approach to language learning speaks to the need for the learner to understand and use appropriate terms and rules of communication in a given culture. Yet the language and culture connection involves more than merely using rules; it also involves employing other channels of communication, including the nonverbal. Articulation of the goals of developing the communicative competence of our students means that we, as teachers, must define language in the broadest terms possible.

To that end, this chapter will review briefly the changing views of language that have dominated the various perspectives espoused by professional linguists in this century, and the influences these theoretical positions have had on the art and science of language teaching and of cultural analysis—both of primary pedagogical concern in the 1980s. The borrowing and lending of methods and perspectives among linguists and anthropologists have not only left their imprint on the forms and methods of second language instruction but have also given us, the pragmatic ethnographers, a set of analytical methods designed to further cultural and linguistic discovery. We should make the best possible use of this legacy.

The primary purpose of the following discussion is to provide an understanding of the roots of present-day linguistic theory and its relationship to our current concern with the teaching of language and culture. In the previous chapter we reviewed some of the changing theories of culture; in this chapter we shall do the same for language. Following that, we shall investigate the various ways in which linguistic models have been used in the analysis of culture and what these experiments have to offer us today.

6.1 APPROACHING LANGUAGE

Table 6.1 lists five shifts in linguistic theory that are of interest to us. Each school of thought has regarded language in a very special way. Although earlier approaches have been rejected in whole or part by some, their insights as well as methods and techniques of analysis still shed light on the complex phenomenon known as human language.

TABLE 6.1 APPROACHING LANGUAGE

Approach	Focus
1. Saussure/Prague School	*langue/parole;* linguistic sign; synchronic study
2. American Structuralism	Bloomfieldian/structural analysis; treatment of surface formal structure; descriptive; language specific; item and arrangement/process
3. British Structural/Functionalism (Firth)	language in context; study of text; meaning in context
4. Transformational/Generative	study of *langue;* item and process; language general
5. Semiotics/Sociolinguistics/ Pragmatics/Neo-Firthism	language in context; functions of language; competence and performance

6.2 LINGUISTICS AND LANGUAGE

Linguistics, as the scientific and systematic study of language, is a discipline that addresses itself to the nature of human language, its description, and its operations. A linguistic description is called a grammar of that language, a grammar being a set of statements about that language and how it works.

There are many kinds of linguistics: *historical linguistics* (language history); *psychological linguistics* (linguistics and psychological mechanisms); *sociolinguistics* (language and its functions in society); *anthropological linguistics* (investigation of language in a given culture and as part of culture); and *applied linguistics* (knowledge from theoretical linguistics put to practical use). It is the last two which interest us most; yet the contributions of all the theorists must be taken into account in adapting their findings to our learning and teaching tasks.

The major theories of language of interest to us are those espoused by the great Swiss linguist F. de Saussure and his followers in the United States and Europe, by Bloomfield in the United States, by Firth and others in England, and by the transformational/generativists set on course by Noam Chomsky. It is from these sources that the current somewhat divided schools of pragmatics, discourse analysis, and sociolinguistics have sprung. Each has provided a unique view of language, has developed very specialized methods of analysis, and has important insights for those who must deal with language both in context and in the abstract. The manner in which language has been approached by each school is of more importance than the search for a direct application of its methods or perspectives in language teaching.

Saussure's Legacy

Important in the development of all schools of linguistics was the force of the ideas generated by the work of Saussure, whose lectures at the University of Geneva (1906–1911) were published posthumously by two of his students under the title *Cours de Linguistique Générale de Ferdinand de Saussure* (1915). Prior to and during the period of Bloomfieldian linguistics in the United States, which began in the early 1930s, linguists in Europe under the influence of Saussure, as well as other European linguists, were examining language from a new point of view. From their work came the concepts of *langue* and *parole*, the importance of linguistic sign, and distinctive feature analysis.

Saussure's formulation of language as a system of signs and their relationships was enunciated in his university lectures. He argued that language should be studied synchronically, not just diachronically. He also distinguished between *langue* (the system) and *parole* (the manifestation or use); *langue* being the larger abstract system that supports *parole* but never appears. *Langue*, as competence or the fundamental linguistic system, was to become the main focus of analysis under the direction of Noam Chomsky and the transformationalists. *Parole*, linked to performance, has come into its own only of recent date.

Saussure described the concept of the linguistic sign as composed of two aspects: the signified (*signifié*) is the concept and the signifier (*signifiant*) is the form (sound). The relationship between the signified (the concept of cat) and signifier (the sound/image of cat) is arbitrary. According to Saussure: "Language is a system of interdependent terms in which the value of each term results solely from the simultaneous presence of the others" (1915:114).

The term *distinctive features* refers to a series of features or characteristics associated with all sounds of all languages. In linguistic analysis distinctive features describe sound contrasts along such dimensions as stridency or voicing (Jakobson and Halle 1956). This method produced a more elegant analytical procedure than had the phonemic analyses of the American structuralist school. The new approach, developed from the work of Trubetzkoy and others of the Prague School, treated classes of sounds as bundles of features, not as individual sound units.

The concepts of *langue, parole,* linguistic sign, and distinctive features influenced the formulation of subsequent theoretical positions concerning language taken by many linguists, especially after Noam Chomsky introduced the transformational/generative model in the late 1960s.

American Structuralism

Linguists of the school of descriptive linguistics, which held sway in the United States from the early 1900s until the Chomskyan "revolution," were interested in uncovering the structure or formal properties of a language by careful analytical dissection. The focus of interest was on the analysis of the structure of the language and the relationships of its various parts. Their data were sets of verbal utterances, or a corpus. The system (*langue*) was to be discovered in the inspection of actual speech (*parole*). The structural model assumed a tri-level model of sound, meaningful units, and their arrangements/processes. The phoneme as a unit of sound in a given system comprised the first level of analysis. These phonemes were combined into minimal meaningful units at a second level of analysis. Structural linguists concerned themselves mainly with descriptive analysis of surface features of a specific language. The assumption was that each language was structurally unique, yet composed of universal analytical levels.

In the early 1900s, linguistic theory in the United States was closely allied with anthropological endeavors. The intensive study of the then vanishing Indian languages of North America brought mountains of data to support the position. Most held that languages (and cultures) must be studied as unique historical products. Because different languages appeared to reflect the concerns of their culture, the study of the language of a given group was a *sine qua non* in anthropological research (Boas 1911). In fact, linguistic analysis was the first order of business in any new anthropological undertaking.

The Bloomfieldian linguistics of the succeeding period (1930–1965) suited exploration procedures very well indeed. Methods were devised to uncover and analyze the meaningful sound and formal patterns of a given language. These proved appropriate to descriptive linguistic purposes; how appropriate they were for cultural analysis remained to be seen.

Contextualizing Language

At the same time that Bloomfieldian linguistics held sway in the United States, the British linguist J. R. Firth, drawing on the field work of the anthropologist Bronislaw Malinowski, proposed that language be studied not only in the linguistic context but in its environmental context. Meaning should be taken into account.

Neo-Firthian theory has formed the basis of the works of Halliday in the functions of language (1970, 1973, 1978), Wilkins' notional syllabuses (1976), and Widdowson's communicative categories (1978, 1979). Halliday's work in the functions and uses of language provided another impetus toward enunciating a theory of communicative competence applicable in the language classroom. Halliday (1970:145) explains: "Linguistics . . . is concerned . . . with the description of speech acts, or texts, since only through the study of language in use are all the functions of language, and therefore all components of meaning, brought into focus."

The T/G Revolution

In the early 1960s Noam Chomsky almost singlehandedly transformed the field of American linguistics by adopting the concept of *langue* as the major focus of linguistic inquiry. The deep structure of language, then, was the fundamental target of analysis, and the description and operation of a native speaker's competence were of primary importance. Performance and the vagaries of language in use were not the concern of these transformationalists. Later known as transformational/generative analysis, the Chomsky model centered on formulating the grammar of a language in terms of its basic syntactic structures and processes. The concern of these linguists was with the specification of the transformations and rules needed to dredge up the surface manifestations or sentences from the deep structure of the language. Much that could be found in the deep structure and in the types of rules and transformations was language-general, although their applications were language-specific. This type of analysis represented, in effect, a reverse approach from that of the American structural linguists who began at the surface level and worked down.

Language in Use and in Context

Of more recent date is the analysis of language in use and the context in which this use occurs. Language in performance and language as social behavior has become of theoretical interest. Questions of semantics (meaning) had been cavalierly postponed by the Chomsky model. In the early 1970s, a turn from the generative grammatical school of linguistic theory shifted interest away from the ideal speaker-listener's linguistic competence to the communicative competence of a real speaker interacting in a real world, ordered by rules of appropriateness and variability.

The view of language held in semiotics, sociolinguistics, modern British functionalism and pragmatics represents a change from the Chomskyan inner-focused scrutiny of a linguistic system uncontaminated by extraneous disturbances of "such grammatically irrelevant conditions as memory limitations, distractions, shifts of attention and interest, and errors (random or characteristic) . . ." (Chomsky 1965:3).

These new approaches have also brought linguistic inquiry closer to anthropological, sociological, and communicative concerns with the nature of communication, culture, and social diversity. The newer models have begun to resemble the models of the social sciences.

Of particular interest to language teachers is the development of sociolinguistics, the study of language in its social context. Dell Hymes focused attention on the concept of *communicative competence* in 1971. This phrase, now so basic in the theory, practice, and research of ESL/EFL, was coined as an umbrella term to emphasize the importance of context and interaction in communication. It recognizes the functions of diversity, register, repertoire, domains, and language styles, as well as their interrelationships with linguistic variables. Justification for such inclusion can be found in the work of Fishman on domains and codes (1966), Joos on the styles of language (1967), and Labov (1966, 1972) on the relationships of dialectical variations and social class.

Thus, the analytical picture began to show such sociocultural variables as age, class, and sex, taken in context or setting, to be important in measuring a given speaker's communicative competence. Communicative competence was defined as the skill to know what to say, when to say it, to whom to say it and how. Language was viewed as social behavior, the speaker as a sociocultural entity. The concerns of linguists, anthropologists, and teachers were closer than they had ever been. If the ambiguities of the mnemonic device Hymes constructed to account for the components of the speech act (SPEAKING)[1] have mercifully been forgotten, the purpose for which it was devised has paved the way for bringing culture into the language learning context as a major and respected element in the language syllabus.

Language as a semiotic system (C. Morris 1939, 1946), now an important part of current linguistic theory, posits a firm link between language and culture. Language as a symbolic system can be viewed in terms of the relationships between various signs (syntactics), between symbols and their referents (semantics), and between signs or symbols and human relationships (pragmatics) (C. Morris 1946).

Theory and Practice

Each model has given us the means to view the interplay of language and culture with different sets of analytical spectacles. The structural/taxonomic model emphasized the importance of the role of cultural meaning and the discovery of culture-specific categories and classification systems. The universalists turned attention from a language-specific to a language-general perspective, providing a method to assess shared features and to understand the formal operations involved in language use and language learning. The present models allow for the consideration of both the general and the specific, language competence and performance, and language in use. They also open the way to the consideration of language as something more than a vocal system. In addition, some have given us methods to bring culture learning into closer synchrony with language learning.

6.3 LANGUAGE AS AN ANALOG OF CULTURE

Because culture and language share many features, it is not surprising that the proposition was put forth in the 1950s that the methods used to analyze language could just as easily serve to analyze culture. This analogy rests on the assumption that some aspects of culture could be treated as language had been; that is to say that the analytical methods used to dissect language were appropriate for cultural analysis. Such analogies were based on the linguistic characteristics of the shared use of arbitrary symbols, hierarchically organized patterns of meaningful structures, and the quality of openness. These features formed the basis for the development of specialized cultural discovery methods. According to Goodenough (1964:37), a strong proponent of such a method: "The relation of language to culture, then, is that of part to whole. Theory and method applicable to one must have implications for the other . . ."

The following section of this chapter reviews several types of adaptations of linguistic analytical methods to cultural exploration in anthropology and second language acquisition—the Pike model, ethnoscience, universalism, French structuralism, and semiotics. Examples of such analyses are briefly discussed. These applications are reviewed because the methods suggested, while exhibiting disadvantages for professional anthropologists, do lend themselves to the structuring of cross-cultural observation and so should be evaluated for their strengths and weaknesses in such a pursuit.

The Pike Model

The proposal that the exploratory methods of structural and descriptive linguistic analysis could be used in cultural analysis was enunciated by K. L. Pike, a professor at the University of Michigan, a missionary, and founder of the Summer Institute of Linguistics. In his 1954 book *Language in Relation to a Unified Theory of the Structure of Human Behavior* (expanded in 1967) and in other articles, Pike put forth the proposition that the analytical methods and analytical structures used in structural linguistics might be gainfully employed in the search for culture-specific units of meaning. This led to a new approach in ethnography, called variously the New Ethnography, ethnoscience, ethnosemantics, or just *-emic* analysis.

That Pike should have made such a suggestion is not at all surprising if one recalls that many of the research methods used in linguistic and anthropological analysis developed together because of the insistence of Boas and others that language held the key to cultural understanding. It was Pike himself who had done so much to develop these analytical methods and who had trained so many budding linguists and missionaries to map as yet unwritten languages.

The descriptive linguistic methods were designed to uncover meaningful phonemic and morphemic units in a language—that is, distinctive sounds and meaningful units as part of a given language's grammatical system. Phonetic analyses described the nature and characteristics of given sounds without regard to their position in a linguistic inventory. Phonemes, or sounds signalling meaning in a given language, formed units of meanings or morphemes. As explained in Chapter 4, these units were distributed according to the position they filled in a given sequence of units in a given language. Thus, the arrangement of these units could be described in terms of their meaning, form, and distribution. For example, in the sentence *The boy ate the sandwich*, the slot for *boy* might be filled by *John*. Its form is a noun and its meaning is a young male person. Thus, strings of meaningful units could be described in terms of the slots they fill (syntagmemes) and the sets of forms (paradigms) that can be substituted in these slots, as Saussure had suggested (1915:122).

It was these proposed analytical units—*-emes*—that could provide the means of discovering units of cultural meaning, just as they had served to isolate units of linguistic meaning. *-Emic* categories were considered "native"; *-etic* were other means of classification and analysis.

Pike suggested that by using the correlation between "spot" or "slot" and "class" or "filler," it would be possible to discover the cultural *-emic* units constituting the list of items suitable for substitution in a particular spot or slot. The *-emic* unit would be culture-specific just as it was language-specific in the case of linguistic phonemes and their variations, or allophones. Working on the assumption that both language and other human behaviors are composed of hierarchical structures, with larger units being formed from smaller ones, Pike proposed the *behavioreme* as the unit of culturally meaningful behavior. He suggested that such behavioremes might be verbal or nonverbal, and used a football game, the recitation of a poem, and a response to a question as examples (Pike, 1964:58).

Pike's suggestion was based on the shared qualities of human language and human culture. Pike's premise (54) was:

> . . . that every purposeful activity of man is structured, and that certain basic characteristics are common to every such activity, so that it should be possible to develop a theory and a technique which would pass without jar from the study of the structure of one kind of activity of man to that of any other kind.

Pike also assumed that the *-emic* event was simultaneously structured in three ways or modes: the manifestation mode, the feature mode, and the distribution mode. The manifestation mode included the "hierarchical, segmental structuring of the physical material which is present in every human behavioral event" (59). The feature mode was the meaningful unit and the point in the system. The distribution mode indicated the slot or filler—a correlation of spot plus all the fillers which could be substituted therein. Pike stressed the importance of the hierarchical structuring of the behavioreme—every *-emic* unit has a physical base and every *-emic* unit within every mode contains a feature mode, a manifestation mode, and a distribution mode (60).

Thus, if what was true for language was also true for culture, then *-emic* analyses should uncover meaningful units of culture. Pike's formulation, as we have noted, provided a bridge between language and other elements of culture. Although the Pike method has proved difficult to use and has been subject to the same attacks aimed at the entire approach to language that it represented, it did and does call attention to the human penchant for classification, categorizing, devising taxonomies of categories, and gathering these together in repeated themes and patterns.

Cultural Contrastive Analysis

Pike's colleague at the University of Michigan, Robert Lado, found the Pike model a means of analyzing cultural items in terms of contrast. Up to that time, second language instruction and methodologies had been limited to grammar translation methods and pattern practice techniques. In his book *Linguistics Across Cultures* (1957) Lado adapts the Pike model to language learning problems. His is a contrastive analytical method based on the premises that thorough knowledge and a comparison between the target language and a student's native language will facilitate the passage from one linguistic system to another, and will also provide a means of predicting errors. This last premise has proved insupportable and inspired second language researchers and practitioners to dismiss the contrastive analytical method as unreliable and, as now seems apparent, to throw out most of the baby with the bathwater. The fact that contrastive analysis did not provide an unfailing method for error prediction does not obviate its utility in other areas. Interest in other language models and other concerns, however, resulted in the ignoring of the methods of contrastive analysis in the years following its rejection in the 1970s. (See Chapter 4.)

Lado had yet another task for contrastive analysis. In the last chapter of his book, he suggests a direct application of the Pike model to cultural data. In a revision of the basic terms, Lado includes both the manifestation and feature modes suggested by Pike in his form mode and substituted *meaning*, which Pike had not mentioned directly. Thus, Lado suggests the terms *meaning, form,* and *distribution* could be used to describe a given functional unit of culture.

For example, Lado applies the Pike model directly to such phenomena as bullfights and tarpon fishing, finding that the meaning assigned to each type of event has to do with the cultural perspective of the observer. As Lado points out, the "alien observer" discerns form and distribution more easily than meaning (115). The cultural meanings assigned to *cruelty* and relationships of human beings to animals are important in interpreting attitudes toward the bullfight. He points out that in the case of the bullfight "the complex form represented by the bull has a different classification, a different meaning, in American culture" (117). On the other hand, tarpon fishing in the American culture does not constitute "cruelty" because fish are distinct from human beings in both American and Spanish cultures. He concludes, "Marginal supporting evidence is the fact that in American culture there is a Society for the Prevention of Cruelty to Animals which concerns itself with the feelings of . . . domestic animals. . . . We would not conceive of a society for the prevention of cruelty to fish" (117).

Thus, variations can be found in form, meaning, and distribution and their permutations. For example, cross-cultural comparison would show several different patterns for the first meal of the day as anyone used to bacon and eggs knows when faced with a Continental breakfast. Misinterpretations may easily occur if the forms are very different. However, often the problems occur when part of the pattern is repeated with the same form but a different distribution, or with the same form, the same distribution, but a different meaning.

Lado provides many examples of contrastive patterns for the problem of same form/different meaning. For example, a hiss communicates disapproval in the United States, calls for silence in Spain, and reveals concentration when used in Japan.

In the case of the same meaning/different form, the problems often lie in the use of different forms to convey similar meanings. For example, respect may be intended, even with the use of first names, in an informal culture. Respect would call for different naming patterns in a formal culture. In the same way, delight at receiving a gift (meaning) may be expressed by different behaviors—eager opening of the gift in some cultures, but postponing it in others.

Finally, in the case of the same meaning/same form with different distribution, the margin for error is even greater. For example, serving salad for breakfast is a source of wonder to visitors in Japan, just as the strange custom of soaping oneself in the bath water must seem to the Japanese.

An example of poor timing or distribution, wrong form, and mistaken meaning has amused and astonished native speakers of English visiting in The Netherlands. The Dutch, a hospitable folk, often greet their visitors with a hearty "hello" at the door, but surprise them greatly by offering an equally hearty "hello" again as they leave. The Dutch speakers are simply using their native language distributional patterns that allow the same form, *dag*, to be used as a welcoming salutation as well as a term of farewell. The meaning conveyed to the English speakers is confusing and amusing; to them the meaning, form, and distribution were right at the coming but not at the going.

Whether or not being aware of areas of differences as sources of misperception could lead to error avoidance in cases of cross-cultural communication, as Lado suggests, remains open to question. In addition, selecting the paradigms to place in the slots may vary intraculturally, so that there may be little consistency in a given culture. All things considered, however, it does seem valuable to bring variant patterns to the level of conscious awareness.

Ethnoscience (The New Ethnography)

The Pike suggestion, which had come from the descriptive school of linguistics and the work of Boas and Sapir, formed the rationale for a new method of cultural analysis in anthropology—ethnoscience or the New Ethnography. This approach uses data collection methods designed to discover categories and contrasts relevant in the cultures under observation and attested to by native informants. (See Chapter 4 for a discussion of ethnoscientific approaches to cultural meaning.)

As Spradley points out: "Ethnoscience took the -emic/-etic distinction seriously; it emphasized that the first goal of ethnography was a thorough -emic description based on native categories" (1979:231). In other words, the insistence on the view from inside resulted in the use of informants or insiders who could describe and explain.

This so-called New Ethnography was in effect only an intensification of the traditional American approach to field work and the emphasis on collecting actual texts from native informants. Inherent in this approach was the assumption that the native's categorizations were the correct ones—for the culture in question. The designation ethno- was meant to imply that the classifications to be uncovered were native and dependent upon native perceptions.

Thus, the ethnoscientists sought to establish the "set of contrasting responses appropriate to a given, culturally valid, eliciting context" (Frake 1962:76). Because these responses were picked up on the verbal channel, culturally appropriate behavior could be analyzed along semantic dimensions. In other words, culturally valid meanings could be uncovered by the analysis of the way people discussed given items and of related units of behavior.

For example, Frake constructed a taxonomy of segregates (units of contrastive meaningful behavioral items) available at an American lunch counter, dividing the items into three major categories: sandwiches, pies, and ice-cream bars (1962:80). After identifying the meaningful units or segregates, the observer must establish the attributes assigned to each unit; i.e., establish the difference between a sandwich and an ice cream bar. This might be as easy as pie for a native observer but not for others. For example, what is the difference between a pie and an Eskimo pie? Would the Eskimos know? The analysis of attributions of given segregates involves the "systematic study of semantic domains" (Pelto 1970:71) and has become known as componential analysis. This is a method to identify the distinctive features of each element in a set of contrasting terms. Such an approach to ethnographic analysis presumably permits the ethnographer to discover "how people construe their world of experience from the way they talk about it" (Frake 1962:74). It has been used in studies of kinship, color categories, weddings, firewood, diseases, and other such cultural areas as represented in the works of Conklin (1955), Frake (1961), Goodenough (1956, 1965), Metzger and Williams (1963, 1966), and others.

An example of these analytical techniques is demonstrated by David De-Camp's schema of the distribution of Jamaican meal terms. (See Figure 6.1.) The distribution of meals is indicated in terms of the dialects spoken and social classes of the speakers, while the meals are contrasted on the basis of time served and the size or heaviness of the meals. Such componential analysis has proved most useful for domains (categories of cultural meaning) for which paradigms are possible—kinship, meals, pronouns.

The Deep Structure of Culture

Finally, the fact that the data derived from -*emic* analyses did not seem to contribute much either to uncovering cultural universals or the testing of generalizable hypotheses drove the anthropologists, most of them quite willingly, into the camp of those who approached language and linguistic systems from the point of view of language in general rather than a specific language. Both the Prague Circle in Europe and the later transformational/generative linguists in the United States turned the focus of study and theorizing from language-specific descriptions to deep structures and language-general characteristics. The identification of universal distinctive features as a means of describing phonological variations, the focus of study on the linguistic system rather than language in use, and the primacy of mapping the system of competence rather than performance, all of which these new approaches to language brought, served to turn the attention of anthropologists to similar concerns. As theories of culture shifted from the shared cognitive patterns of given cultural groups to a consideration of the nature of culture as a cognitive and, later, a symbolic system, anthropologists turned to the search for universals of cultural behavior and fundamental operations. The search was for the same universality in culture apparently being demonstrated in language.

For those interested in the relationship between language and culture there was little practical benefit to be derived from research aimed at finding underlying and fundamental properties of the human mind, human language, and human culture. Indeed, Chomsky himself stated that he was "rather skeptical about the significance, for the teaching of languages, of such insights and understanding as have been attained in linguistics and psychology" (1966:43).

Chomsky notwithstanding, the transformational/generative model provided a rule-oriented approach to language instruction and emphasized the universal foundations—deep structure—of all language systems. The use of the descriptive and analytical techniques of this model focused attention on what was shared among all human speakers rather than on what was not. It has provided a common ground for linguistic analysis.

Jamaican Meal Terms

Dialect	5:00–7:00 A.M.	11:00–Noon	4:00–6:00 P.M.	7:00–8:30 P.M.	10:30–Midnight
Upper middle class	*breakfast* medium	*lunch* medium	*tea* light	*dinner* heavy	*supper* light
Lower–middle class	*breakfast* medium	*dinner* heavy	*supper* medium	*supper* light	
Estate laborer	*tea* light	*breakfast* medium		*dinner* heavy	
Peasant farmer	*tea* light	*breakfast* heavy	*dinner* medium	*supper* light	

Only two dimensions of semantic contrast are needed to distinguish the meanings of these various terms: (1) the time at which the meals are eaten, and (2) the size or heaviness of the meal. T can stand for the dimension of time and the segments of the day which must be recognized as distinctive can be symbolized as follows:

T^m morning—5:00–7:00 A.M.
T^n noon—11:00–noon
T^a afternoon—4:00–6:00 P.M.
T^e evening—7:00–8:30 P.M.
T^l late—10:30–midnight.

Similarly H can stand for the dimension of heaviness of the meal. The three degrees of heaviness recognized by the Jamaicans can be shown as follows:

H^l a light meal, usually including a hot drink, but lacking hot food
H^m a medium meal
H^h the heaviest meal of the day.

Jamaican Meal Terms (2)

	Breakfast	Lunch	Tea	Dinner	Supper
Upper-middle class	$H^m T^m$	$H^m T^n$	$H^l T^a$	$H^h T^e$	$H^l T^l$
Lower-middle class	$H^m T^m$			$H^h T^n$	$H^m T^a/H^l T^e$
Estate laborer	$H^m T^n$		$H^l T^m$	$H^h T^e$	
Peasant farmer	$H^h T^n$		$H^l T^m$	$H^m T^a$	$H^l T^e$

Figure 6.1.

Source: From *Man's Many Voices: Language in its Cultural Context* by Robbins Burling. Copyright © 1970 by Holt, Rinehart & Winston, Inc. Reprinted by permission of CBS College Publishing.

Lévi-Strauss and the Human Myth

The application of the structuralist (European) model as exhibited in the work of Claude Lévi-Strauss, the French anthropologist, illustrates the application of formalistic, linguistically related analytical methods to cultural data, especially myths and kinship systems. To Lévi-Strauss "the phenomena of kinship are phenomena of the *same type* as linguistic phenomena" (1964:41). Thus, influenced by the methods of the Prague Circle and its approach to phonology, he sought logical relations, binary contrasts, and correlations in human myths and social relationships. His thesis was that by noting how mankind looked at nature, as revealed in myths and by observing the qualities of classifications used, crucial facts about human logic and similarities across cultures could be isolated.

For example, Lévi-Strauss examines the *avunculate* (uncle) relationship as a fundamental or elementary kinship structure widely distributed in human groups. Four terms (brother, sister, father, son) are "united among themselves by two pairs of corollative oppositions, and such that, in each of the two generations implied, there exists always a positive relation and a negative relation" (1964:48). The use of universal terms and oppositions speaks to the influence of European models of language.

Semiotics and Language in Use

Modern schools of linguistics, eclectic in nature, reflect the insights gained from the various models that preceded them. Linguistic theory, linguistic forms, anthropological theory, and cultural focus are synchronized more closely than they have ever been. In our present approach to language instruction and in our notions and functions and dedication to communicative competence, we have opted for all that sister theories and perspectives have to offer us. We shall examine the nature of cultural competence as well as communicative competence in a later chapter. The promise of the present approach to language by linguists, anthropologists, and language professionals makes the establishment of the language and culture connection in the language classroom not only possible but imperative.

6.4 THE VALUE OF LINGUISTIC ANALOGIES

Of what value is the fact that elements of culture may be analyzed using methods developed for linguistic analysis? What were the main advantages and disadvantages of such applications? What use do any of these methods have for the language teacher and the language learner?

Let us address the last question first. The methods emphasized, especially in the application of the *-emic* model by the New Ethnographers and as used later in anthropological studies of given cultures, the strong connection between language in use, linguistic and/or cultural domains, and language and culture learning, as should be clear. That there are theoretical disadvantages is also clear, but such disadvantages should not lead us to dispense with the analytical tools given us.

The main advantage of the Pike model is its provision of a means of looking at and understanding native categories. That it did not prove adequate to the task of mapping an entire culture is not surprising. Culture is too complex—too vast a territory—to be so easily charted. Critics complained that linguistic analogies produced lifeless descriptions of human events (Berreman 1966:350).

Yet what might fail to serve the theoretical anthropologist may well benefit others. As Goodenough points out "ethnographic description, then, requires methods of processing observed phenomena such that we can inductively construct a theory of how our informants have organized the same phenomena. It is the theory, not the phenomena alone, which ethnographic description aims to present" (1964:36). This would appear to be a strong recommendation for the intercultural communicator to heed the value of such an approach.

Anthropologists who did not share the fascination of some with the techniques of the New Ethnography warned that their colleagues should search for "scientific rigor" lest they should succumb inadvertently to scientific *rigor mortis* (Berreman:353). The critics called for *-etic*, or "scientific categories" of analysis, and the use of empirical, inductive research methods, in their zeal to eliminate observer bias, be it native or non-native. Anthropologists who had been hoping for the establishment of cultural universals to aid in the understanding of the processes of cultural change and the development of valid cross-cultural theory condemned the ethnoscientific approach as being not only too mentalistic, and dependent upon verbal behavior, but also too boring, cumbersome, and nitpicking (Harris 1968).

Furthermore, the critics of the New Ethnographers faulted the latter for placing too much emphasis on descriptive validity, reliability, and exhaustiveness. There were even questions concerning the validity of informant categories. Were they real or only personal constructs? The very appropriateness of the linguistic analogy to the study of culture was also questioned. Greenwood and Stini (1977:236) comment:

> To begin with, the treatment of language in formal terms as a code represents a very restricted view of language. It usually means that all the uses of space and of the body in communication and that the immense variability within a single linguistic community are ignored in favor of listing the smallest possible set of elements and rules that can account for observed utterances. Language is particularly amenable to this sort of treatment. . . . Whether the rest of culture is amenable to such treatment is much more questionable.

On the other hand, the universalist approach brought the means to examine the syntax of a language. It has also provided a method to look at the deep structure and/or universal features exhibited in cultural units. Structural anthropologists forced consideration of the underlying, and perhaps fundamental structures of language, culture and even of the human mind. The disadvantages of this approach lie in the inability of its practitioners to construct tests for some of the universals "discovered." Some critics have observed that to assume a universal grammar (linguistic or cultural) conflicts with an evolutionary approach. Greenwood and Stini add: ". . . structuralism operates *as if* the mind were static when *in fact* it is not static" (241).

Such interdisciplinary squabbles between the -*emicists* and the -*eticists* should not cause undue concern to the intercultural explorer. For the latter the use of what has been termed an "imbedded emicism" (Silverman 1966:899) combining both approaches seems to offer the means both to remain sensitive to native (and individual) categories of meaning, and at the same time to maintain the observational distance necessary to distinguish both similarities and differences, universals and specifics, in human behavior and interaction.

Language teaching methods and views about language have followed those of the current schools of linguistics—faithfully in spirit, yet only partially in practice. The application of the analogy of language and linguistic methods of analysis to cultural behavior, while not wholly successful, has been largely ignored. This somewhat haphazard connection between theory and practice has become outmoded in the quest for communicative competence. Yet, the legacies of the linguists and anthropologists who have spent so much effort in understanding the relationships of language and culture have left us important clues, some very sophisticated discovery methods, and many ways of looking at language and culture; these gifts may still serve us well.

6.5 CONCLUSION

For those interested in the practical relationship between language and culture, there was little to expect from research and analysis aimed at finding underlying and fundamental properties of the mind, human language, and human culture, or from the diligent application of linguistically spawned analytical methods. Today, a broadened definition of language and revived interest in semantics, language in use, and the social context of language call for the rejection of direct applications of methods of linguistic analysis to cultural phenomena. The relationship between language and culture must be viewed in broadened terms and from all aspects. Both *langue* and *parole*—competence and performance—play a part in this reciprocity. Modern linguistic theory and anthropological theory, in tune as never before, offer theoretical foundations as well as practical methods to bring language and culture together in the classroom.

It is good to recall that the application of the linguistic analogy to culture, and linguistic models to cultural analysis, should not be construed as explanation. As Durbin (1972:405) points out, no linguistic model has been applied in its entirety to cultural data, nor is any model adequate for all aspects of a given set of data. "Each different model uncovers a portion of structural facts from the data; one must decide what kinds of information about the data one wants to unfold."

In conclusion, it is suggested that those who are so intimately concerned with language and culture should selectively partake of the feast of methods, techniques, perspectives, approaches, and formal operations offered by the models discussed.

This review of the changing theories of language and the applications of the models of linguistic analysis to cultural data may appear to have taken us far afield from our main concern with teaching and learning. As Greenwood and Stini (241) write: "A good analogy helps the analysis, but analogy is often misused. . . . [It] requires the use of self-conscious, formal methods of analysis. . . . But it must not be forgotten that formalization is simplification. . . . We do not have any guarantee that the really significant aspects of human realities are amenable to formal treatment."

The next chapter will treat language and culture in their total context. As our inquiry continues, we must broaden our definition of language to cover the forms accompanying language (paralanguage) and that of communication to include both verbal language and nonverbal forms of communication. In the later chapters we will investigate the nature of beliefs and values in the process of intercultural communication, as well as methods, techniques, and materials fashioned to serve the objectives of a culturally sensitive language curriculum.

FOR STUDY AND DISCUSSION

1. Identify the following terms:

   componential analysis

   behavioreme

   New Ethnography

   meaning/form/distribution

   sociolinguistics

2. Discuss the premises upon which the applications of the linguistic analogy in cultural analysis were based. What features of language supported such premises?

3. How have changing theories of language affected the application of linguistic analytical techniques to cultural analyses?

4. What are some of the advantages of the application of the -emic discovery methods to cultural units? What are some of the disadvantages?

5. Explain the meanings of the terms "slot" and "filler" as used in the Pike model. How are they related to the designations of meaning, form, and distribution in the Lado application?

6. What did Frake mean by stating that "people construe their world from the way they talk about it"? Does such a statement support the application of linguistic analytical methods to cultural data? What can we learn about a culture by analyzing the terms people use to describe the world around them?

7. Define the terms *langue* and *parole*. How are they used in linguistic analysis? What is implied by the statement that communicative competence concerns both?

8. Can you think of any features of language not discussed in this chapter but which are also reflected in cultural elements? What type of cross-cultural variation might be expected?

CULTURE LEARNING EXERCISE

1. Apply the techniques suggested by Lado concerning meaning, form, and distribution to an analysis of one of the following:

   a baseball game

   a birthday party

   an examination in a language class

2. Make a componential analysis of meals in the native country of your informant. Compare and contrast this analysis with one that would reflect your own dining patterns.

FOR FURTHER READING

It goes without saying that any serious student of language and language learning should be familiar with the works of Chomsky, Bloomfield, Firth, Lado, Saussure, and others referred to in this chapter. In addition, the following books and articles should be of interest:

M. Durbin. 1972. "Linguistic Models in Anthropology" (383–410). This article treats the application of linguistic models in anthropology and their attendant advantages and disadvantages. While this material might be difficult for readers not well versed in the intricacies of the various linguistic models, it does call attention to the methods by which linguistic models have been applied.

J. Gumperz and D. Hymes (eds.). 1972. *Directions in Sociolinguistics. The Ethnography of Communication.* This volume, with an "Introduction" by Gumperz (1–25) and a first chapter, "Models of the Interaction of Language and Social Life," by Hymes (35–71), presents some of the basic formulations that were to influence the development of the field of sociolinguistics in the United States. Hymes' chapter contains his well-known SPEAKING mnemonic device.

C. Lévi-Strauss. 1964. "Structural Analysis in Linguistics and in Anthropology" (40–53). The author explains and exemplifies the European structuralist (anthropological) approach to cultural analysis, based on the position that the structures of both language and culture reflect underlying structures of the mind.

K. Pike. 1964. "Towards a Theory of the Structure of Human Behavior" (54–62). This article sets forth the main thrust of Pike's -*emic* model of cultural analysis as discussed in this chapter. The complete formulation is contained in Pike's 1954 volume *Language in Relation to a Unified Theory of the Structure of Human Behavior* and its later revision in 1967.

M. Saville-Troike. 1982. *The Ethnography of Communication. An Introduction.* This textbook puts into practice the suggestions of Hymes for an ethnography of communication. It is concerned with the ways in which social meanings are conveyed in a speech community. Such an approach focuses upon the "modes and functions of language" (3). It investigates the ways in which language is used and how these uses vary cross-culturally.

H. Stern. 1983. *Fundamental Concepts of Language Teaching.* This book reviews theories of language teaching and the theoretical foundations for good teaching practice. Of particular interest to readers of this textbook are the chapters in Part Three, "Concepts of Language," and Part Four, "Concepts of Society" (119–288).

NOTE

1. Dell Hymes, in his discussion of the interaction between language and social life, not only identified major components of the speech act but also called attention to the social elements and factors at work in language in use. In so doing, he gave new meaning to the term "communicative competence" and provided impetus to the development of the field of sociolinguistics. He also devised a mnemonic device, SPEAKING, as an aid to the recall of the elements of importance in the speech act.

   Hymes identified the following components of the speech act:

   S   settings

   P   participants

   E   ends

   A   act sequences

   K   keys

   I   instrumentalities

   N   norms

   G   genres (types)

   Settings includes the time and place of action. The terms *participants, ends,* and *act sequences* vary according to the demands of the situation in which the speech event occurs. *Keys* refers to the tone and manner in which the event occurs. It includes both verbal and nonverbal behavior. *Instrumentalities* refers to the channels and forms of speech used, including dialects, register, and style. *Norms* are the rules governing speaking, and *genres* refers to the types and categories of speech.

   These terms identify the major sociolinguistic variables affecting the speech act in a communicative setting and are useful as points for observation in the classroom.

Chapter 7

Public Views and Private Worlds

In previous chapters we have been concerned with the definitions of the key concepts of *culture* and *communication*. Yet a third major variable in the culture/communication riddle must be considered—*language.* Several questions must be answered if the riddle is to be solved:

1. How are language and culture related?
2. How do they both relate to thought?
3. How do they relate to world view, or a system of beliefs and values associated with a given cultural group?
4. How do the relationships of language, culture, thought, and world view fit into the puzzle of intercultural communication?

7.1 LANGUAGE: MANKIND'S SPECIAL TOOL

We have defined *communication* and *culture* in previous chapters but have not yet defined *language.* It is time to do so now. *Language,* as the term is used in this text, refers to a special mode of communication, unique to the human species. Animals, indeed all living things, communicate; none uses all the features of the human linguistic system.

Charles Hockett, in 1960, listed 13 "design features" characteristic of human language. Hockett suggested that these features of human language may have emerged as evolutionary changes and might indicate how the human language originated and evolved. Although Hockett's list has been questioned and revised, it remains a useful exposition of the major features of human language. The features he listed were:

1. use of the vocal/auditory channel;
2. broadcast transmission and directional reception;

3. rapid fading (transitoriness);

4. interchangeability;

5. total feedback;

6. specialization;

7. semanticity;

8. arbitrariness;

9. discreteness;

10. displacement;

11. productivity;

12. traditional transmission;

13. duality of patterning.

Hockett suggested that the first nine are present in some animals, such as other primates, but features 10 through 13 are unique to human communication (1960:92).

Let us consider these features briefly with an emphasis on the last four. Use of the *vocal/auditory channel* is self-explanatory; it does emphasize the advantage of leaving the body of the speaker free for other than communicative activities. *Broadcast transmission* and *directional reception* indicate that the significant units of language are sent over the air and are received by auditory systems. *Rapid fading* refers to the transitory nature of the oral communication system. *Interchangeability* refers to the constant shift from speaker to listener; it means that any communicator can both send and receive messages. *Total feedback* refers to the fact that speakers can monitor their own communication patterns.

Specialization, the signalling function, supports the fixed association between the signifier and the signified. *Semanticity* refers to the assignment of meaning; *arbitrariness*, to the lack of an isomorphic relationship between the referents to a vocal sound and the symbol itself; and *discreteness*, to the use of discrete units of sound (phonemes) to form meaningful and differentiated units of meaning (morphemes) in given languages. For example, while there is no connection between *tin* (the word) and *tin* (the object), except as the meaning has been arbitrarily assigned, the discrete sounds of /t/ and /d/ signal the difference between *tin* and *din* when used by English speakers. These features are found in all languages, although the units providing these distinctions differ. Phonemes have the power to change meaning, but have no inherent meanings.

The last four features are unique to human communication. *Displacement* involves the language user's ability to refer to events not of the moment but of the past or future. *Productivity* means that the system can change; human language is considered an open system. This feature also refers to the ability of the human speaker to produce totally new sentences. *Traditional transmission* is the most characteristic feature of human language; it links language to culture. Hickerson (1980:19), in discussing this feature, comments:

> Although the potential for using languages . . . is biologically transmitted, specific languages are taught and learned. They are passed on traditionally, generation after generation, from older speakers (who already know the language) to younger ones (who acquire it). In turn, language enables humans to learn other things through tradition rather than by direct experience.

Finally, *duality of patterning* refers to the fact that human languages are built of two types of elements: a pool of sounds and their combinations into significant units. These distinctive sounds, limited and language-specific, are drawn from the reservoir available to human speakers and combined into distinctive and meaningful units—words, phrases, and sentences. Thus, the relatively limited number of sounds produced by the human vocal tract are woven together in the linguistic tapestries of the more than 3000 languages of the world.

Because these design features of language are also observable in some degree in human cultural patterns, linguistic researchers and analysts have called attention to the similarities between spoken language systems and cultural systems. In the past the force of these likenesses has led to several attempts to apply what was known about the analysis of language to the analysis of culture. It has also brought about the present commitment in the field of language teaching to the development of the communicative and cultural competence of language learners.

In the following portion of this chapter, some of the cultural aspects of language (vocal communication) will be discussed as will several as yet unanswered questions concerning the relationships of *language* and *culture* and *thought*.

7.2 DEFINING LANGUAGE

As a special form of communication, human language may be viewed as a system, as a vehicle for cultural transmission, as a formative force whose structures place their stamp upon the minds and actions of its speakers, or as only one of many modes of communication, albeit a crucial one.

Language approached as a system of communication can be isolated and studied like any other human system. As such, it is just one of many ways human beings communicate; others include the use of the senses (feel, touch, smell), facial expressions, body movement (kinesics) including gestures, and other means of physical contact.

The system definition serves the purposes of theoretical linguists concerned with the characteristics and operations of language *as a system*. Their field of inquiry is the mapping of the rules for transforming and combining the significant units of a language—i.e., the grammar of a language. Such inquiry may be related to the phonological level, the morphological level, the syntactic level, or the semantic level—that is, the meaningful sounds, the significant units of meaning, the rules for combining these units, and the meanings attached to them.

Yet language is that and more. It is "the primary symbol system that encodes cultural meaning in every society" (Spradley 1979:99). The processes of naming, identifying, and classifying are carried out largely by means of language.

A language itself not only carries and describes shared symbols but also has symbolic importance to its users. The mother tongue demands loyalty; the emotional torment over the selection of a national language and/or the consequences of suppressing one are too well-known to need explanation. A language reflects and reinforces the value and belief systems that form such a large part of the subjective reality shared by members of the same culture. Our cultural givens remain alive in our proverbs, mottos, songs, and metaphors—all shared by means of language. Goodenough (1964:37) states: "In this sense, a society's language is an aspect of its culture."

In his discussion of the relationship between language and thought, Sapir (1921) points out that speech has a cultural function. This cultural function has recently been ignored by linguists caught up in the search for the universal features of language as a human system. Their single-mindedness, of course, has brought deep insights into the nature of language. Yet language is a tool that human beings have used as a special mode of adaptation and communication in conjunction with culture to change their environments, to manipulate nature, and to protect themselves. It is the cultural functions of language that are our major focus of interest.

7.3 THE LANGUAGE AND CULTURE CONNECTION

The details of the development of human linguistic and cultural systems remain anthropological mysteries buried in unrecorded human history. Although no certainty is possible, many anthropologists believe language must have developed very early in human history as a means of communication for the foraging creatures hunting in bands in the forests and savannahs of Africa and Asia (Hockett 1960). Hockett felt that the design feature called displacement developed quite early in order to enable human beings to talk about what was not present, seen, or heard. Other features, such as duality of patterning and productivity, were strong forces for change. How strong and for how long cannot be known.

Which comes first—language or culture? This question brings us to the recurring puzzle of the influence of language on culture or of culture on language. Although the nature of the language and culture connection is unclear, the binding tie is secure and cannot be ignored. Insight into the nature of these connective strands can be found in positions *vis à vis* language taken in the fields of linguistics, anthropology, and anthropological linguistics. And, as in all matters cultural, these statements often appear contradictory and obscure as much as they reveal.

Let us, then, look at the language and culture connection in terms of human systems of classification, cultural foci, and world view. In addition, the intriguing but probably unanswerable questions posed by the Sapir-Whorf hypothesis regarding language, culture, and thought will be addressed. The intercultural implications of the hypothesis necessitate a brief review of the long-standing controversy.

Classification

Language serves to facilitate classification and order. Language enables those who use it to relate to their environments, to identify and classify natural and cultural objects, and to organize and coordinate their activities. These categories and classifications, or folk terms, are used to refer to human experiences and are related semantically within given cultures. Although there are certain *types* of universal classifications, such as kinship, naming of natural objects, and color coding, there are variations due to cultural influences in the manner in which these relationships are classified and linked cross-culturally.

For example, there are universal semantic relationships such as inclusion, function, space, cause and effect, rationale (purpose), means-end, location of an action, sequence, and attribution (Spradley 1979:111). Thus, all languages provide means to express the condition that X is Y, or that X is the result of Y, or that X is a reason for doing Y. Yet the terms associated with these categories and the ways these categories are grouped are culture-specific. Native categories of concepts or domains reflect a native organization. Examples of a cultural domain might be systems of organizing time, space, or patterns of kinship.

Two examples of such classifications are given below. The first indicates how the human hand and arm may be divided in three languages—English, Arawak, and Papago. (See Figure 7.1.) Hickerson (1980:107) points out that these differences are easily ignored. To ask the question, "What is the word for *hand?*" is to elicit the answer *dakabo* in Arawak and *nowi* in Papago. Clearly a hand is not just an English hand. This is an example, not of the universal aspect of spatial relationships, but of differences in the inclusiveness of the terms.

The second example illustrates the division of time by the Aymara of the *altiplano* of Bolivia and Peru. (See Figure 7.2.) In Aymara patterns, the past, present, and future are positioned in a different manner from that familiar to most speakers of Indo-European languages. Our language reflects this spatial relationship, as we say, "Our future is ahead of us; the past is behind us." We look forward to the new and backward to what has occurred. On the other hand, in Aymara, time is divided into the future and other time. Such divisions are reflected in the very inflections of the language. There is no obligatory division between present and past. One Aymara speaker explained:

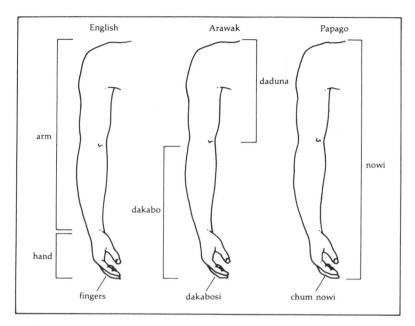

Figure 7.1. English, Arawak, and Papago terms for the hand and arm.

Source: Linguistic Anthropology by Nancy Parrott Hickerson. Copyright © 1980 by Holt, Rinehart & Winston. Reprinted by permission of CBS College Publishing.

The future in Aymara is what has not been seen. We cannot see the future. . . . In Aymara the future is *behind* you—you cannot see it. In English, the future is *ahead* of you; you can look into it. [Miracle, Jr., and Yapita 1981:33]

Aymara language forms indicate this division. *Q"ipüru* translates as *tomorrow* and is a combination of the term *q"ipa*, meaning *behind* or *back*, and *uru*, meaning *day*.

Cultural Foci.

Languages reflect cultural emphases. There is a connection between folk categories in a given language and elements of the culture in which they are used. Franz Boas first emphasized the need to pay close attention to these connections. He urged his students to study lexical items and degrees of differentiation made in specific areas. The width and depth of this differentiation, or lack of it, could be associated with areas of cultural emphases or foci.

Hickerson (1980:108) writes:

. . . points of cultural emphasis are usually directly reflected in language through the size, specialization, and differentiation of vocabulary. That is,

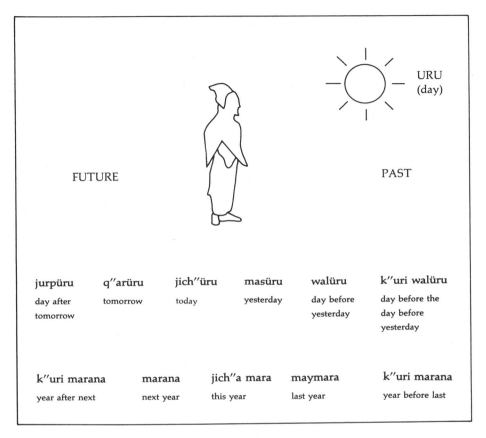

Figure 7.2. Aymara time orientation

Source: From *The Aymara Language in Its Social and Cultural Context* edited by M. J. Hardman. University Presses of Florida. Used by permission.

there are more separate terms, more synonyms, and more fine distinctions made in reference to features of environment or culture with which the speakers are the most concerned. There are fewer terms and they tend to be more generalized when they refer to features which are given less cultural emphasis. "Cultural emphasis" may indicate environmental or economic factors which are critical to subsistence; it can also comprehend esthetic, religious, or other kinds of values.

An example of such an emphasis is found among the Barai of Papua, New Guinea, who have 30 different words for *yam* and only one for all of the following: *bed, chair, table, bench, desk, counter,* and *cupboard.* As Olsson (1985:3) points out, "In a yam cult society, fine distinctions among types of yams are to be expected as is one term for any furniture with a flat surface in their mild tropical climate where most of their time is spent out-of-doors."

World View

Languages are related to the world views of their speakers. Language is not only a means of communication; it is also a powerful tool available to human beings in coping with reality. Different languages help form and express different means of dealing with the "real" world. Yet no language is in any sense able to provide its speakers with a means of describing and dealing with an exact and perfect copy of reality. *World view (Weltanschauung)* is a term that describes categories and their relationships, or the particular way of dealing with social life identified with a given cultural group.

A world view, according to Kraft (1978:407–410), serves five functions. It helps its adherents explain phenomena and events, validate and evaluate, receive psychological reinforcement, integrate, and adapt. A given world view is most closely associated with the value and belief system of a cultural group and is concerned with what that group believes to be true, valuable, and significant.

In short, world view refers to sets of culturally shared "realities." These realities are the culturally constructed world of perception, meaning, and practice that members of any culture take to be absolutely correct and genuine. To put it simply, reality equals experience plus perception. Such reality is considered true and serves as a basis for action; it is often expressed in the language use of its faithful. Through individual and group experience, cultural codes are formed and defined; they "reflect" these "realities." World view, then, is a cover term that refers to the particular sets of realities associated with a given cultural group. It includes attitudes, beliefs, and assumptions about the environment, human relations, social organization, and all that constitutes human life. Cross-cultural variations in world views are discussed in Chapter 10.

7.4 ANSWERING THE UNANSWERABLE

The close and symbiotic relationship between language and culture is fundamental and universal. All human beings, unless handicapped, are language users; all are culture bearers. The nature of the relationship between language and culture remains a question of profound implication in linguistics, anthropology, and intercultural communication. In each discipline it is interpreted in a different manner and fashioned to "fit" the particular perspective taken. The fundamental problem lies in trying to find valid responses to several questions raised by anthropologists, psychologists, and linguists in their search to identify the missing links. Some of these questions as formulated by Dell Hymes (1964a:115–116) are: To what extent and in what ways is a language related to the world view of those who speak it? Are linguistic habits related to other habits and behavior? Can the linguistic habits and differences be taken as determining the others?

The Sapir-Whorf (Whorfian) Hypothesis

The sorting out of the puzzle of language—world view, thought, and culture—has been a source of controversy among linguists, psychologists, and others for many years. It was the focus of the celebrated Sapir-Whorf or Whorfian hypothesis of linguistic determinism or relativity, which was an attempt to make a theoretical statement concerning the cultural implications of linguistic differences. Put very simply, the Whorfian hypothesis, for it was more Whorf's than Sapir's, states that a causal arrow can be drawn from language categories and forms to cultural items and meanings, which in turn add up to a unique world view or system of cultural meanings, postulates, and theories. This is the strong version. The weaker version of the hypothesis (linguistic relativity) states that there is a relationship between language categories and cultural thought patterns, that languages have special effects on mental activities, and that the "mental activity is to at least some degree relative to, and dependent on, the language in which it takes place" (Carroll 1973:126). Whorf states (1956:214):

> We are thus introduced to a new principle of relativity, which holds that all observers are not led by the same physical evidence to the same picture of the universe, unless their linguistic backgrounds are similar, or can in some way be calibrated.

In its strong or deterministic version, the hypothesis can been seen as a statement that languages structure perception and experience, and literally *create* and *define* the realities people perceive. The weaker version simply extends the principle of relativity and cultural synthesis to the language and culture relationship, indicating that different languages are associated with different world views.

It is important to trace the roots of the hypothesis before opting for acceptance, rejection, or modification. Who was Whorf and why should he have set forth such a hypothesis? In the first place, he did not enunciate the hypothesis in the traditional way, but rather made statements in his various writings on American Indian languages, based on his own field work and linguistic data, as well as on the writings of his teacher, the celebrated Edward Sapir, also a linguist and psychologist, and of *his* teacher, Franz Boas, the American anthropologist. In addition, it is important to locate the time and circumstances of the statements that led to the hypothesis, for they bear upon the interpretations given both by Whorf and by others who have refuted his conclusions.

The relationship of language, thought, and/or culture had been the object of inquiry in the past. In the last half of the eighteenth century, German philosophers were concerned with the question of whether languages had a world view. Von Humboldt stated bluntly that every language has a particular world view or

Weltansicht. The declarations of Von Humboldt and others, such as Herder, were made at a time when the languages of several European nations, such as Italy and Germany, were being threatened. To preserve the language was said to preserve its own *ethos*, its world view.

Boas, in studying American Indian languages, pointed out that common phenomena seemed to call for various degrees of differentiation by people in different cultures. He noted the many terms the Eskimos had for "snow," including *aput* (snow on the ground), *qana* (falling snow), *piqsirpoq* (drifting snow), and *qimuqsuq* (a snow drift) (1911:25–26). Boas' comments, which seem so pedestrian today, were somewhat startling at the time he wrote. His work in the early 1900s with the American Indians provided information about people who were generally considered "savages," unsophisticated folk with rudimentary social and linguistic systems. The work of Boas and the other field anthropologists he trained forever discredited those guilty of condescending attitudes toward Indian cultures.

As other linguists and philosophers of the time, Boas was concerned with the relationship of language and world view (1911:67).

> It does not seem likely, therefore, that there is any direct relation between the culture of a tribe and the language they speak, except in so far as the form of the language will be moulded by the state of culture, but not in so far as a certain state of culture is conditioned by morphological traits of the language.

He found that languages "differ not only in the character of their constituent phonetic elements and sound-clusters, but also in the groups of ideas that find expression in fixed phonetic groups" (24). While not directing the causal arrow from language to culture, Boas did point out the unconscious nature (and power) of linguistic phenomena.

He also believed that the study of language was of great importance in ethnological study as noted in Chapter 4. In suggesting language study, he wrote (73):

> . . . the study of language must be considered as one of the most important branches of ethnological study, because, on the one hand, a thorough insight into ethnology can not be gained without practical knowledge of language, and, on the other hand, the fundamental concepts illustrated by human languages are not distinct in kind from ethnological phenomena; and because, furthermore, the peculiar characteristics of languages are clearly reflected in the views and customs of the peoples of the world.

Any reader who is able to unravel the ponderous syntax of the preceding statement may recognize the suggestion, later so widely accepted, that language might be considered an analog of culture.

Edward Sapir, a student of Boas, suggested that speech is a "non-instinctive, acquired, 'cultural' function," and contrasted it to walking, which is organic and instinctive (1921:4). What his position might have been on the Sapir-Whorf hypothesis is unclear, for, in general, the statements he made about language and thought leave room for speculation. At times he did appear to reject a causal relationship (1921:218):

> Culture may be defined as *what* a society does and thinks. Language is a particular *how* of thought. It is difficult to see what particular causal relations may be expected to subsist between a selected inventory of experience (culture, a significant selection made by society) and the particular manner in which the society expresses all experience.

Yet Benjamin Lee Whorf, Sapir's student, later could find support for his position in statements from his mentor. Sapir, in discussing language and in his zeal to support the recognition of linguistics as a science, also wrote (1931:578):

> Language is not merely a more or less systematic inventory of the various items of experience which seem relevant to the individual, as is so often naïvely assumed, but is also a self-contained, creative symbolic organization, which not only refers to experience largely acquired without its help but actually defines experience for us by reason of its formal completeness and because of our unconscious projection of its implicit expectations into the field of experience.

Thus, language must be seen as more than a neutral medium through which thoughts or ideas are filtered. Statements concerning this relationship appear contradictory. Sapir saw language as "a guide to social reality." He concludes (1929:209–210):

> Human beings do not live in the objective world alone, nor alone in the world of social activity as ordinarily understood, but are very much at the mercy of the particular language which has become the medium of expression for their society. It is quite an illusion to imagine that one adjusts to reality essentially without the use of language and that language is merely an incidental means of solving specific problems of communication or reflection. The fact of the matter is that the "real world" is to a large extent unconsciously built up on the language habits of the group. No two languages are ever sufficiently similar to be considered as representing the same social reality. The worlds in which different societies live are distinct worlds, not merely the same world with different labels attached. . . . We see and hear and otherwise experience very largely as we do because the language habits of our community predispose certain choices of interpretation.

True or False?

Benjamin Lee Whorf, a student of Sapir, elaborated upon these ideas in his writings as presented posthumously in *Language, Thought, and Reality* (1956). Whorf chose to rest his case for linguistic relativity/determinism on the evidence of language samples taken from Hopi, an Indian language spoken in the North American Southwest. Data were selected to illustrate his contention that speakers of different languages viewed the world in different ways.

Using examples from the Hopi language, Whorf postulated that language was not only a means of transmitting culture, but also was, in and of itself, a force in the delineation of the world of its speakers. In his analysis of Hopi, Whorf noted that certain grammatical categories in Hopi did not "fit" the SAE (Standard Average European) system. From these examples he concluded that the habitual thought worlds of the SAE and the Hopi were different (Whorf 1956:147). He suggested that when two language systems show radically different grammars and linguistic characteristics, their speakers inhabit a different thought world—a world circumscribed by their respective languages. He apparently believed the content of thought influenced cognitive processes (Carroll 1956:26).

In comparing SAE and Hopi, Whorf concluded that SAE had been linguistically conditioned to objectify time. According to Whorf, (1956:57–58) the Hopi had:

> . . . no general notion or intuition of TIME as a smooth flowing continuum in which everything in the universe proceeds at an equal rate, out of a future, through a present, into a past. . . . In this Hopi view, time disappears and space is altered, so that it is no longer the homogeneous and instantaneous timeless space of our supposed intuition or of classical Newtonian mechanics. At the same time, new concepts and abstractions flow into the picture, taking up the task of describing the universe without reference to such time or space—abstractions for which our language lacks adequate terms.

Whorf commented on the subject in the 1930s, but much of his work was not collected until after his death. The controversy generated by his views has never been stilled. Attempts to prove or disprove their validity, especially in the strong version, have produced more fire than light (Berlin and Kay 1969; Carroll 1964; Cole and Scribner 1974; Hoijer 1954, 1968; Lenneberg 1953). Whorf himself in discussing the matter stated that he was concerned with language, culture, and *behavior*. He asks (1956:156):

> Which was first: the language patterns or the cultural norms? In [the] main they have grown up together, constantly influencing each other. But in this partnership the nature of the language is the factor that limits free plasticity and rigidifies channels of development in the more autocratic way.

Thus, his main emphasis was the primary position of language in the language, culture, and behavior equation.

The hypothesis has been easy to attack for several reasons. The data were questionable. Conclusions were supported by rather than discovered in data. The statements attributed to both Whorf and Sapir were contradictory and reflected their continuing efforts at clarification of their own positions. At times, Whorf seemed to indicate a strong position of linguistic determinism, at other times, to lean toward a more relativistic position, and at still other times, to endorse a universalistic position. No set of statements has engendered more comment, more arguments, more position papers, and more acrimony than those that have come to be known as the Sapir-Whorf hypothesis. Its somewhat brutal dismissal by anthropologists and linguists in the first blush of the dawn of the Chomskyan reign in linguistics can be attributed to selective quotation and fascination with the new and the universal. Whorf's insistence on taking cultural and linguistic differences seriously was, at that time, *démodé*. His data and most deterministic statements have been dismissed as false at worst or unprovable at best. According to Carroll (1973:136):

> At the present time we must draw the conclusion that no satisfactory evidence exists for thinking that languages reflect particular world views. Indeed, the evidence from common knowledge would seem to point in the opposite direction, namely, to the effect that any world-view can be expressed in any language.

Those who still wish to continue to explore the language and culture connection must reply, "Yes, that is true, but why, then, are there so many different world views? Why is it that those who speak the same language so often share world views?" The questions the Whorfian hypothesis addressed have yet to be answered.

Reprise

Carroll suggests a modified version of the hypothesis: "Insofar as languages differ in the ways they encode objective experience, language users tend to sort out and distinguish experiences differently according to the categories provided by their respective languages. These cognitions will tend to have certain effects on behaviour" (1973:139).

Rejection of the strong version of the hypothesis seems well supported and so justified. A modified version may be equally suspect, for the arrow still points from language to culture. As pointed out in Chapter 5, the basic insights of the Whorfian approach form the rationale for the application of the principle of relativity and its relationship to perception. Whorf's statement that "all observers are not led by the same physical evidence to the same picture of the universe, unless their linguistic backgrounds are similar, or can in some way be calibrated" (1956:214) was revised by Singer (1982:55) as follows:

> We would go a step further and substitute the word "perceptual" for the word "linguistic." We would argue that every culture has its own language or code, to be sure, but that a language is the manifestation—verbal or other-

wise—of the perceptions which the group holds. Language, once established, further constrains the individual to perceive in certain ways, but we would insist that language is merely one of the ways in which groups maintain and reinforce similarity of perception.

Thus, subjective reality, or the way in which the world is perceived, resides in the individual, but both culture and language conspire to reinforce similarity of perception by those who eat, love, die, and speak together.

That Whorf (1956:239) himself did not intend to maintain a totally deterministic stand is attested to in the following quotation:

> . . . the tremendous importance of language cannot, in my opinion, be taken to mean necessarily that nothing is back of it of the nature of what has traditionally been called "mind." My own studies suggest, to me, that language, for all its kingly role, is in some sense a superficial embroidery upon deeper processes of consciousness, which are necessary before any communication, signaling, or symbolism whatsoever can occur. . . .

One last word is in order in defense of Whorf and the Whorfian approach to language and culture. Whorf was a chemical engineer and a fire insurance assessor. His interest in the power of language over people's actions was sparked by his observation of the use of the term "spun limestone" to designate a product considered not flammable or dangerous simply because it was called a type of "stone." In point of fact it burned easily. Whorf noted that the meaning (not able to be burned) assigned appeared to be derived from the linguistic form (*spun limestone*). Behavior was apparently being directed by the meanings assigned the linguistic forms.

The so-called Sapir-Whorf hypothesis remains unproved, and yet not easily dismissed. There are the nagging clues bilingual speakers give us as they report that speaking another language involves more than just uttering sets of different sounds and modifying gestures. The language, thought, and culture connection is strong, its strands tightly intertwined, and its relationships as old as human society.

We must then subscribe to the view set forth by Gudykunst and Kim (1984:137):

> Thus the true value of the Sapir-Whorf hypothesis is not in providing a definitive and deterministic relationship between specific linguistic categories and the thought patterns of the people in a cultural system but in articulating the profound alliance of language, mind, and the total culture of the speech community. Few students of language, cognition, culture, or communication today doubt such an interpretation of this hypothesis.

And neither should any language teacher.

7.5 CONCLUSION

This chapter has been devoted to defining language and its relationship to culture, world view, thought, and reality. We have found that:

- Language is more than speech; it's a rallying symbol, a means of identification, a tool, a lens through which reality is seen.
- Language responds to and at the same time influences the observations of its speakers and mediates their experiences.
- Language provides the embroidery for the world of its speakers.
- Language provides easy and familiar ways to classify the world of its speakers.
- Languages contain categories that reflect cultural interests, preoccupations, and conventions.
- Language is "a tool rather more than a prison, but we are still limited by our particular tools" (Condon and Yousef 1975:181).

The old argument over the Sapir-Whorf hypothesis should be given a decent funeral and attention turned toward the truly monumental insights of both Sapir and Whorf, each in its turn, and applied in the continuing study of language, culture, and reality. Ardener (1983:154), in discussing the hypothesis, concludes:

> The major contribution of anthropology results from the experience of trying on a multiplicity of cultural spectacles: the illusion of total truth is amended by the revealed discrepancies. Where all the spectacles agree we have a universal. Is it simply a universal of spectacle construction? To find out we try to deconstruct the spectacles. We have added a semantic materialism [real world] to the approaches available for such purposes. It is inevitably in part linguistic, for our worlds are inescapably contaminated with language . . . the contamination extends into materiality. . . .

Language, then, impinges upon and in turn is affected by the world in which it is used. It is only one form of human communication, but a major one. As such it defines, gives form to, supports, limits, and sometimes obscures shared cultural patterns.

As we have seen, all these special attributes of language led to the application of methods of linguistic analysis to cultural elements. These also ensure that the language teacher cannot provide instruction in language without dealing with culture, nor can the students learn a language without learning about its cultural aspects and connections. The following statement from a student essay may not prove the Sapir-Whorf hypothesis, but it should serve to remind the teacher of the power of the word:

> It is evident that a Swiss *kindergarten* is not very different from an American, because we already use the same German expression for this institution.

FOR STUDY AND DISCUSSION

1. Identify the following terms:

   linguistic relativity

   linguistic determinism

   semanticity

   world view

   cultural emphases

2. Hockett listed 13 design features of language. How many of these features are also characteristic of cultural patterns? Which ones? Can you give examples of each of the features? To what practical use could knowledge of these features be put in intercultural interaction?

3. What is meant by the statement that language is the primary symbol system? What is the "cultural function" of language?

4. What is the Sapir-Whorf hypothesis? Why has it caused such controversy among linguists and anthropologists? Why do psychologists and cross-cultural researchers find value in the proposal? What are the differences between the strong and the weak versions?

5. It has been stated that the Whorfian insights have been more valuable in practice than in research. How could these insights be applied in the language-learning context?

6. How can the concept of the "thought world" as defined by Whorf (1956:134–159) be correlated with modern theories of culture, which propose that culture itself is a theory of reality and that an individual's theory is both personal and public?

7. Sapir once wrote (1929:214) that "Language is primarily a cultural or social product and should be understood as such." What characteristics of language and culture would justify such a statement?

8. Whorf suggested that the Western method of scientific investigation was based on Western views of time and space and was essentially ethnocentric. Is the scientific method a Western tool? If so, has its bias been overcome? After all, many scientists are able to communicate in spite of language barriers.

9. What applications might the knowledge of the Aymara culture and linguistic emphases upon source of information have in a language classroom in which Aymara children are being taught Spanish?

10. Valerie Quennessen, a French actress, in discussing the making of films in French and English, has been quoted as saying: "We spoke English in the film which is not difficult for me. I studied English in school and in Spain. I can think in English as well as French, although I think differently in each language. Every French word has a history for me. Each has many inflections and nuances which I must consider before I use it. English is new. I don't worry about the nuances. I go directly to the idea. I try to communicate with the camera without wasting time on the meaning of the words

themselves" (*St. Petersburg Times,* May 22, 1982). Does Mademoiselle Quennessen "think" in English? Is she communicating? If so, in which language?

11. Whorf wrote (1956:213):

> We dissect nature along lines laid down by our native languages. . . . the world is presented in a kaleidoscopic flux of impressions which has to be organized by our minds—and this means largely by the linguistic systems in our minds. We cut up nature, organize it into concepts, and ascribe significances as we do, largely because we are parties to an agreement to organize it in this way—an agreement that holds throughout our speech community and is codified in the patterns of our language. The agreement is, of course, an implicit and unstated one, *BUT ITS TERMS ARE ABSOLUTELY OBLIGATORY;* we cannot talk at all except by subscribing to the organization and classification of data which the agreement decrees.

What position does this imply concerning language and thought? Contrast this statement with Dorothy Lee's (1950, 1959) statement that as soon as a person conceptualizes a "thing" it has been objectified and language has intervened. Condon and Yousef (1975:180) suggest Lee's statement posits linguistic intervention rather than determinism. Do you agree? What evidence might support either statement?

CULTURE LEARNING EXERCISE

Make a brief report concerning the characteristics of the major language or languages spoken by your cultural group or by your informant. In this report try to provide the following information:

1. General features of the language
   a) Family
   b) Number of speakers
   c) General characteristics
2. History of the language
3. Writing system
4. Unique features

In order to complete this assignment locate three bibliographic sources concerning this language and use your own judgment concerning points of interest. For example, a report on Arabic should contain some discussion of the relationship of that language to the Islamic religion. From the sources you are able to locate, and with the help of your informant, write up a brief summary of your findings.

FOR FURTHER READING

E. Ardener. 1983. Chapter 7 (143–156) "Social Anthropology, Language, and Reality," in Roy Harris (ed.). *Approaches to Language.* Ardener examines contrastive cultural classifications in light of his interpretation of Whorf's work. He concludes that cross-cultural mis-understandings on "supposedly trivial matters" are a human universal, rooted in the characteristics of human classification and in the role language plays in giving these categories the qualities of reality.

R. Burling. 1970. *Man's Many Voices: Language in Its Cultural Context.* The content of this book addresses the language and culture connection and the many ways in which nonlinguistic factors affect language use.

M. Cole and S. Scribner. 1974. *Culture and Thought. A Psychological Introduction.* This book does just what it sets out to do; it provides an introduction to the subject of culture and thought from the psychological perspective. It is highly recommended.

J. Fishman. 1973. "The Whorfian Hypothesis" (114–125). Fishman reviews the evidence relating to the Whorfian hypothesis in terms of four analytical levels and the types of language structures which show what Fishman calls "the Whorfian effect."

J. Fishman. 1982. "Whorfianism of the Third Kind: Ethnolinguistic Diversity as a World-wide Societal Asset (The Whorfian Hypothesis: Varieties of Validation, Confirmation, and Disconfirmation" (1–14). The title of the article tells it all. Fishman argues for the recognition of a third type of Whorfianism related to cultural diversity, W3 being seen as more valuable for the message it carries than for its scientific enlightenment.

V. Fromkin and R. Rodman. 1978. *An Introduction to Language.* 2nd edition. This introductory linguistics text covers the major features of language study, including language origin, animal "languages," language diversity, language change, language acquisition, and writing forms. It could provide a solid foundation in linguistic matters because it demands no previous knowledge on the part of the reader. This is one for the novice.

M. Hardman (ed.). 1981. *The Aymara Language in Its Social and Cultural Context.* This collection of essays concerning the Aymara language contains edited versions of student term papers or professional papers concerning aspects of the interrelationship of language and culture as evidenced in the forms and uses of the Aymara language, spoken by the people of the *altiplano* around Lake Titicaca in Peru and Bolivia. The section titled "Aymara Grammatical and Semantic Categories and World View" (31–122) is of particular value to those interested in such matters, among whom it is hoped are numbered many of the readers of this book.

E. Haugen. 1977. "Linguistic Relativity: Myths and Methods" (11–28) is a discussion of the problems raised by the Whorfian hypothesis and its relationship to bilingual behavior.

N. Hickerson. 1980. *Linguistic Anthropology.* This is a basic textbook with a strong focus on the interplay of language and culture. It is a fine introduction to this field.

D. Hymes (ed.). 1964a. *Language in Culture and Society. A Reader in Linguistics and Anthropology.* A collection of readings in linguistics and anthropology, containing excerpts from the writings of Boas, Sapir, Whorf, and Pike, as well as many others.

E. Sapir. 1964. *Culture, Language, and Personality. Selected Essays,* and E. Sapir. 1921. *Language.* These two volumes contain some of the basic positions taken by Sapir in regard to language, personality, and culture. Because Sapir's observations remain germane, especially in the field of intercultural communication, a review of these two major works is highly recommended.

M. Singer. 1982. "Culture: A Perceptual Approach" (54–62). Singer proposes that human perception is culturally colored and that language is one of the ways cultural groups "maintain and reinforce similarity of perception" (55). This perceptual approach to the riddle of the relationships between and among language, culture, thought, and reality has been widely endorsed in the literature of intercultural communication.

B. Whorf. 1956. *Language, Thought, and Reality: Selected Writings of Benjamin Lee Whorf* J. Carroll (ed.). This is a posthumous collection of the writings of Whorf. Because so much has been extracted from Whorf's writings and so many comments have been made about what he meant, it is good to let the man speak for himself.

Chapter 8

A Voyage of Discovery: Learning a New Culture

Moving about in an unfamiliar environment, at home or abroad, is often not unlike a voyage into the unknown, the uncharted, and, alas, the incomprehensible. Yet these inevitable sallies into the new and unfamiliar that mark all our lives can become less fearsome if they are simply regarded as exercises in culture learning.

One might well ask why the meeting of the new and strange so often brings embarrassment, confusion, or even anger. Why do so many visitors, sojourners, and immigrants feel as though they have become invisible in a strange country or, if not invisible, adrift without any sense of personal or cultural identity? The answers to these questions lie in the processes of cultural change and acculturation; they also lie in the examination of these processes at work in episodes of intercultural contact.

8.1 INTERCULTURAL ENCOUNTERS OF THE DISTURBING KIND

Learning a new culture can be embarrassing . . .

The grateful Latin American student, hoping to express his appreciation to his teacher for her efforts to improve his English, chose to send her the following card. After all, she was so *simpatica!*

. . . maddening

The Japanese hosts to a group of North American teacher/students arranged for their guests to be housed in pairs in the student dormitory on the campus of the university they were visiting in Japan. After all, reasoned the hosts, it would be frightening to be alone in a foreign country. Yet these honored guests soon staked out their own ranges and settled down, one to a room, in red, white, and blue solitude. These inscrutable *gaijin!*

Figure 8.1.

. . . and confusing.

Abdul Aziz never came to class on Friday afternoon. As a result, he often missed tests, which were scheduled for the end of the week. When his teacher pointed out that the seeds of failure lay in these absences, he shrugged his shoulders and muttered, *"Inshallah."* "I understand that you must pray, but," countered the teacher, "you are in a foreign country and you may be excused from these responsibilities." After all, she concluded, first things first.

These vignettes of cross-cultural encounters illustrate not only the perils of unwarranted cultural assumptions as to what is translatable, what is frightening and what is not, and where priorities lie, but also the pain of learning the hard way.

Culture learning, or understanding the new ways of another group (or even one's own), is very like looking into a shadowed mirror. The broad lines of the reflected images are clear enough, but the muted light obscures details and forces viewers to fill in the gaps from their own experiences and cultural assumptions.

One means to cast some light on the nature of culture learning and cultural investigation is to review some of the methods and techniques that have been employed by professional cross-cultural researchers in the past. Valuable insights can be gained by assessing the hazards involved in such research and the solutions proposed. First, however, we must come to terms with some important concepts.

8.2 COMING TO TERMS

The field of intercultural communication has been a debtor in its exchanges with other social sciences; not only methods of analysis but also terminology have been freely borrowed. Because basic terms, such as *perception, acculturation, enculturation,* and even *culture* itself, have been defined in different ways in these disciplines, the unwary may find themselves confused by the variety of terms and seemingly contradictory definitions. This state of affairs is not necessarily detrimental; it does force the student of the field to accept various points of view and avoid a one-dimensional approach to basic concepts.

Before proceeding to a discussion of the nature of culture learning, several fundamental concepts, already introduced, need a more formal introduction. These include:

acculturation/enculturation

cross-cultural awareness

cultural identity

perception

cultural patterns, themes, and postulates

Each of these definitions will be further refined and exemplified in ensuing discussions of the methods of cultural analysis and culture teaching. Additional definitions are included in the Glossary.

Acculturation/Enculturation

Culture learning is a natural process in which human beings internalize the knowledge needed to function in a societal group. It may occur in the native context as *enculturation* or in a non-native or secondary context as *acculturation*. Fundamentally, learning a first culture is a process of indoctrination. Enculturation builds a sense of cultural or social identity, a network of values and beliefs, patterned ways of living, and, for the most part, ethnocentrism, or belief in the power and the rightness of native ways. Acculturation, on the other hand, involves the process of pulling out of the world view or *ethos* of the first culture, learning new ways of meeting old problems, and shedding ethnocentric evaluations.

Presumably, the major enculturative processes take place only once, during childhood, and are largely molded by the individual's family, native institutions, and experiences. Individuals even in the same culture, however, do not have the similar personal experiences, so the cultural identity achieved is partly private and partly public; partly similar to that of others and partly idiosyncratic.

The process of acculturation involves dealing with new ways and systems of beliefs and patterns of an unfamiliar cultural group. The term *acculturation* is frequently used in the sense of a terminal state to be reached *vis-à-vis* the new group. Thus, we might say, "Adel has acculturated well." Or, if the person in question does not seem to cope well with the new ways, "He hasn't acculturated at all." In its simplest form, the term refers to an individual's adjustment to the new and the strange. For our purposes, the term acculturation should be regarded more as a series of steps taken to close the gap between the patterns of the native culture and that of the target culture than as a prescribed goal or end state. This definition is a far cry from the traditional one which identified processes at a group level representing the "modification of a primitive culture by contact with an advanced culture" (*American Heritage Dictionary* 1969:9). The latter definition obtained under the strictures of the old immigrant model of acculturation, which called for obliteration of first culture patterns and their replacement with those of the new, and presumably better, culture. Because many of our students or clients are *not* immigrants but merely sojourners or visitors—selective culture learners— the traditional definitions appear inappropriate.

A more culturally sensitive definition would identify acculturation as an individual process of learning to adjust to a new culture, either within the native culture or among strangers, at home or in a foreign land. As used in this text, then, *acculturation* is approached as a series of processes and as Kim (1982:360) states, "not as an either-or phenomenon, but as the continuous process in which the immigrant adapts to and acquires the host culture, so as to be directed toward ultimate assimilation."

Assimilation, then, is a form of complete acculturation—i.e., an adoption of the characteristics and behaviors of the new culture, or, in the parlance of earlier times, disappearance into the "melting pot." It is only one of several possible destinations on the road to acculturation.

The above distinctions are important in the context of second language and second culture learning because of the varied natures and purposes of the cultural contact in which we, as teachers, are engaged. Our students' goals are idiosyncratic; therefore, it is clear that the teacher's role is to understand, foster, and encourage the processes of culture learning rather than set prescribed goals for desired degrees of acculturation.

Cross-cultural Awareness

Cross-cultural awareness involves uncovering and understanding one's own culturally conditioned behavior and thinking, as well as the patterns of others. Thus, the process involves not only perceiving the similarities and differences in other cultures but also recognizing the givens of the native culture or, as Hall says, our own "hidden culture" (1969).

Hanvey (1979:53) describes several levels of cross-cultural informational awareness: (1) awareness of superficial or very visible cultural traits (stereotyping); (2) awareness of significant and subtle highly contrastive traits; and (3) awareness of an insider's point of view of a given culture. Hanvey correlates methods of learning and interpretation with these levels. Thus, Level 1 is associated with using secondary sources of information and a usual feeling of "Oh! Wow!"; Level 2 is associated with conflict and feelings of frustration; Level 3, which repeats the information level of 2, moves into intellectual analysis and some understanding. The last level is associated with "going native," or total immersion and becoming bicultural.

Cross-cultural awareness is the force that moves a culture learner across the acculturation continuum from a state of no understanding of, or even hostility to, a new culture to near total understanding; from monoculturalism to bi- or multiculturalism. Of course, the polar states are seldom observed. One cannot live very long and remain totally monocultural in the modern world. On the other hand, achieving a full state of acculturation is equally difficult. The facilitation of the journey along this acculturation continuum is of primary concern to the teacher. The final destination is a matter for the learner to decide.

Cultural Identity

Cultural identity refers to the relationship between the individual and society. Lum (1982:386) writes that "identity cannot be found by drawing apart from society. Identity is a social process in which one balances what s/he thinks oneself to be and what others believe that one to be. . . ." It is the cultural or social identity that is at stake when the process of acculturation is under way. To become bicultural is to develop an altered cultural personality and identity.

Perception

Perception refers to the process of evaluating stimuli from the outside world. Singer (1982:54), in explaining his perceptual approach to culture, states:

> . . . man behaves as he does because of the ways in which he perceives the external world. . . . While individuals and the groups which they constitute can only act or react on the basis of their perceptions, the important point is that the "same" stimuli are often perceived differently by different individuals and groups.

He continues (55):

> Not only the languages he speaks and the way in which he thinks, but even *what* he sees, hears, tastes, touches, and smells are conditioned by the cultures in which he has been raised.

Singer described an individual society as an aggregate of the identity (cultural) groups which exist within it (58). Identity groups are formed by aggregations of persons sharing similar perceptions of the external world (55). Those familiar with the literature concerning the relationship between language and thought and the Sapir-Whorf hypothesis (see Chapter 7), will recognize that Singer has altered the elements of the equation to read language/culture/*perception* as interrelated factors in intercultural communication. In so doing, he has brought a new perspective to an old puzzle.

Cultural Patterns, Themes, and Postulates

The term *patterned* has been used repeatedly in this book. No definition has been given, for it was felt that the reader should first explore concepts before being saddled with somewhat arbitrary definitions. This having been done, it is time to consider just what is meant by cultural patterns, as well as cultural themes and cultural postulates. The term cultural patterns, as used in anthropological and sociological literature, describes the systematic and often repetitive nature of human behavior, interaction, and organization. This is to say that human behavior is channeled and constrained by underlying systems that impose regularity and rules on what otherwise might be random activity. These systems permit the development of "patterns" of customary or expected behavior. The linguistic analogy is helpful here. Just as language users must recognize and obey the rules, conventions, norms, and system of the language they speak if they are to communicate with other speakers of that language, so must culture bearers recognize and be constrained, albeit in lesser degree, by the regularities or customs of the cultures in which they function.

This means that cultural behavior is more ordered than might appear from superficial observation; it is affected by the presence of customary or normative patterns. These patterns represent expected or acceptable behavior in given cultures. The anthropologist studying a specific group will not only observe individual and idiosyncratic behavior but will also observe modal or expected behavior. A member of a given group when queried concerning a specific modal pattern is likely to answer, "That's the way we do it," or "That's our custom." For example, behaviors related to family relationships in any culture are not simply random, but will follow in some degree the expected and customary norms. The constellation of the behaviors and norms surrounding the family relationship constitutes a different pattern in Culture A than it does in Culture B. Thus, although we all take nourishment, there are culture-specific rules concerning what to eat, when, on what kinds of tables, and even for what purposes. Caterpillars, anyone?

Edward Stewart (1972) discussed American culture in terms of patterns of behavior, thinking, and values. He saw these patterns as the dominant forms of cultural components identified with the dominant social group—the middle class. The patterns he described were those observed, expected, and associated with "typical" American behavior. That one or another American wouldn't be caught dead indulging in some of the patterned behavior described is a truism often overlooked.

Cultural patterns do not represent expected individual behavior but rather provide a means of speculation as to probable or valued behavior in a given group. Recognition of cultural patterns forms the basis for cross-cultural observation; using these patterns as the justification for predicting individual behavior is the foundation of unwarranted stereotyping. Patterns are found in all cultures; they can be observed in styles of dress, relationships to the external world, perceptions of time and space, the sense of self, and values and norms.

In cases in which some patterns of a given culture are closely entwined and interrelated, cultural themes or central organizing principles can be identified. Opler (1945) first introduced the concept of cultural theme. According to Opler (198), "a limited number of dynamic affirmations, which I shall call *themes,* can be identified in every culture." The aggregate of these affirmations form themes, a theme being "a postulate or position, declared or implied, and usually controlling behavior or stimulating activity, which is tacitly approved or openly promoted in a society." He used the pervasive postulate of male superiority in Apache culture to illustrate his point. Male superiority was expressed and reinforced in religious, political, and family life.

Spradley (1979:186) explains: "Cultural themes are elements in the cognitive maps which make up a culture . . . They consist of a number of symbols linked into meaningful relationships."

These themes, fashioned from sets of cultural postulates or assumptions (dynamic affirmations) about the world, provide blueprints for behavior. Postulates spell out positions taken about the world and human experience; cultural themes reflect the orientations taken. Both themes and postulates are transmitted during the period of enculturation so their power is often unconscious. They form the hidden basis for value judgments. For example, most Americans do not believe that the external world has a spirit or soul; others on the globe do not share this assumption. Yet from this basic belief or orientation to nature and the external world flow sets of behavior and patterns that treat the external world, in the case of the Americans, as an entity outside the individual to be manipulated, exploited and/or destroyed.

Where do we find evidence of themes and postulates? They are echoed in the expression of folk wisdom or common sense found in our proverbs and metaphors; they are preserved in the amber of our crystallized systems of values and beliefs. They are the rationale for the observation made so frequently in anthropological literature that cultural patterns, taken on the whole, seem to form logical worlds for their believers.

Consider what the following statements reveal about the American theme of individualism.

- A man's home is his castle.
- Variety is the spice of life.
- Live and let live.

The concepts of cultural themes and postulates led several anthropologists, especially those associated with the culture and personality school of American anthropology in the 1930s and 1940s, to propose that the themes and patterns of a culture could be subsumed under a general master pattern or configuration. Some have suggested that these patterns even produced a kind of modal or typical personality configuration (DuBois 1944). Ruth Benedict in *Patterns of Culture* (1934), proposed that the Zuni Indians had an "Apollonian" type modal personality, marked by balance and restraint, while those such as the Kwakiutl Indians were "Dionysian," or more prone to violent and unpredictable behavior. Data have failed to substantiate this grandiose explanation for several reasons. One is that the modal personality traits were extracted more from the observer's perspective than from the data. Another is that cultures do not focus on one major theme, but appear to be organized around a series of variations on several related themes and patterns. In any case, these *caveats* notwithstanding, Benedict's concern with the power and pervasiveness of cultural themes should not be dismissed lightly.

That the cultural themes do not always accurately reflect cultural reality is clearly demonstrated by the American aphorism: Silence is golden.

Themes and postulates often linger long after the patterns they justify have disappeared. As shown above, they may reflect more the desired than the real world. They may speak to patterns idealized but seldom realized. A following chapter deals more completely with the subject of cultural themes as expressed in systems of values and beliefs. In the meantime, don't believe everything you say.

8.3 CROSS-CULTURAL RESEARCH: SOME QUESTIONS AND A FEW ANSWERS

As Kleinjans (1972b) states in discussing the effects of culture learning, cross-cultural experiences may open up new insights, lead to discovery of additional similarities between cultural groups, and even bring into question our most treasured paradigms and/or explanations. He concludes (31):

> If a culture is the living storehouse of the learning of a group, if it dissects nature according to its own system, if it is a way of seeing, thinking, and believing, then different cultures will have different paradigms. It is possible that, as a consequence of learning a second culture, a scientist may begin to see "new and different things when looking with familiar instruments in places [he has] looked before" [Kuhn 1962]. If this is so, then science done cross-culturally may have greater validity than that done within a single culture.

In other words, there are many ways to skin a cat. Culture as mankind's adaptive mechanism has provided various paths; diversity has been a strong factor in human survival over the millennia. It may serve the individual cultural traveler as well as it has served the species.

Diversity also brings complexity to cross-cultural research and, at the same time, adds a measure of adventure to the search for cross-cultural generalizations. In this section of the chapter, then, we shall review some of the perils of looking at cross-cultural patterns with instruments forged in monocultural contexts and point out some of the ways to avoid chauvinistic bias in research.

Some Problems

In the past what had been labeled "cross-cultural research" had often been simply research related to testing known hypotheses or retesting already "validated" data among diverse cultural groups. Thus, instruments and research models devised and employed in monocultural contexts were taken, largely unchanged, to another cultural group. Psychological tests, considered validated and reliable, were used by anthropologists, sociologists, and psychologists without much consideration of their possible appropriateness in other than Western cultures.

An excellent example of the penchant to come to the field with testable hypotheses, ready-made instruments, and a pre-determined set of correlations to be tested can be found in the work of the American anthropologists of the culture and personality school of the 1920s and 1930s. Enchanted by the exciting new field of psychology, they scrutinized and explained such matters as incest, child-rearing practices, and modal personalities from a distinctly Freudian perspective and with Freudian precepts in mind.

Price-Williams, commenting on this tendency to explain in terms of Freud, observes (1982:73):

> The notion that it [Oedipus complex] might be the product of a particular social structure operating in Central Europe, and that in other cultures there might be variants of the situation or even that it might not exist, did not occur to anybody at the time. It is, of course, no criticism of Freud that this cultural aspect was lacking; the data were supplied only considerably later by the anthropologist Malinowski. . . .

As Malinowski found, there were indeed "variants." In Trobriand society, the tension existed, not between father and son, or in terms of illicit relations between mother and son, but between sons and uncles and sisters and brothers respectively. The principle was similar; the manifestations were not. The roles of father and procreator were not joined in one person as they were in Freud's Western family model. Thus, the permutations made cultural sense for the Trobrianders. Price-Williams writes (1982:73): "While there is a similarity in principle between the Trobriand and the European model, the different relationships enable us to view the Oedipus complex as a function of a social and not a biological factor."

The problems such research approaches can bring are obvious. Generalizations, conclusions and, for our purposes, recommended remedies to problems of cross-cultural contact and effective teaching methods may be quite suspect unless tested in a cross-cultural context. Perhaps it is necessary, as Kleinjans suggests, not only to look in different places with familiar instruments but also to look in different places with new and unfamiliar instruments—or at least with those best fitted to elicit the data needed in different cultures and in a form that lends itself to cross-cultural analysis. One way this can be accomplished is to ground the theory by investigating evidence that may lead to the formation of working hypotheses; these speculations then may be tested against empirical evidence. Another is to develop instruments of measurement and forms of data collection that are appropriate to the cultures in question. Cross-cultural research should not be carried out with methods and instruments developed in monocultural contexts. Researchers in language learning and acquisition would be well-advised to consult some of the more recent studies in intercultural communication and cross-cultural psychology in order to acquaint themselves with the problems of such research and with some suggested research designs and testing instruments.

Apart from the problems of finding suitable theoretical approaches to cross-cultural research, other dilemmas arise from the most basic problem in intercultural contact—similarity and difference. Which is most important? Should research be focused on that which human beings share or that which divides and distinguishes them?

These questions are as persistent and baffling today as they were when the first traveler in a foreign land looked around and saw that things appeared strange. The ways of the strangers or "them" were puzzling to the observer ("us"), even threatening, and certainly not to be adopted. Yet the most obtuse visitor could not fail to notice that those "strangers" had homes, families, griefs, and joys, that they prepared food, loved or hated each other, and all eventually died. This paradox of human existence not only plagues the wondering traveler but also remains of continuing concern to all cross-cultural researchers and theorists. The paradox is particularly difficult to deal with if the methods and techniques being applied call for rigorous application of nonparadoxical scientific methods of observation and data collection. Differences or variables may be manipulated in controlled experiments, but in so doing, crucial cultural variations may have been obscured.

Some Nagging Questions

Several fundamental questions must be answered by all who would investigate human similarities and differences.

- Are there universal generalizations pertaining to human organization and interaction that transcend the individual and specific groups or cultures?

- How may such laws be established and observed?

- Do differences really make a difference?

- If so, how? Furthermore, how can differences be measured?

These questions are still being pursued. Because they are as yet unanswered, any approach to intercultural communication and research—and ultimately culture learning—that focuses only on similarities *or* differences, is doomed to slice only half of the research loaf, and in this case, half a loaf is perhaps not enough.

While the balancing of the same and different remains an unresolved paradox, the problems of focus and method must also be considered in designing cross-cultural research. Measurable equivalencies and suitable cross-cultural frames of reference, both of which are essential in personal culture learning as well as in general research, must be established. In addition to the usual methods of qualitative research—interviewing, participant observation, use of informants, and such ethnographic techniques—other methods have been developed to serve the special circumstances of cross-cultural research. Several such methods and their attendant problems are discussed in the following section of this chapter.

Finding Equivalencies of Terms

As should be clear from the preceding discussion, the discovery of testable cross-cultural variables is difficult. Sechrest, Fay, and Zaidi (1972) list several types of problems involved in trying to establish translation equivalencies. They point out that there are difficulties in relation to vocabulary, use of idiom, and grammatical/syntactical patterns. They also add two more troublesome areas: experiential and conceptual equivalencies. The first three are familiar to the language teacher; the last two may not be as well-known. Experiential and conceptual equivalencies rest in the realm of personal and cultural variation. Experiential variability, of course, is a function of each communicator's personal experience. Conceptual problems imply that the concepts covered by an "accepted" translation do not cover the same ranges of meaning (48–49). For example, in American English the term *pharmacy* is generally synonymous with *drugstore*. In French, the term *pharmacie* only partially covers the range of meaning implied by the English word *drugstore*. Again using French as an example, the English word *attic* may be translated by the French word, *grenier*. The French word covers two terms in English, *attic* and *granary*, but in English an attic is not a granary.

Although the grammar translation technique is out of favor, second language teachers should remember that their students are manipulating such experiential and conceptual translations as these while learning a new language. If such mistranslations are not recognized, then exercises in vocabulary development are often reduced to exercises in confusion.

On the other hand, Sechrest *et al.* warn cross-cultural learners not to be too quick to look *only* for equivalencies. They comment (1972:49):

> We have gone into some detail concerning the problems of achieving equivalence across two or more languages as if equivalences were the fundamental problem. Actually, in certain respects it is not, for there may be a distinct paradox involved in translation for the sake of achieving equivalence. The paradox is that if one demands that a form of a test or other measure yield comparable results in two cultures in order to demonstrate equivalence, then the more equivalent two forms become the less the probability of finding cultural differences.

Because both similarities and differences must be considered in cross-cultural research and intercultural communication, the search for true equivalencies and ranges of meaning cannot be ignored by either researchers or teachers. One of the means to uncover them is the method of back translation—that is, translation and retranslation from one language to the other.

Needless to say, cross-cultural generalizations cannot be effected unless the same concepts are being measured; this involves what Price-Williams called *transcultural variables*. In speaking of the difficulties of undertaking cross-cultural psychological studies, he wrote (1982:84):

> A difficulty which faces the psychologist concerns the basis of comparison between cultures in the study of some psychological process. In order to assess, say, concept formation in two widely separate regions of the world, we have to be sure that the methods of interrogation can be equated for both regions. This is more difficult than it may superficially seem, for many psychological techniques are very sensitive to environmental influences, and to the way in which they are applied. The ability to create *transcultural* variables, so that they are measurable on an equivalent basis anywhere in the world, is a challenge which always faces cross-cultural research.

Two such attempts to form a basis for transcultural variables have been: (1) the *semantic differential technique*, which weds linguistic definitions to cultural meanings by means of ethnosemantics and extrapolates terms valid cross-culturally and identifiable in each culture on its own terms; and (2) the *associative group analysis* and *semantographs*, which are means of defining cultural frames of reference of similar concepts for contrastive purposes. Both of the procedures are designed to uncover dimensions of equivalency for scientific analysis.

Charles Osgood, in *The Measurement of Meaning* (1957) and later with May and Miron in *Cross-Cultural Universals of Affective Meaning* (1975), developed the semantic differential technique to establish universal contrastive attributes. He reasoned that human beings "apparently abstract about the same properties of things for making comparisons, and they order these different modes of qualifying in roughly the same way in importance" (1975:189).

These studies isolated three pancultural factors of affective (emotional) meaning: *evaluation, potency,* and *activity*. These pancultural values were identified and described in the terms of the cultures studied; for each language group involved, the individual measurement scales devised were based on rigorous testing and statistical verification in that group. The establishment of the measurement scales for each group was a long and arduous process. The technique is difficult to administer, but it has paved the way for additional efforts at devising cross-culturally valid measurement scales. This type of research also demonstrated the means to use qualitative and quantitative methods in eliciting culture-specific descriptions of transcultural variables.

The second approach, associative group analysis, is related to the types of questions Osgood and his collaborators were addressing. Such analysis was undertaken for the purpose of establishing culture-specific frames of reference composed of the characteristics or attributes assigned to certain pancultural relationships or concepts by native culture bearers.

Szalay and Fisher (1979) gathered their data by asking samples of native speakers in two languages to respond by free association to certain stimulus words. By charting the salient differences in the components of subjective meaning (beliefs, values) and differences in the dominance or strength of these subjective meanings, they produced what they called culture-specific frames of reference, or a list of attributes assigned a given concept. Contrasting frames of reference formed a *semantograph*. A semantograph, then, is a graphic portrayal of the contrastive meaning components identified by given groups. The longer the bar for each component, the more important the attribute. As these researchers state, nonshared elements point to possible areas where miscommunication might take place (62). The differing frames of reference to *education* for a priest and a coach are shown in Figure 8.1.

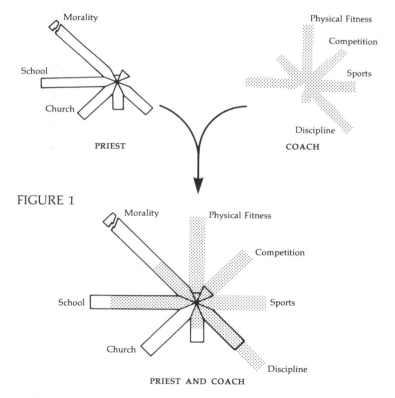

FIGURE 1

Figure 8.2. Differing Frames of Reference

Source: Reproduced by permission of the Institute of Comparative Social and Cultural Studies, Inc. (ICS).

These researchers suggested that their associative analysis method might be used to compile a communication lexicon to supplement conventional dictionaries. This is an intriguing idea. The cultural frame of reference would be described "through its natural units of meaning, which happen to be the natural units of language as well" (82). No doubt this is a good deal easier said than done.

Yet, there are practical applications. For example, consider the associative analysis you might draw for your own personal frame of reference for "mother." First, write down five components to describe *mother* as a role, as a person, in terms of status, relationship to the family, and duties. What characteristics would you assign to each component of meaning? How much strength would you assign to each component? Are you surprised at your answers or associations? How do they compare with those of a classmate, a fellow teacher, or your informant?

Asking the Right Questions

Osgood *et al.* (1975), in the course of developing and testing the semantic differential technique, asked some fundamental questions. The following list* summarizes their questions and observations about these questions.

Question: When is the same really the same?

Comment: When it is the same even though expressed differently.

Question: When is the same really different?

Comment: When there are problems of hidden assumptions and hidden culture.

Question: When is the different really the same?

Comment: When the surface structure represents the same deep structure and a common evaluative factor.

Question: When is the different really different?

Comment: When it can be attributed to semantic and/or cultural differences, when it can be used to test a hypothesis, or when it makes a real cultural difference.

---

* These questions and answers have been summarized from a discussion in *Cross-Cultural Universals of Affective Meaning,* C. Osgood, W. May, and M. Miron. (Urbana, IL: University of Illinois Press, 1975), pp. 31–36.

After reading these questions and comments, can you relate them to the language/culture learning context? When is the same really the same? How many languages and cultural universals are there? What are the attributes of the good or successful language learner? Are these universal or are there cultural variations? Could it be that what seems the same is truly different? Can we safely assume that basic human relationships are similar, but that their manifestations are variable?

If we assume that they are really the same, will we fail to recognize the differences in manifestations? For example, can we separate friendship from the ways in which we show friendship? When is different really different? Does Sunday have the same cultural significance everywhere that it has in the United States or Western Europe? We know it does not, but do we expect the stranger to notice the differences? What *is* different about Sunday? In the United States, it isn't solely a matter of religion. Osgood (35) found that Wednesday has a special meaning in The Netherlands because it is associated with school holidays. Wednesday is just the middle of the week for most in the United States, but Sunday is Sunday.

8.4 CONCLUSION

In this chapter we have defined such basic concepts as *acculturation/enculturation, cross-cultural awareness, cultural identity, perception,* and *cultural patterns, themes, and postulates.* In the final portion of this chapter, the problems and concerns encountered by cross-cultural researchers were discussed as were the insights they offer the pragmatic ethnographer. In the next chapter, we shall continue our investigation of the very special and powerful codes and channels of communication not yet examined—the nonverbal.

FOR STUDY AND DISCUSSION

1. Identify the following terms or concepts:

   back translation

   cultural postulates

   semantic differential technique

   cultural identity

   associative group analysis

   cultural patterns and themes

   transcultural variables

2. Comment on the following quotation from Edward Sapir: "Cultures . . . are merely abstracted configurations of idea and action patterns, which have endlessly different meanings for the various individuals in the group . . ." (1964:200–201).

3. Read the following student theme. Identify any cultural themes and comment on the student's explanation.

   There are many races in the world, and they have each national characteristics. They are quite different from other countries.
   We seldom tell somebody our real feeling clearly. When we have a disagreeable thing, we usually should get angry. But we don't do that. Then, we think like this: "If

I endure it now, it will not be a problem." Second, when we fail something, we seldom show angry faces, and we smile a little. Because we know somebody saw our failure.

Third, we are very shy, especially young ladies. We always look down, and we bring our hands to our mouths. When we have a class, we don't talk to our teacher. We are always waiting for the teacher's indication. In this, we have our characteristics. They may be very strange for other countries, and foreign people may have many questions about them. But they are never strange to us. We shall keep them forever!

4. Some experts point out that cultural emphasis will tend to provide the needed vocabulary, which is then used metaphorically in other contexts. Hickerson suggests that speakers in the United States emphasize food and make wide metaphoric use of culinary terms (1980:117). For example, we say, "She's a cupcake." "We're in the soup." Can you enlarge the list? Are English speakers hung up on food? Can you identify another North American cultural theme? Such themes are often identifiable in folk sayings, mottos, proverbs, or recurrent expressions.

5. Look at the cartoon shown in Figure 8.3. How does this cartoon relate to the topics discussed in this chapter? Would this type of material be useful in discussing cultural differences with a group of students either learning a second language in their own culture or in a foreign context? How would you explain the cartoon? What examples would you use?

THE FAMILY CIRCUS®   **By Bil Keane**

"Mommy said 'We'll see.' That means 'no.'"

Figure 8.3. How Does She Know?

Source: Cowles Syndicate, Inc.

CULTURE LEARNING EXERCISE

Simulation: How Hard Is It to Learn a New Set of Rules?

1. The class is to be divided into three groups. One group will consist of two or three persons who will serve as consultants, or pragmatic ethnographers. Their job is to discover why the two groups do not seem to get along well.

2. Those who are chosen to be ethnographers will leave the room. They will be given special guidelines. (See below.)

3. The two other groups will place themselves in different parts of the room. During a 10-minute planning session, each group will agree to three rules of cultural conduct that must be observed when communicating with strangers or among themselves. Each group will be given suggestions concerning these rules. (See below.) It is a fact that these two groups are not friendly to each other.

4. The consultants return to the room. Their task is to discover the cultural rules being used. They may use any device or line of questioning to discover these rules.

5. After 15 minutes, the inquiry session ends. The consultants must then report what appears to be the problem in communication between these groups. In no case should the rules be revealed except by the procedures indicated above. A cultural secret is a cultural secret.

GUIDELINES SHOULD NOT BE SHARED BETWEEN GROUPS.

Guidelines to Pragmatic Ethnographers

You are going to be asked to discover the reasons for the hostility between the two groups. They live side by side, but there is frequent dissension. Apparently, they don't share many cultural patterns. It is feared that open warfare may erupt unless the sources of such hostility are made clear.

Try to talk to them and find out what is going on. Observe their manner of communication. Neither group is easy to talk with. You have exactly 15 minutes to avert war! Good luck!

Guidelines to Groups

Your neighbors are strange folk and don't follow your ways at all. Review (devise) three rules for proper communication. These rules might include restrictions as to when a person is required to answer, to whom an answer may be given, what kinds of questions deserve an answer, body position, eye contact, or degree of proximity. Your group might think that men should only reply to men and women to women. Of course, your way is the right way. You wish to communicate but you aren't going to say a word unless your rules are followed. Each group should write out its rules and present them to the supervisor before those ethnographers arrive.

FOR FURTHER READING

L. Barzini. 1964. *The Italians.* Barzini's book is a lucid, entertaining, and informative introduction to the Italians and their ways as described by a native Italian whose cultural blinders have been lifted.

R. Benedict. 1934. *Patterns of Culture.* Although this book was written more than fifty years ago, it is still of interest as an example of ethnographic analysis using psychological traits as organizing principles with which to view entire cultures. One of the moving spirits behind the culture and personality school of anthropology, Benedict considered cultures as "individual psychology thrown large upon the screen, given gigantic proportions and a long time span" (1932:24).

R. Benedict. 1946. *The Chrysanthemum and the Sword.* This discussion of Japanese culture and the Japanese modal personality is still widely quoted and is recognized by Japanese experts as an insightful discussion of Japanese ways and character.

R. Hanvey. 1979. "Cross-cultural Awareness" (46–56). This article in the Smith and Luce reader is reprinted from a larger work by Hanvey. It is a cogent discussion of the dimensions of cross-cultural awareness and the various levels through which the cultural traveler may pass. Hanvey provides an excellent introduction to the concepts of cross-cultural awareness and empathy.

Latin America. 1977. This is one of the Communication Learning Aid Series published by the Kennedy Center for International Studies, Brigham Young University. The volumes in this series, along with *Culturgrams* also published by the Brigham Young Center, are short, readable introductions to the life styles, customs, and manners of various cultures. *Latin America* is a fine example of a contrastive approach to cultural complexity. This volume emphasizes the "characteristics of the people with whom the majority of visitors will come in contact" (1).

E. Lee. 1980. *The American in Saudi Arabia.* This small volume details the problems of transporting one's "cultural baggage" to a "foreign" country. It examines the "personal disruption which often occurs within individuals as a result of a clash of cultures . . ." (vii). Because clashes are bidirectional, such a book as this provides insights into the problems that might be encountered by Saudis or other students from the Middle East as they travel and study abroad. This book is an excellent eye-opener and consciousness-raiser.

M. Mead. 1942. *And Keep Your Powder Dry. An Anthropologist Looks at America.* Mead's book is one of the many national character studies produced during World War II. The content of this book makes for interesting contrastive analysis when placed side by side with Benedict's book (see above), or compared with the United States forty years later.

C. Osgood, G. Suci, and P. Tannenbaum. 1957. *The Measurement of Meaning.* This book describes the work of Osgood and his associates in the identification of cross-cultural variables of affective meaning. The cross-cultural methods employed in his studies are discussed in detail.

C. Osgood, W. May, and M. Miron. 1975. *Cross-Cultural Universals of Affective Meaning.* In this book the authors report the methods and techniques they have developed to identify and compare cross-cultural evaluative dimensions.

D. Price-Williams. 1982. "Cross-cultural Studies." (73–87) Price-Williams provides an excellent review of cross-cultural research in perception, cognition, socialization, and personality as well as commentary on the problems encountered and methods used.

N. Sakamoto and R. Naotsuka. 1982. *Polite Fictions: Why Japanese and Americans Seem Rude to Each Other.* The title is self-explanatory. Read it; you'll like it even if you are not going to Japan. The many ways in which we can misunderstand each other are far greater than any of us dream. If you don't believe this, just read this book.

F. Schuon. 1976. *Understanding Islam* (translated by D. Matheson). This is an excellent introduction to the main tenets of Islam, its history, and philosophical foundations. This author explores and explains the pervasive quality of the Islamic influence in all aspects of the societies founded upon its principles.

L. Szalay and G. Fisher. 1979. "Communication Overseas" (57–82). In this article Szalay and Fisher explain and exemplify their method of associative group analysis in cross-cultural research and the development of semantographs.

Chapter 9

Other Channels — Other Messages

In the previous chapters the concepts of language and culture were discussed in relation to communication. One other form of communication must be considered—the nonverbal. As stated previously, much of the transmission and reception of information in communicative acts is effected in other than the verbal codes. Thus, the impact of nonverbal communication, so semantically loaded and so varied cross-culturally, deserves more than a passing nod. Nonverbal communication (NVC) has to do with what Edward Hall termed "the silent language" and "the hidden dimension" (1959, 1969).

Its messages are transmitted by hand signals, body movements, silence, distance, eye movements, and even by uses of time and space. It is the sometimes silent but highly communicative accompaniment of verbal speech. It may also replace language. The complexities of verbal language, so overwhelming to those being initiated to the field of language study, pale in comparison to the subtle nuances of NVC.

In addition to being very complex and exhibiting wide cross-cultural differences, NVC is also largely used unconsciously. As a result, its power to foster miscommunication is very great indeed. Hall writes: "Most Americans are only dimly aware of this silent language even though they use it every day" (1959:10). One may also add that the majority of those from other cultures are equally unaware of the swirling storm of nonverbal stimuli directed toward and emanating from them as they move through their daily lives. We all toss our heads, wave our hands, and position our bodies in both conscious and unconscious ways in the firm conviction that messages are being sent and received. As we shall see, we are often not even aware of transmitting such messages and cannot be sure that they are even being noticed—much less correctly "read."

Hall (1959:10) also comments: "In addition to what we say with our verbal language we are constantly communicating our real feelings in our silent language—the language of behavior." Is it true that we are more honest in our silent language than we are in our verbal language? The proverbial belief shared by many North Americans that actions speak louder than words would seem to support this view. In any case, the lack of conscious intention that marks so much NVC speaks to the need to consider just what messages are being received as well as what messages are being sent.

The symbol shown in Figure 9.1 is a case in point. It was designed to be used to identify American-made products. The okay sign with a star between the thumb and index finger was chosen in a nationwide contest as a "winner." The caption should perhaps have more rightly been labeled a "slip of the hand," for it could easily be taken for an obscene gesture in Brazil and several other countries. If the hand is held lower and closer to the body, this same sign, used in Japan, may indicate "money." Such are the complexities of cross-cultural symbolization.

Nonverbal communication is carried on many channels and employs various codes of behavior. It carries a major percent of the social meaning of a given message, perhaps as much as 65% (Birdwhistell 1970:158; Mehrabian 1972). In addition, in its paralinguistic forms, it affects the decoding of, or may even give lie to, the spoken word.

In the following portions of this chapter we shall consider major types of nonverbal behavior and cues, their various guises, and some obvious cross-cultural variations. Finally, we shall compare and contrast some of these variations particularly pertinent to the multicultural language classroom, concentrating on student/teacher interaction and possible areas of confusion.

9.1 NVC: GENERAL CONSIDERATIONS

In the following discussion, the term nonverbal communication (NVC) will be used as a cover term to refer to all forms of nonverbal interaction, including paralanguage, body language, and contextual arrangements used in human interaction and communication. Like language, NVC forms are part of a system, learned, culturally related, and cross-culturally varied. Messages are sent and received, understood or misunderstood. We have not chosen to use Hall's term "the silent language" because NVC is not always silent, as anyone knows who has heard the expression, "I don't like your tone of voice." The use of the term "nonverbal" is in no way meant to imply that it is less important than the verbal. This is patently not so. NVC is mankind's most fundamental and pervasive means of communication. It is the language we use when words aren't enough. It manifests itself in our uses of time and space and the movements of our bodies and the placing of our buildings and all else involved in human interaction. It sometimes speaks louder than words and is often the most persuasive of the communicative channels. Its cultural variations are easily overlooked.

'Made in America' symbol a sleight of hand

Made in America

SEATTLE (UPI)—It's a deceptively simple design—the sihouette of a hand making an "OK" sign, with a star replacing the hole made by the thumb and index finger.

If two California manufacturers and their Beverly Hills publicist have their way, the emblem will become a nationwide "Made in America" symbol proudly displayed on packaged goods here and abroad.

For design student Joan Nielson of Seattle, who came up with the logo, it means $2,000 and a head start on a career in commercial art.

"When they called and told me I won the contest I just giggled and giggled," said Nielson, 22, who studies at the Art Institute of Seattle.

"I mean, Saul Bass (one of the country's leading graphic designers), giving me first prize—this isn't like winning 'Most Artistic Gal of the Year' in high school," she said.

"This is the largest student prize that I've seen in my 25 years of teaching and 42 years in commercial art," said Jess Cauthorn, president of the school where Nielson is in her sixth quarter.

"Most of all, it will improve the heck out of her portfolio. You can't even put a dollar sign on its value. Most students have a real problem showing prospective employers any professional-quality examples of their work," Cauthorn said.

It all began when two businessmen told

their public relations agency they wanted to broadcast their pride in American-made products by affixing a logo to packaged goods.

"I got to thinking about it and learned that, my gosh, this country is 200 years old and we've never had a universal 'Made in America' symbol," said Alex Litrov, a public relations man from Beverly Hills, Calif.

So Litrov last summer launched a contest among design students, attracting more than 500 entries from universities and art institutes. By mid-January, the three-member panel of professional design artists had chosen the winning emblem.

The labor and art that went into its creation showed as much sleight of hand as the finished product.

"I pared and pared and pared," Nielson said at the comfortably scruffy art school in central Seattle, housed in a part of an old three-story building.

"I can't really describe the process that went into creating the symbol of the hand," said Nielson.

First, she went through lists of "what I thought was 'American'—stars and stripes, liberty bells."

After days of stripping her emblem of nonessential frills—the essence of good design work—computer graphics instructor Tom Price approached her.

"Had you thought of just Xeroxing a hand and working from there?" he asked.

Figure 9.1. "Made in America" Symbol

Source: Reprinted with permission of United Press International, Inc.

9.2 CULTURE-GENERAL OR CULTURE-SPECIFIC?

In general, research in NVC has centered on the old question of same or different. Are nonverbal behaviors, such as facial expressions and gestures, universal or culture-specific? Questions abound not only as to the specificity or universality of given forms but also as to the functions of nonverbal behavior and its relationship to verbal behavior. Even though these questions are difficult, the intercultural communicator must furnish some type of response and attempt to deal with them even if only on an *ad hoc* basis.

Much of what is known about nonverbal behavior and NVC is contained in a hodgepodge of lists of "differences" and is described in fascinating anecdotes that tell us little about how to handle these differences. Should we concentrate on understanding universally shared expressions of NVC or continue to add to our lists of "strange" behaviors?

Universal aspects of nonverbal communicative behavior, such as blushing, appear to support the position that some nonverbal behaviors are innate and related to human physiology (Pennycook 1985). But is not a smile a sign of happiness and a furrowed brow of anger or concern? Aren't we all able to read the expressions of despair on the faces of those ravaged by war or the pride in the faces of gold-medal winners? Aren't basic emotions clearly marked in the faces of friends and strangers alike? Well, yes and no. Charles Darwin in his book *The Expression of the Emotions in Man and Animals* (1872) felt that all human beings expressed basic emotions in a common way. Ekman and his colleagues (1969, 1971, 1975) support Darwin's suggestions in their writings on universal facial expressions of fear, happiness, surprise, anger, sadness, and disgust. Yet the rules for display of these emotions vary from culture to culture. Thus, pictures of happy faces, sad faces, frightened faces appear to be read correctly among many diverse peoples, even very small infants. Another characteristic of nonverbal behavior seems to be the connection between the expression of emotions and the subsequent engendering of the feeling; that is, an angry face brings forth feelings of anger both to those who pull their faces into the furrows and folds of rage and those who observe them. The *when, where, how, why, to whom,* and *to what degree* these emotions are revealed, however, are subject to cultural, situational, and individual variation (Wolfgang 1979a). The human facial expressions of joy, anger, perplexity can be recognized cross-culturally, but what cannot be read so easily are the human messages associated with them.

Although there are literally thousands of separate physical ways to move the human body available to most of us, the number of gestures, signs, movements, and positions actually used to transmit messages to others is limited in any given culture. However, they are much greater in number than those used in the verbal code. In addition, all those smiles, nods, bows, and sighs by which we transmit culturally shared messages are often similar in form, and perhaps even in distribution, but are accorded very different meanings cross-culturally. Any North American who has been summoned with what he or she considers to be the baby's "bye bye" sign would agree with the previous statement.

Birdwhistell concludes: ". . . although we have been searching for 15 years, we have found no gesture or body motion which has the same social meaning in all societies. . . . Insofar as we know, there is no body motion or gesture that can be regarded as a universal symbol" (1970:81).

For example, the avoidance of eye contact in public between strangers is considered proper behavior in Japan. In the subway, on trains, and in other public places the great masses of people pass each other with heads lowered and eyes vacant or cast down. To engage in eye contact is to acknowledge the presence of another. Not to do so is to pass unhindered through masses of people. The utility of such public behavior in a heavily populated country of such limited space seems to make cultural sense. It is often observed in larger cities everywhere, but the Japanese pattern is different. There is a studied avoidance. It seems to be related to the Japanese habit of falling asleep on public transportation. Closed eyes mean no contact (Morsbach 1982:313).

Yet such behavior often disturbs and sometimes even enrages the visitor who comes from a culture in which to pass a human being without some acknowledgment that another human being is present is culturally unsettling. The slightest nod of the head or flicker of the eye will do, but to make no such move is insulting and often arouses hostility. This Japanese public behavior transferred to most American contexts represents inadmissible behavior. On the other hand to engage in American public behavior in Japan is to engender surprise, court rebuff, and demonstrate once more the strange ways of the *gaijin*.

Because nonverbal codes are in many ways even more rigid than the verbal, the American who is struggling up a set of steep stairs with a heavy suitcase and is buffeted about by hordes of seemingly indifferent Japanese men, women, and children finds it hard to fathom the Japanese logic or find it acceptable. Where are all the Boy Scouts? Those who understand know that in Japan assistance is bound up with personal acquaintance, assumption of responsibilities and duties, and other personal interrelationships. The helping hand once offered is committed to additional interaction. The stranger in Japan must either solicit the friendly hand before starting up the stairs or send the heavy baggage by other means. There certainly is more to NVC than meets the eye!

9.3 DEFINING NONVERBAL COMMUNICATION

Before discussing the various types of nonverbal behavior and their communicative meanings, let us clarify the relationships between verbal and nonverbal behavior and communication. First, how does NVC differ from nonverbal behavior? Not all nonverbal behavior involves nonverbal communication, but all nonverbal communication involves communicative behavior carried out in other than verbal codes. However, some nonverbal communicative behavior may accompany verbal behavior, as we shall see.

Nonverbal communication has been used to refer to many different human activities, including everything from traffic patterns to nose twitching. Harrison and Knapp conclude that "there is no complete consensus on what should be fenced in and fenced out of the nonverbal range" (1972:347).

The term *nonverbal communication* must be reserved for those behaviors and other cultural symbols and cues that serve to "communicate" culturally specific meanings and are understood and shared by others in the same cultural group. For example, an up-and-down motion of the head is physical behavior. It is nonverbal and nonvocal but may accompany a verbal sign or replace it. This body movement becomes nonverbal communication (NVC) when it transmits some cultural message, such as assent, dissent, or confirmation. It is not NVC if it has no such shared meaning.

Thus, NVC may encompass a wide range of phenomena including gestures, sounds accompanying language, body movements, communicative styles, or lack of each of the above. Samovar, Porter and Jain (1981) identify NVC as involving "all those stimuli within a communication setting, both humanly generated and environmentally generated, with the exception of verbal stimuli, that have potential message value for the sender or receiver" (156). Broadly defined, nonverbal communicative behavior includes all the ways in which human beings behave, interact, and communicate except in their use of language. When these behaviors are accorded meaning and evaluation, they become part of the NVC system or code of a given cultural group. In cases in which such behaviors vary cross-culturally (and most do), they must be understood, and perhaps learned, if intercultural contact is to lead to effective communication. If they are not, the messages may be lost, garbled, or misinterpreted. As noted previously, not all behavior "communicates." Just as it is necessary to discriminate between random and meaningful linguistic sounds in a new language so is it necessary to discover meaningful nonverbal behaviors and environmental cues related to NVC. It is not enough to know that people use their bodies, senses, and cultural artifacts to communicate in the nonverbal code; we must know how these cues are incorporated into the overall cultural patterns of the groups in question.

If this appears difficult, it is. That it is not impossible is attested to by the fact that despite all the barriers rising before us as we try to cross cultural boundaries, we do succeed in communicating more often than not and reasonably well. We must be warned that use of the nonverbal code or other cues does not constitute communication unless cultural meanings have been assigned. Nor does it if the individual culture bearer elects to ignore such assigned meanings. Thus, arriving two hours late to an appointment may indicate personal patterns of procrastination that allow for great latitude in the matter of determining the definition of "too late" rather than a shared cultural pattern. Furthermore, because much nonverbal communication takes place at an unconscious level, messages may be sent without intention and received without awareness.

9.4 THE VERBAL VS.
THE NONVERBAL

Because nonverbal forms often occur in conjunction with verbal forms, there may be difficulty in distinguishing between them. Muriel Saville-Troike, in her book *The Ethnography of Communication* (1982), suggests a division on the basis of code and channel. Codes are divided into the verbal and nonverbal and channels into vocal and nonvocal (143). The verbal/vocal is spoken speech. The nonverbal/ vocal is often called paralanguage (prosodic features accompanying or replacing linguistic forms). The verbal/nonvocal includes such systems as the Morse code and written language. The nonverbal/nonvocal is most often what is meant when the term nonverbal is used; it includes kinesics (body movement), proxemics (use of space) and even pictures and cartoons.

In another formulation, Taylor (1980:560) divides NVC into four categories along the dimensions of verbal supportive or verbal nonsupportive and conscious or unconscious. Thus, a pointed finger accompanied by the word "there" may be verbal supportive and conscious. A sneer may be verbal nonsupportive but conscious. A widening of the eyes while one says "No kidding!" would be verbal supportive but probably unconscious. Finally, finger snapping or doodling in a boring situation is a verbal nonsupportive and probably unconscious message. The verbal and nonverbal codes are woven into patterns of synchrony in human communication so that the nonverbal may complement, emphasize, repeat, or even contradict the verbal, and vice versa.

Several characteristics are particularly important in comparing the nature of the nonverbal and the verbal codes. Nonverbal communicative behavior tends to be analogical, while verbal behavior is more digital in nature (Watzlawick *et al.* 1967:62). This is of importance to the classroom teacher who so often depends upon analogy or parallelism between the sign and the message, especially when dealing with students at the beginning levels of language learning. But Condon and Yousef warn us that the analogical characteristics of nonverbal behavior render learning the patterns of NVC of another culture easier only if the basis of the analogy is known (1975:133). They use the example of differing forms of beckoning gestures—either with the palm turned toward the summoner or with the palm down. In both gestures there is an analogical pulling motion with the fingers. The positions of the palm, however, are given different interpretations cross-culturally. Try them out and you'll understand how an analogy may be misleading. Counting behavior is also analogical but culturally varied.

The nonverbal code shares certain features with the verbal: both are symbolic, subject to individual variation, learned, and capable of conveying meaning. Also, like language, nonverbal systems are formed of smaller units of behavior.

These units may be combined into higher level structures, molded in turn into culturally meaningful patterns of interaction. While verbal codes tend to be discrete, arbitrary, invariable, and denotative, nonverbal codes have been described as continuous, natural, variable, and connotative. According to R. Harrison (1972:490) "Each proposition raises interesting research questions."

Nonverbal communicative patterns are acquired, as are linguistic systems, during the period of enculturation in the native culture. They are polished by both instruction and imitation. Wolfgang (1979b:161) points out that much of the learning and instruction concerning nonverbal behavior in school involves manners, deportment, and courtesy. Is this not also true of the type of NVC instruction that takes places in our language classrooms, consciously or unconsciously?

On the other hand, because nonverbal communicative behaviors may be involuntary, as, for example, in the case of pupil dilation, they may also be unintentional and unconsciously transmitted. It is also very difficult to falsify nonverbal behavior. Wolfgang writes: "It is easier to get out of verbal mistakes than body language mistakes. On the verbal level you can always say, 'you didn't understand what I was trying to say.' On the other hand, try to tell someone that your angry face is not angry" (161–162).

In examining differences between the verbal and nonverbal codes it is useful to consider why the nonverbal is needed and why it carries such a heavy load of social meaning. One of the functions of NVC is to express affect and interpersonal attitudes. Indeed, gestures such as clenching the jaw and gritting the teeth, not to mention shaking the fist, may well be not only panhuman but also very ancient human behavior. Such signals, which may or may not accompany language, carry powerful messages. Nonverbal signals also carry information that may be difficult to put into words. For example, consider the difficulty of describing all the information gathered by the mere touch of a hand or the wink of an eye or the smell of home-baked bread.

Nonverbal signals may also be used in social interaction to provide feedback and synchronize signals. These relate to communicative procedures and are often those which our non-native speakers either miss or misuse. All those "Uhhuhs" and nods help to keep the conversation going.

Finally, nonverbal signals, as Argyle (1975:132) points out, convey information concerning other messages perhaps best left unsaid. For example, negative aspects or dislike may be communicated silently or by tone of voice.

9.5 SOME WARNINGS

Nonverbal communicative behaviors are learned very early, even earlier than verbal language, and hold a deeper and less conscious hold upon their users than verbal patterns. Those who would observe, understand, and monitor nonverbal behavior and understand NVC in all its cross-cultural variations should be warned of the enormity of their task and of some of the problems they are likely to encounter. First, the popularization of bits and pieces of information concerning NVC in the lay press has served to make people aware of the phenomena, but often seems to distort rather than clarify, to pass over lightly instead of providing in-depth explanations, and to engender fear of error rather than provide means of coping with differences. Just because we know that touching conventions vary cross-culturally, should we monitor our behavior so that we touch the touchers and leave the rest alone, as suggested in Chapter 1 of this text?

Several writers (Jensen 1970; Samovar, Porter and Jain 1981; Wolfgang 1979a) note that superficial approaches to NVC may lead to serious errors—not of commission but of understanding—in the context of intercultural contact. Shallow generalizations concerning body language, the uses of time, and other aspects of nonverbal behavior may lead the observer of such behavior either to overgeneralize and thus fail to note idiosyncratic behaviors, or to overlook differences. Observers may also ascribe their own cultural meanings to such universal gestures as leg-crossing, head-bowing, or smiling. In addition, there may be a tendency to take note of trivial or relatively meaningless activities simply because they are different. Jensen (1970:136–138) warns that such superficial approaches may ultimately strengthen tendencies to exaggerate differences and their effects, to indulge in stereotyping, and to reinforce prejudices.

The following portion of this chapter reviews five types of nonverbal communicative behavior and some of their cultural variations. Each has significance in intercultural communication and each has relevance to the multicultural classroom, if not all classrooms.

It is very tempting to investigate in great detail all the ways in which each of these categories is realized in various cultures. The exotic is easy to discover and titillating to contemplate. In no other area of intercultural communication is the temptation to chuckle over the strange and the danger to evoke miscommunication so great. The following discussion is designed not to add to the chuckle list but to indicate some major variations in these categories. Readers are urged to observe their own nonverbal behavior and assess their NVC patterns as they should in the context of real interaction. They should then learn the true meaning of the old cliché: "It ain't what you say, it's the way that you say it." And may we add that actions, or their lack, may indeed speak louder than words.

9.6 NONVERBAL COMMUNICATIVE BEHAVIOR

Nonverbal communicative behavior may be divided into three major categories: those most directly related to language use (paralanguage); those manifested in individual movement and actions; and those stimulated by the context or environment.

Paralanguage does much to elaborate, to embroider, and to give affective depth to the verbal message. Its forms reveal themselves in the pitch, rate, intensity, and quality of the speech generated. They are found in the sighs, quivers, and grunts that tell our listeners that we are bored, frightened, or simply listening.

They may replace the verbal in the form of a "Tsk! Tsk!" to indicate disapproval in North American NVC. They may add meaning to a simple statement as falling intonation does to the statement "You didn't!" The sliding curve from high to low adds the element of resignation to disbelief; a rising tone invites a response.

Body language involves systematic movements of the human body assigned communicative meaning; *kinesics* is its formal, systematic study. Kinesic cues are those body movements and indications which "communicate." Finger-pointing and head-shaking are cases in point if they are attributed meaning. Kinesic movements may accompany verbal communication or may, just as paralinguistic elements do, supplement and replace verbal speech. In addition to body movements of all types, nonverbal behavior may also include uses of the human senses, such as touch (haptics), taste, and smell.

A third form, external or contextual cues, seems to include "and everything else." These refer to the communicative content contained in the environment or context in which interaction or communication may occur. They are often, although not always, behavioral in nature, and sometimes modifiers of behavior. These stimuli are external to the speaker/listener and may under given circumstances be assigned specific cultural meanings. Included under such a classification are the uses of time (chronemics), space (proxemics), communicative styles and habits, group behavior, and other interpersonal interaction. They may also include housing arrangements, city plans, business activities, manners of dress, eating, food, or other variables of human interaction.

Let us examine these major categories and some variations in greater detail and in a less abstract fashion.

Paralanguage

The term *paralanguage* includes various types of acoustical elements that accompany language, as well as the vocalizations that replace or supplement speech. Both are carried on the vocal channels but are nonverbal. Paralanguage, as described by Trager, is comprised of the acoustical elements accompanying, supplementing, or replacing verbal sounds. They include voice set, voice qualities, and vocalizations. Trager (1964:276) defines voice set as the background for language.

> Voice set . . . involves the physiological and physical peculiarities resulting in the patterned identification of individuals as members of a societal group and as persons of a certain sex, age, state of health, body build, rhythm state, position in a group, mood, bodily condition, location. From the physical and physiological characteristics listed are derived cultural identifications of gender, age grade, health image, body image, rhythmic image, status, mode, condition, locale—and undoubtedly others.

Voice qualities include such elements as pitch range, vocal lip control, articulation control, glottis control, rhythm control, pitch control, resonance, and tempo. Vocalizations are "actual specifically identifiable noises (sounds);" they include vocal characterizers, vocal qualifiers, and vocal segregates (276). Vocal characterizers are the sounds made in laughing, crying, moaning, groaning, belching, hissing, tongue-clicking, or sneezing. Vocal qualifiers include intensity, pitch height, and extent (drawl or clip). Examples of vocal segregates are the "uh-huh's" and "uh-uh's" which so often replace "yes" and "no" in English.

In general, the vocal cues of paralanguage provide information about the emotional states of the speakers, their personalities, and even their intentions. The paralinguistic deals with the *how* of a statement. Such cues may also include hesitations and periods of silence.

Certain paralinguistic features are so clearly verbally linked that they are part of the linguistic system. This is the case for the suprasegmentals of intonation and pitch in English. We know that in some languages tone is used phonemically; however, in English, a nontonal language, stress or intensity may be used to change the meaning of a word. For example, consider the difference between *record* as a noun and *record* as a verb. In the noun the stress falls on the first syllable, in the verb, on the second syllable.

We also know that intonation in English can describe the differences between questions, statements, and exclamations. Consider the following sentence: *You are a fool.* By allowing their voices to rise or fall, English speakers may indicate surprise, disbelief, or anger, make a statement, or ask a question. In written form, some of the affective messages are conveyed by exclamation points, question marks, and other punctuation. Any composition teacher who does not utilize the paralinguistic connection between written and spoken communication in English is ignoring the nonverbal aspects noted in the written message.

Such paralinguistic patterns vary in different languages and are often the source of speaking and comprehension difficulties encountered by the speaker whose language does not possess the target language forms. Because these patterns are so natural to the native speaker, a teacher may overlook the differences, fail to explain them, or simply continue to correct without pointing out the precise problems.

For those whose languages are tonal in nature, the tendency to place their native paralinguistic features on specific words or syllables in English may lead to pronunciation problems and difficulty in comprehension. Also, because voice features such as stress, pitch, or loudness may convey affect, the margin for miscommunication is very great. For example, many observers conclude that speakers of Arabic are angry when they are not. The intonation and stress patterns of Arabic often fall upon ears accustomed to English as harsh, angry, and aggressive. Coupled with the tendency to maintain close personal distance with frequent touching, the intention of the Arabic speaker may be *unjustly* regarded as pushy, aggressive, or even hostile.

The acoustical sounds or vocalizations that replace or accompany language, such as tone, stress, or intonation, but are *not* part of the actual verbal system, may also carry a heavy load of meaning. As the cartoon (Figure 9.2) suggests, these sighs, hisses, moans, discreet coughs, heavy breathing, or clicks of the

Figure 9.2. Coughs and Sighs

Source: Reprinted by permission: Tribune Media Services

tongue may carry broad cultural meanings or simply be highly idiosyncratic. Such sounds may replace language forms; they are as much a part of the speaker's lexicon as words found in the dictionary. Most Americans would understand what the sharp intake of breath means to fellow North Americans, but what does it convey in Japanese NVC? And what about a Latin American hiss?

Imagine you are giving a test in class. After you have handed out the papers, you hear a sharp intake of breath from your Japanese students. Have they been burned? Have they cut their wrists? What is the matter? If you asked yourselves these questions, then you have misread the extralinguistic clues that should have told you that your Japanese students were looking over the test and were concentrating very hard before they took any action.

On the other hand if your students from France were emitting highpitched *Ou! la la's!*, you may be sure that they were not only concentrating but also expressing some dismay at the difficulty of the test. The Japanese may be scratching behind their ears, shaking their heads, or breathing in again, but they are not likely to be mixing the linguistic and paralinguistic as do our French friends.

On the other hand, over in the corner a student from the Middle East, a speaker of Arabic, bounds out of his chair, rushes to the teacher's side, and asks for an explanation of the first question even though the directions are clearly written out. Apparently written instructions are not to be trusted; oral commands are. He returns to his seat emitting moans and groans of obvious dismay. A student from Latin America holds up her hand, signals for the teacher to help her, and looks up inquiringly. Does she want the answer?

Each student was sending out both vocal and nonvocal, verbal and nonverbal messages, but in different patterns. Which reaction would an American teacher operating under the rules of American classrooms be most likely to overlook, most likely to condone, or most likely to consider improper? Should the teacher have understood that to an Arab loudness means strength and the spoken word holds more power than the written? Would she miss the drawing in of the breath and decide that because no questions were asked, there were no problems? Would she understand that personal attention is a vital ingredient in Hispanic communicative patterns? The answers to these questions lie in the ability of such teachers to lay aside their own cultural blinders and observe the scene through other cultural spectacles.

It is doubtful that the full intent of any of the NVC would have been clear to the uninitiated. Consider such nonlinguistic vocalizations as laughing, crying, yawning, or coughing. We can often uncover the meaning of such nonverbal signals by the way in which we describe them. Isn't there a belly laugh, an embarrassed cough, a bored yawn, a suppressed yawn, a warning clearing of the throat, and a sneering smile? The native English speaker could probably identify these nonverbal signals easily. The difficulty arises when what appears to be happiness masks grief, and what appears to be inappropriate is appropriate in another cultural system.

Body Language: Messages without Words

In discussing paralanguage, we have described behaviors that included not only the acoustic elements but also their accompanying body movements. In fact, it is very difficult to talk about any one of the categories of human behavior without talking about them all. Few patterns are exclusively vocal or nonvocal, verbal or nonverbal. The more likely situation is that demonstrated by the smile, kinesic in nature but accompanied by and supplementary to language and its paralinguistic overtones.

Kinesic behavior, or body movement, includes an extensive array of communicative modes and codes; it encompasses movements of all parts of the body, facial expressions, eye movements, head movements, torso positioning, and hand gestures. Much work in this area was done by Birdwhistell (1970, 1972) using linguistic methods of phonemic analysis, as suggested by the Pike model (see Chapter 6) to identify meaningful units of bodily movement, or *kinemes*. He defined kinesics as "the study of the visual aspects of nonverbal, interpersonal communication" (1972:492) and developed an elaborate method of noting the meaning, form and distribution of meaningful "kines," using the linguistic analogy of the Pike model. The complexities of the resulting studies attest to the intricacies of NVC.

Let us now take a look at some cross-cultural variations in body movement that are often encountered and sometimes misinterpreted in the language classroom. The purpose of the following discussion is not to present a definitive list of all NVC—a patently foolish and impossible task—but to call attention to some well-known gestures that carry cultural messages. Because there are so many different facets of NVC and nonverbal communicative behaviors, this discussion can call attention only to some of the cultural variations of particular significance for the classroom teacher. Additional sources of information on specific cultures are included in the list of suggested readings at the end of this chapter.

As an exercise in "reading nonverbal" messages, inspect the eight illustrations that follow. Each indicates a nonverbal message associated with a specific cultural group. First, can you identify what message the person is illustrating, and can you then match this message to the one shown in the second set of illustrations representing American messages?

The answers are contained in the following pages. Play fair! Take the test before you look up the answers! First, try to determine what the person is "communicating" and then try to match the gesture or posture with its North American counterpart. Warning! Some messages may be contradictory!

Write down meanings you would assign these gestures and body positions if you observed them in your classroom. Then study the second set of illustrations. Which ones are variations on the theme? Can you identify the "come here," the "who me?", the silent hello, counting to six, and the measuring height motion? What about the wrinkled noses? Were the messages the same? Which two gestures have no counterparts? How would the ideas expressed by these gestures be communicated verbally or by other gestures?

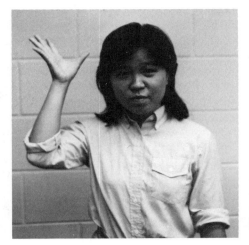

1.A.1

1.A.2

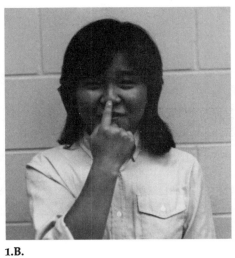

1.B.

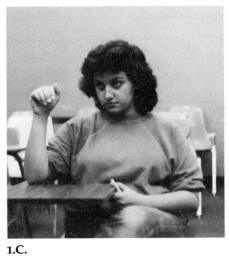

1.C.

1.D.

1.E.

1.F.

1.G.

2.A.

2.B.

2.C.

2.D.

2.E.

2.F.

2.G.

Photos by Ann Morris

If you did not pass this test, do not despair. Unless you have been introduced to some of these variations, you are not likely to have passed.

Now for some answers. In the first set of illustrations, **1.A.1** and **1.A.2** indicate lunacy in Japan and Lebanon respectively. There is no North American counterpart shown. **1.B.** is a gesture which might be used by a Japanese student for self-identification. It is matched by **2.A. 1.C.** is a method of beckoning used widely outside the United States, especially in Latin America and Southern Europe. It is matched by **2.E. 1.D.** relates to counting behavior in Japan and is contrasted with **2.G. 1.E.** is the gesture to indicate human height in Latin America; it contrasts with **2.C.** The North American gesture for measuring height is used in Latin America for animals; that shown in the first set is reserved for people. To mix up the gestures is to commit a serious *faux pas*. **1.F.**, the nose wrinkle, matches **2.D.** In the first instance, however, it is used to indicate an informal greeting in Latin America; in the second it is the North American sign that "something smells bad." The informal American greeting gesture is indicated in **2.B. 1.G.** is a gesture used by Arab students to ask how long a written assignment should be. There is no American counterpart. Such information would most likely be transmitted verbally, although fish (fictitious and real) are generally measured by hand positioning. **2.F.** apparently is strictly North American and is differentially distributed in the population. It symbolizes a personal triumph or success.

Ethnic insult with feet blamed in Laotian's death

LOS ANGELES (AP) — A foot gesture that would be considered innocuous by most people was interpreted as a grevious [sic] insult by a singer from Thailand, and he is accused of shooting the offender to death about seven weeks ago.

The ethnic insult — pointing the sole of a foot at a Thai — has been disclosed as the motive in the March 9 shooting at a Thai restaurant in Hollywood. Deputy District Attorney Josephy Martinez said Tuesday.

"No matter what the insult, it doesn't justify the killings," Martinez said.

Ponsak Trakulrat, 35, pleaded innocent at his arraignment Tuesday to one count of murder and three counts of attempted murder. A preliminary hearing has been scheduled for May 21.

Prosecutors allege that Trakulrat killed Korakanh Piousourinha, 29, a Laotian, and wounded a companion after the Laotian raised his feet to his chair while Trakulrat was singing at the Thai Town restaurant.

Police said Trakulrat, who regularly sang at the restaurant as an amateur, believed Piousourinha was pointing the soles of his feet at him.

Anything to do with the foot can be insulting in some Asian cultures because it rubs in dirt and muck and "it is the lowest part of the body," said Officer Woody Saeaee of the Police Department's Asian Task Force.

Figure 9.3. The Unforgivable

Tampa Tribune, May 1985.

The preceding illustrations should provide some insight into the ways in which kinesic behavior may vary cross-culturally. There are many, many others. In general we can divide the types of significant kinesic behavior into those associated with facial expressions, eye movements, head movements, shoulder and torso movements, hand movements, postures, pantomime, and affective positions (deference, embarrassment, shame) (Taylor 1974: 67–73).

In the classroom particular teacher behavior may convey unexpected messages. Showing the sole of the foot can lead to serious confrontations as can be seen from the newspaper clipping shown in Figure 9.3. Several reviews of significant points of nonverbal impact in the classroom are available (Galloway 1976; Saville-Troike 1978; H. Smith 1979). Miller (1981) lists some characteristics of NVC at work in all classrooms. They include, not surprisingly, paralanguage (intonation), touch, spatial distance, facial expressions, and dress.

That cross-cultural variations occur is also not surprising. A study based on replies of 154 foreign students at the University of Texas and reported at the TESOL 1983 Conference (McMichael and Orr) revealed that the following postures and gestures used by American teachers were offensive, at least to some observers:

hands on hips

slouching

yawning

touching the heads of others

counting people with the index finger and wide arm movement

beckoning with the index finger

Gestures identified in this, and similar studies, as potentially offensive to East Asians include: touching a student on the head, hugging, passing something over another person's head, and pointing or pushing with the foot. To Arabs, offensive gestures involve touching a student of the opposite sex, hugging a student of the opposite sex, showing someone the sole of the foot, handing someone something (especially food) with the left hand, turning the back during a conversation, and winking. To some Latin Americans, the "okay" sign is taboo. (See Figure 9.1.)

It should go without saying that the teachers must be aware of the body language of their students. What is a listening posture? A student from the Middle East may turn his head away and his ear toward the listener when assuming a listening posture; others may close their eyes and turn the head upward. Obligatory eye contact as practiced in the United States is not the universal listening position.

Counting procedures differ. Referential gestures related to people and animals differ. Ways of showing respect differ. In the United States we stand up, but in some parts of the world deference is shown by a bow, a lowering of the body, or even sitting down (Polynesia). Greeting gestures and bodily movements in the United States tend to fit the general pattern of informality. Shaking hands and the prescribed patterns of respect are practiced much less frequently in the United States than abroad.

As previously noted, the values, norms, and beliefs or subjective culture of a particular group will be reflected in the patterns of both its verbal and nonverbal codes. Thus, in the United States the emphasis is upon informality, non-contact, verbal accompaniment to nonverbal kinesic motion, action-oriented gestures often expressing personal feelings of joy, despair, or contempt (clenched fists in the air, head bowed, the finger). Americans are less likely than others, as, for example, the Japanese, to modify gestures or employ a particular pattern in reference to the status of those with whom the communication is made. Americans are more likely to reveal their emotions nonverbally in a pattern of rugged individualism in contrast to the pattern of group harmony found elsewhere.

As we have seen, nonverbal behavior often carries a heavy affective load. How much emotion it is proper to reveal varies cross-culturally. The suppression of negative feelings may result in a smile in the face of appalling tragedy. Most of us had heard of, read about, or seen the "Asian smile," which serves to hide embarrassment, dismay, failure, and grief as well as to signal joy and happiness. Because many cultures limit smiling to the happy side of life, observers of the "Asian smile" may be baffled, disconcerted or even angered by its appearance. To have a student who has failed a course smile, giggle, or even laugh is disconcerting to a teacher. How could anyone laugh lightly when admitting to failure or when saying "I'm sorry"? Should such paralinguistic, linguistic, and body movements be interpreted as representing grief, joy, callousness, or simply insanity?

But, then, let us note what a Japanese student studying in the United States has to say about the matter.

It is a rather annoying task to describe something about body language used in our country because most often we use body language without thinking much about it. But I am afraid there is one thing widely known, that is our queer system of smile. Of course, I myself never thought it queer. Often Japanese people smile when they are angry, sad, or even after they have failured [sic]. Why do we Japanese smile in such a bad condition? Probably because the exposure of sadness or anger is considered "impolite." Why are these expressions considered "impolite"? Although I am Japanese, I am not sure why. Here in America I can have so great a chance to know what is foreign, what is American that someday, surely, I will be able to understand more exactly the secret of the Japanese smile. It is often said that by knowing the characters of other country's people, we can realize those of our own country's people. American people probably say it is natural for a man to express his anger in his face when he feels angry and it is a little crazy for a man to smile when he is really angry. Sometimes we also smile when we do not understand people in front of us while talking.

This student has not only opened the door to understanding more about the smiling behavior of his countrymen, but has also told us how important it is to seek to understand specific cultural patterns and how these patterns are related to the beliefs and values of a given culture. Thus, the focus upon group behavior and group well-being is reflected in the use of the smile to hide what might be unpleasant, disruptive, sad, or incomprehensible.

Finally, we shall do well to think about the meaning of the Japanese term *haragei*, which means "wordless communication." It reflects the value in which communication without words is held. Silence communicates much. Yet, as teachers we exhort our students to speak in order to communicate. Silence is generally considered noncommunication. Saville-Troike (1982:144) points out that such patterns of silence are not just pauses but are deliberate communicative acts. In contrast, verbal reaffirmation is constantly sought by those who come from the oral cultures of the Middle East where to take a man's word as his bond is a mark of respect and confidence.

Because nonverbal communicative behaviors are learned, it follows that students in our classrooms will engage in some conscious as well as unconscious nonverbal learning. However, it is very difficult to know when the cultural switch has been made. As we shall see in a following chapter, culture learning differs greatly from language learning and one of the ways in which it differs is in the recognition of code-switching. For example, if a student from a culture in which showing the sole of the foot to another is taboo displays this behavior toward the teacher or other students in a classroom in the United States, whose code is being used? Is this behavior a mark of disrespect or an attempt to emulate the informality of American college students? Such dilemmas are daily fare in the multicultural classroom. Disrespect lies in the meanings attached to the elements of the code being used. Observations such as those made by the Japanese student emphasize the important relationship between NVC and other cultural patterns, especially those associated with value orientations.

Environmental and Contextual Cues

Finally, there are factors outside the individual that affect interaction, either directly or contextually. Three of these factors are proxemics and spatial arrangements, temporal attitudes, and interactional patterns.

Proxemics. In considering the mechanics of spatial orientation (proxemics), it is important to examine the values often attached to the use of space and how they are reflected in variant cultural patterns.

Edward Hall in *The Hidden Dimension* (1969) points out some ways in which the use and organization of space varies cross-culturally. He classifies spatial distribution in relation to general categories of human proxemic behavior as follows (101–112):

1. *fixed-feature* —behavior associated with fixed features such as buildings, town organization, arrangement of neighborhoods;

2. *semi-fixed feature* —behavior negotiated between the individual and elements of the environment, such as furniture arrangement and organization of living space;

3. *dynamic or informal feature* —behavior regulated by human interaction.

These three categories act together to produce given proxemic behavior. All of these features come into play in the classroom and teaching context.

Given proxemic behavior varies cross-culturally. People in the United States use space generously and measure it by its outside limits or boundaries. They are primarily concerned with the arrangement for given activities and their boundaries. Hall finds contrastive patterns in the design of cities and houses elsewhere. He identifies two European patterns: the radiating star of France and Spain, whereby the cities spread out from the center, and the grid in England, where crossings are made at major intersections. He contrasts these with the Japanese system of marking intersections rather than streets and focusing upon the concept of the center (146–154).

It is easy to find examples of varying cultural patterns in housing plans and in room and furniture arrangements. One has only to contrast the closed walls of the houses of southern Europe and the Middle East with the broad lawns and gardens that surround many American homes and provide the required "elbow room." The former type homes enclose the family; American homes advertise the occupants' financial state, need for space, and a type of outer privacy which says, "Do Not Trespass. My home begins here." On the other hand, the Japanese home, in which furniture is sparse and rooms serve many purposes also allows personal privacy—not by surrounding space but by ordered inner space and moveable partitions. Each arrangement serves to illustrate the cultural values of the given group. Americans like to draw boundaries and mark off turf. The peoples in Middle Eastern and Mediterranean cultures live in close proximity in enclosed spaces with unobstructed views but separated by high and often inviolate domestic walls. The Japanese also live in close proximity in separate private worlds enjoyed in group contexts.

In terms of interactional space, Hall's four spatial zones of social relations are almost too well-known to repeat. He simply suggests that the American pattern can be described in terms of intimate distance (0–18 inches); personal distance (1.5–4 feet); social distance (4–12 feet); and public distance (12–25 or more feet). Each range has a near phase and a far phase (Hall 1969:116–125). It is the particular genius of Edward Hall to state such generalizations, based upon his own powers of observation, and seldom be called to recant.

Hall reminds us that Americans are generally considered to be part of a non-contact culture, all the back slapping and social kissing notwithstanding. People from other cultures, especially Hispanic, often consider Americans to be very cold. On the other hand, the Japanese, who frown upon kissing in public and other tactile communication, may find North Americans to be overly demonstrative. It is certain that the Japanese professor who had come to the airport in Japan to bid a group of visiting Americans farewell was shocked and disconcerted when one husky and enthusiastic American woman embraced him warmly and said, "I just *had* to do that!"

Temporal Behavior.

"Time is money."

"Don't waste time!"

"I need to spend some time with you."

"You are just in time."

"Be on time!"

If there is truth in our proverbs and metaphors then these expressions, familiar to most North Americans and subscribed to, at least superficially, by many, reflect an attitude toward time as a commodity, an entity, something to be earned, spent, not wasted, and even saved.

Edward Hall has pointed out (1969) that North Americans regard time in a monochronic manner (M-time), while much of the rest of the world operates on polychronic time (P-time). That is to say, North Americans are very task-conscious but are habituated to doing one thing at a time. The type of cultural time which allows for multiple activities is very likely to upset M-time people.

To Hall P-time cultures stress time as a "point rather than a ribbon or a road, and that point is sacred" (Hall 1977:17). This in part then explains the fact that punctuality is a sometime thing in P-time cultures, while it is a matter of little or no negotiation in the North American M-time culture. In the latter, time is a road to be traveled from past to future.

To Americans, who pride themselves on punctuality and a fast-paced life, at least in the urban areas, the recent revelation that Japanese clocks were more punctual than theirs and that the Japanese hurried through the daily chores of life at a faster pace was probably not only surprising but also disappointing (Levine and Wolff 1985).

Attitudes toward time form an important foundation for a web of appropriate behaviors concerning time in the North American context. Invitations should be issued in advance; guests should arrive within a given period of time; and students should observe deadlines for homework, class arrival, and departure. Yet an American teacher who arrives at a class in Japan within the approved time (plus or minus the approved leeway) is likely to find she is already late and the class patiently awaiting her delayed arrival. Students are expected to arrive five to ten minutes before the class and seat themselves; *she* was expected to make her entrance on the dot. It is disconcerting to be beaten at one's own game.

Again Hall points out the Arab cultural time patterns divide sets of time into 1. no time at all; 2. now (of varying duration); and 3. forever (too long) (1959:137). Coupled with adherence to ritual forms of greeting and hospitality, this approach to time often presents problems for those who would conduct business negotiations at a faster pace.

Time relationships in Latin cultures have been parodied to the point of stereotyping. Although by North American standards, these cultures appear to "squander" time, its uses are carved to fit personal commitments to cultural patterns that emphasize personal contact, class and status, and the exchanging of social pleasantries. The latter being seen as essential in appropriate human interaction, time thus spent is not wasted but put to good social purpose.

Most language teachers who are dealing with multicultural groups are painfully aware of how difficult it is to keep to a schedule of "five-minute speeches." The reports seem to wander off in all directions and what should, according to the teacher, take only a class period, stretches over days. It all depends on whose "five minutes" are being counted.

Interactional Patterns. Interactional patterns are units of behavior and their attendant attitudes; they are related to the manner, content, and purposes of communication.

Let us consider the phases of communication first. There are culturally approved ways of greeting, beginning conversations, taking turns, and leave taking. For example, North Americans are well known for their desire in business encounters to "get down to business" and "not waste time with preliminaries." Anyone who has tried to approach Latin Americans or people from Middle Eastern or Far Eastern cultures with such direct behavior knows that "getting down to business" is an important part of the negotiation. As noted above, in cultures in which status and role are clearly defined and in which formality is de rigeur, launching communicative episodes can be very lengthy indeed.

Hall states that the temporal and spatial orientations of a given group may have a great deal to do with what takes place where. For example, in the United States, as Gudykunst and Kim (1984:155) point out, business "can be discussed almost anywhere, except perhaps in church" (155). It can be discussed even there if it pertains to church business, or the business of the elders.

Once communication has been undertaken, the communicants interact in a kind of synchrony, which Hall finds is culture-specific. This synchrony is revealed through body motion and language. Hall has suggested that all interactional movements occur in an action chain whose links lead from a beginning to an end. These action chains vary cross-culturally. Hall proposes that the commitment to the completion of the action chain is greater in a high-context culture than in a low-context culture. He attributes this to the degree of involvement between people and sensitivity to nonverbal and other context cues in high-context situations. (1977:150). (See Chapter 5.) Conversely, low-context cultures, such as in the United States, allow for greater individuality and less commitment to the finishing off of a chain.

In connection with interaction patterns, differences in the degree of expressiveness, intimacy of address, degree of emotion and animation, degree of frankness, degree of intensity and persistency, as well as volume are all areas of cross-cultural variations, according to Jensen (1970:154–158).

9.7 BACK IN THE CLASSROOM

The preceding discussion of the major features of nonverbal behavior and NVC and some cross-cultural variations should serve to alert the reader to the importance of these codes and channels.

What should be done in the classroom? Should NVC be taught explicitly? Should our students be instructed in all the taboos, niceties, and values associated with the NVC code of the target group? More detailed answers to these questions will be given in the chapter dealing with goals and objectives of culture training. Take a look at the classroom we encountered at the beginning of the chapter. Would you change your answers to the questions posed? Can you imagine what types of NVC were taking place?

No one should be more aware of the communicative power of nonverbal behavior than a teacher, and no teacher should be more aware than the one who steps into a multicultural classroom and assumes the posture and expression of the friendly, smiling, responsive, supportive facilitator considered to be the very model of a modern language teacher. The impression given to the astounded students may be quite at odds with the intended message.

FOR STUDY AND DISCUSSION

1. Identify these terms:

   kinemes

   paralanguage

   nonverbal communication

   digital/analogical expression

   kinesics

   proxemics

2. Identify ten hand or body gestures used in classrooms in the United States or in a culture with which you are familiar. Would all of these patterns be "understood" by natives of other cultures? How could we discover their meanings for these students? What modifications in the use of gestures would you suggest in dealing with your cultural group?

3. Can you identify any significant patterns of paralanguage associated with your cultural group which might be of significance in intercultural communication? Illustrate one for the class.

4. Should the patterns of nonverbal communication be taught along with the linguistic forms of a language? What problems might be encountered in trying to incorporate this type of instruction in an ESL/EFL program?

5. Devise a short (five-minute) demonstration for an ESL/EFL class illustrating one gesture or set of gestures identified in question 2.

6. Which of the hazards of the superficial study of nonverbal communication patterns as discussed by Jensen is most important in the language teaching/learning context?

7. Bruneau (1982:297) stated that "the temporal dimension is a most significant factor in intercultural communication." Do you agree? If so, what types of cross-cultural variations might be expected in the classroom? Try to go beyond the stereotypic examples of "mañana" and prompt trains. Look for what is considered time well spent and time wasted, the division between business and pleasure, and the various definitions of being "on time" and "in time."

CULTURE LEARNING EXERCISE

1. Taylor (1980) suggests four categories for NVC: plus or minus verbal supportive, and plus or minus conscious. Using these cells explore your behavior or that of a colleague. Are there some messages being sent of which you have been unaware? Try to identify at least one example in each cell.

2. Explore nonverbal behavior in your target culture. Check out the examples used in this chapter. Does your informant indicate any differences? What are they? Try to discover some new ones.

3. Refer to the list of teacher behaviors identified in this chapter as potentially offensive to various cultural groups. Would these behaviors be considered inappropriate or offensive in your target culture? Are there others that have not been listed that would not be suitable? Inventory your own teaching behaviors. How often do you engage in any of these activities? If you use them, have you noted any student reaction, either negative or positive?

FOR FURTHER READING

R. Birdwhistell. 1970. *Kinesics and Context. Essays on Body Motion Communication.* This book contains Birdwhistell's formulation of the field of kinesics or the study of body movement. The terminology and methods of analysis he devised are explained in this volume.

V. Clark, P. Eschholz, and A. Rosa (eds.). 1972. "Space and the Language of the Body." Part V. *Language. Introductory Readings.* This section contains readings on various facets of NVC by Hall, Birdwhistell, Fast, and others. The nearly one hundred pages contained in this section offer a general selection of readings on the subject.

P. Ekman, E. Sorensen, and W. Friesen. 1969. "Pan-cultural Elements in Facial Displays of Emotion." As a general discussion of the universal features of human emotion, this article, as well as many others written by Ekman and his associates, is recommended reading for those interested in the cross-cultural similarities and differences exhibited in emotional displays.

J. Fast, 1970. *Body Language.* This is a discussion of the subject of nonverbal communication, couched in popular terms and from the American perspective. It is a good introduction to the field, but do not be bewitched into thinking that "reading" nonverbal behavior is quite as easy as this author would have us believe.

E. Hall. 1959. *The Silent Language.* This small volume remains a still fresh and powerful statement about the complex nature of human culture, its unseen power, and its many manifestations. Although much of the terminology and analytical categories suggested have not been embraced in the field of intercultural communication, the insights Hall offered as to the many ways and means by which communication takes place—in time and space—have immeasurably enriched the field of cross-cultural inquiry. Of particular interest are Chapter 3, "The Vocabulary of Culture," and Chapter 5, "Culture is Communication." Enough of us have recognized ourselves in Hall's examples to feel the power of his observations and to become more aware of contrastive patterns in other cultural groups. Although anecdotal in nature, Hall's examples prod the reader into the process of cultural self-examination so necessary to cultural consciousness-raising. His "Map of Culture" (174–175) is reproduced in this book as a guide to cultural inquiry. Perhaps Hall's work remains so challenging today because all of us must be continually reminded that we are not only served by our cultures but also, to some degree, enslaved by them.

E. Hall. 1969. *The Hidden Dimension.* This volume, which followed his immensely popular *The Silent Language*, concentrates on cross-cultural variations in the use of space, elaborating on many of the themes presented in his first volume concerning the uses of space and the contrastive patterns among Germans, English, French, and Arabs. Few readers of English are unfamiliar with his description of the four distance zones observed in a group of "non-contact, middle-class, healthy adults, mainly natives of the northeastern seaboard of the United States" (116). Hall coined the term "proxemics" to describe the "interrelated observations and theories of man's use of space as a specialized elaboration of culture" (1).

E. Hall. 1977. *Beyond Culture.* This volume continues in the same vein as the two previous works, but is more explicit in defining Hall's position on the nature of culture, particularly in its covert mode. Following in the footsteps of his mentors, Boas, Sapir and Whorf, Hall, the anthropologist, brings into question some assumptions concerning the "truth" and "reality" of Western logic. He makes a strong case for the existence and power of that which is cultural but hidden. The chapters covering the relationship of context and meaning (Chapters 7 and 8) are quoted in this book and in nearly every other volume devoted to language and culture. The reader is urged to read these chapters and those already recommended in order to comprehend more fully the force of Hall's conceptualization and the many allusions to be found in the literature of the field of intercultural communication and in second language acquisition.

P. Harrison. 1983. *Behaving Brazilian. A Comparison of Brazilian and North American Social Behavior.* This book compares social behavior (NVC) in Brazil and the United States. Types of behavior associated with conversation, food, business, and family are among those described. In addition, the contextualization of the behavior and gestures discussed is an additional bonus for the reader.

J. Jensen. 1970. "Perspective on Nonverbal Communication" (133–161). This chapter in Jensen's book is an excellent discussion of the main categories of nonverbal cues in body movement and gestures. Of particular interest is the section dealing with the problems attendant upon superficial study of nonverbal communication in the intercultural context.

M. Knapp. 1972. *Nonverbal Communication in Human Interaction.* This is a general review of nonverbal communication. It includes a selected bibliography for each unit.

R. Levine and E. Wolff. 1985. "Social Time: The Heartbeat of Culture" (28–35). This is an interesting discussion of the social uses of time with some very enlightening examples of cross-cultural variation.

H. Miner. 1956. "Body Ritual Among the Nacirema" (503–507). This satirical ethnographic account of life among a group known as the Nacirema is must reading for all North Americans and great fun for all who are not. To be seen through the eyes of the friendly ethnographer is a privilege none of us should miss.

D. Morris, P. Collett, P. Marsh and M. O'Shaughnessy. 1980. *Gestures: Their Origins and Distribution.* This is a report of a study of 20 key gestures and their distribution in Western Europe. The methods used to map gestural distribution in 40 locations were developed for this study and represent adaptations of methods used in mapping the distribution of linguistic variations. This book is interesting to the student of NVC both for its content and for the description of data collection methods and analysis. It also contains an extensive bibliography on the subject of gestures.

C. Nine Curt. 1976. *Non-Verbal Communication in Puerto Rico.* Nine Curt's observations concerning contrasts between American (Anglo) and Latin American NVC are those of a sensitive, knowledgeable, and astute observer. Although this author's descriptions are generally limited to Puerto Rican culture, much of what she reports is also generalizable to other Latin American contexts.

A. Pennycook. 1985. "Actions Speak Louder than Words: Paralanguage, Communication, and Education" (259–282). This article reviews the subject of nonverbal communication, which is termed paralanguage, and provides very concrete suggestions for the development of paralinguistic competence in second language learners. Although the author's insistence upon subsuming kinesics, proxemics, and paraverbal features under the term "paralanguage" serves more to confuse than to clarify, the discussions of the components of "paralanguage" and research in the field are very succinct and helpful. The many bibliographic references not only attest to a high level of scholarship but also provide a rich source of information for those who would delve further into the mysteries of NVC.

K. Scherer and P. Ekman (eds.). 1982. *Handbook of Methods in Nonverbal Behavior Research.* This handbook reports on the various methods and problems associated with nonverbal communication research. As a joint publication of the Cambridge University Press and *Editions de la Maison des Sciences de l'Homme*, it represents an international and "authoritative critical review of each of a number of separate research methods relevant to nonverbal behavior" (ix). It is heavy going but well worth the effort.

A. Wolfgang (ed.) 1979a. *Nonverbal Behavior: Applications and Cultural Implications.* This book of readings contains articles relating to the role of nonverbal behavior in interpersonal and intercultural communication. Part 3 is devoted to discussions of the implications of nonverbal behavior in teaching. Wolfgang's article in this section, "The Teacher and Nonverbal Behavior in the Multicultural Classroom" (159–174) is especially instructive.

Part II

Practicum: Theory in Practice

Chapter 10

My Way, Our Way, Their Way: Cultural Values, Beliefs, and Assumptions

Our perception of foreign cultures is usually based not on their complex reality, but on the simplified image they project. The clearer and more sharply defined that image is, the more convinced we will be that we are intimately acquainted with it: it is a mere outward confirmation of knowledge we already possess.

—Juan Goytisolo
"Captives of Our 'Classics'"
The New York Times Book Review
May 26, 1985:1

In the course of human interaction, evaluations are assigned to given types of behavior, attitudes, and kinds of social contact. Taken together they form the belief and value system, the cultural premises and assumptions, and the foundation for law, order, and the world view of given cultural groups. These systems embrace a number of assumptions about how the world is put together. Hiebert and Winans in their book *Cultural Anthropology* (1976:356) write:

> Some of these assumptions, called "existential postulates," deal with the nature of reality, the organization of the universe, and the ends and purposes of human life. Others, values and norms, differentiate between good and evil, right and wrong. Some of these assumptions are made explicit in the beliefs and myths of the people. Others appear to the anthropologist to be implicit in people's behavior. Taken together, the assumptions the anthropologist uses to explain a people's total response to their universe are sometimes called a "world view."

You may recall that the connection between the world view of given groups and their language was one of the major points of discussion in connection with

189

the Sapir-Whorf hypothesis (Chapter 7). In addition, the power of perception in the interpretation of intercultural contact has been emphasized in the publications of Singer (1982), Condon and Yousef (1975), and others cited in previous chapters. Beliefs, value systems, and world view often combine with other features of social and cultural organization to provide shared cultural symbols.

10.1 A SURPRISING CASE IN POINT

For example, all types of human organization provide rules for relationships between the sexes. Not only do these rules show great variation cross-culturally and interculturally through time, but they also give expression to the cultural values, beliefs, and assumptions concerning these relationships. Marriage is a universal institution, but the roles of wife and husband, child and parent differ in practice and in evaluation. Let us listen in on a brief conversation between an interviewer (Speaker A), a young woman from New Delhi (Speaker B), and an American female graduate student (Speaker C), concerning marriage arrangements.

> A: In an arranged marriage, do you meet each other before the wedding?
>
> B: Sometimes. It depends on the situation you are in. There was no way we could see each other until the day of the wedding.
>
> C: Your marriage was arranged? Weren't you afraid?
>
> B: I had just met him once, and that was six months ago on top of that and not very personally because the whole family was present. And there is a limit that you can know somebody in the presence of the whole family.

In a previous exchange Speaker B had commented on the closeness of family ties in India and emphasized her trust in their choice. She added: "If the families arrange the marriage, you just do it. . . . I wasn't afraid."

The clashing of assumptions about the role of family and the individual was clear; beliefs or expectations about the "problems" of arranged marriages on the part of the graduate student were a surprise to Speaker B. She later added that "In India, the family is such a big part of your life. It is what you value most. . . . Your grandparents always live with you."

10.2 DEFINITIONS

It is useful at this juncture to make some distinctions between *beliefs* and *values*.

Beliefs

Beliefs are generally taken to mean a "mental acceptance or conviction in the truth or actuality of something." (*American Heritage Dictionary*, 1969:121). A belief links an object or event and the characteristics that distinguish it from others (Samovar, Porter and Jain 1981:39). These authors explain:

> The degree to which we believe that an event or object possesses certain characteristics reflects the level of our subjective probability [belief] and, consequently, the depth or intensity of our belief. The more certain we are in a belief, the greater is the intensity of that belief.

This is well attested to in the power of religious beliefs. Samovar, Porter, and Jain identify three types of beliefs, all of which are of concern to us. They are experiential, informational, and inferential (39–40). Experiential beliefs come from direct personal experience, of course; they are integrated at the intrapersonal level. The second type involves information. This is transferred on the interpersonal level and shows great cultural variation. Here cultural beliefs are stated, transferred, learned, and practiced. Informational beliefs are connected with what these authors call "authority belief," or credible information sources. If a group of people believes that exercising increases the individual's physical and mental well-being, these believers may also be willing to accept athletes as authority figures even though the testimonies of these idols range beyond their physical prowess. Witness the selling success of Olympic champions and football stars in promoting breakfast food or panty hose.

Inferential beliefs are those which go beyond direct observation and information. These concern rules of logic, argumentation, rhetoric, and even establishment of facts (the scientific method). They involve the ways of thinking discussed in Chapter 7 in relation to the Sapir-Whorf hypothesis. Samovar, Porter, and Jain comment (1981:40):

> Although internal logic systems differ from one individual to another within a culture, they differ more from one culture to another. The most dramatic difference in cultural variance in thinking lies between Western and Eastern cultures. The Western world has a logic system built upon Aristotelian principles, and it has evolved ways of thinking that embody these principles. . . . Eastern cultures, however, developed before and without the benefit of Athens or Aristotle. As a consequence, their logic systems are sometimes called non-Aristotelian, and they can often lead to quite different sets of beliefs.

The pedagogical implications of cultural variation in patterns of thinking and argumentation are considered in Chapter 15.

Values

Values bring affective force to beliefs. Some of these values are shared with others of our kind; some are not. Thus, we all adhere to some of the beliefs and values generally accepted within our cultures; we reject others. Values are related to what is seen to be good, proper, and positive, or the opposite. Values are learned and may be normative in nature. They change through time and are seldom shared in specifics by members of different generations, although certain themes will prevail. For example, the positive attributions placed upon competitiveness, individualism, action, and other general principles that pervade the belief and value orientation of members of the North American culture of the United States remain. They include the constitutionally guaranteed and socially valued "unalienable rights to life, liberty, and the pursuit of happiness" in individualistic, action-oriented, and competitive ways. These values have endured; their expression varies from generation to generation.

A cultural value system "represents what is expected or hoped for, required or forbidden." It is not a report of actual conduct but is "the inductively based, logically ordered set of criteria of evaluations" by which conduct is judged and sanctions applied (Albert 1968:288).

10.3 THE VALUE/BELIEF PUZZLE

Value and belief systems, with their supporting cultural postulates and world views, are complex and difficult to assess. They form an interlocking system, reflecting and reflective of cultural history and forces of change. They provide the bases for the assignment of cultural meaning and evaluation. Values are desired outcomes as well as norms for behavior; they are dreams as well as reality. They are embraced by some and not others in a community; they may be the foundations for accepted modes of behavior, but are as frequently overridden as observed. They are also often the hidden force that sparks reactions and fuels denials. Unexamined assignment of these characteristics to all members of a group is an exercise in stereotyping.

Attributions and Evaluations

Often values attributions and evaluations of the behaviors of "strangers" are based on the value and belief systems of the observers. Have you heard or made any of the following statements? Guilty or not?

- Americans are cold.
- Americans don't like their parents. Just look, they put their mothers and fathers in nursing homes.
- The Chinese are nosy. They're always asking such personal questions.
- Spaniards must hate animals. Look what they do to bulls!
- Marriages don't last in the United States.
- Americans are very friendly. I met a nice couple on a tour and they asked me to visit them.

- Americans ask silly questions. They think we all live in tents and drink nothing but camel's milk! They ought to see our airport!

- Americans just pretend to be friendly; they really aren't. They say, "Drop by sometime," but, when I did, they didn't seem very happy to see me. Of course, it was ten o'clock at night!

How should such statements be received? With anger? With explanation? With understanding and anger? Should one just ignore such patent half-truths, stereotypic judgments, and oversimplifications? Before indulging in any of the above actions, consider what can be learned from such statements. First, what do these statements reveal? The speakers appear to be concerned about families, disturbed by statistics, apt to form opinions on limited data (friendliness), given to forming hasty and unwarranted generalizations (Spanish bullfighting), and angered by the ignorance of others. No one cultural group has a corner on such behavior. Second, we might be able to guess how certain speakers might feel about divorce, hospitality, or even animals. Third, the observations, while clearly not applicable to all members of the groups about which the comments were made, represent the speakers' perceptions. To many, Americans *are* seen as cold and uncaring. Because perceptions and native value and belief systems play such important roles in communication, it is important to recognize and deal with these perceptions—correct or incorrect, fair or unfair.

In the following section of this chapter the concept of value orientations will be explored. This will be followed by a review of the major value orientations associated with people from the United States. These orientations will be contrasted with those of other culture groups. Such an approach to cross-cultural variations in values and beliefs is far more productive than flat denial or even anger. As we form evaluative frames of reference for ourselves and hold them up to the frames of others we shall, at the very least, learn a great deal about ourselves.

Value Orientations

Compiling a list of cultural values, beliefs, attitudes, and assumptions would be an almost endless and quite unrewarding endeavor. Writers in the field of intercultural communication have generally adopted the concept of value orientations suggested by Florence Kluckhohn and Fred Strodtbeck (1961).

In setting forth a value orientation approach to cross-cultural variation, Kluckhohn and Strodtbeck (1961:10) pointed out that such a theory was based upon three assumptions:

1. There are a limited number of human problems to which all cultures must find solutions.

2. The limited number of solutions may be charted along a range or continuum of variations.

3. Certain solutions are favored by members in any given culture group, but all potential solutions are present in every culture.

In their schema, Kluckhohn and Strodtbeck suggested that values cluster around five universal human problems involving man's relationship to the environment, human nature, time, activity, and human interaction. The authors further proposed that the orientations of any society could be charted along these dimensions. Although variability could be found within a group, there were always dominant or preferred positions. Culture-specific profiles could be constructed. Such profiles should not be regarded as statements about individual behavior, but rather as tendencies around which social behavioral norms, rules, values, beliefs, and assumptions are clustered. As such, they might influence individual behavior as other cultural givens do; like other rules, they may be broken, changed, or ignored.

In the Kluckhohn and Strodtbeck classification, three focal points in the range of variations are posited for each type of orientation. In the man-to-nature continuum variations range from a position of human mastery over nature, to harmony with nature, to subjugation to nature. Most industrialized societies represent the mastery orientation; the back-to-nature counterculture of young adults during the 1960s and 1970s, the harmonious stance; and many peasant populations, the subjugation orientation.

The time dimension offers stops at the past, present, and future. Human nature orientation is charted along a continuum stretching from good to evil with some of both in the middle. The activity orientation moves from doing to being-in-becoming to being. Finally, the relational orientation ranges from the individual to the group with concern with the continuation of the group, as an intermediate focal point. Examples of such orientations are contained in Chapters 3, 4, and 5 in Condon and Yousef (1975). These chapters examine cultural variations in the five dimensions listed. Also Chapter 3 in Gudykunst and Kim (1984: 39–60), "Cultural Influences on the Process," contains a very cogent discussion of these orientations with explanatory comments and examples.

Value orientations only represent "good guesses" about why people act the way they do. Condon and Yousef warn us that statements made or scales constructed are only part of an "as if" game. That is to say, people act as if they believed in a given set of values (118–119). Because the individuals in any cultural group exhibit great variation, any of the orientations suggested might well be found in nearly every culture. It is the general pattern that is sought. Value orientations are important to us as intercultural communicators because often whatever one believes, values, and assumes are the crucial factors in communication.

10.4 CONTRASTIVE ORIENTATIONS

Let us take some American cultural patterns that have been identified as crucial in cross-cultural communication and consider what assumptions, values, and attitudes support them. Edward C. Stewart was a pioneer in examining such American behavior in a cross-cultural perspective. His book, *American Cultural Patterns. A Cross-Cultural Perspective* (1972) describes dominant characteristics of middle class Americans. Stewart distinguishes between cultural assumptions and values and what he called cultural norms. Cultural norms are explicit and repeatedly invoked by people to describe or justify their actions. They represent instances in which the behavior and the value attached to it seem at odds. Stewart writes, "Because cultural norms are related to behavior as clichés, rituals or as cultural platitudes, they provide inaccurate descriptions of behavior" (19). He points out that Americans are devoted to the concept of self-reliance but accept social security, borrow money, and expect a little help from their friends. Culture bearers are usually more aware of their cultural norms than their systems of values and assumptions. As Stewart explains, "being fundamental to the individual's outlook, they [the assumptions and values] are likely to be considered as a part of the real world and therefore remain unquestioned" (20).

Table 10.1, based on references in Stewart (1972) and Condon and Yousef (1975), illustrates some of the general value orientations identified with North Americans. The left-hand column indicates what the polar point of the orientational axis might represent. The Contrast American column does not describe any particular culture, but rather represents an opposite orientation. Of course, the American profile is drawn in broad strokes and describes the mainstream culture; ethnic diversity is of necessity blurred in this sweeping treatment.

TABLE 10.1 SOME IMPLICIT CULTURAL ASSUMPTIONS

North American (USA)	Contrast American
Personal control of the environment	Nature dominating man
Change inevitable and desirable	Unchanging; traditional
Equality of opportunity	Class structure dominant; hierarchical
Individualism	Interdependence but individuality
Future orientation	Present or past orientation
Action orientation	Being orientation
Directness and openness	Suggestive; consensus-seeking; group orientation
Practicality; pragmatic; rational	Feeling orientation; philosophical
Problem-solving orientation	Inactive; enduring; seeking help from others
Cause-and-effect logic	Knowing
Informality	Formality
Competition	Group progress
Do-it-yourself approach to life	Intermediaries

Thus, with the reservations noted above, it can be said that in the relationship of human beings and nature, Americans assume and thus value and believe in doing something about environmental problems. Nature can and should be changed. In addition, change is right and good and to be encouraged. That the pace of change has increased to a bewildering point in the United States at the present time presents problems, but, as yet, change has not been seen as particularly detrimental.

Equality of opportunity is linked to individualism, lack of rigid hierarchies, informality, and other cultural givens. It is manifested in American laws regarding social conduct, privacy, and opportunity. This contrasts with an ascriptive social order in which class and birth provide the bases for social control and interaction.

The achievement orientation calls for assessment of personal achievement, a latter-day Horatio Alger (Lee Iacocca) orientation. A future orientation is joined to the positive value accorded change and action. Directness and openness are contrasted to a more consensus-seeking approach in which group harmony is placed above solving problems.

Cause-and-effect logic joined to a problem-solving orientation and a pragmatic approach to problems defines the much-vaunted scientific method. Intuition and other approaches to evidence, fact, and "truth" are associated with being orientations and philosophical approaches to knowledge and knowing. Competition and a do-it-yourself approach to life are well served by a future orientation, individualism, and the desire for change.

The statements above simply point out some very general orientations that have driven and, to some degree, still guide North American society. Change is always in the air. Many have pointed out, as Stewart himself does, that these orientations represent white middle class American values. They do. They serve the purpose, however, of providing a frame of reference for cross-cultural comparison.

Table 10.2 offers a contrastive look at some American and Japanese values. Such culture-specific contrast alerts us to the need to examine our cultural values and assumptions from the perspective of others. As one studies the dimensions of contrast, one cannot help but marvel at the communication that does take place despite such diversity. Okabe, in drawing upon Japanese observations about some well-known American values, reveals a new perspective to us. For example, the bamboo whisk and octopus pot metaphors refer to a reaching out tendency in the United States as opposed to the drawing inward of the Japanese.

Omote means outside and *omote/ura* combines both the inside and outside world. Okabe (1983:25) quotes Professor Yuji Aida of Kyoto University:

In the heterogeneous, egalitarian, *sasara*-type, doing, pushing culture of the United States, there is no distinction between the *omote* and the *ura* aspects of

TABLE 10.2 VALUE ASSUMPTIONS OF EAST AND WEST: JAPAN AND THE UNITED STATES.

Values concerning	United States	Japan
1. Nature of Society and Culture	heterogeneity; horizontal society	homogeneity; verticality
	guilt	shame
	sasara (bamboo whisk)	*takotsubo* (octopus pot) (draws in)
	doing	being
	pushing	pulling
	omote predominates	*omote/ura* (outside/inside) (*ura* more real)
2. Interpersonal Relationships	independence; I/You clash	We over I; *amae*
	symmetrical relationships	complementary relationships
	informality	formality
	achieved status	ascribed status

Source: Roichi Okabe, "Cultural Assumptions of East and West: Japan and the United States," W.B. Gudykunst (ed.) *Intercultural Communication Theory: Current Perspectives* (Beverly Hills, Ca.: Sage, 1983), pp. 21–37.

culture. . . . In the hierarchical *takotsubo*-type, being, pulling culture of Japan, . . . a clear-cut distinction should always be made between the *omote* and the *ura* dimensions of culture, the former being public, formal, and conventional, and the latter private, informal, and unconventional. The Japanese tend to conceive of the *ura* world as being more real, more meaningful.

Interpersonal relationships contrast on the basis of the role of the individual and group interaction. Japanese patterns are characterized by formality and complementary relationships that stress the value of dependence or *amae*. Doi (1973:28) identifies *amae* as the key to understanding Japanese society. Okabe comments (26):

The concept of *amae* . . . underlies the Japanese emphasis on the group over the individual, the acceptance of constituted authority, and the stress on particularistic rather than universalistic relationships. . . . In the homogenous, vertical society of Japan . . . the dominant value is conformity to or identity with the group: The Japanese insist upon the insignificance of the individual.

Symmetrical relationships focus on the similarities of individuals; complementary relationships exploit differences in age, sex, role and status. J. Condon (1984:20) points out:

There are many ways in which the Japanese publicly acknowledge a social hierarchy—in the use of language, in seating arrangements at social gatherings, in bowing to one another and hundreds of others. Watch Japanese greet each other and the principles will become quite apparent. Notice who bows lower, who waits for the other to go first, who apologizes more: (1) younger defers to older; (2) female defers to male; (3) student defers to teacher; (4) the seller's bow is lower than the buyer's; and (6) [sic] in a school club or organization where ranks are fixed, the lower ranked is, of course, subordinate.

These features of interpersonal relationships lead to an emphasis on the public self in the United States and on the private self in Japan, Americans being more open in the demonstration of personal feelings and attitudes than the Japanese (Barnlund 1975).

Contrast in forms of thought and rhetoric discussed in the Okabe article are summarized in Chapter 15. The observations made in this article refer to Japanese patterns, but they are useful in alerting any teacher in a multicultural classroom to the areas of critical variation.

10.5 MYTHS AND MATCH

How are these cultural assumptions, values, and beliefs woven into our daily lives? They are often hidden in our conversations, social behaviors, and unconscious evaluations. They may represent what we wish were true rather than what is. They are sometimes the clues by which strangers try to understand and, perhaps, often judge us. They are called myths because they represent our traditional stories and reflect our world views, real or imagined.

Apple Pie, Motherhood, and . . .

Complete Exercise 10.1. First, label the statements true or false according to your assessment of the prevailing American orientation. Mark them according to your own "version." Then translate or paraphrase each of these in terms of cultural meanings and their accompanying behavioral norms. For example, Number 1 speaks to individual responsibility and might informally be paraphrased as "Get cracking!" Finally, contrast these terms with those evidenced in your target culture. Try to elicit contrastive statements.

Exercise 10.1. Apple Pie, Motherhood, and. . . .

Answer the following questions in the manner in which you believe most North Americans would respond. Then relate them to any of the cultural values and assumptions listed by Stewart or other authors cited.

TRUE/FALSE

_____ 1. It is better to help yourself than to take help from another person.

_____ 2. Someone should always be in charge of a group activity.

_____ 3. What you do is less important than what you think.

_____ 4. Men should not cry when hurt.

_____ 5. To die for a friend is a great virtue.

_____ 6. Everyone should have an equal chance.

_____ 7. The future is behind us; what counts is the past.

_____ 8. Obedience and respect for authority are goals for education.

_____ 9. Time is money and it is a sin to waste either.

_____ 10. It is better to try and fail than never to try at all.

_____ 11. It is better to do something than just sit around.

_____ 12. Group improvement is better than self-improvement; indeed, self-improvement is achieved through group improvement.

_____ 13. There are no answers to some problems.

_____ 14. Everyone needs breathing room.

_____ 15. Man and nature, animate and inanimate, are one.

_____ 16. Education is the doorway to success.

_____ 17. Success is just around the corner.

_____ 18. There is a solution to every problem; we just haven't invented it yet.

_____ 19. Smile and the world smiles with you.

_____ 20. Life is a lottery; it can be won with a little luck.

_____ 21. It's not whether you win or lose but how you play the game.

_____ 22. One should mix business with pleasure. After all, life is short.

Values Clarification Practice

Bringing to a conscious level the assumptions and premises underlying belief and value systems can be an important step in culture learning. In Exercise 10.1 you were asked to examine and discuss some expressions that carry culture-specific evaluative force. We used the American perspective. Gaining the perspectives of others is, of course, important, but is hard to achieve until native orientations are understood. The following exercise is an example of how proverbs and aphorisms can help clarify cultural values and beliefs and their force.

Exercise 10.2 is similar to the preceding exercise. In this case, familiar proverbs are used to facilitate both language and culture learning. The statements of "Apple Pie, Motherhood, and . . ." are useful to provide some values clarification training for native speakers of American English and those of the majority culture. They serve other ethnic groups and foreign students less well because the cultural secrets are hidden and the form of a given statement is unlikely to be presented in quite this way in the real world. Proverbs are universal; often the students will express the same idea in their native proverbs. When comparisons are made, it is often found that although the values appear the same, their expressions and attendant behaviors are not.

Exercise 10.2. And That's the Truth

A. The proverbs or statements below will be familiar to many North Americans. Try to identify the cultural value underlying each statement; then determine to what degree each is reflected in cultural patterns and behavior.

1. Cleanliness is next to godliness.
2. God helps those who help themselves.
3. A penny saved is a penny earned.
4. A man's home is his castle.
5. A woman's place is in the home.
6. Actions speak louder than words.
7. It's not whether you win or lose but how you play the game.
8. Winning isn't everything; winning is the only thing.
9. Seeing is believing.
10. Time is money.

B. What do you think about . . .

1. The individual in a group is more important than the group.
2. You shouldn't worry about the past or the future; the present is what really counts.
3. You should work to live, not live to work.
4. You're as young as you act.
5. A free man or woman owes nothing to anyone.
6. The sky's the limit; you can do anything you wish if you just try.
7. Better late than never!
8. That's your problem!
9. Put up or shut up!
10. Don't just stand there! Do something!

In Part A respondents are encouraged to make the language and culture connection between what is believed and what is done. Such clarification is useful in eliciting discussion of contrastive values and behavioral rules and norms. The 10 statements in Part B are designed to promote discussion of some value orientations such as human relations, action, time, or problem solving.

Using these statements or similar ones, the instructor who is cognizant of the various dimensions of contrast and probable focal points should be able to provide some very useful guidance in the fine art of learning about a new culture. In the hands of teachers who find their primary instructional goal is simply to "teach American culture," such approaches are usually unsuccessful and eminently unfair.

Finally, values clarification and examination, as steps in culture learning, can be integrated with the teaching of specific language skills, such as reading and composition, or discussion. They can form a specific culture learning project. Exercise 10.3 reproduces excerpts from student essays on the subject of "*Americans Are . . .*" As classroom exercises, the essays served two purposes: first, they gave the students a chance to express personal opinions and describe personal observations; second, they brought these opinions to a conscious level and prepared students to complete a subsequent assignment to describe their own cultures.

Teachers who elicit such essays are likely to suffer a twinge of shame or anger at what might be construed as stereotyping or just plain error. The value of such exercises is not in their validity or reliability but in their doing.

The student observations about observations are intended as signposts for the culturally sensitive language teacher. A brief review of what others have seen may make us better guides. According to these students, Americans are lively, quick-speaking, time-driven, mechanistic, ruled by machines, politically naïve, polite, pragmatic, organized, uncaring, friendly, overly friendly, and addicted to sending greeting cards.

Will the real American please stand up?

Exercise 10.3. Americans are . . .

What response would you give to these students? Do you consider their observations biased? naive? limited? unfair? interesting? useless?

Student No. 1—from Saudi Arabia: "I have learned three important things about Americans since I came to the United States. First, I have learned that all Americans are lively; they move and speak quickly . . . because time is very important to them. Second. . . . Americans are the same as the machine, they do their work . . . worthily but without any thinking, they just use the instructions even if it is not completely right. Finally, they do not know anything except their job, they do not know what is happened in their country."

Student No. 2—from Venezuela: "I have observed that Americans are polite, pragmatic, and organized. Wherever you are in the United States you can hear words of friendship and cordiality like, "May I help you?", "Excuse me", "Have a nice day.", "Thank you", and many others. . . . Another characteristic is their pragmatism. Along years, Americans have worked a lot in order to create many devices which have made their life more comfortable. These devices not only save time but they also make things easier. . . . Last, but never least, Americans are very organized. Perhaps, for the same fact that they are very pragmatic people, they have developed different ways of organization that assure them better services."

Student No. 3—from Japan: "I have been learning about Americans since I came here last September. . . . First, Americans don't care what other people do or what happened. For example, when I come out of my room . . . my roommate never ask me where you are going or where I went. . . . Second, Americans are friendly and open-minded. . . . When I went to my roommate's home, I was welcomed by her family. Her mother said to me immediately: "Help yourself to everything in my home," and I was surprised to hear it. I thought that the words indicated friendliness. . . . In Japan . . . we never open refrigerators or use my friend's things without permissions. Because to serve is a virtue in my country. . . . Third, Americans like cards . . . sometimes I can find cards are delivered to my American friends without special reasons. . . . As far as I look at Americans, they seem not to care what other people do as a whole, while they think it's important to keep relationships between them and their friends and them and their parents."

Reprinted from *Gulf Area TESOL Newsletter*, "Cultural Content in Student Compositions." Summer 1980.

FOR STUDY AND DISCUSSION

1. Identify the following terms.

   belief systems   value orientation   *amae*

   value systems   inferential beliefs

2. List the adjectives you would use in describing most young adult Americans (aged 20–30). Ask your informant to do the same, then compare notes.

3. Describe three types of behavior that you feel would be inappropriate for a foreign newcomer in the United States. Please rate these warnings on a scale of importance from: a. do with care; b. shouldn't do; c. positively never do. Ask your informant to list three such types of behavior which would be taboo in his/her country.

4. A Gallup poll (1982) (Exercise 10.4.) lists a number of values in their order of importance reported by a sample of Americans. Look over the list and match any of these to the list of values identified in this chapter as points of orientation for Americans.

   Would you personally add others to the list? In your opinion, does the order of importance reflect the "real" scale of values in the United States at that time. Do you agree with the order of importance? In what order would you rank them?

Exercise 10.4.   Cultural Hide and Seek
Answer discussion question 4.

WHAT'S IMPORTANT TO AMERICANS?

(Percent rating importance very high or high)

HAVING A GOOD FAMILY LIFE — 82%
BEING IN GOOD PHYSICAL HEALTH — 81%
HAVING A GOOD SELF-IMAGE — 79%
PERSONAL HAPPINESS OR SATISFACTION — 77%
FREEDOM OF CHOICE TO DO WHAT ONE WANTS — 73%
LIVING UP TO ONE'S POTENTIAL — 71%
HAVING AN INTERESTING JOB — 69%
HAVING A SENSE OF ACCOMPLISHMENT — 63%
FOLLOWING GOD'S WILL — 61%
HAVING MANY FRIENDS — 54%
HELPING PEOPLE IN NEED — 54%
WORKING TO BETTER AMERICA — 51%
HAVING AN EXCITING, STIMULATING LIFE — 51%
FOLLOWING A STRICT MORAL CODE — 47%
BEING ACTIVE IN CHURCH OR SYNAGOGUE — 40%
NICE HOME, CAR, OTHER BELONGINGS — 39%
HAVING A HIGH INCOME — 37%
HAVING ENOUGH LEISURE TIME — 36%
SOCIAL RECOGNITION — 22%

WHAT'S IMPORTANT?
A 1982 Gallup Poll asked Americans to rate the social values they consider important or very important.

5. Review the following list of phrases, commands, signs, and comments heard frequently in the United States. Do they reflect any norms and assumptions identified in question 3? Would a newcomer to the United States understand the cultural meanings of these terms? How would you explain their meanings?

a) Get going!
b) Stand on your own two feet!
c) Join the Pepsi generation!
d) Reach out and touch someone.
e) Do your own thing!
f) Take care of Number One!
g) Have a nice day!
h) Enjoy!
i) You get what you give!
j) Clean teeth and fresh breath. . . .
k) She's a winner!
l) I believe in me!

6. Evaluate the use of culture-specific material, such as contained in the article by Miner (Suggested Readings, Chapter 9), "Body Ritual Among the Nacirema," to introduce a discussion of American cultural values.

7. Draw up a list of value orientations for your target group, using the information in this chapter. Organize your list around the value orientations suggested by Albert.

CULTURE LEARNING EXERCISE

Same Theme—Different Perspectives

On the following pages excerpts from student textbooks are reproduced. They show different approaches and information on the same cultural themes.

A. Will The Real American Stand Up?

1. How many different kinds of "Americans" can you find?

2. What are the characteristics of each?

3. Which one would you feel most comfortable in "introducing" to your students? Why?

[1] *People*

| a miser | tightwad
moneygrubber
cheapskate
penny pincher
skinflint | an unenthusiastic person | wet blanket
killjoy
party pooper |

in hot water (a jam, a pickle, a fix, a bind, Dutch)

Eugene is *in hot water (in trouble)* with his wife because he forgot her birthday.

up a creek

You'll be *up a creek (in a hopeless situation)* if you don't take enough food and water when you go camping.

up against the wall (it)

Poor Eric is *up against the wall (trapped);* if he doesn't find a job soon, he'll have to move out of his apartment.

From *Colloquial English. How to Shoot the Breeze and Knock'em for a Loop While Having a Ball* by Harry Collis. Copyright © 1981. Regents Publishing Co., Inc., p. 5, 63.

The Washington Gay Community

[2]   *Brainstorming Questions—What Do You Think?*
First, look at the picture and read the title. What information do they give

you about the article? Remember, sometimes there isn't enough information in the title and picture to answer the questions.

1. Where are the people in the picture?

2. Is it possible to know if they are gay or straight?

Vocabulary in Context

The following sentences have the new vocabulary from this article. Do you or the other students know what the *underlined* words mean?

1. People are *conscious of* the conservative *mood* in Washington.

   1. _____

   2. _____

2. A *homosexual* has advertised in a *gay* newspaper.

   1. _____

   2. _____

3. There is advertising in gay newspapers for social *disguises.*

   _____

4. Gay white male, good-looking, *straight*-acting young *professional*, looking for gay white female.

   1. _____

   2. _____

5. I'm looking for a companion in our straight *circles.*

   _____

From *Americana Articles. An Intermediate ESL Reader.* Vol. II by Tacey Ruffner, p. 162. Copyright 1982 by Tacey Ruffner.

[3]   *MARY'S FEELING BLUE*

Mary Rathbun, 57, spent a restless night in the San Francisco jail thinking about the "magical cookies" that she baked to add to her fixed income. "The police wouldn't let me have one before I went to jail," she said. "I might have slept better if they had." Mary started her home baking business six months ago after a back injury forced her to quit her job as a grave-yard shift waitress. "I was a waitress for 43 years. I *was good at it.*"

Mary's 54 dozen magical brownies, which were baked with a lot of marijuana, were taken Wednesday night from her apartment, along with 20 pounds of *pot* and large amounts of sugar, margarine and flour. Mary, who has no previous criminal record, admitted doing a great business out of her home selling her "health food cookies." She said that she wouldn't give away her special recipe.

Mary advertised her "original recipe brownies" for $20 a dozen. Her lack of carefulness, especially taking orders over the phone from anyone, amazed and amused the police officers who arrested her. "Life is a gamble. I played by the rules for 57 years. Then I gambled and lost."

From © San Francisco Chronicle, January 16, 1981, by Paul Liberatore. Reprinted by permission.

[4]   True, Americans enjoy money and the things it can buy. But in defense of the so-called materialistic American, one expert in American culture points out, ". . . however eager we are to make money, we are just as eager to give it away. Any world disaster finds Americans writing checks to relieve distress. Since the war we have seen the spectacle of the United States sending billions and billions of dollars' worth of goods to countries less fortunate than we. Write some of it off, if you will, to a desire to buy political sympathy; there is still an overplus of goodwill strictly and uniquely American. Generosity and materialism run side by side."

The average American is also accused of being "rough around the edges"—that is, of lacking sophistication in manners and understanding of things cultural. He tries hard to polish those edges through education and travel. But no matter how much he learns and sees, his interests are less with the past than with the present and future, less with the decorative than with the functional. He may be bored by medieval art but fascinated by modern engineering. Foreigners will find him always ready to compare cultures, though he may conclude that American methods are more efficient and therefore better. In expressing his views, he may be blunt to the point of rudeness. He admires efficiency and financial success. Eager to get as much as possible for his time and money, he is sometimes impatient, tense, and demanding. Often, he is in a hurry and unable to relax. His intensely competitive outlook is probably his greatest fault. But one must give him credit for his virtues: he is friendly, spontaneous, adaptable, efficient, energetic, and kindhearted. All things considered, he is a likable guy.

From *The USA: Customs & Institutions. A Survey of American Culture & Traditions.* Vol IV. by Ethel & Martin Tiersky. Copyright 1975 by Regents Publishing Co. Inc. p. 13.

B. Whose American Dream?

1. Two versions of the American dream are presented. What are the characteristics of each?

2. What supplemental information would you provide if you used the Tiersky and Tiersky text?

3. What information would you provide if you used the Levine and Adelman version?

4. Might there be other versions?

[1]   "All men are created equal," says the Declaration of Independence. This statement does not mean that all human beings are equal in ability or ambition. It means, instead, that all people should be treated equally before the law and given equal privileges and opportunities, insofar as government can control these. In practice, this ideal often does not work perfectly. There have always been those who would deny the rights of others for their own self-interest. There are times when the American people need to be reminded that *any* denial of basic rights is a weakening of the total system. However, equal treatment and equal opportunity for all are ideals toward which American society is moving ever closer.

The American belief in equality of opportunity is illustrated by the Horatio Alger myth. Horatio Alger was a nineteenth-century American novelist who wrote stories about poor boys who became successful. His books told about the little newsboy or bootblack who, because he was hardworking, honest, and lucky, grew up to become rich and respected. These popular "rags-to-riches" stories exemplified the American Dream—the belief that any individual, no matter how poor, can achieve wealth and fame through diligence and virtue.

From *The USA: Customs & Institutions. A Survey of American Culture & Traditions.* Vol. IV. by Ethel & Martin Tiersky. Copyright 1975 by Regents Publishing Co. Inc., p. 5.

The "American Dream"

[2]   In the United States there is a belief that people are rewarded for working, producing, and achieving. Many people believe that there is equality of opportunity that allows anyone to become successful. This belief is illustrated by stories written by a nineteenth-century American *novelist*, Horatio Alger, who wrote about the "American Dream." In his stories he described poor people who became rich because of their hard work, honesty, and luck. The stories *reinforced* the idea that all individuals, no matter how poor, were capable of becoming wealthy as long as they were *diligent* and virtuous. For many Americans, however, Horatio Alger's *"rags*-to-riches" stories do not represent the reality of opportunity. Many poor immigrants who came to the United States in the nineteenth and twentieth centuries were able to rise on the social and economic scales. Today, however, the poor generally do not rise to the middle and upper classes. The "American Dream" is now described as a *myth;* it is still difficult for several million Americans to "get ahead."

From *Beyond Language. Intercultural Communication for English as a Second Language* by D. R. Levine & M. D. Adelman. Copyright 1982 by Prentice Hall, pp. 132–133.

C. Which Kind of University?

1. These excerpts provide two versions of life on North American university campuses. Which version would be most helpful to foreign students in general? Should a choice be made?

2. Which version reflects cultural norms most directly?

[1]   A college community is an interesting and lively place. Students become involved in many different activities—extracurricular, religious, social, and athletic. Among the extracurricular activities are college newspapers, musical organizations, dramatic clubs, and political groups. Some of these have faculty advisers. Many religious groups have their own meeting places where services and social activities can be held. Student groups run parties of all types—from formal dances to picnics. Most colleges have a *student union* where students can get together for lunch, study sessions, club meetings, and socializing.

At many schools, campus life revolves around fraternities (social and, in some cases, residential clubs for men) and sororities (similar clubs for women). These organizations exist on more than 500 campuses. The best known are national groups with many *chapters* at schools throughout the country. Their names are Greek letters such as Alpha Delta Phi. These groups have been much criticized for being cruel and prejudiced because membership is limited and selective. A student must be invited to join. There is often great competition among freshmen and sophomores who want to join. Those who seek membership must go through *rush* (a period when prospective members visit different *houses* to meet and be evaluated by current members). The whole experience can be very painful if a student goes through *rush* and then is not asked to *pledge* (become a trial member of) any of the houses he or she has visited. Sororities and fraternities also tend to limit membership to one particular racial and religious group, thereby depriving its members of the wonderful opportunity that college offers for broadening social contacts. However, these groups do help students find friends of similar backgrounds; thus, they help combat loneliness for those away from home.

From *The USA: Customs & Institutions. A Survey of American Culture & Traditions, Vol. IV.* by Ethel & Martin Tiersky. Copyright 1975 by Regents Publishing Co., Inc., p. 157.

[2]   Student life at American universities is *chaotic* during the first week of each quarter or semester. Registering for classes, becoming familiar with the buildings on campus, buying books, adding and dropping classes, and paying fees are confusing for everyone. During this busy period there is little time for students to anticipate what they will later encounter in the classroom.

International students, *accustomed* to their countries' educational expectations, must adapt to new classroom *norms* in a foreign college or university. Whereas in one country prayer may be acceptable in a classroom, in another it may be *forbidden*. In some classrooms around the world students must *humbly* obey their teacher's commands and remain absolutely silent during a class period. In others, students may talk, eat, and smoke during lectures as well as criticize a teacher's methods or *contradict* his or her statements. It is not always easy to understand a new educational system.

Diversity in Education

There is considerable variety in university classrooms in the United States. Because of *diverse* teaching methods and non-*standardized curricula*, no two courses are identical. Undergraduate courses are considerably different from graduate courses. The classroom atmosphere in expensive, private universities may differ from that in community colleges which are free and open to everyone. State-funded universities have different requirements and expectations than do *parochial* colleges. Nevertheless, there are shared features in American college and university classrooms despite the diversity of educational institutions of higher learning.

From *Beyond Language. Intercultural Communication for English as a Second Language* by D. R. Levine & M. B. Adelman. Copyright 1982 by Prentice Hall, p. 109.

FOR FURTHER READING

J. Condon and F. Yousef. 1975. Chapter 3, "Something of Values"; Chapter 4, "An Outline of Value Orientations: Self, Family, Society"; and Chapter 5, "From Values to Beliefs: Human Nature, Nature, the Supernatural" (47–121) in *An Introduction to Intercultural Communication*. These chapters contain very helpful discussions of the concept of value orientations, their use, and examples of cross-cultural variation. As indicated in this chapter, these discussions are most informative.

J. Fieg. 1976. *The Thai Way: A Study in Cultural Values* examines various Thai cultural values. Read in connection with discussions of American values as in Stewart, it provides a means of contrasting very different cultural orientations.

R. Gorden. 1974. *Living in Latin America: A Case Study in Cross-Cultural Communication*. This book focuses on critical differences to be expected in intercultural contact between North Americans and Latin Americans. The chapter on the role of the guest in the family is approached in terms of the values attached to the role and expected behavior. This chapter is reprinted in *Toward Internationalism: Readings in Cross-Cultural Communication* by E. Smith and L. Luce (1979:196–213).

The diligent researcher can locate such culture-specific articles and books about nearly every country or cultural group in the world. Please consult the list of informational sources, the bibliography, and the area-specific bibliography contained at the end of this book.

W. Gudykunst and Y. Kim. 1984. Chapter 3, "Cultural Influences on the Process," (39–59) in *Communicating with Strangers: An Approach to Intercultural Communication*. This is a review of the concept of value orientation and its relation to cultural meaning and intercultural communication. The authors' discussion of norms and rules, their definitions and relationship to value systems should be of particular interest to teachers who are so often put in the position of either explaining or enforcing norms and rules unfamiliar to their students.

P. Harris and R. Moran. 1979. *Managing Cultural Differences*. This book is concerned with intercultural communication in the business world. Although its focus is on business relations and management problems, it contains very broadly informative units on the cultural influences affecting international management and problems of cross-cultural differences. There are five case studies, covering American macro- and microcultures, Western culture (England and Ireland), Japan, the Republic of China, and the Middle East. These case studies address topics of interest to anyone planning to work in these cultures. They also touch on cultural values, norms, and rules of behavior. Because many of us will be teaching English to businessmen and businesswomen from these areas, it is not unlikely that some of the insights contained in these case studies will be valuable some day.

R. Okabe. 1983. "Cultural Assumptions of East and West: Japan and the United States" (21–44). Although portions of this article have been included in this chapter and in Chapter 15, readers are urged to study the article itself.

R. Patai. 1983. *The Arab Mind*. Rev. ed. As the title suggests, this book touches on the foundations of the Arab world view and the role of religion in that perspective.

E. Stewart. 1972. *American Cultural Patterns: A Cross-Cultural Perspective*. This is the classic analysis of American values and assumptions. Although often quoted and sometimes criticized, this discussion has much to offer those who would learn more about those inscrutable Americans.

C. Welte. 1977. "Interrelationships of Individual, Cultural, and Pan-human Values" (441–468). This author discusses values in terms of individual, cultural, and universal frames for classifying types of cultural values. This article should be of interest to those who are concerned with developing a generalized approach to cultural diversity.

Chapter 11

Culture Learning

"When you learn another language, you learn another culture. Part of me is French, and part of me is American. Sometimes I think my home is an island in the middle of the Atlantic."

—Kit Ballard, an 18-year-old senior, who has lived most of her life in France

"Expatriate Students Are Often Innocents at Home."
The New York Times, May 26, 1985. Section E. p 16.

As has been stated before, just as language and culture are inextricably bonded in human society, so are language learning and culture learning. In addition, the processes of language learning and teaching are also joined in a cause-and-effect relationship, some learning being the effect of teaching if all the fervent wishes of teachers and curricula planners are realized. Failure to achieve these expectations often lies in the nature of culture learning itself, in the goals and objectives of both teachers and students, and in the impact of the many external sociocultural variables affecting the teaching/learning process.

Thus, in planning, directing, and evaluating culture learning and teaching in the language classroom, teachers should be aware of the general nature of culture learning as a process and the major variables that stimulate or hinder its progress. They must become aware of the nature of the stages of acculturation, their relationship to language and culture learning and their influences in the classroom context. These variables, as well as the limitations and strengths of the language classroom as a culture learning locus, are examined in this chapter.

11.1 THE CHALLENGES OF COMMUNICATIVE COMPETENCE

This book is concerned primarily with exploring the symbiotic relationship between language learning and culture learning. It was written with the purpose of enhancing teachers' understanding of these learning processes. Such understanding, it was felt, must form the foundation for the necessary professional competencies to guide culture as well as language learning.

Our present-day commitment to developing student communicative competencies and assessing subsequent performances mandates that teachers not only be willing to direct the development of such competencies and to monitor the performances of their students but also to understand and, if possible, to duplicate this development.

Why? In adopting a communicative approach to second language learning, we, as teachers and program administrators, have embraced several assumptions, largely implicit, concerning our pedagogical roles and goals as cultural guides.

In general, we assume that the concept of communication has been broadened to include a wide range of behavior, verbal and nonverbal. Communicative competence includes concern with styles and purposes of communication, both of which show great cross-cultural variation (Barnlund 1975; Gudykunst and Kim, 1984; Hall 1959, 1969, 1977). Indeed, as Canale and Swain (1980:29) point out, "a theory of communicative competence interacts . . . with a theory of human action and with other systems of human knowledge (e.g., world knowledge)." We are thus constrained by having joined the communicative competence bandwagon to expand our field of instruction and practice.

Furthermore, we are committed by the communicative approach to provide opportunities for meaningful communicative interaction for the learner and to give priority to learner needs. The hidden assumption supporting these objectives is that "meaningful" is culture-bound and culture-specific. Yet, paradoxically, learner needs are both partly idiosyncratic and partly universalistic—that is, both personal and human in nature.

Table 11.1 details other hidden assumptions and their consequences. Most of these assumptions have been discussed in the previous chapters but not in relation to culture teaching and instruction. Teachers, planners, and trainers should examine their personal commitments to these assumptions before, after, and during training periods. To fail to do so is to stack the cultural deck in favor of shock, failure, or increased ethnocentrism.

The first assumption, that nothing human is off limits nor to be arbitrarily ignored, implies that the gospel of cultural relativity must be welcomed and practiced in language classrooms. Cultural relativity, the nonevaluative acceptance of the logic and holism of a given cultural system, precludes attitudes of chauvinism, especially on the teacher's part.

The second hidden assumption relates to the nature of culture learning as discussed in this chapter. In the classroom this implies that the goals and objectives of culture learning should be carefully selected and honed to the needs and *desires* of the learner. Third, because culture learning and language learning occur together, there can be no question as to whether culture should be taught or not. The fundamental questions in relation to bicultural instruction have to do with the selection of content and approach. This, of course, implies that no students

TABLE 11.1 WHILE RIDING THE COMMUNICATIVE COMPETENCE BANDWAGON. . . .

We Assume That. . . .	Which Means That. . . .
1. Nothing human is off limits nor to be arbitrarily ignored.	1. Cultural relativity is the golden rule for those who would communicate interculturally.
2. Culture or cultural patterns are learned or taught. Such learning is additive rather than replacive.	2. Learning a new culture is part and parcel of learning a new language, but it is not a similar process.
3. Culture learning and language learning are inextricably linked so that the question is not whether to teach culture, but whose culture to teach and how.	3. There are many ways to approach cultural instruction and learning. No one approach will serve all students and all teachers in all contexts. Choices must be made.
4. Cultural patterns within a given culture are as parts to the whole; they exhibit a cultural rationality within that context.	4. Cultural patterns reflect a general consistency at any given time, although individual manifestations vary.
5. Ethnocentricism is not necessarily a dirty word.	5. Man is a culture bearing animal. Loss of cultural identity should not be a goal of cultural instruction.

are either linguistic or cultural *tabulae rasae* when they enter a second language classroom. Pedagogical determinism, which sets predetermined cultural learning attitudinal results, is not only inappropriate but also useless. Research in relation to attitudes, motivation, and other psychological barriers to language learning and acquisition supports this statement (Gardner and Lambert 1972; Oller *et al.* 1977).

Fourth, to embrace the concept of cultural relativity is to recognize that the cultural patterns within a given culture function as parts to the whole and exhibit a general consistency at a given point in time. Thus, to change one portion of the overall cultural web is to send vibrations throughout the entire network. There are discontinuities as change takes place because not all members of a cultural group share the same perceptions. Stereotyping, or blind categorization, can lead to false cultural hypotheses and often ineffective interaction. Yet classification and categorization are major processes of human learning. Gudykunst and Kim (1984:87) write:

> Our initial predictions about strangers' behavior must, out of necessity, be based on the stereotypes we have about the strangers' culture, race, or ethnic group. To the degree that our stereotypes are accurate, we can make accurate cultural level predictions about strangers' behavior. If our stereotypes are inaccurate, we cannot make correct attributions about strangers' behavior.

Finally, the last hidden assumption has to do with the individual's need to maintain a psychocultural identity. Ethnocentricism, or adherence to a given set of cultural options adjudged right, is a natural and necessary human attitude. It is the source of cultural and personal identity.

An ethnocentric orientation is not intrinsically bad. Hoopes (1979a:18) comments:

> *Ethnocentrism* is a basic human survival response. . . . Strength lies in the group. Yet as civilization becomes more advanced and complicated, as the population increases, and as culture groups become more accessible to each other, another, more negative aspect of ethnocentrism becomes a threat. . . .

It is destructive when it is used to shut others out, provide the bases for derogatory evaluations, and rebuff change. This face of ethnocentricism is very ugly, indeed. As Sumner (1940:13) has stated:

> *Ethnocentricism* is the technical name for this view of things in which one's own group is the center of everything, and all others are scaled and rated with reference to it. . . . Each group nourishes its own pride and vanity, boasts itself superior, exalts its own divinities, and looks with contempt on outsiders.

Thus, cultural identity represents the bright side of ethnocentrism, but when such cultural bias is used to support negative and capricious evaluation of the new and strange, then it is very dark.

To understand another set of rules for living does not necessarily mean that old patterns are wrong and to be rejected. To do so may mean a loss of cultural identity and relegation to the permanent status of the marginal stranger everywhere. Such decisions are personal and can only be answered by the individual involved.

The final assumption points to the need for specialized training for student and teacher alike. Learning to deal with one's own psychocultural identity while maintaining a posture of cultural relativism should be the focus of all training courses.

Thus, we must, as Savignon (1983:10) points out, regard communicative competence more as a particular view of language than in terms of measurable student goals.

> The notion of communicative competence goes *beyond* narrowly defined linguistics and learning psychology to the fields of anthropology and sociology. . . . People and the languages they use are viewed not in isolation but in their social contexts or settings.

We must also recognize that communicative competence may consist of several types of components including: grammatical competence, sociolinguistic competence, and strategic competence (Canale and Swain 1980:27). The characteristics of the first three should be clear. Strategic competence refers to coping behavior used when the flow of messages is interrupted or diverted.

Thus, communicative competence must be seen as composed of knowledge and many other elements. Saville-Troike (1982:22–23) writes:

> Communicative competence extends to both knowledge and expectation of who may or may not speak in certain settings, when to speak and when to remain silent, whom one may speak to, how one may talk to persons of different statuses and roles, what appropriate nonverbal behaviors are in various contexts, what the routines for turn-taking are in conversation, how to ask for and give information, how to request, how to offer or decline assistance or cooperation, how to give commands, how to enforce discipline, and the like—in short, everything involving the use of language and other communicative dimensions in particular social settings.

Perhaps we can address these communicative needs only in part in our classrooms. In any case, as teachers, we are, like it or not, intimately involved in directing the acquisition or learning of many new rules for interaction.

The discovery and description of these rules is the major purpose of the sociolinguistic approach proposed by Hymes and christened "the ethnography of communication." Hymes proposed a focus on patterns of communicative behavior in a given culture and suggested the use of ethnographic methods to uncover these patterns (Hymes 1972b, 1974).

As Saville-Troike notes, the development of the methods of the ethnography of communication has helped identify "what a second language learner must know in order to communicate appropriately in various contexts in that language, and what the sanctions may be for various communicative shortcomings" (10). Thus, such methods of analysis and explanation are the sources of much of the cultural content that can be brought into the second language classroom. They provide the means to deal with what is often totally ignored in second language classrooms: the sociolinguistic variables of language, such as those related to geography, ethnicity, class, sex, role, and setting.

Finally, the so-called communicative competence approach to second language teaching and learning is a misnomer, for it implies not only competence but also performance. Thus, how and to what degree communicative competence is desirable and attainable depend to a large extent on the goals and objectives of the learner, the context, and other external sociocultural variables that affect performance. Performance is what one *does*; competence is what one *knows* (Savignon 1983:9).

It may be that the terms *communicative competence* and *communicative performance* should be broadened to include *cultural competence* and *cultural performance* in order to compensate for the Western bias which generally equates communication with verbal, intentional, conscious activity. In any case, the many cross-cultural variations in communicative styles, functions, and patterns should not be set aside in the context of the second language classroom.

11.2 MEETING THE UNKNOWN

Although we know relatively little about how first or second languages are acquired or learned, we do know that the processes are not entirely similar. The same holds true for the processes of enculturation (native culture learning) and acculturation (second culture learning). Neither are we very certain about the relationship of second language and second culture learning. If it is true that biculturalism represents a two-skills-in-one-skull phenomenon, we must explore the relationship between the processes of second language and second culture learning and some of the intervening variables affecting these processes.

Culture Learning

Human learning is a complex process. It involves change, acquisition, retention, storage, and retrieval. Teaching implies the facilitation of these processes. Yet, as Brown (1980:8) suggests, they cannot be defined separately. "Teaching is guiding and facilitating learning, enabling the learner to learn, setting the conditions for learning."

Culture learning is simply a particular type of human learning related to patterns of human interaction and identification. Because it is so deeply concerned with norms, values, beliefs, world views, and other aspects of subjective culture, it is a type of learning subject to the action of many variables and often accompanied by feelings of discomfort or even shock. Kleinjans (1972b:18), in discussing culture learning, observes:

> . . . all cultures provide men with façades to protect their egos. However, that which serves as a façade in his own culture may be stripped away by exposure to another culture and the learner may suddenly find himself standing psychologically naked. Therefore, the main prerequisites to second culture learning are receptivity, plus normal intelligence and a good measure of inner security.

That not all of us are able to bring all three to the task of culture learning goes without saying and should not be overlooked in setting learning and teaching goals, objectives, and outcomes.

Culture learning, like all learning, should be seen as a process; the general goals of all cultural training programs should be to facilitate this process. There are several ways to regard cultural learning. It may be seen as a series of stages along the road to the development of intercultural communicative skills and personal change. It may be marked on a path leading from ethnocentrism, which finds only value, right, and logic in one's own cultural patterns, to varying stages of awareness, understanding, acceptance, and a variety of outcomes.

Kleinjans has suggested that the use of the concepts of domains and levels as developed in the work of Benjamin S. Bloom (1956) and others in educational psychology, would be useful to structure an examination of these "levels" of

TABLE 11.2 HIERARCHY OF CULTURE LEARNING MATRIX

Cognition	Affection	Action
Information	Perception	Awareness
Analysis	Appreciation	Attending
Synthesis	Revaluation	Responding
Comprehension	Orientation	Acting
Insight	Identification	Interacting

Source: E. Kleinjans. *On Culture Learning.* Paper No. 13, (1972b:20) for presentation at the Japan Association of College English Teachers' Annual Conference, Hachioji, August 1971.

culture learning. Table 11.2 reproduces Kleinjans' hierarchy of culture learning matrix.

In Kleinjan's matrix the first level is the most superficial. Complexity grows as each level is passed. This book has been designed to carry the reader at least through the first three levels of this process. The final levels relate to behavior and values change, which may accompany cultural instruction but should generally not be stated classroom goals or objectives.

The most superficial level involves information, perception, and awareness. At the second level, observation and data management are essential. At the level of synthesis (the third level) patterns and themes should emerge. As Kleinjans (21) points out, "Synthesis enables one to see the coherence of cultural patterns." At the fourth level comprehension is joined by orientation and behavior. The fourth level calls not only for understanding, but also values change and action. The final level involves what has been called "empathy," or the feeling of being inside the head of others, especially those who do not share our cultural patterns. It is the ability to identify with and understand the *-emic* view—literally to stand in the shoes of another.

Table 11.3 incorporates the domains and levels of the Kleinjans' matrix with the concept of perceived social distance and degrees of acculturation, to present a schema of the general processes involved in culture learning. The stages of culture learning are not necessarily experienced by all learners. The process is carried out along a continuum rather than by set stages. The scientific validity of the stages is, perhaps, open to question. They do reflect the types of emotions and experiences that travellers to strange lands often report. They are also sign posts along the road to culture learning. Let us now consider each of the processual stages shown in Table 11.3. They are interactive both on the horizontal and vertical axes.

Cultural and Social Distance

In intercultural communication, cultural distance, or dissimilarity, has been of interest in terms of the effects of such distance upon communication processes

TABLE 11.3 THE PATHS OF CULTURE LEARNING

Stage	Cultural/ Social Distance	Levels of Culture Learning (cognitive/affective)	(action)	Degree of Acculturation
1	Maximum	Little or no knowledge of THEM Low awareness	Little interaction; stereotypic	Ethnocentrism
2		Some knowledge; brief experience Awareness of superficial or "exotic" features	Intellectual interest; some analysis	Euphoria
3		Much more knowledge and contact Greater awareness of differences	More analysis; evaluation; disorientation	Conflict !!!!SHOCK!!!!!
4		Knowledge, experience, and understanding Awareness of important similarities/differences	Accepting; tolerance of the new	Reintegration
5	Minimum	Understanding; insight Empathy; -emic point of view	Interactive; mediating	Assimilation Adaptation Adjustment

and ultimately, acculturation. Porter and Samovar (1982:35) constructed a sliding scale of cultural differences along a continuum from maximum to minimum, from cultures to individuals. At the top of their scale was the canyon experienced by the meeting of the twain of the East and the West, and at the bottom was the much more bridgeable gap between environmentalist and developer. The subjectivity of such a scale is self-evident, as some Sierra Club members might be quick to point out.

Acculturation, or adaptation in varying degree to new cultural patterns, is affected by what has been termed social distance and its effect on communication patterns. Social distance, generally defined as a subcategory of cultural distance, refers to the affective and cognitive dimensions of cross-cultural differences as measured in terms of social categories such as social group characteristics and variables affecting social interaction. Kim (1982) pointed out that the acculturation process is related to patterns of personal communication and social communication. Personal communication has to do with how the individual communicates or "the process by which the individual informationally fits himself into (adapts to and adapts) his environment" (Ruben 1975:168–169). Social communication, on the other hand, is interactive or occurs between individuals. It can be further classified into interpersonal communication and mass communication (Kim: 363).

Because an individual's acculturation potential is affected by the degree of similarity of the native culture to the target culture, among other factors, cultural distance is an important factor in the degree of acculturation achieved. Other elements affecting acculturation potential are those related to social factors such as the age at the time of immigration, educational background, personality characteristics, and other sociocultural variables.

Degrees of Acculturation

Hanvey's matrix of the levels of cross-cultural awareness, as shown in Chapter 8, as well as Kleinjans' levels of culture learning are combined in Table 11.3 to indicate cognitive, affective, and behavioral characteristics of the various levels of culture learning. They identify a process by which the learner moves away from a state of little or no knowledge of THEM (an unknown and faceless group). Ethnocentricism rules supreme. This is a stage of culture learning in which enculturation has taken a firm hold and acculturation is at ground zero.

In Stage Two of the learning continuum, some knowledge has been acquired either by contact with a THEM Group on home turf or contact in the target culture. This might be the case of a vacationer, the two-week tripper, or the casual visitor to the target culture. In the case of the immigrant or sojourner (one who will stay for some time in the target culture), the level of awareness is superficial and generally confined to the "exotica" of the target culture. There is intellectual interest and often feelings of euphoria. All appears new and fresh and interesting.

The third stage, often called "culture shock," represents a plunge into conflict, or even rejection. There is more analysis, more noticing of the strange, the distasteful, the unacceptable, the intolerable. Feelings of anger, depression, illness, and even disorientation occur.

In the fourth stage, recovery from the miseries of Stage Three begins. More knowledge, experience, and understanding are gained as contact continues. The learner is increasingly aware of major similarities and differences. In addition, feelings of acceptance and tolerance for the new and the strange develop. The melding of the patterns of Culture One (C1) and Culture Two (C2) begins to take place in an expanded cultural competence, representing elements of both cultures.

In the final stage, the social/cultural distance has been substantially narrowed, understanding and insight have been developed, an -emic point of view achieved both in C1 and C2. A mediating role can now be played by the learner. Whether the culture learner, who has progressed so far along the road of culture learning, chooses to assimilate, adapt, adjust, or just go home is a matter of personal choice. Many outcomes are possible.

No learner travels through these stages quite so neatly and directly as these schema would indicate. Some skip stages; others exit at some particular stage. There are those who reach the fifth stage. Some remain in a permanent state of culture shock; others reject their native cultures so that they truly "cannot go home again." They have what is called the shock of re-entry. The native culture seems strange and different.

A Visit to the Land of THEM

All good people agree,
    And all good people say,
All nice people, like Us, are We,
    And everyone else is They:
But if you cross over the sea,
    Instead of over the way,
You may end by (think of it!) looking on We
    As only a sort of They!*

Just for a moment, let us translate this thought into the words of a cultural traveller. Let us ask the visitor to the Land of Them the question that every sports commentator asks the winner: "What was going through your mind when . . . ? (See Table 11.4.)

Note that these bits of dialogue are accompanied by emotional highs at stages one and five and a deep low at stage three. Giving up the game at any stage is always possible and with probable consequences. This is the well-known U-curve of cultural adjustment (Lysgaard 1955). A similar process experienced upon re-entry into the native culture produces a W-curve of adjustment (Gullahorn and Gullahorn 1963).

Finally, anyone who plays the game of culture learning should return to *Go* as often as possible. The experience is never the same twice.

11.3 CULTURE AND LANGUAGE LEARNING: SAME OR DIFFERENT?

How does culture learning relate to language learning? Kleinjans (1972b) has stated that language and culture learning are analogous. Certainly, as we have seen in previous chapters, language and culture are bound together in many ways. Indeed it would be surprising if language and culture did not share many features.

Kleinjans' position, based on the old linguistic analogy (See Chapter 7), assumes there are cultural as well as linguistic universals. Just as those who use the

---

* *Source:* Rudyard Kipling, *The Collected Works of Rudyard Kipling*, Vol. 27 (New York: Doubleday, Doran and Company, 1970), pp. 375–376.

TABLE 11.4 A VISIT TO THE LAND OF THEM

GO

Social/Cultural Distance

High	**Stage 1**	Aren't THEY of THEM interesting? I'd like to visit there someday. THEM was featured in the *National Geographic* last week.	EXIT—No change
	Stage 2	Isn't this exciting? Look at those buildings! THEY are so polite! And this food! I think I'll try to get a job here. I wonder *what* THEY are saying?	EXIT—On euphoric note. Never returns but shows slides frequently.
Low	**Stage 3**	Well, this trip is getting long. I should've stayed home. So there's another temple. I *know* what THEY are saying! Did you know that you just ate a curried THAT? When do we leave? I feel terrible. These people are so rude!	EXIT—In depressed state; goes home where they do things right
	Stage 4	So they eat THAT. Well, why not? I'm beginning to like it. I not only know *what* they are saying, I know *why* they *said* it.	EXIT—I shall return or maybe stay.
High	**Stage 5**	Look you just don't understand THEY of THEM. THEY have always eaten THAT. It is an excellent source of protein. Besides WE eat a kind of THESE! THEM would never eat THOSE. I really feel like one of them.	EXIT—Go home Go native Go back to GO

linguistic analogy, he also assumes that a "grammar" of a culture could be compiled and that contrastive analysis would reduce miscommunication. Although such a "grammar" of any culture has yet to appear, we must consider the value of the analogy in terms of learning. As Kleinjans notes, the process of culture learning accompanies language learning, although in many ways it is more complex because of the nature of culture and its many manifestations. In addition, culture learning is likely to cause greater change in the individual. It may force the transcending of native and familiar culture patterns and, in some cases, result in their being discarded. This may produce culture shock, disorientation, and temporary loss of cultural identity. If prolonged, these side-effects can lead to marginality and even alienation.

Finally, one can generally learn the formal system of a language without much culture learning, but one cannot learn much about a culture without knowledge of its language or languages.

11.4 BICULTURALISM AND BILINGUALISM: SAME OR DIFFERENT?

In the following discussion and throughout this book, the term *biculturalism* is defined as the development of expertise in communication and culturally appropriate behavior with members of a cultural group not native to the individual involved. The term *biculturalism* is often linked with *bilingualism* (fluency in another language). They influence each other, but do not necessarily develop at the same rate or in the same depth.

Biculturalism is a slightly misleading term, for most of us are multicultural in our own cultures. Pure states of monoculturalism are rare. We all display cultural fluency in a number of subcultural groups (churches, schools, age-related groups). In addition, the term biculturalism is often used to indicate the addition of a second, third, or fourth area of cultural competence, so it is hardly "bi-." However, because biculturalism is the term generally appearing in the literature, it will be employed in this book to indicate additional fluency in other than the native culture.

Christina Paulston, in an excellent discussion, "Biculturalism: Some Reflections and Speculations" (*TESOL Quarterly*, 12 (4), 1978), explores biculturalism and its relationship both to bilingualism and to the dichotomy of performance/competence postulated in modern models of language, performance being actually observable behavior, and competence, the knowledge of the language system.

Paulston questions the cavalier use of bicultural/bilingual as permanently wedded terms, pointing out that becoming bicultural is probably an "eclectic process which results in an idiosyncratic mixture of the two (C1 [culture 1] and C2 [culture 2]) cultures with one basic 'cultural competence' but with two sets of 'socio-cultural performance' . . ." (1978:369). That is, the cultural competence of an individual remains unitary and only modified by cross-cultural experiences and learning. On the other hand, performances (sociocultural behavior) might be observably different.

Using an ideational definition of culture, Paulston observes that the nature of cultural competence is different from that of linguistic competence. According to Paulston, cultural competence does not show the same conformity between individuals that linguistic competence does (372–373).

> . . . becoming bicultural differs from becoming bilingual. It is perfectly possible to learn a foreign language from non-native speakers. . . . It is also possible to become bilingual without becoming bicultural, while the reverse is not true. Many . . . claim that to become bilingual is to become bicultural; but apart from trivialities, this need not follow.

Thus, we may make two observations, while reserving judgment on the relationship of cultural proficiency and the attainment of a high level of linguistic proficiency. First, culture learning is additive and supplementary rather than replacive. It is not certain that this is true of second language learning. Second, the distinction between sociocultural performance and an eclectic unified competence base helps explain the feeling of "being different" that bilingual persons often report when they speak one or the other of "their" languages. They are perhaps using added cultural dimensions of which they are more conscious than are monolingual speakers.

Paulston makes an interesting statement in relation to this concept of biculturalism and language teaching. She points out that because becoming bicultural is an individual matter, "what a bicultural program should hope to do is to allow the student the right to pick and choose his own individual make-up as a bicultural person . . ." (379). She was speaking to the purposes of bilingual/bicultural programs in the United States. The same warning is valid in all language and culture learning contexts.

11.5 VARIABLES IN SECOND LANGUAGE AND CULTURE LEARNING

Because we are first and foremost teachers of language, we must consider the sociocultural variables affecting second language acquisition and their relationships to the processes of acculturation.

Sociocultural Variables

A taxonomy of the factors affecting second language acquisition compiled by Schumann (1978) includes social, affective, personality, cognitive, biological, aptitude, personal, input, and instructional variables. They are all subject to cultural effects, except perhaps for the biological factors. Some writers might question the inclusion of cognitive factors, but some evidence suggests that specific societies and cultures favor given kinds of cognitive processes including patterns of rhetoric and argumentation (Condon and Yousef 1975; Kaplan 1966). These variables reside partially in the individual and partially in the cultural context in which that individual operates.

Social factors include length of residence in target area, relationships between the native group and the target group, and other such factors. These are powerful forces in the learning situation. (See the discussion in 11.7.) Affective variables have to do with motivation (instrumental or integrative), culture shock, and attitude. Personality factors include tolerance for ambiguity, self esteem, and ego orientation. Cognitive factors relate to cognitive style, field-dependence or field-independence, and other such constructs. Biological factors are those which form the bases for learning. Aptitude and personal factors relate to factors internal to the learner. Input factors and instructional factors are inherent in the classroom context (Schumann 1978:28).

Thus, cultural influences abound in the second language learning process, just as they do in first language acquisition. While we cannot examine all of them in detail, it is useful to discuss some of the major variables, their possible effects and relationship to the general process of learning another language.

Affective Variables

Much of the research in ESL/EFL as well as in intercultural communication relates to the many affective factors influencing second language and second culture learning.

The work of Gardener and Lambert (1972) and others regarding attitudes, motivation, personality traits, and other egocentric factors focused on the characteristics of the individual language learner. Yet, it must not be forgotten that the expression of these traits, and even their measurement, may be subject to Western interpretation and instrument bias. This is not to say that there are not universal traits that mark the successful or unsuccessful language learner; it is to say that these qualities may be manifested in many different ways, and measures taken to enhance the desired traits may produce unexpected results.

Most certainly attitudes relative to the target language and culture are of direct influence upon the learning process. Again the work of Gardener and Lambert (1972), Oller, Hudson, and Liu (1977), and Oller, Baco, and Vigil (1977) have shown that positive attitudes toward the target language group, as well as toward self and the native culture, were enhancing factors in second language and culture learning. Clearly, one goal of cultural instruction should be to provide valid information to dispel any misinformation a student has received that might contribute to negative attitudes.

Acculturation and Second Language Learning

Acculturation is the general term for the process of becoming adjusted to another culture. It should not be seen as a set of stages, although it is often illustrated as such, but rather as points on a continuum along which the learner proceeds in the process of gaining an understanding and appreciation for another culture.

In relation to second language acquisition (SLA), Schumann in 1978 proposed two types of variables—social and affective. The former referred to relations between social groups; the latter were related to individuals. These factors clustered into a single causal variable—*acculturation*. He defined acculturation as the social and psychological integration of the learner with the target group. Second language acquisition (SLA) was seen as just one aspect of acculturation. The degree to which learners acculturate to the target language group would control the degree to which they acquire a second language. Lack of acculturation may lead to a permanent "pidginized" interlanguage, according to Schumann (1978:29–34).

Whether this acculturation model or the monitor model proposed by Krashen (1978) tells us more about second language acquisition is neither the focus of this discussion nor of this text. Both models call for lowering the affective filter (which appears to limit language acquisition), for natural input, and for the development of language acquisition rather than language learning. (See Note, Chapter 1.)

The Schumann model has limitations, for it applies only to language learning in the target area and over a long term. It cannot be applied easily to situations in which there are other types of clients and other goals as noted above. Schumann (48) himself notes that among the problems with the acculturation model is the difficulty in ascertaining that acculturation is the causal variable in second language acquisition. In any case, what is known about communication and social organization appears to support the suggestion that cultural or social distance plays a major role in second language learning and acquisition. Acculturative processes that bridge these differences must then, perforce, affect language development.

The Power of Culture Shock

Culture shock, an intermediate stage in the acculturative process, is particularly painful as it follows an initial period of euphoria and joy at the new and strange, which has been termed the "streets of gold" syndrome. This state may endure for some; for others it is quickly followed by a devastating period of depression, dislike of the new and strange, illness, discouragement, and despair.

The term, *culture shock* was coined in 1958 by Oberg who suggested that it resulted from anxiety over losing familiar signs and symbols. He listed symptoms such as excessive washing of the hands, excessive concern over the water, food dishes, and bedding; fear of physical contact with attendants; the absent-minded stare, a feeling of helplessness, and a desire for dependence on long-term residents of one's own nationality; fits of anger over minor frustrations; great concern over minor aches and pains and skin eruptions; and finally "that terrible longing to be back home." (1979:44) These fears and frustrations are often compounded for the refugee who cannot go back home. Who has not observed or even felt such symptoms?

Individuals vary greatly in their reactions to the effects of culture shock. The state has been compared to that of the schizophrenic who cannot deal with reality; in the case of the second culture learner, the reality has changed (Clarke 1976:378). While there are instances in which the effects of culture shock, or the second stage of culture learning, are great, they are not always so traumatic. Culture shock is a natural process and should be treated as such. We all suffer from culture shock at one time or another, even if we do not leave our own cultures. Modern cultural change is effected so rapidly that an episode of culture shock might well be expected regularly. Harris and Moran (1979:93) write: "Culture shock is neither good or bad, necessary or unnecessary. It is a reality that many people face when in strange and unexpected situations."

Thus, to regard culture shock as a disease or a disorder is not only a generalization from a few instances, but is also a denial of the naturalness of its occurrence. Fear of the new is universal among human beings and probably most animals. It is an evolutionary survival mechanism. There is no reason to consider it any more than one stage in the process of learning to cope with change.

A Cultural Critical Period

What is the relationship between this period of disorientation and second language acquisition? In discussing this question H. Douglas Brown, in his book *Principles of Language Learning and Teaching,* suggests that the interaction might be clarified by considering several factors. Drawing on the concept of social distance, or the cognitive and affective dissimilarity between two cultures as defined in the work of Schumann (1976a,b), Acton's (1979) refinement of the concept of perceived social distance"[1] as experienced by the learner, and the implication of Lambert's (1967) hypothesis that mastery in a second language (within a second culture) occurs somewhere at the beginning of the third stage of acculturation, Brown (138–139) concludes:

> The implication of such a hypothesis is that mastery might not effectively occur before that stage, or even more likely, that the learner might never be successful in his mastery of the language if he has proceeded beyond early Stage 3 without accomplishing that linguistic mastery. Stage 3 may provide not only the optimal *distance,* but the optimal cognitive and affective *tension* to produce the necessary *pressure* to acquire the language, yet pressure that is

neither too overwhelming . . . nor too weak. . . . According to my hypothesis, an adult who fails to master a second language in a second culture may for a host of reasons have failed to synchronize linguistic and cultural develop- ment. . . . What I have suggested here might well be termed a culturally based *critical period* that is independent of the age of the learner. . . .

If the stages of acculturation and of cross-cultural awareness are considered in conjunction with perceived social distance and the process of second language learning, the "window" of the critical period coincides with a feeling of tension, awareness of significant contrastive differences, and a period of minimum social distance. Table 11.5 illustrates the relationships of these concepts. It may be what has been called the "teachable moment" or the moment of optimal desire to learn and be taught (Knowles, 1970:46).

Brown noted that the hypothesis was just that—an educated guess. It has appeal and certainly deserves to be considered in all language classrooms. It may account for the students whose linguistic mastery remains at the "how you say" level while their cultural skills are near native. Then there are those who have achieved a commendable level of linguistic mastery but are unable to deal with the local butcher. Often those who have developed a communicative but ungram- matical control of the target language feel they have "learned" enough and have no need to attain linguistic mastery because their cultural adaptation is sufficient. Such a person is unlikely to achieve full linguistic mastery, according to the hypothesis and the predictions of Schumann's model. Such a situation often oc- curs if the student has wide communicative contacts with the target culture and spends a minimal amount of time and/or effort on formal language learning. Often in these cases, nonverbal signals plus a kind of fractured version of the target language enable the learner to "get along." On the contrary, the students who remain in close contact with their native cultures or cultural group and shuttle between class and the safety of their compatriots are likely to achieve more formal language skills but be unable to use them productively in the "real" world. Neither situation is desirable. The hypothesis certainly underscores the need for attention to acculturative processes in second language instruction. Brown suggests that "teachers could benefit from a careful assessment of the current cultural stages of learners with due attention to possible optimal periods for language mastery " (139).

11.6 OF CLIENTS AND CONTEXTS

Language and culture instruction and presumably learning take place in a variety of contexts. (See note, Chapter 1.) For the purposes of the following discussion, a second language not a foreign language context is presumed. Our students or

TABLE 11.5 ACCULTURATION AND LANGUAGE LEARNING

I. Stages of Acculturation	euphoria	disorientation and culture shock	tentative recovery	assimilation or adaptation
II. Stages of Awareness	awareness of superficial traits— stereotypes (curiosity)	awareness of significant contrastive traits (conflict)	awareness of significant contrastive differences (intellectual analysis)	awareness of insider's view (believable)
III. Optimal Perceived Social Distance (Schumann 1976b) (Acton 1979b)	maximum ------------------			------ minimum
IV. Language Learning (Brown 1980a)		Cultural Critical Period	Mastery or skillful fluency in a second language (within a second culture) occurs . . . at the beginning of the third stage of acculturation	

This chart does not contain the complete information of the original works cited.

clients may be divided into several types; each with a different set of needs and goals. (See Table 11.6.)

TABLE 11.6

Learners

Types	Goals
sojourner	accommodation; short-term; return to native culture
immigrant	acculturation desired; assimilation
refugee	accommodation; survival; restricted assimilation
visitor/traveler	study; professional or personal interest

These categories and goals are very broad. They are useful only as indications of what type of learners are met in our classroom and the variety of goals they may bring with them. As pointed out earlier, because acculturative outcomes are highly personal, the goals suggested above are only very general and should not be attributed to an individual learner without careful consideration. (See Chapter 12 for additional discussion.) Within these contexts and among these clients may be found circumstances that could lead to hypothetically good or bad learning situations as a function of the social distance between two cultures. Although the measurement of social distance is difficult to effect (Brown 1980:137), the identification of sociocultural elements at work in a second language classroom will at the very least alert the observer to crucial context variables.

For example, John Schumann (1976b) suggests that effects of social distance can be observed in terms of several societal factors. These include:

1. Degree of dominance of target language group (TL) to second language group (2LL)

2. Degree of integration of 2LL to TL

3. Degree of enclosure of 2LL

4. Degree of cohesiveness and size of 2LL

5. Degree of congruence between 2LL and TL

6. Attitude toward other group

7. Length of residence of 2LL

As noted previously, it is clear that social distance involves many personal factors, affective factors, and situations. Schumann suggested that these factors affected second language acquisition and that the greater the social distance between two cultures, the more difficulty members of the second language learning group would have in mastering the language of the target group. This has not yet been proved, but it is apparent that cultural (social) distance does play a part in the effectiveness of communicative processes and so would affect culture learning.

Using these factors listed above Schumann describes hypothetical learning situations. "Bad" learning situations would involve either a feeling of domination by both the target group and the language learners, or a feeling of domination by the target group and a feeling of subordination by the learning group. Both groups would desire preservation for the second language group. The second language group would be large, cohesive, and expect a short sojourn in the target language area. Negative attitudes would abound. There would also be a high degree of cultural incongruency between the two groups. A "good" situation would include a non-dominant second language group with both groups desiring assimilation or some form of acculturation. Its characteristics would be the opposite of a "bad" situation. In these cases, "social distance would be minimal and acquisition of the target language would be enhanced" (1976b:141).

To these "good" or "bad" learning situations come the many types of clients or students whom we serve in a variety of settings from universities to store fronts to church basements to elementary school rooms to private sessions.

Consider an ESL or EFL class you have taught, observed, or attended. How would you assess the characteristics of the learning context? What was the perceived social distance between the students and the culture of the target language? Of course, private opinion is not a scientific manner of assessing social distance but there are observable clues. Did the students communicate with members of the target culture? How were they perceived by the members of the target culture? Where did they live? With whom did they communicate? Much can be uncovered by simple observation. Were their complaints and discomforts the result of culture shock or incongruency between the goals and objectives of the course, their own personal agendas, or the learning context?

Although the answers to these questions remain matters for more in-depth analysis, the teachers who pose them, as they deal with the daily ups-and-downs of the language classroom, will be rewarded with deeper understanding and skill in ameliorating the negative effects of affective and sociocultural variables on the processes of adjustment and hence language mastery.

11.7 WHAT CAN BE DONE?

What should be done about culture shock? Larson and Smalley (1972) suggest that we treat culture shock sufferers as we would a child trying to be socialized, that is take them into the "family." This is a possible solution under some circumstances, but such attention might be very difficult to achieve, or inappropriate in the classroom context. It does appear to be helpful to inform the student that culture shock exists (and an amazing number of young adults who come to study here have already been so informed), and what is more to the point, that what they are feeling has been experienced before and will pass. It is also helpful to provide some cultural solutions to the problems at hand—for example, explaining the postal system or how to deal with the intricacies of the local transportation system. It is usually impossible to ward off culture shock; it is useful to find some of the sources of shock and treat these causes.

One student who appeared to be very well adjusted to study in the United States said: "I can stand culture shock because I am not sensitive and I have my goals." He had found his way alone through the slough of shock.

In addition, teachers can make adjustments to the learning environment. They may be able to do little to alter patterns of dominance and non-dominance, but they can mitigate the problem by approaching the cultural patterns of the second language learner positively. Integrative patterns can be adjusted through discussion and explanation of variant cultural patterns. Cohesiveness and enclosure are serious problems. Opportunities must be provided to lower enclosure and provide intercultural contacts. Congruence is a delicate matter for it involves values and beliefs. Recognition of differences and knowledge concerning these differences may help to provide smoother interaction among those who hold very diverse value orientations. Finally, many believe that attitudes can be changed by behavior modification techniques. Information, demonstration, and discussion serve to clarify problem areas. Certainly, the development of positive attitudes toward *differences* facilitates the process of acquiring empathy or understanding of the ways of others.

11.8 CONCLUSION

If culture learning is such hard going, why not simply decide that what happens happens and let well enough alone? This, of course, cannot be, for culture learning will take place, even unaided. It should be facilitated, as there are several good reasons to nurture successful culture learning.

First, intercultural adjustment certainly would be welcome in a world seemingly forever torn by war, dissension, distrust of the stranger, and virulent ethnocentric behavior.

Second, because all human beings are unique, there are many differences among those who can be classified as Brazilian or French or Hispanic-American or Indochinese. Indeed, there may be more individual differences within cultural groups than we imagine. We may, then, find more like-minded among so-called "strangers" than we do among our own.

Third, we must recognize the value of human diversity. Learning a new culture is a means of uncovering the great variety of human cultural patterns and behavior. Kleinjans (1972b:28) comments:

If the adages "Know thyself" and "The unexamined life is not worth living" are valid, then learning another culture is one avenue toward examining one's life and knowing one's self. A person cannot learn a second culture beyond the information/perception level without sensing some challenge to his cultural and individual ways of thinking and feeling. He should also gain a much better perception of the nature of man and his possibilities, for no culture exhausts all the possible alternatives open to it.

Learning a new culture brings these and other personal benefits. It is a difficult process but offers rich rewards. Ursula K. Le Guin, daughter of A.L. Kroeber and a well-known author and anthropologist herself, in a short story in the *New Yorker* called "She Unnames Them" recalls to us that the act of unnaming, or looking at the world without labels, brings the individual into our consciousness. Names stand between the reality and the individual, or, as Lee (1950) suggests, give reality to the nameless. Without names one must proceed slowly in single file, scrutinizing all that passes. So it is with the cultural traveler. In the un-naming/renaming process familiar classifications and categories into which we place individuals and experiences are removed. The resulting clarity is often blinding; it *can* be illuminating. That it is also painful and difficult and only for the strong of purpose should not be surprising.

FOR STUDY AND DISCUSSION

1. Identify the following terms:

   culture shock

   communicative competence

   U-curve of adjustment

   perceived social distance

   W-curve of adjustment

   acculturation model

2. Identify the major sociocultural variables affecting second language learning.

3. Explain the importance of social distance in the acquisition of a second language/culture. What is the difference between social distance and perceived social distance (Acton)? (See Note 1.) How does this concept relate to intercultural communication?

4. Explain the cultural critical period hypothesis suggested by Brown. What are its implications for second language teaching and learning?

5. Various types of clients (students) and contexts (settings) in which second or foreign language learning takes place were discussed in this chapter. Can you name others?

6. Schumann identified several factors which might be combined to produce "good" or "bad" language learning settings. How would you rate a familiar or typical setting in which you have worked? How could the negative characteristics be changed into positive forces?

7. What are the main stages of acculturation as identified in the literature? When is culture shock likely to occur?

8. What types of "shock" might a student encounter in entering the North American educational system?

9. What type of problems might a person who has traveled or studied abroad for some time encounter on re-entering his or her native culture? What might cause problems for a member of your target group upon returning home after a sojourn in the United States?

10. What should be the major goals of culture learning in your opinion?

11. How does Paulston define biculturalism? What are the implications of this definition for teachers? What is the relationship of biculturalism to bilingualism?

CULTURE LEARNING EXERCISE

1. Fill out the form shown in Figure 11.1. Follow these inflexible rules!
   a) Write from right to left
   b) Write very clearly. Sloppy writing will be discarded.
   c) Fill in every blank.
   d) Do not answer number 7 unless you have a green and white card.
      Complete this task within three minutes!
      Ask no questions!
      After you complete the form, try it out on one of your friends.

(The following form is printed in mirror-image / reversed lettering.)

THE FORM

1. NAME _____	6. FAVORITE COLOR
FAMILY	_____
BIRTH	WHY? _____
2. YEARS _____ *	7. LANGUAGE
3. SEX ___ YES	YES ___ NO ___
___ NO	8. IF ENGLISH
4. STATUS	WHAT KIND?
	KOJAK
5. DEGREES	REAGAN
CHECK ONE O, V, X	EDITH
PHD	9. FAVORITE DISEASE
PDQ	
AM	
MA	
PM	

Figure 11.1. Culture Learning Exercise
* Use the Moslem calendar, which begins July 16, A.D. 622.

2. Explore the communicative contacts your informant has had with native speakers of the language being studied. List all the types of communicative events, what problems were encountered, and how your informant feels about the contact.

3. Discuss your informant's experiences in the United States or in any other foreign context. What were his or her feelings at the time of arrival and subsequently? Does your informant expect to encounter any adjustment problems upon returning home?

4. Several types of "coping strategies" used by bicultural adults have been identified (Seelye and Wasilewski 1979b) such as avoidance, substitution, addition, synthesis, or resynthesis. These are steps taken to alleviate cultural problems by avoiding them, substituting native patterns, adding first culture patterns to second culture patterns, or devising a recombination of C1 and C2 patterns (Seelye 204–205). Interview your informant to discover which of the strategies have been employed during a cross-cultural encounter or sojourn.

FOR FURTHER READING

P. Adler. 1975. "The Transitional Experience. An Alternative View of Culture Shock" (13–23). This article approaches the occurrence of culture shock as a natural and "transitional experience." This positive appraisal of a universal phenomenon shows more promise than some of the more depressing views as those found, for example, in Clarke's article "Second Language Acquisition as a Clash of Consciousness" (1976).

H. Brown. 1980a. Chapter 7, "Sociocultural Variables" (122–146). This chapter covers a host of sociocultural variables that affect second language learning, including culture shock, social distance, and perceived social distance. It also contains Brown's formulation of a "cultural critical period hypothesis" (138–139). His treatment of the language and thought puzzle, characterized as it is by a rejection of the Whorfian hypothesis, is somewhat disappointing.

M. Canale and M. Swain. 1980. "Theoretical Bases of Communicative Approaches to Second Language Teaching and Testing" (1–47). This article is an exhaustive review of the major theoretical bases for the development of communicative competence, its major components, and their implications in pedagogical practice.

P. Harris and R. Moran. 1979. Chapter 7, "Managing Culture Shock" (82–100). In this chapter, these authors chart the symptoms associated with their five stages of transitional experience adjustments (acculturation).

E. Kleinjans. 1972b. *On Culture Learning.* In this short monograph, Kleinjans discusses the relationship of language and culture learning and the elements involved in culture learning. His discussion of the implications of the linguistic analogy in cultural analysis is excellent.

K. Oberg. 1979. *Culture Shock and the Problem of adjustment to New Environments.* Reprinted in E. Smith and L. Luce (177–182). This is the classic discussion of the effects of culture shock. The symptoms Oberg discusses are those most commonly associated with this stage of adjustment.

C. Paulston. 1978. "Biculturalism: Some Reflections and Speculations" (369–380) is an interesting discussion of the nature of biculturalism and the implications of recent theories of culture. As an expert in the field of second language learning/teaching, Paulston's comments concerning the relationship of these theories to the ESL/EFL classroom are of particular interest to language teachers.

J. Schumann. 1978. "The Acculturation Model for Second-Language Acquisition" (27–50). This article presents Schumann's acculturation model of second-language acquisition. The first chapter in Gingras's volume in which the Schumann article appears is Krashen's description of his Monitor Model of second language acquisition (1–26). These two chapters represent succinct statements of the two language acquisition models. Additional sources on Schumann's position are listed in the bibliography (Schumann 1976a, 1976b). A more detailed discussion of the Monitor Model is contained in Krashen, 1982.

G. Trifonovitch. 1980. "Culture Learning/Culture Teaching" (550–558). This is a general discussion of some of the problems related to culture learning and teaching. The author identifies the stages of culture shock in terms of a series of mnemonic H's: honeymoon, hostility, humor, and home.

NOTE

1. Acton refined Schumann's hypothesis by developing a measure for *perceived social distance*, or what the learner perceived to be the social distance. Acton's Professed Difference in Attitude Questionnaire (PDAQ) was designed to measure the social distance perceived by the learner *vis à vis* the target culture, that is, the distance between his views and that of his fellow countrymen as well as that of his countrymen and members of the target culture. The measures of social distance were extrapolated by means of a semantic differential technique. In his study, Acton reported that an optimal perceived social distance ratio among the three scores existed, and further that the successful language learners held themselves at some distance from both the target and native cultures.

Chapter 12

Plots and Plans

Facilitating culture learning as a process and developing intercultural communicative skills can and should be part of any language curriculum. To achieve these, careful plans must be laid.

This chapter and a following one review, discuss, and exemplify several approaches to cultural training and culture learning as well as the ways and means of planning culture learning components for implementation in a second language learning context. The array of choices on the cultural training menu available to any teacher is very rich, indeed. Those described in this and subsequent chapters should be regarded as mere appetizers. It is hoped that these brief tastes will whet the appetites of those who read this book so that they will avail themselves of the many courses available.

To that purpose this chapter discusses several approaches to cultural training. Following this review, guidelines for the planning of specific cultural learning projects will be presented. Thus, first for the plots and then for some plans.

12.1 TWO PERSPECTIVES ON RESEARCH AND TRAINING

From the outset there have been two basic points of view or schools of thought concerning intercultural communication theory, research, and practice. Supporters of these two perspectives have been called respectively: cultural critics and cultural dialogists (Asante *et al.* 1979b:11–22).

This dichotomy represents two approaches associated with intercultural communication and the choice of methods to serve given training goals. Adherents of the cultural critical point of view regard cultural differences as potential barriers. They advocate understanding these barriers, and respecting the differences. They promote training to bridge the inevitable cultural gap. The somewhat unfortunate term "critic" refers to the emphasis upon "critical" or vital differences that might be sources of communication breakdown. Methods suited to such an approach are those that explain, illustrate, or exemplify culture-specific differences. Critics operate at three levels: classificatory, analytic, and applicative. Asante, Newmark, and Blake (1979b:20) comment:

> At the classificatory level, the researcher attempts to identify the "barriers" to communication across cultures; at the analytic level, he or she explores the barriers in terms of priority, intensity, or difficulty. When the cultural critic has made the classification and analysis, application to specific settings becomes possible; this level is called applicative.

Cultural dialogists are those whose research and training efforts are directed toward the investigation of cross-cultural communication. Their concern is with the honing of communicative skills fostering higher levels of both self-awareness and cross-cultural awareness, and the development of personality characteristics to enhance cross-cultural communication.

Cultural dialogists have been guided largely by Western rhetorical assumptions in their investigations of cross-cultural communication, according to some observers. Asante, Newmark, and Blake (18) conclude:

> Their work emerged not from concentrated study of the phenomenon of humans interacting across cultures, but rather from the application of rhetorical or symbolic categories to intercultural behavior. Concepts seem to have preceded percepts. The relevance of this work is in the application of one discipline to another, or, rather, in the use of a familiar set of tools for problems for which tools had not yet been invented.

The perspective of the cultural critic was extracted from the rich descriptive lode found in the work of Franz Boas, Ruth Benedict, Alfred Kroeber, and other American anthropologists who made field work an art form and cultural relativity a major dogma. The perspective of the cultural dialogist emerged from the long search for generalizations about behavior led by Freud, Jung, and other psychologists, by those in communication who rejected mechanical models and looked at the intricate process of communication in all its complexity, and by anthropologists and linguists engaged in defining cultural and linguistic universals and general linguistic processes.

Today, few practitioners are exclusively wedded to one approach or the other. Yet, because these schools of thought represent emphases on two different aspects of intercultural communication still reflected in training models, methods, and techniques, it is interesting for us to consider their underlying assumptions. The cultural dialogue school emphasizes internationalism, world-wide communication, and humanism, while cultural criticism seeks to find points of conflict and isolate them as researchable issues in transcultural interaction. The activities of the critics are aimed at sensitizing the researcher and/or trainee to differences; the dialogists bend their efforts primarily to the overcoming of these differences.

12.2 TRAINING MODELS

Not surprisingly, the two approaches outlined above have been associated with specific training models. These models, as well as specific methods and techniques, have been developed, refined, clarified, and combined over the last twenty years. The evolution of these models has not only provided trainers with many choices as to the ways and means to their goals, but has also made planning decisions somewhat difficult.

Understanding the forces that have shaped these models is one way to make certain that the right model, method, and technique are used at the right place and at the right time. A brief review of the development of the major models, as well as their advantages and disadvantages, should simplify the selection process. The evolution of training models has, of course, been greatly influenced by developments in the field of intercultural communication as discussed in Chapter 2.

The first efforts at organized cross-cultural training in the United States after World War II were aimed at preparing those who were to travel abroad for the cultural rigors they would encounter in the unknown cultural worlds. This was the type of instruction supplied in the most part to Peace Corps volunteers in the 1960s and 1970s. It has been called the " university model" and was generally confined to presenting "factual" secondary material chosen to enlighten and prepare the recipient of the training for the rigors of life among THEM. This model was called the "university model" because most of its programs were carried out in the classroom format and by cognitive/didactic methods. Classroom sessions and lectures were primary methods of training.

Hoopes, in discussing the evolution of cross-cultural training, writes (1979b:4):

> It was not long, however, before word began to seep back from the field (then deluge them during the debriefing of returnees) that the "university model" of cross-cultural training they were using left the trainees largely unprepared for the realities of functioning in a radically different socio-cultural environment.

Yet there was the call for practical training for Peace Corps volunteers, for foreign students studying in the United States, for soldiers and diplomats involved in the sporadic but painful American military forays abroad (Korea and Vietnam), and for teachers charged with bringing to their classrooms the promise of the civil rights movement. This call was intended to nurture a climate of cultural pluralism and serve the goals of multicultural education.

Increased attention then was paid to developing training methods to explain and illustrate cross-cultural differences. Several methods and techniques, still part and parcel of any culture trainer's stock in trade, emerged. For example, as noted in Chapter 10, Edward Stewart described mainstream American cultural patterns, assumptions, and values in a contrastive framework in his well-known book, *American Cultural Patterns: A Cross-Cultural Perspective* (1972). Hoopes (1979a:11) writes: "Stewart's work was particularly important because it not only compared and contrasted cultures but examined them from the perspective of cross-cultural *interaction*." From Stewart's work and that of others in the field were developed some major cross-cultural training devices, including "contrast American" role play and Triandis' "culture assimilators." These emphasized the identification of critical differences and culturally appropriate solutions.

These now traditional types of exercises were similar in many ways to those of many foreign language programs. They differed in that the emphasis in cross-cultural training was on culture with a small "c" rather than with a large "C" (civilization) as was the practice in foreign language classes. The new-style training programs were designed to highlight critical points of possible conflict and misunderstanding. This implied that the learners should have knowledge about the target culture as well as be aware of the contrasts which their own cultural patterns might show in relation to the new.

The need for increased self-awareness and understanding gave rise to yet other types of training programs. These emphasized personal growth and self-awareness rather than information and rule-oriented training. The National Training Laboratories instructed business personnel in organizational and human relations skills. Methods and techniques included group interaction and sensitivity training, values clarification, and other interactional activities.

The cultural sensitivity training model, which came into prominence as the problems of the culture-specific approach became critical, emphasized experiential training and held promise for the development of intercultural communicative skills. The model has not been without problems and criticism. Reservations expressed stem from concern over some of the theoretical assumptions on which the model rests as well as upon the use of certain training methods and techniques.

What are some of these principles? As practiced today, modified cultural sensitivity and experiential training rests on the assumption that human beings are fundamentally similar. In some models training for the "cross-cultural mind" is based upon the tenets of Jungian psychology, which hold that the structure of the human psyche is the same for all human beings.

Pierre Casse, a proponent of the Jungian model, *Training for the Cross-Cultural Mind* (1981:ix–x) explains:

> To understand other people requires a minimum of commonality. We have it. All human beings do actually share something in common: a *psyche*. That psyche is "programmed" differently according to the cultures which exist (or have existed) around the world. Furthermore, the content of the psyche varies in relation to the individual genetic inheritance as well as the situational experiences he or she has gone through . . . Deep down inside our psyche, it

seems that we can find a set of what the Swiss psychologist C.G. Jung called the ARCHETYPES which make you and me alike and capable of reciprocal understanding.

Casse continues:

It is our contention that, by its own nature and structure, the mind is cross-cultural, meaning that it has the capacity to understand other people, comprehend the world in a meaningful way and, even more, cope with its own internal dialectics. . . . There is no need for you and me to go around the world to experience some kind of cross-cultural adventure. . . . Talk and listen to the person next to you. The interaction is cross-cultural. Watch the world and discover its "truth." The confrontation between what actually is and your perception of what is or what seems to be is also intercultural.

Casse's training approach, which carries the stamp of European structuralism and echoes the Lévi-Straussian approach to culture, is based on two assumptions: 1) there is no absolute truth; 2) to learn how to learn is the answer (xiii). It would be hard to fault these assumptions. Yet there are others, more fundamental, which have been called into question as will be noted below.

Hoopes (1979b:4), comments on the human relations training approach in general:

. . . it soon became apparent that while the communication and self-awareness skills which resulted from human relations training were of some relevance and value overseas, there were major deficiencies in the methodology. First, human relations training spawns its own behavioral and attitudinal norms that are no more universal than any others. The frequent result was a cross-cultural blindness hardly less dysfunctional than unregenerate ethnocentrism. Such qualities as openness, directness, confrontiveness, which tend to become norms in sensitivity training, translate into biases and stumbling blocks in the encounter with contrasting cultures.

Second, human relations training too often failed to deal directly and substantively with such central cross-cultural issues as perceptual differences, cultural assumptions and values, and cultural awareness. It produced self-insight within the American cultural context, but it did not consistently result in self-awareness in cross-cultural situations. Finally, from the cross-cultural perspective, human relations training suffered the same shortcoming it did elsewhere—it tended to be so thoroughly experiential that it left participants without a conceptual framework within which to turn it into a usable tool. In the end, for most people, the benefit lay in a behavioral residue rather than in a cognitively integrated self-management skill.

In a book review of the Casse manual in the *International Journal of Intercultural Relations* (1981) Cornelius Lee Grove, AFS International/Intercultural Programs, echoes Hoopes' comments by pointing out that some of the assumptions of the Casse model may not be "universally appreciated." He writes (409–410):

Some of these assumptions are:

- that trainees recognize that they have needs, that they are willing and able to assess their needs, and that they share responsibility with the trainer for meeting those needs;
- that self-directed "learning by doing," often involving trial-and-error procedures, is the most effective way of acquiring knowledge and skills;
- that role playing in artificially contrived situations can so realistically reproduce the circumstances of everyday life that the skills gained in the former can be easily transferred to the latter; and
- that open self-disclosure of one's private thoughts and feelings in a public forum is beneficial in terms of learning and personal growth.

Grove concludes that the approach advocated in *Training for the Cross-Cultural Mind* is "culture-bound." He notes that it appeals primarily to an "American middle-class audience . . . but it's hardly appropriate for everyone" (410).

In addition, current research in social psychology and related fields warns us to proceed with caution in the embracing of the "universals" on which some models rest. Shweder and Bourne (1984:195), in discussing the concept of person observe:

People around the world do not all think alike. . . . What's not yet fully appreciated is that the relationship between what one thinks about (e.g., other people) and how one thinks (e.g., "contexts and cases") may be *mediated* by the world premise to which one is committed (e.g., holism) and by the metaphors by which one lives (Lakoff and Johnson, 1980).

12.3 CULTURE TRAINING AT HOME AND ABROAD

Thus, the problem of choosing the most effective training model remains. In addition, a division in the field of intercultural communication developed early in the United States between those whose interest lay with international problems and those with intracultural or interethnic ones. Internationalists have tended to emphasize mainstream American culture and problems of cross-cultural communication. Interethnic groups have supported the development of cultural pluralism and multicultural education in the schools.

Experiential and affective training methods have been suggested as particularly appropriate in domestic multicultural situations and as a means of reducing the effects of ethnocentrism and ethnic bias. Their application has been urged in programs of multicultural education in the United States in which the fostering of cultural awareness, attitudes of cultural relativity, the development of intracultural communicative skills, and the experiencing of cultural differences are program goals (Hoopes and Pusch 1979a; Pusch, Seelye, and Wasilewski 1979:96). Internationalists have tended to support cross-cultural awareness training models and methods. Sensitivity training techniques emphasize the understanding of one's own self and culture, so may serve the purposes of the cultural pluralists and multiculturalists better than they would those of the internationalists.

Some Choices

Because teachers and other professionals trained in the field of ESL/EFL must deal with both of the faces of cultural diversity, internal and external, in terms of possible positions as bilingual teachers in our elementary and secondary schools, as directors of programs to develop a sense of cultural pluralism and the value of multiculturalism, and as second language teachers using texts combining both approaches (see Chapter 13), the division between those who are mainly concerned with cross-cultural variation and those concerned with intra-cultural variation is a gap to be bridged both personally and professionally.

That there are similarities in cross-cultural or intercultural communication and intracultural communication seems evident. Misunderstandings arise because of different styles of communication, shared meanings, experience, and other sociocultural factors. Yet to treat intra- and intercultural differences as only ranges of variations within a culture, or between cultures, will mask the different values found within minority groups of that culture. To take note only of "mainstream" culture, as so many of our textbooks have in the past, is to risk subscribing to a misleading one-dimensional view of a culture; to present only given subcultures is equally misleading for it misses the ways in which the parts relate to the whole.

Achieving the correct balance is a problem faced daily by teachers, and most particularly by language teachers, who are asked to guide the culture learning of their students. Whose culture are they to teach? If a textbook presents a description of a particular cultural group within the target culture, must the teacher balance the cultural load and point out variations? These questions and problems, as so many we have posed in this book, do not lend themselves to standardized answers; their solutions must be found in the context of the communicative moment. The conclusion that neither the inter- nor the intra- approach supplies the exclusive sets of answers is surely the better part of pedagogical wisdom.

A Solution

Today the perspectives of the cultural critics and cultural dialogists, of the internationalists and the interethnicists, of the sensitivity trainers and the cross-culturalists should not represent "either/or" propositions but rather a range of methodological choices, each appropriate and productive under given circumstances in given contexts for given trainees. The richness of the choice calls for careful consideration by the trainer; such scrutiny will bring rewards to trainer and trainee alike. Similarities and differences, culture-general and culture-specific perspectives, all have a place in the curriculum of a language classroom in which culture learning is a recognized part of the daily lesson plans.

Let us then reconsider the two approaches discussed at the beginning of this chapter: those of the cultural critic and the cultural dialogist. Let us call them, for the sake of simplicity, a culture-general approach and a culture-specific approach. We need not employ one or the other approach exclusively. Let us choose a combined approach. A cultural-general approach emphasizes intercultural communicative skills and is most closely allied to the cultural dialogists' point of view. The culture-specific approach focuses on the need to understand cultural processes and components, but is most directly concerned with understanding the *whys* and *wherefores* of a particular group. It may well be that a combination of both points of view and methods will prove most effective. Thus, the double perspective may not have to be a matter of choice but simply a bonus.

To benefit from this double perspective the lesson planner then must take careful stock of the context, clients (students), and content of any training program. Sensitivity training may be quite in order if the training involves those who are comfortable with the methods used (native students in a multicultural classroom in the United States); it may be less successful if the training is planned for those who are not (students in a multicultural second or foreign language classroom). Planning projects to facilitate cultural discovery and learning, then, becomes a matter of balancing the variables of student characteristics and needs, appropriate content, and effective methods and techniques.

12.4 PLANNING STUDENT CULTURE TRAINING PROJECTS

At the present time those planning training programs to develop intercultural communicative skills and cross-cultural awareness must consider several aspects. First, what training model and methods are to be chosen? We have already suggested one might choose a culture-specific, a culture-general, or a combined experiential and didactic model designed to develop both types of skills. A choice must be made between implementing integrated or specific learning projects. That is to say, are the units to be part of the language instruction (integrated), or are they to be independent projects? How structured should the instructional episodes be? Second, the goals, objectives, and rationale of instruction must be delineated. Third, appropriate content, methods, and techniques should be chosen to present the instructional material. Fourth, the project should be administered, student responses evaluated, and the project itself re-evaluated.

In the following portion of this chapter, a plan for the development of teaching units (project) will be presented and the first two points of decision will be addressed. This project is to be carried out in four phases. The first phase, Presentation of the General Plan (Form A), is discussed in this chapter. Phase Two, Lesson Plans (Form B), is covered in Chapter 14, and Phases Three and Four in Chapter 15. Four completed projects are contained in Appendix B. The planning and execution of your project need only be limited by your own imagination and situation. If possible, focus on your target group. If you cannot, then tailor your project to the circumstances that obtain for you. Although the examples given in this book are predicated upon the availability of second language students in an academic classroom context, the method of planning and implementation may be adapted to any teaching context.

Choosing Training Models and Orientation

Training models may be designed to develop intercultural communicative skills and sensitivity or cross-cultural awareness or both. In addition, the type of training may be intended to develop: a) behavioral changes (attitudes, attributions, or conduct); b) insight into one's own cultural patterns or those of others; or c) culturally appropriate hypotheses about the behavior of others.

The teacher planning culture training projects must not only choose which general orientation to take—culture-general or culture-specific, intercultural or intracultural—but also decide how the instruction should take place. Figure 12.1 indicates the relationship of these elements in the form of a circle with four polar points. The axis AB represents the degree of structure of the learning exercise. Unstructured projects would include general discussion, a field trip, or some open-ended situational exercises. General learning goals may be set but specific objectives are not. Structured exercises are less flexible and should be developed in terms of the learners' needs. For example, in a class consisting of newly arrived students on a university campus, an exercise that permits the students to learn about the services of the university could be planned as a treasure hunt. Such an exercise directs the students to find certain locations, uncover specific information, and to report their findings to the class within a given period of time. The axis CD represents the orientational continuum, AD/BD representing the culture-general orientation and AC/BC, the culture-specific.

Each quarter of the learning circle indicates a different type of orientation and calls for a different instructional format. For example, cross-cultural awareness training in a structured format might include a presentation, discussion, and illustration of American jazz (AC). A structured intercultural communicative skill project might be designed to illustrate differences in perception as a function of cultural and individual differences (AD). A magazine illustration is often enough to spark such discussions. A general discussion of the problems of foreign students can serve to enhance intercultural communicative skills. Many of the recent

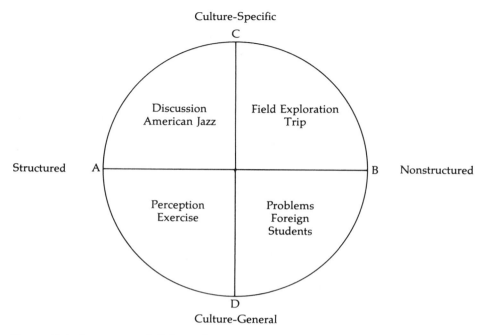

Figure 12.1. Language and Culture Planning Circle

textbooks designed to encourage "discussion" propose these kinds of activities (*BD*). A cross-cultural nonstructured activity might include a field trip to a local school in order to encourage observation of cultural patterns and set up contrastive frames of reference (*BC*). The students would be encouraged to observe, comment, and discuss their perceptions.

Setting Goals

As should be evident from the previous discussions in this book, some cultural groups share characteristics, while others seem far removed from each other. As might be expected, wide differences may give rise to a range of variation in social perception and problems of communication. They also lend more power to the affective variables, which are so entwined in personal and cultural values, orientations, norms, and taboos. The greater the social distance of the two cultures, as perceived by the individual learner, the greater the impact of culture shock and culture stress is likely to be.

Thus, the addition of the cultural dimension in the language classroom will focus attention on processes, many of which have either been passed over or given mere lip service in the past. Recognition of the cultural connection will not make teaching and learning languages simpler; it may afford more satisfactory outcomes. A culturally sensitive approach does mandate that the goals of the learner be given serious consideration in the design and implementation of training programs.

The incorporation of culture learning into a traditional classroom setting is no easy task, as many warn us (Krashen 1976, 1978, 1982; Paulston 1974, 1978; Schumann 1978). Yet because such learning does take place in our classrooms every day, teachers must attempt to facilitate culture learning and reduce the acculturative stress that often accompanies language learning. One way to do so is to understand where our students are "coming from," literally and figuratively.

Several possible outcomes of the process of acculturation have been listed: rejection, assimilation, biculturalism. Often these end states have been taken to constitute goals and objectives of cultural training. Such conclusions pre-empt the learner's right to choose and also place a heavy burden on the culture guide.

On the contrary, the goals and objectives of cultural training should serve to enhance the processes leading to culture learning rather than to specific competencies. This does not mean that culture-specific information is not desirable; it does mean that the *ways* of culture learning are more important than the *whats* of culture learning. Explanations, elucidations, and rule-setting-forth should be only a small part of the culture learning process. More important are provisions for practice in culture learning as a self-directed process. In this way the teacher serves not as a judge and dispenser of the code of cultural rights and wrongs, but as a guide, a facilitator, and a mediator.

General Goals. In general the goals of any cross-cultural and intercultural training should be:

1. to expand cultural awareness of both the student's native culture and the target culture;

2. to increase tolerance and acceptance of the existence of different values, attitudes, and belief systems as part of a target culture;

3. to encourage a seeking to understand the new and different cultural patterns;

4. to develop intercultural communicative skills in areas in which cross-cultural similarities occur;

5. to develop a perspective of cross-cultural awareness that recognizes cultural differences and fosters understanding of the strength found in diversity; and

6. to develop an attitude of acceptance toward change and personal adjustment; to foster personal flexibility in order to open avenues for learning and growth throughout a lifetime; and to understand that culture shock is a natural process.

General Objectives. Some general objectives of any culture learning program should include activities relative to a target culture and designed to foster:

1. discovery of salient cultural themes, patterns, and values orientations;
2. awareness of the affective and culture-specific attributions given verbal and nonverbal behavior;
3. skill in forming appropriate cultural hypotheses related to behavior, perceptions, and expectations;
4. skills of observation and information gathering that will facilitate all of the above;
5. maintenance of a posture of delayed evaluation of the new and strange;
6. an understanding that learning a new culture means taking risks, being willing to change, and enduring much discomfort.

Instructional Goals. H. Ned Seelye, in his book *Teaching Culture: Strategies for Intercultural Communication*, first published in 1974, provides a nuts-and-bolts approach to planning units of cultural instruction. The lesson plans described in this book are based on his suggestions with some additions for the second language context. Although his book is aimed primarily at foreign language teachers, it is an excellent resource for all language teachers.

In the 1984 edition of his book, Seelye presents seven goals of cultural instruction. They represent the first decision point in any instructional planning. They answer the question: why? Seelye's goals (9) relate to student behavior; they involve culture-specific knowledge and the understanding of:

1. the sense, or functionality, of culturally conditioned behavior;
2. interaction of language and social variables;
3. conventional behavior in common situations;
4. cultural connotations of words and phrases;
5. evaluating statements about a culture;
6. researching another culture; and
7. attitudes toward other societies.

Seelye illustrates each of these goals with numerous examples. Readers of this book should be able to supply their own examples, as each of the learning exercises has in one way or another addressed these very general instructional goals. They represent the processes of culture learning. These instructional goals, delimited by the general goals and objectives listed above, must be translated into learning objectives or expected student behavior.

12.5 ORGANIZING THE PROJECT

The general format for the planning of culture training projects follows. The planning of a project includes four main steps: A—setting goals; B—module planning; C—implementation; and D—evaluation.

Four examples of these steps in cultural instructional planning are reproduced in Appendix B. The first is a structured, cross-cultural module on American
education, which was integrated as a part of the general instruction in an advanced writing class. The students were being instructed in the development of
comparison and contrast essays. The background information upon which these
essays were to be based was provided by the content in the cultural units.

The second example is that of a cultural unit that was designed as a noninte-
grated structured module with both cross-cultural and intercultural implications.
It stresses the power of euphemisms as carriers of cultural meaning and their
cross-cultural variations. The third example is a structured learning project developed for an intermediate reading class. The fourth example is a structured project
for an advanced composition class.

The format for planning a module (a series of lessons on the same subject)
should be as follows:

A. Presentation of General Plan
    Cultural Focus
    Target Group
    General Goals
    Instructional Goals
    Theoretical Support

B. Lesson Plans (for each unit)
    Cultural Focus
    Performance Objectives
    Requirements
    Evaluation Bases
    Resource Materials
    Conditions

C. Implementation (lesson plan)
    Cultural Focus
    Learning Activities
    Resources
    Methods
    Sequencing

D. Evaluation (oral or written)

Each planning stage is important. Careful consideration of the rationale or
"reason" for presenting the information is essential (Form A). It is at this stage
that information and knowledge gained from informants and secondary sources
are incorporated into the overall plan.

The planning of the complete module involves detailed consideration of each
unit (Form B). At this stage the focus of a particular module is determined, and

specific performance objectives and desired terminal behavior are set. It is also at this stage that the criteria for evaluation are determined. Each lesson, then, is planned in terms of the cultural focus involved, specific learning activities, resources (actual materials), methods, and sequencing or order of introduction.

The final stage (D) involves unit evaluations of given lessons in whatever form desired. In the examples supplied in Appendix B, these evaluations took various forms, including short written reports and discussions with fellow class members.

12.6 CONCLUSION

This chapter has been concerned with the beginning stages of cultural instructional planning. Several different approaches and perspectives in relationship to cultural training have been discussed. Those who plan such lessons should remember that the selection of an approach, an orientation, and, as we shall see later, the methods and techniques to implement the planned instruction should be matters of choice, but reasoned choice. Setting global goals and understanding the purposes of the instruction constitute the first stage in effective lesson planning.

The following chapters contain information to assist you in developing a culture learning project of your own. You are urged to follow the steps suggested above and to try your hand at developing, administering, and evaluating your own project. No doubt many of you now incorporate cultural information in your lesson plans. The exercise of conscious planning, however, should help focus your efforts and provide more guidance than is possible without such planning.

FOR STUDY AND DISCUSSION

1. Discuss the two approaches to cultural training (cultural critic and cultural dialogist) discussed in this chapter. What general assumptions underlie each approach? What are the advantages of each approach? What are their disadvantages? Under what circumstances might one or the other approach be more suitable?

2. There has been some criticism of the use of sensitivity training methods in cross-cultural instructional contexts. What types of problems have been identified? What consequences might be expected in the use of such techniques in some contexts?

3. How is the approach to intercultural training as presented in the Casse book related to the approach to cultural analysis used by Lévi-Strauss and European structural anthropologists?

4. If you were presented with a textbook in which the content was limited to discussions of minority groups in the United States, how would you "balance" this cultural perspective? Should you try to achieve such a balance?

5. What elements should be considered in setting student learning goals for cultural instructional units?

6. Some general objectives to be achieved in a culture learning program are listed in this chapter. Review each one and suggest the types of activities that might be used to reach these objectives.

7. A notional/functional syllabus that organizes language content by semantic and functional categories (Savignon 1983:308) appears to offer more opportunities than some other more traditional methods for the presentation of cross-cultural training. What might be some of the drawbacks in using this approach exclusively? Be specific!

CULTURE TRAINING PROJECT

Review the following examples of the first stage in planning a cultural training project. Choose a focus for your project. You are to plan at least three units or modules. Include the information requested on Form A (page 252). Examples of completed projects are contained in Appendix B.

In the following chapters you will be asked to submit a plan for *one* of the modules, present it to a student group, and evaluate its outcome. Planning form examples will be supplied in the chapters to follow.

FOR FURTHER READING

The following list of suggested readings includes a variety of manuals and textbooks designed to help the trainer formulate plans. All of them contain information and exercises upon which instructional units may be based. These are only a few of the many available. Others may be located by reviewing bibliographies listed in the major intercultural communication textbooks and training manuals, the publications lists of such organizations as SIETAR (Intercultural Press), and the publications of the David M. Kennedy Center for International Studies, Brigham Young University, Provo, Utah.

P. Casse. 1981. *Training for the Cross-Cultural Mind* is a manual for cross-cultural trainers and consultants. The exercises and activities described are carefully explained and are designed to facilitate intercultural communication. Although this manual was designed for a workshop format, the exercises and activities can be easily adapted to the classroom context. This is a very handy guide for the practiced trainer.

M. Pusch (ed.). 1979. *Multicultural Education: A Cross-Cultural Training Approach.* This volume is recommended for anyone charged with planning and implementing cultural instructional modules or units. Of particular interest to the novice is Chapter 1, "Definitions of Terms" by David S. Hoopes and Margaret D. Pusch.

M. Pusch, A. Patico, G. Renwick, and C. Saltzman. 1981. "Cross-cultural Training" (72–103). This chapter in *Learning Across Cultures*, G. Althen (ed.), presents an overview of the steps in planning a training program. Various approaches, methodologies, and evaluation procedures are described. There is an excellent bibliography of general references and sources of supporting materials, such as films, guides and organizations.

H. Seelye. 1984. *Teaching Culture. Strategies for Intercultural Communication.* This is "must" reading for the instructional planner. It was first published in 1974 and has been one of the very few training textbooks for language teachers concerning specific procedures for teaching culture. The many examples and lesson plans are invaluable as sources of ideas, procedures, and even mistakes to be avoided. There is much to recommend in this textbook. It has been used by this author in a course on "Teaching for Cross-Cultural Understanding." It served students and teacher well.

CULTURE TRAINING PROJECT

FORM A

GENERAL PLAN

I. Cultural Focus

II. Target Group

III. General Goals

IV. Instructional Goals

V. Theoretical Support

Chapter 13

Textbook Selection and Evaluation

The process of selecting a student textbook is often a hurried procedure carried out before a class has been formed and with more hope than certainty that the choice will be right. In practice, the selection method sometimes appears more like a game of Russian roulette than an exercise in a rational process. Consequently, teachers may be asked to use textbooks chosen on a "try-it-you'll-like-it" basis—textbooks that may be ill-suited to teacher and student alike.

13.1 WEIGHING THE CULTURAL LOAD

In all fairness to those making these choices, it must be admitted that the selection of a textbook is generally a difficult process. There are several reasons this should be so. First, there are many texts from which to choose. This is a mixed blessing unless the bases of choices can be well-defined. Second, the selection process is predicated on a set of probabilities concerning the types of skills to be taught, the needs of students likely to form the class, and the curriculum objectives to be met. Only rarely are all these exigencies fully served. Although many textbooks are available, the method of selection is often only marginally effective.

13.2 THE SELECTION PROCESS

In the case of selecting textbooks for use by second, or foreign language students, additional problems and hazards make the process even more difficult. The appropriateness of the content, the methods to be used to reach curriculum goals, and the relationship of these goals to the learning goals of students must be reconsidered when the additional variables of a new language and a new culture are added.

Yet textbooks must be selected. Indeed, this process may lead to the most critical decision taken by planners and designers. Joiner has written, "With the exception of the teacher . . . , perhaps, the single most influential 'culture bearer' in the language classroom is the textbook" (1974:242). Clearly, the choice should not be taken lightly.

The selection process is more complex than might be expected. There are two points at which selection is effected. The first occurs when the initial choice is made; the second when the text is brought into the classroom. There are hazards associated with both actions. In the first place, the process is often hurried. As Cowles (1976:300) states:

> Haphazard is a word which can often be applied to the manner in which foreign language textual materials are evaluated by harried teachers, pressured curriculum committees, and others charged with making decisions on this important aspect of today's foreign language courses.

He further points out (300) that "no text or set of materials has 'all the answers,' and that no reviewer can foresee all the situations in which textual materials might be used."

As if that were not enough, when the chosen textbook is taken into the classroom, a second selection process takes place. This process, in contrast to the initial procedure, is not based on a set of probabilities as to the characteristics of students, their levels of competence, and the skills of the teachers. It is rather a process of selection, enhancement, avoidance, or reinforcement of pre-selected textual material by students and teachers alike. As Daoud and Celce-Murcia (1979: 306) point out, "The ultimate evaluation of a text comes with actual classroom use." Neither students nor teachers come to the second language classrooms as cultural or linguistic novices. They bring "ideas about, and an attitude toward, the foreign culture" (Joiner 1974: 242). Thus, the selection process continues as the textbook is added to the pedagogical balance between curriculum and course objectives.

13.3 STUDENT TEXTBOOKS: NO EASY CHOICES

In the past, the criteria for choosing a textbook were generally limited to the prospective students' levels of proficiency, the linguistic skills to be developed, and a set of pre-determined course goals. Today the communicative approach to second language learning and teaching mandates the practice of meaningful communication as language exercises (Munby 1978; Paulston 1974; Widdowson 1978). The current emphasis on cultural as well as linguistic instruction has meant that questions regarding the type of cultural content to be presented, and its purpose must be accorded equal consideration in the evaluation process.

While the question of textbook selection has become more critical as the flood of culturally sensitive textbooks increases, the implications of their language and culture content has long been recognized. Robert Lado in his book, *Linguistics Across Cultures,* already warned us in 1957 (2–3) that we should pay more attention to such matters:

> On the surface, most textbooks look pretty much alike. Publishers see to it that their books look attractive and that the titles sound enticing. This is part of their business. If a teacher is professionally trained, however, he will be able to look beyond attractive illustrations and handsome printing and binding. He should be able to see whether the book presents the language and culture patterns that form the system to be studied, and does not merely list disparate items from here and there. He should also be able to discern whether the book gives due emphasis to those patterns that are difficult because they are different from those of the native language of the students.

He further suggests that textbooks should be "graded as to grammatical structure, pronunciation, vocabulary, and cultural content" (3). At the time Lado made these comments, language texts were focused primarily on grammatical instruction, vocabulary development, and pronunciation. Cultural content was covert, lurking unrecognized in the vocabulary studied and the sentences used for practice. Students generally remained blissfully unconscious of the currents of cultural meaning running through their classrooms.

Reading excerpts, which were often limited to vignettes of life in a specific foreign context, were more likely to be structurally enlightening than culturally comprehensible. These episodes of "life in . . ." were rendered even more puzzling by the usual insistence upon the use of the now largely rejected grammar translation method of instruction. The inadequacies of translation, linguistically and culturally, were further compounded by the assumption on the part of the authors of texts, teachers, and students alike that "culture" meant "high culture" (civilization), as manifested in the art, music, literature, or poetry of a given group. The concept of culture as patterns for living shared by interacting groups of individuals, as it is generally defined today, was seldom explored in those texts. The "civilization" approach reflected stereotypic conceptions more frequently than it did ethnographic reality. Few who struggled with such texts escaped confusion and disappointment when they moved from the gallery of one-dimensional natives who graced the pages of their textbooks to the real world. Students searched in vain for those merry-making, carefree Italians, eternally dancing Mexicans, Indian-fighting American cowboys, or blue-frocked, sabot-clad Frenchmen. To those fortunate enough to take their stereotypic visions abroad and test them against reality, the joy at the sight of the new usually far outweighed the disappointment of the imagined.

If, in the past, attempts to offer cultural content as well as linguistic instruction in our language textbooks fostered more stereotyping than cultural understanding, today we are more fortunate. The current emphasis on the development of the communicative competence of our students has brought culture into our classrooms and textbooks, explicitly and intentionally. Sociolinguistic competence has been seen as one of the major components of communicative competence (Bachman and Palmer 1982:451). Thus, in addition to meeting the demands of the teacher, the students, and the curriculum in making a proper textbook selection, those in charge of the process must consider another element, content.

Happily, we have come a long way from the days of teaching culture as an unplanned and often serendipitous addition to our language curricula. We have been helped along the way by the work of Dell Hymes (1972 a, b, 1974); J. J. Gumperz and Dell Hymes (1972); Joshua Fishman (1966); M. A. K. Halliday (1978); and others who have focused our attention successively on the importance of the speech community, the social context and rules of language use, code switching as a function of context, and functions of language as sociosemantic options.

These new considerations in language learning—context, cultural rules, sociosemantic options—provide a rich pool from which to draw instructional material. This richness, however, also confers a heavy responsibility on those in charge of curriculum development. Questions about the type of cultural content to be included, the role of the teacher, the context in which the text is to be used, and student goals can only be answered by carefully weighing the cultural implications or "load" of all factors.

The torrent of culturally oriented student textbooks, spurred by the demands for communicative material, is now at flood stage. The innovative and absorbing content is a welcome relief from the unrealistic and tiresome episodes of less culturally sensitive texts.

Anyone reviewing current student textbooks cannot fail to be aware of their virtually universal mission: the development of the communicative competence of students. What may seem less clear is the connection between the organization of the content and the stated mission.

Textbooks designed to serve communicative curricula and syllabi may be organized in various fashions. Thus, some texts are designed to elucidate the notions and functions of the target language. Students are instructed in the forms and their uses, as, for example, the ways and means of greeting, leave-taking, getting rid of unwanted guests, or dealing with the local police. Others exploit given situations, such as going to the dentist or visiting a sick relative in the hospital. Others are organized in a manner to develop the language skills and vocabulary for special purposes (medicine, law, engineering). Then there are those that employ a more traditional format, presenting grammatical forms in a spiral of increasing difficulty, but, in the spirit of the times, encouraging the practice of these forms in various formats.

The communicative emphasis in all these formats ensures the addition of a cultural emphasis. The choice of one or the other of these formats, however, influences and, at times, even mandates the cultural content to be presented. For example, the omission of a general category, such as communicative style, in a notional-functional format implies that there are no significant differences between the patterns of the target culture and that of the students. This may or may not be true.

Selecting and using a student textbook must include more than choosing a given organization form. In point of fact, the format, or organization, of the textbook should not form the first point of selection as it frequently does. That decision should be delayed until other matters are weighed.

Thus, although many administrators and teachers are more at ease assessing the linguistic than the cultural impact of a given text, there is more reason to celebrate than to despair; there is more reason to be grateful than overcome by the current *largesse*. Although the discovery of the perfect textbook remains an impossible dream, the odds of making reasonable and reasoned choices will be considerably enhanced if evaluation and selection processes are based on a systematic analysis of the cultural load or affective force impinging on the bases of choice: communicator (teacher), client (student), context, and text.

13.4 IN THE BALANCE

The following portion of this chapter describes a set of procedures that may be followed in the process of textbook evaluation and selection. These procedures are based on the identification of key elements or "weights" that must be assessed according to the bases of choice (context, client, communicator, and text) to achieve an appropriate pedagogical balance between curriculum demands and course objectives. Figure 13.1 indicates the relationship of these elements. This illustration is meant to convey the need to examine various elements related to the linguistic and cultural content of a textbook and to determine their weight or load. The weight assigned is, of course, determined by a subjective evaluation, yet the consideration of all these elements by the evaluator assures that the major variables are considered in a systematic fashion.

The language elements (weights) are *content, skills, approach,* and *level* are familiar to most evaluators. Those related to culture—*content, method,* and *perspectives*—may be less so. In the following discussion, different types of content, methods, and perspectives will be examined, along with types of clients, communicators, contexts, and finally, texts. Several working classifications to assist in identifying the major characteristics of dominant groups or divisions are suggested. The *ad hoc* nature of these typologies permits their use as heuristic devices only; as such, they are, of course, open to modification or expansion.

In the following discussion it is assumed that those who select textbooks must still answer the traditional questions—Is the text suited to the prospective students? Is it too complex? Is the subject matter linguistically appropriate? Is the approach suitable? Is it too expensive? How does this text fit in with other texts being used? These are familiar questions.

But in assessing the cultural load, other questions must be asked. For example, we need to know to what purpose the cultural information is presented. Is the focus on culture in general or on a specific culture? What ranges of subcultures are described? Is the cultural information hidden or secondary to linguistic drills?

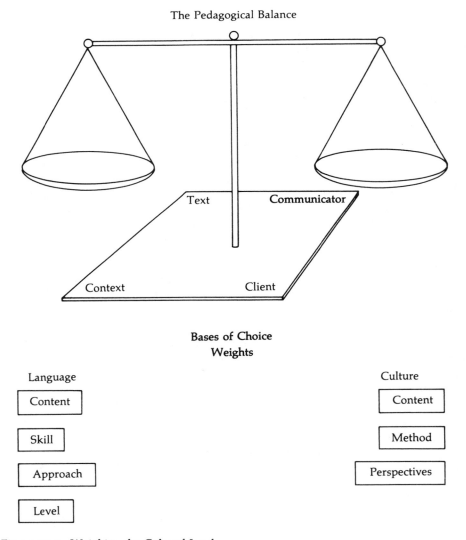

Figure 13.1. Weighing the Cultural Load

Would any specific cultural group be offended by any illustrations or content? Would some teachers find it "difficult" to handle given content?

Answers to these questions lie in a systematic consideration of the basic variables for the purpose of measuring the weight of the cultural load in a given text for given students in a given context. In this discussion the term "load" is used to designate the emotional, affective, and often culturally specific power associated with given types of content, approaches, and perspectives. Thus "heavy" cultural loads are those that carry great emotional and evaluative impact. Often the weight of the cultural load is hidden or covert, to both instructor and student. Those who would weigh this load—that is, bring to a conscious level the hidden assumptions, covert givens, and the affective evaluations of specific content, method, or perspectives—may, and perhaps must be, native culture bearers. It is well to recall the admonition of anthropologists such as Edward Hall, who warn us that it is the hidden, the most "taken-for-granted and therefore the least studied aspects of culture that influence behavior in the deepest and most subtle ways" (1977:17). The weight of cultural content lies in its unrealized emotional impact. As Hall points out, it is, as in the case of the purloined letter, the obvious, the least noted aspects which are of the greatest import.

Thus, weighing the cultural load calls for pushing aside the natural cultural screen and assessing the cultural content with as much detachment as we do the linguistic content of a textbook. We must, in fact, step outside our own cultural identities and walk in the shoes of others if we are to make honest evaluations and suitable selections.

Finally, by their subscription to a communicative approach to second language teaching, with its assumptions of cultural relativism, definitions of communication and culture, and the nature of culture learning as outlined in previous chapters, program directors and teachers commit themselves to dealing with the cultural questions mentioned. Although these questions may only be answered in relation to real students in real classrooms who are taught by real teachers, careful textbook evaluation and selection procedures provide a major step in the direction of achieving a communicative, culturally sensitive approach to second language instruction and learning in a variety of contexts and for a variety of clients.

Bases of Choice

As any practitioner in the field of second language learning is aware, many of the current communicative texts are designed for teachers who are native speakers of the language and presumably bearers of the "culture" presented. This is often not so. In addition, the types of clients and contexts are also variables which must be weighed during selection procedures. Table 13.1 lists a series of classifications of these major variables: client, context, communicator, and text. In the following portion of this chapter the implications of the characteristics of these variable types will be discussed.

TABLE 13.1 IN THE BALANCE

	Types	Goals
Clients (Students)	sojourner	accommodation; return to native culture
	immigrant	acculturation; assimilation
	refugee	accommodation; survival; restricted assimilation
	visitor/traveler	study; professional interests; personal goals; personal pleasure
Context	Types: formal; informal on-the-job/classroom; native/foreign; planned/serendipitous	
Communicator	Types: native; non-native; sociocultural variables	
Text	**Culture**	
	Content: culture-specific, culture-general; themes; facts-realistic, values-idealistic; institutional, eclectic	
	Perspectives: process of learning a new culture; cultural components; language and culture; nature of culture	
	Methods: problem solving; case studies; discovery; explanation; discussion; implication; role play; contrast; rule presentation	

Types of Clients. Four general classes of clients (students) are posited: *sojourner, immigrant, refugee,* and *visitor/traveler* (see Chapter 11). Each type exhibits certain features and goals that must be considered in the textbook selection process. The term "client" rather than "student" identifies this classification as the latter designation could be misleading. Many of those who attend classes, using the textbooks we select, are not "students" in the usual sense. They may be travelers, short-term visitors, or refugees. If we fail to recognize their different goals, we may be baffled by their behavior. They often behave in a quite unstudent-like manner. For example, "travelers" only temporarily identifying themselves as "students" may do little or no studying. This may be especially upsetting if these "students" come from cultures, such as Japan, in which education is highly respected and "hitting the books" is a way of life. Teachers may feel somewhat relieved if they recognize these "students" as "travelers" with special goals.

The first type of client, the *sojourner,* may be unfamiliar. These clients have been identified as "relatively short-term visitors to new cultures where permanent settlement is not the purpose . . ." (Church 1982: 540). The term, as it is used in published literature, is generally applied to foreign students in a host culture, although it may designate technicians, professional scholars, and business people who spend considerable time abroad for purposes other than immigration.

The learning goals of the sojourner are usually directly linked to the specific purpose for which the sojourn is undertaken. In the case of foreign students these purposes are usually related to professional training, or specialized studies, and often are subsidized by the sojourner's home government. Under these circumstances the acculturation process is geared toward accommodation rather than acculturation and focused toward a return to the native culture. In many cases, the sojourners themselves are unaware that a process of change and accommodation is taking place.

Sojourners, as most others entering a new culture, are subject to culture shock, or shock of the new. The sojourner experiences the problems of fatigue, sleeplessness, anxiety, depression, anger, and malaise—all recognized signs of culture shock—not once but often twice. Gullahorn and Gullahorn (1963) state that the sojourner curve of adjustment is a double U or a W curve. The sojourner presumably passes through the stages of acculturation or adjustment, sinking from a high point of enthusiasm at the beginning of the episode to a state of despondency as culture shock is experienced, and then rising to higher levels of adjustment both in the host culture and in the home culture.

Some researchers have expressed doubt as to the validity, or even their empirical reality and predictive value, of such stages of acculturation (Church 1982:542). No one, however, questions the reality of the *problems* sojourners face. Patterns of adjustment are highly individualistic, but the types of academic, personal, and sociocultural problems academic sojourners may experience are predictable, as attested to in the long lists of "student problems" enumerated in the literature on sojourner adjustment.

The value of these speculations about sojourner problems in relation to selecting textbooks lies in the recognition that "adjustment" involves both accommodation to a new culture and readjustment to the native culture. This means that the sojourner's culture learning goals are predicated on the premise of a return to the home culture. Seldom, however, is the problem of readjustment met directly by either students or teachers. Classroom content directed toward assimilation to the new culture, or which reflects cultural patterns at odds with that of the native culture, may be rejected by the sojourner. On the other hand, if new ideas are embraced too warmly, the sojourner's return to the native culture may be even more painful than the first encounter with the new culture (Foust *et al.* 1981). For example, a North American visitor returning from an extended stay in Japan is likely to feel almost physically assaulted by the decibel level of personal communication in the home territory. Conversely, imagine the feelings of disorientation experienced by those accustomed to the academic amenities in the United States upon returning to their less technologically developed homelands. A graduate student from India commented, "Do you know that we had to make carbon copies by hand of the research material? Can you imagine?" After several years in such a technological paradise, neither could she. While this deprivation might seem trivial, it may well loom large as a source of dissatisfaction upon her return.

Types of Contexts. There are, of course, many different types of contexts for second language and second culture learning. These contexts may be found, for example, on the job or in native or foreign environments. Thus, a learning context may be an informal but a planned program of orientation in the target culture. It may also be a formal classroom in the student's native culture in which learning about a foreign culture occurs by happenstance. These are only two examples of possible contexts.

Each context may enhance or impede both language and culture learning. Textbook evaluation, selection, and use must be executed within a given context. That some contexts enhance language learning better than others cannot be denied. The choice is seldom up to the teacher; therefore, it is important to consider characteristics of a given context carefully in choosing and using textbooks.

Types of Communicators. Just as contexts, clients, and textbooks vary, so do those who serve as teachers or communicators. In the case of culture learning, the teacher's role is particularly sensitive. Variations may be measured by such sociocultural dimensions as age, social class, sex, experience, country of origin, and education. Different types of texts call for special expertise on the teacher's part. Some call for a practiced intercultural communicator, others for a native culture bearer. Still others call for a cultural mediator who is able to bridge all intercultural gaps—perhaps not at a single bound—but with alarming regularity in a multicultural classroom.

Types of Textbooks. Textbooks may be analyzed in terms of content, perspective, and methods.

The cultural content contained in a textbook may be seen as culture-specific (related to the patterns of a particular culture), or culture-general (related to general aspects of culture as a universal adaptive human mechanism). This is the first major division. There are far more of the former than of the latter. We are all familiar with books that "explain" the United States to refugees from Southeast Asia (Kuntz 1982), or Japanese businessmen (Okada and Okada 1973). These books tend to carry fairly general information about major themes and patterns of the dominant culture. Culture-general textbooks, as we shall see later in the discussion of specific types of textbooks, emphasize cultural universals, need for understanding, and promotion of empathy. An example of such a textbook is *Communication and Culture* (Gregg 1981); an example of a culture-specific textbook might be *Living in the USA* (Lanier 1978).

Content may also be analyzed in terms of the presentation of cultural patterns. Are these patterns presented in a factual or "realistic" approach or as an "idealized" system? For example, a textbook using a factual approach would be more likely to present actual case studies, real life examples, and specific data about a cultural group. The "idealized" approach tends to "explain" given cultural behavior. It is often disguised as an "Introduction to. . . ."

Content may also be analyzed according to its approach to cultural elements. Is the emphasis on learning a new culture, explaining given cultural components (the ways of greeting or organization of schools), tying together language and culture and learning, or simply learning about the nature of culture? As we shall see later, some textbooks combine some or all of these elements.

The types of approach to cultural content and the perspectives chosen are related. Culture-specific content is likely to contain information about cultural components and themes, whereas the modern culture-general texts are more concerned with the processes of learning a new culture and understanding the nature of culture.

Methods of presenting cultural content also vary. As will be discussed in Chapter 14, there are many methods and techniques to present cultural data. They may be divided into two general categories: those that promote understanding of new cultural themes, patterns, and behavior, and those designed to produce appropriate behavior. In the former we find such methods and techniques as case studies, explanation, discussion, and implication or inference. The latter employ such methods as role play, rule presentation, practice of expected behavior, and cultural hypothesizing.

In the section of this chapter concerning the types of textbooks available, the nature of the cultural content is discussed more specifically, as cultural content itself serves best as the means to weigh the cultural load of the texts now available.

Table 13.2 presents a proposed textbook taxonomy. The three major classes posited are: *traditional, communicative,* and *cultural/linguistic.* Each general class has two or more subclasses. These types are differentiated on the basis of the approach or format used to present cultural content. The student textbooks cited in the chapter are listed in the bibliography.

In general, textbooks that might be classified as traditional (I.A.) are familiar to most teachers. Such textbooks focus primarily on linguistic skills; any cultural information presented is implicit or merely part of the linguistic data used for linguistic practice or to demonstrate linguistic points. Examples are grammar, reading, or writing textbooks which place the major emphasis on linguistic skill development. Cultural instruction or explanation, which, of course, emerges through the use of language, is left to the teacher.

Another type of traditional textbook is one in which linguistic skills training is still primary, but the cultural focus is less implicit (I.B). These texts provide practice of language in use, promote vocabulary development, and may explore semantic ranges. The cultural content is more extensive than in Type I.A. General reading texts, especially for advanced levels, are of this type. The cultural information is more apparent, but still the burden of explanation and instruction is

TABLE 13.2 TYPES OF STUDENT TEXTBOOKS

I. *Traditional*	
A. Linguistic skills	culture implicit; peripheral; linguistic skills primary focus
B. Linguistic skills	culture focus still secondary, but less implicit; language in use; vocabulary development; semantic range
II. *Communicative*	
A. Notional-functional; situational	culture and communication primary focus; often heavy emphasis on development of oral skills
B. Supplemental	focus upon idiom; language use; specific functions for target group
III. *Cultural/linguistic*	
A. Thematic	cultural content and focus, plus complementary linguistic drill or practice
1. Universal	content related to universal human problems; an emphasis on similarities of difficulties and differences in solutions
2. Specific	
a. Stated linguistic focus	content culture-specific; emphasis on culturally relevant vocabulary; discussion encouraged
b. Descriptive or explanatory	linguistic focus minimal or absent; components of target culture examined
c. Directed discovery	readings relating to cultural themes; culture-specific and culture-general; often in form of anthologies of selected readings
B. Developmental	related to individual change
1. Acculturative	examines process and methods of change; survival; problem solving; culture-general or culture-specific
2. Intercultural communicative	focus upon development of intercultural communicative skills
C. Eclectic	combination of IIIA or IIIB above

usually left to the teacher. Examples of such texts, which are directed toward the development of advanced language skills, are *Reader's Choice* (Baudoin *et al.*) and *Skillful Reading* (Sonka). The choice of reading excerpts and the emphasis on discovering context clues in such texts call not only for an understanding of English syntax but also for familiarity with cultural patterns.

A second class (II.A.) includes textbooks of more recent origin than those just described. These are the communicative texts, which often focus on the development of oral or reading skills, with the transmission of cultural communicative information and practice being of primary importance. Some of the material prepared for use with refugee training programs and immigrants is of this type. Explicit cultural information is presented; survival skills are emphasized. Three examples of this type of text are *Fitting In* (Coffey), *Speaking of Survival* (Freeman), and *Japanese for Beginners* (Yoshida *et al.*).

Another type of communicative textbook may be called supplemental (II.B.). These texts are ordinarily targeted for given types of students or language learners, and supply basic information to be used either in conjunction with more traditional or linguistically oriented textbooks or simply as guides in less formal language learning situations. Examples of this type of text are: *Colloquial English* (Collis), *Do's and Don'ts for the Japanese Businessman Abroad* (Okada and Okada) and *American Cultural Encounters* (Ford and Silverman). They supply culture-specific information, usually in simple discourse form. As such, they are informative and culturally sensitive; they are a welcome improvement on traditional guidebooks.

The third major class of textbooks are those labeled cultural/linguistic (III). These are further divided into three subclasses: thematic, developmental, and eclectic. The newest and most innovative textbooks on the market, they are designed to incorporate language and culture learning and to develop students' communicative competence. In the cultural/linguistic texts, cultural content and focus plus complementary linguistic drill, practice, and content may be found. In some cases the cultural content is related to linguistic patterns. These texts may be distinguished from traditional texts in that the latter give primary emphasis to linguistic skills development.

Thematic texts are concerned with the presentation of cultural patterns. They may be either universal or specific. In the first type the context is related to universal problems such as family relations, old age, employment, pollution, and the status of women. These texts may approach the cultural content from a universal or a specific perspective. A universalistic approach (III. A. 1.) treats the general processes of culture and often communication. The main focus is not so much on linguistic skills as on communicative skills and cross-cultural understanding. An example of this type of text is *Communication and Culture. A Reading-Writing Text* (Gregg), previously cited. The readings contained in this text are unadapted selections in introductory cultural anthropology. As stated in the Preface (vii), "The content, drawn from American and foreign cultures, is appropriate and interesting for both native and nonnative students." Chapter headings include such topics as "Culture and Human Behavior," "Culture and Reality", and "Culture and Food Habits." The theme of the reading selection is also the theme of the accompanying exercises. Key concepts presented in this text represent fundamental anthropological dogma. The teacher using such a text would need more than a nodding acquaintance with this dogma and its implications to field the questions students will surely raise.

Specific thematic texts, on the other hand, are culture-specific; that is, they present cultural themes and patterns shared by a given cultural group. These texts are of three types: linguistic, descriptive, and directed discovery. The first type (III.A.2. a.) is probably the most familiar. The content is concerned with various cultural patterns, sometimes of one culture and sometimes of several cultures. The culture-specific texts treat a single culture, using the content to present cultural information, which in turn provides data for practice in the development of language competence. Again, the linguistic drills and exercises are related to the reading content, thus reinforcing culture learning. An example of this type of text is *American Mosaic: An Advanced ESL Reader* (Live and Sankowsky). The Preface (ix) clearly states:

> The function of this book is to enhance the language competence of non-English-speaking people in the United States. . . . At the same time these people are introduced to the richly variegated composition of this nation.

These texts differ from the more traditional readers (I.B.) in that the subject matter is selected and presented in connection with cultural learning goals.

The authors continue (x):

> The subject matter of the book is the ethnic and racial groups which together have built up the population as well as the cultural diversity of this country. This theme should appeal to the readers not only because of the current widespread interest in folklife and ethnic heritage, but also because of a special meaning it bears for students of ESL. It shows them that they are not outsiders facing a monolithic society, but newcomers in a land of newcomers. The result should be a positive approach to the material, which will help to stimulate learning.

This text presents readings concerning various ethnic and racial groups in the United States. Another example of such a text is *American Topics* (Lugton). Each of its fifteen chapters "centers upon some aspect of American life" and "treats contemporary issues of concern to older adolescent and adult students" (xiii). The themes are universal—pollution, marriage, wildlife management; the focus is North American (culture-specific).

These texts (III. A. 2. a.) demand increased cultural input from the teacher to round out the cultural picture and supply cultural explanations. Authors choosing such formats and content must assume that the teacher or other user of the text is not only able but also willing to provide these supplementary insights.

Another type of specific thematic textbook (III. A. 2. b.) is primarily descriptive or explanatory. It can be distinguished from the preceding type by its focus, which is cultural, and the relegation of linguistic skill development to a relatively minor role. Examples of these types of textbooks are: *Speaking of the USA: A Reader for Discussion* (Neustadt) and *The USA.* Vol. IV (Tiersky and Tiersky). A main aim of the Neustadt text is to "introduce the contemporary United States with some relevant historical background" (vii). Although exercises to develop linguistic and academic skills are included, cultural content is the primary focus. The cultural information in the *USA* series is dispensed over four volumes whose topics include *The Land and the People* (Vol. I), *Men and History* (Vol. II), *Men and Machines* (Vol. III), and *Customs and Institutions* (Vol. IV). In the last volume, the authors present some analyses of aspects of American life, but do not engage the reader in the process of analysis. The bearer of the culture described is a "mythical 'typical' American."

In these books the approach is historical and descriptive, the content mainly confined to generalizations concerning modal cultural and behavioral characteristics of "Americans."

The teacher using such books should have access to a fairly extensive fund of general knowledge about American cultural patterns, a strong historical background, and the expertise to weave together the many threads of the tapestry of the American culture. The content presented is excellent for developing a cultural comparative framework for the student. For example, knowledge of the educational system in the United States may provide a framework for comparing and contrasting such institutions in the student's native culture. As was stated previously, the setting up of a comparative framework is a vital step in the process of adapting to another culture.

An additional type of specific thematic text (III. A. 2. c.) is one that presents the cultural content in the form of readings that reflect social and cultural problems and that have shaped or are shaping the human experience. These texts are often designed to stimulate discussion and encourage analysis.

Two examples are: *Insights. A Contemporary Reader* (Flint) and *Crossing Cultures* (Knepler and Knepler). Such textbooks are usually aimed at advanced language students and often for both native and non-native speakers. Recently, however, books of this type for intermediate level ESL students have appeared. One example, *Reflections: An Intermediate Reader* (Griffin and Dennis), is designed to develop critical and analytical skills, especially in reading, and contains reading selections about such topics as racial prejudice, self-discovery, and the feminist movement. These excerpts, according to the authors, "represent the material currently being read and discussed by American young people in academic and nonacademic settings" (vii).

The teacher using such texts will be called upon to serve as an "interpreter" as well as a linguistic mentor and, in the case of the first two mentioned, a literary critic. These texts have been placed in a separate classification, for they place a special burden on the teacher. In the case of a text such as *Reflections*, the format, which resembles a traditional reader (I. B.) or a cultural/linguistic type text (III. A. 2. a.), masks important differences in approach. In the traditional text the reading content is meant to be culturally interesting, but the learning objectives are very different from those proposed for the directed discovery (III. A. 2. c.) type. In the latter, issues rather than simple themes are presented and in current rather than historical perspective; the student/reader's role is to interact with the content rather than just understand. The addition of critical and analytical discussion has added a new dimension to the culture-learning game.

Although all of these texts are labeled "readers," the content involved is directed mainly toward understanding and interpreting textual material rather than simply affording reading practice. The teacher using such textbooks would need to supply additional information, balance the content of subcultural variations, and discuss the issues involved. Many of the issues met head-on in these books are highly sensitive and carry heavy cross-cultural implications.

Developmental textbooks (III. B.) are of two types: acculturative and intercultural communicative. Acculturative textbooks (III. B. 1.) are directed toward the rapid acculturation of the student. The bulk of the materials created for the instruction of refugees as well as those used in programs of adult vocational education for second language learners (VESL) are of this type. An example is *The New Arrival* (Kuntz) for U.S.-bound Far Eastern refugees. These are similar to the communicative, notional-functional books (II. A.) but differ in respect to the emphasis placed upon culture learning and adjustment rather than simply explaining how, when, and where an action or behavior takes place in the target culture. For example, in *The New Arrival* the adventures of a mythical Laotian refugee in Laos and in the United States are recounted.

To date, there are few intercultural communicative texts (III. B. 2.). An example is *Beyond Language* (Levine and Adelman). Each chapter of this intermediate reading textbook contains a section about a segment of American culture and supplementary intercultural communication exercises. The primary focus is on the development of intercultural communicative skills. In such textbooks culture learning is placed on an equal footing with language learning. It differs from the thematic/universal (III. A. 1.) type of text in its focus upon the culture-learning process rather than the identification and understanding of the concept of culture and its many cross-cultural manifestations. Thematic universal texts emphasize the tenets of anthropology and other social sciences concerned with human society and interaction; the intercultural communicative texts seek to develop personal skills in bridging cultural gaps.

Finally, there are what might be called cultural/linguistic eclectic texts. They are both thematic and developmental. Examples are: *Points of View* (Pifer and

Mutoh), *Contact USA* (Abraham and Mackey), *Americana Articles* (Ruffner), and *Living Language* (Johnson). These texts are generally culture-specific and explanatory. They are eclectic for there are culture-specific exercises as well as other content to foster the development of intercultural understanding and attitudes concerning culture and cultural differences. For example, in *Points of View* two types of case studies are presented: one for analysis and one for problem solving. The students are expected not only to understand the content but also to "make value judgments" (xvii). Such exercises demand not inconsiderable linguistic skills, cultural hypothesizing, and understanding of cultural themes. Such a text appears deceptively easy, yet it calls for the highest level of teacher input as well as for extensive knowledge of the specific cultural patterns and an understanding of the processes of culture learning.

13.5 LEARNING BY DOING

The preceding typology attempts to focus the selection, evaluation, and classroom use of given kinds of texts. Although there is no "perfect" text, guided and informed choice, which weighs the cultural load of a textbook in terms of method, content, and perspective, and balances this weight in relation to the client, communicator, and context will surely tip the balance in favor of making a satisfactory selection. We are fortunate to have such a large current pool of textual resources. Because we do, it is important that the right choices be made. At the moment, textbooks in the cultural/linguistic category are fewer than those in the first two classes. We can expect more type III texts to be published if the present emphasis on communicative competence continues, although there will always be a place for the traditional and communicative texts.

The challenges of type III textbooks lie in the changing and demanding role assigned the teacher or guide. Because no one person can encompass and internalize all cultural patterns, the teacher cannot pass simply as the all-knowing "native" as can be done in linguistic study. The teacher's role is very different and calls for increased sophistication in terms of intercultural communicative skills and cross-cultural awareness. The challenge is great, but the rewards of taking on a heavy cultural load may also be very great indeed. In so doing we are underscoring our support of the proposition that language and culture learning must proceed in some type of synchrony, if the desired degree of mastery is to be achieved in each.

In the belief that practice makes perfect, you are now asked to "play" the selection and evaluation game in a simulation of the process of choice. The evaluation guide (Culture Learning Exercise) that follows will help you focus on the salient characteristics of any textbook under consideration. It is hoped that this practice will make your future choices easier, better, and more satisfactory to you and your students.

FOR STUDY AND DISCUSSION

1. Some problems of the readjustment to the home culture often experienced by sojourners are discussed in this chapter. Can you think of other problems which might arise? In what ways might the sojourner be "prepared" in advance to meet these problems?

2. It has been suggested in this chapter that the more culturally sensitive a textbook is the greater the demands upon the teacher as a cultural guide might be. Are there types of content that you would find "unacceptable?" Please explain.

3. If you as a teacher are handed a textbook with which you are not "comfortable" because of given cultural content or approach, what should you do?

4. Have you ever "censored" or skipped over certain portions of student textbooks because you felt they were "inappropriate"? If so, describe such content and your reasons for circumvention.

5. Choose a selection from a student reading textbook. Analyze the selection according to the type of textbook, client, context, and communicator (See Table 13.1) for which it is best suited.

6. Choose a student textbook. Analyze the nonverbal "messages" contained in the illustrations. Are there any hidden cultural messages? Do these illustrations carry heavy social and affective meaning? Would explanations of these meanings be needed?

7. What is meant by the term "cultural load" as used in this chapter? Which element (communicator, text, context, or client) appears to you to be the most decisive?

8. Type III textbooks (thematic, developmental, and eclectic) call for a high level of teacher input. What problems might a teacher encounter in using these textbooks without specialized intercultural training?

9. Current textbooks for ESL students often contain examples of informal speech and even what has been termed "nonstandard" dialectical forms. Should such excerpts be used? To what speech varieties should students be exposed? How would you approach the double negatives and faulty case assignment in such standard "nonstandard" American speech as: "I don't know from nothing" and "It's me"?

CULTURE LEARNING EXERCISE

Textbook Selection Simulation

This is a simulation of the textbook selection process. Naturally, as in all simulations, real circumstances can only be approximated, not duplicated. Thus, the selection process practiced here must be hasty, limited, and fragmented.

No textbook could be properly evaluated within the period of time allotted to this exercise. We can, however, consider basic questions that must be asked in order to make valid selections and to achieve a balanced cultural load for given types of clients, contexts, and communicators.

Indeed, the questions asked are as important as the answers you may find. It is hoped that this exercise will assist you in asking the right questions and adding a few of your own.

If this simulation is carried out in a workshop format, use the following procedures. If not, proceed individually, but consider the use of the textbook in a multicultural class, or, if you prefer, in a class composed of members of your target culture.

Selection Procedures

1. Form small groups to serve as *ad hoc* selection committees.

2. Choose a current student textbook to review. This textbook will be used in a class consisting of students from the general areas of the Far East, Middle East, and Latin America. You may assume that their numbers are balanced.

3. In the time you are allotted, answer as many of the questions on the guide sheet as you can. Please *do* complete the questions in Part II.

4. You will be asked to return these forms and, if time permits, make a brief report to the group.

5. Please add any additional questions or comments you think would be appropriate.

TEXTBOOK EVALUATION GUIDE

EVALUATION OF CULTURAL LOAD = SELECTION
(client, communicator, context, content)

Part I. General Descriptive Information

Name of Textbook _____ Author _____

Publisher _____ Date/Place of Publication _____

_____

Rationale

1. For whom is the textbook intended?

2. What is the rationale for the textbook?

3. What is the primary goal of the presentation of cultural information? Is this goal secondary to other goals? Is the goal of the cultural instruction explicitly stated?

4. What type of textbook does this book represent?

Content

1. General subjects covered

2. Specific language skills targeted

3. Cultural content

    a) Are specific cultural items covered? If so, which ones?

    b) Are these items the main teaching focus?

    c) What cultural or social groups are represented? Are members of these groups presented as modal personalities (average) or as individuals?

Presentation of Content

1. How is the content presented (description, example, problem)?

2. Are specific cultural items "explained"? Would additional information or explanation be necessary?

3. Is the cultural content given a historical dimension?

4. Is the cultural content presented with evaluative comment, either direct or implied? Give any examples you find.

5. Is the content reprinted from original sources without change, reprinted with adaptation, or written for this textbook?

6. Are there illustrations? If so, are they appropriate? Would additional explanation be necessary to explain these illustrations?

   Do the illustrations supplement the content effectively?

7. Would students need additional hints from the teacher to understand the cultural implications of the illustration or content?

Method

1. By what method is the cultural information presented?

2. Is the information presented in relation to one culture, or is it presented in a comparative frame of reference?

3. Describe briefly the methods of presentation. Are they appropriate to the subject matter?

4. Would a teacher using this book need specialized training in order to use it effectively?

Part II. Evaluation of Cultural Content (personal opinion)

1. Is the information presented authentic?

   a) Is it timely?

   b) Is it fair?

2. If it is problem-oriented, are solutions provided? If so, are they adequate?

3. Is the descriptive vocabulary appropriate? Unbiased?

4. Please list three adjectives which you might use in describing your overall impression of the cultural information presented (adequate, biased, incomplete, boring, limited, comprehensive, mainstream, quaint).

5. If you were using this book would you delete, change, or supplement any of the cultural material in the text? Give examples.

6. What changes appear to be expected on the part of the cultural learners (students)? Are these expectations realistic in view of the type of student for whom the book has been written?

7. Comment on these expectations in view of the multicultural nature of your prospective class (see selection procedures). Would you wish to adjust any of the materials, exercises, or methods for the various cultural groups?

Part III. *Summary*. Balancing the Cultural Load.

Identify the ideal combination of circumstances under which this text-book might be used.

> Client: sojourner; immigrant; refugee; visitor; other
>
> Context: formal; informal; on-the-job; foreign; serendipi-tous; academic
>
> Communicator: native; non-native; representative mainstream culture; representative ethnic minority; age 20–30, 40–50, 60–.

Other Characteristics:

FOR FURTHER READING

As Daoud and Celce-Murcia (1979) comment in their chapter on textbook selection and evaluation, "relatively little" has been published on the topic of textbook selection. This author agrees. The following list includes some informative articles. In addition, any reader interested in more in-depth discussions of the complex process of content analysis is referred to the many textbooks on the subject.

Asia in American Textbooks. 1976. This report by The Asia Society contains the results of an intensive study of the ways in which Asia is shown in American textbooks. The study was co-sponsored by The Asia Society and the Ford Foundation and was compiled from data gathered in 1974–1975 from 100 scholars and teachers reviewing 306 social studies textbooks in 50 states. The document, available from ERIC (ED 127 232/ SO 009 331), is well worth looking over for those interested in pursuing the processes of textbook selection and assessing their cultural impact. A highly detailed evaluation guide was used for the purpose of listing "the variety of themes and source materials which can contribute to an understanding of Asia, and on the other hand, those which can distort Asian reality (6)." The study contrasted an "Asia-centered approach" (culturally relativistic) with what was called a "progress-centered approach" (change is good, necessary, and historically inevitable) and "a Western-centered approach." The first approach appeared only in 30% of the books studied and predominated in only 18%. In the final analysis of the 261 books evaluated, 63 were deemed "excellent," or "can be used with some problems," 118 were recommended only for use with some revisions, and 80 were rejected as totally inadequate (29). The full report is worth reading for two sections: its discussion of the ethnocentricity of much of the textbook literature about the Far East being used in American schools at the time of the study, and the observations the evaluation guide elicited.

H. Cowles. 1976. "Textual Materials Evaluation: A Comprehensive Checklist" (300–303). Cowles' article contains a 26–point evaluation checksheet soliciting circled responses to set choices. The checksheet calls attention to important elements to be considered in textbook selection, but is only briefly concerned with matters cultural (item 14). This is useful as a general guide.

A. Daoud and M. Celce-Murcia. 1979. "Selecting and Evaluating a Textbook" (302–307). This chapter in the Celce-Murcia and McIntosh textbook presents a step-by-step approach to the process of textbook selection. The authors do not specifically discuss the cultural implications of content.

S. Foust (ed.). 1981. "Dynamics of Cross-Cultural Adjustment: From Pre-Arrival to Re-Entry" (7–29) This is an excellent review of sojourner literature with a list of references on the subject.

E. Joiner. 1974. "Evaluating the Cultural Content of Foreign-Language Texts" (242–244). In this article Joiner presents a form for evaluating the cultural content of foreign language texts. Briefer and more general than the form suggested in this chapter, it offers a quick checklist for those involved in textbook selection.

Chapter 14

Ways and Means

There are almost as many ways to bring cultural instruction into the classroom as there are students to teach—or so it appears sometimes to those planning culture teaching units. As noted in the preceding chapter, many current teacher training textbooks contain very helpful suggestions, techniques, and methods. Making choices is no easy matter. In developing culturally sensitive instructional training projects, the choice of appropriate methods and techniques to present the cultural content requires as careful an assessment as does the choice of theoretical approach.

You have already been requested to choose appropriate material or content, delineate learning goals, and select instructional goals for your Culture Training Project. You are now asked to plan teaching units. To help you do so, some methods, techniques, and evaluation procedures specifically designed for cultural training, or suited to given types of such instruction, are reviewed in this chapter. The methods and techniques discussed represent only a fraction of those available. You are urged to consult the list of suggested readings at the end of this chapter for further guidance in planning cultural instructional units.

14.1 PURPOSES OF CULTURAL TRAINING

The purpose or purposes of cultural instruction should be clearly specified before completing the processes of planning and setting instructional goals.

Triandis (1975:68–70), emphasizes the need for cross-cultural training to familiarize the student with critical cultural differences, enhance the transfer of learning to new situations, and increase isomorphic (-*emic*) attributions. He lists several types of information needed by the student. These include, among others, knowledge of norms, role structures, behaviors that express intentions, kinds of self-concepts, valued and disvalued cultural behavior, and types of differentiations. Such information is culture-specific.

To develop intercultural awareness, other methods and techniques have been developed. For example, experiential (hands-on) training demands the direct participation of the learner. Exercises in values clarification, examination of personal value systems, and self-evaluation pave the way to dealing with the assumptions and values of others, a major step toward effective intercultural communication.

14.2 SELECTED METHODS AND TECHNIQUES

This section is an alphabetical listing of several methods developed and used successfully in cultural training projects. Each one of these is described briefly, with examples of some particularly effective methods and their accompanying techniques. Many of these will be familiar to you; however, there are cultural implications in their use in a cross-cultural context. In planning your own training project, choose the method and technique that best suits the type of client (student), content, and context involved. Do not forget that you should also consider your own teaching strengths, talents, and skills.

Area-Specific Studies

This type of training is cognitive in approach and focuses upon a specific country or cultural area. Kohls, in an article titled "Conceptual Model for Area Studies" in Hoopes and Ventura (1979), presents a model for the development of area studies. He lists three divisions under which the information gathered may be organized: briefing or factual background information; profile information concerning subjective culture (attitudes, personality traits); and integration problems faced by foreigners. Kohls' article contains a model of a report on Korea which presents ideas for types of information to be sought (172–178).

Area studies are culture-specific. When used as training devices, they should be structured so that the student or students must uncover the information by means of using library resources, interviewing informants, taking polls, making surveys, "treasure hunting" for important information, compiling reports, or searching through culture-specific literature. You will recall that your first ethnographic report was a mini-area studies exercise.

Case Studies

Ross (1979), in an article in the Hoopes and Ventura handbook identifies case studies as "analogues of actual situations written as close to reality as possible. . . . Case studies open up the opportunity . . . to think carefully, analytically, and understandingly about the experiences that the cases describe" (142).

A case study, or actual problem-solving, is a technique long used in business and legal studies. Moran (1981:vii) writes:

> The case study method in intercultural education is based on the assumption that working effectively in a multicultural environment is a *skill* more than it is a collection of techniques or ideas. An effective way of learning these skills is to practice them in a simulation type process. . . . The case method does not provide *the answer*. Several viable answers will be developed and supported by various participants discussing the case.

Participants are asked to analyze given cases, identify basic issues, and suggest solutions. As Moran points out, in cross-cultural case study there are intercultural issues involving values, assumptions, communicative styles, role expectations, expressions of opinions, need for verbalization, nonverbal behavior, problem-solving strategies, and background (ix).

Much of the material being used so effectively in the training of businessmen and businesswomen who must deal with members of other cultures is fashioned around the case study method. For example, the case study method forms a major portion of the training program for Japanese businessmen at the Language Institute of Japan in Odawara. While the focus is on the improvement of English language skills, the program is also designed to acquaint the participants with the ways and means of handling business dealings abroad. Case studies and other teaching materials have been developed to deal with the intercultural issues listed above (J. Brown 1979).

Contrast American

Although frequently applied to American culture, this social-psychological contrastive method can be used with any group. It involves the setting up and systematic examination of the contrastive qualities of one or more cultural groups. Edward Stewart used this method in his book *American Cultural Patterns. A Cross-Cultural Perspective* (1972). Stewart examined major American cultural assumptions and values as a means of developing cultural awareness on the part of Americans and providing a foundation for cross-cultural comparison and contrast. In a teaching context, this method can serve the same purpose and can be implemented by the use of selected readings followed by discussions, role play, case studies, dramatizations, televised materials, or other student projects. The project on American education (Appendix B) employs this method.

Training may be effected by the use of simulation, specific readings, or special case studies. The contrastive approach should be part of every language lesson. (See Chapter 10 for a contrastive treatment of Japanese and North American value orientations.)

Critical Incidents

These are exercises that focus on a critical difference. The incident or situation presents a problem related to interaction. There are no rights or wrongs to be discovered. The incident marks a critical point; the value of the use of incidents is in the discussion which evolves from this point.

In developing critical incident exercises the trainer should attend to the guidelines proposed by Barnak (1979:134):

- the incident should represent an area of conflict, such as values, goals, or standards;
- the solution should neither be apparent nor overly controversial;
- the context of the situation should be presented; and
- the situation should be presented clearly and concisely.

Critical incidents should be short and contain a cross-cultural problematic situation; they are most useful in handling day-to-day problems. Participants are asked to comment upon the incident and to reach a group consensus (Holmes and Guild 1979:137). Several critical incidents likely to occur in a multicultural language classroom context are given in Example 14.1. What values are clashing? What explanations or solutions might be proposed in such situations? Some hints are given below.

Example 14.1. Critical Incidents

Look at the following critical incidents which might occur in a multicultural situation in the United States. Some hints as to possible explanations, or culturally appropriate attributions follow. First, however, do your own explaining and problem solving.

1. The class took a field trip. Most of the students appeared to have fun and interact with each other. However, the Japanese students remained apart and somewhat aloof.

2. You invited one of your Saudi Arabian students and his wife to a pool party at your house. He said he would come, but he never showed up. Don't they like swimming?

3. You offered a Filipino student a piece of cake at a class party, but she refused. You made a second effort with the same result. Well, no one should be forced to eat.

4. The end of the term class party started at noon. The Latin Americans didn't arrive until 2 p.m. when most of the food had been eaten. However, they did begin singing and dancing and didn't appear to mind the lack of food. Indeed, they stayed until 11 p.m.!

5. One of your students from Vietnam has great difficulty in making himself understood. It is embarrassing both for you as a teacher and for the student to have

to ask for repetition so frequently. You didn't call on him in class today and now you feel guilty about his silence.

6. A Chinese student asks his female teacher how old she is even though he has been informed that American women are sensitive about their ages. Is he just being rude?

7. Your student from Jordan eagerly answered every question in class today while the student from Thailand never opened her mouth. How can you encourage active class participation on an equal time basis?

8. One of your Japanese students wished to repeat a class which he had passed, stating that he felt he needed more practice at that level. After due consideration and a conference with you, it was decided that the student should not repeat this course. When told of the decision he nodded his head. Two weeks later he made the same request! Why couldn't he take "no" for an answer?

Some Hints

1. Think about Japanese group behavior.

2. Social customs vary greatly concerning the inclusion of wives in social gatherings.

3. Appropriate behavior between host and guest is very culture-specific. Find out more about how many times food must be offered.

4. Social time is very culturally sensitive as is social behavior. It may be time for you to do some "explaining."

5. It may be that a period of listening silence is working more miracles than you imagine. In addition, some private tutoring may help the situation.

6. Age is accorded respect in many cultures. Don't underestimate the power of the North American accent on youth. It may blind you to patterns of other cultures.

7. Appropriate classroom decorum is culturally colored. Both groups need some cultural counseling if they are to operate in the North American context.

8. In this case, the nod meant what it means in the Japanese NVC pattern. He had heard you; he wasn't answering.

Culture Assimilators

This is a programmed technique designed to assist adjustment to another culture. Developed at the University of Illinois (Fiedler, Mitchell, and Triandis 1971; Triandis 1975) and based on an attributional approach to intercultural communication, the culture assimilator is composed of a series of short descriptions of episodes of intercultural conflict. The trainee is asked to analyze or choose the appropriate explanation of the causes of each incident. Four possible attributions may be listed. Three will be typical of attributions expected to be made by members of the trainee's culture and one will be typical of the target culture or cultures. If the incorrect choice is made, the trainee is asked to think the matter over and make another choice. The construction of assimilators is exceedingly difficult and time-consuming. As Triandis points out (1984:301), creating culture assimilators requires identification of critical incidents (several hundred) and their causes (attributions) by members of two relevant cultures. This is followed by verification that the attributions are statistically different and the compilation of feedback concerning the rationale for given attributions.

Clearly behavioristic in nature, the culture assimilator approach is a culture-specific training model formulated upon the premise that making proper attributions should increase a person's intercultural effectiveness in cross-cultural contexts. (See Example 14.2.) It is designed to expose the participants to the cultural values, attitudes, and beliefs of another cultural group (Harris and Moran 1979:150).

Where does one find culture assimilators? Many exist in the literature. Training handbooks and other teaching materials listed in the suggested readings at the end of this chapter and in other materials in the bibliography often contain examples of useful incidents. *American Cultural Encounters* (Ford and Silverman 1981) brings together a series of assimilators related to education and the school context and includes a very useful discussion of the possible attributions.

Teachers or trainers may write their own assimilators although they should be warned that it is easy to make mistakes and mislead more than lead. Seelye (1984) recounts some of the hazards of constructing and testing assimilators. Wrongful attributions can increase confusion. Harris and Moran point out that the assimilator may be ethnocentric as it focuses on the peculiarities of another culture (151). Yet carefully constructed and used well, the culture assimilator is a powerful tool in the development of skilled cultural hypothesizing—a vital intercultural communicative skill. Example 14.2 presents an assimilator exercise adapted to a multicultural problem for the teacher in connection with "party" behavior.

Example 14.2. Culture Assimilator

My English language class at a North American university was having a picnic and I wanted to be sure all the students would attend. There were students from many different countries in my class and I thought it would be a very good way for them to get to know each other. We had planned games, swimming, cooking, and hiking as activities. Surely everyone could find some way to have fun. Well, the Latin Americans came two hours late, the Japanese didn't come at all even though they had said they would, and the Middle Easterners sat stiffly on the picnic benches and ate little or nothing at all. I guess these students just don't like to have a good time. What's a teacher to do?

What was the problem?

1. The students were just burned out and too tired to go anywhere.

2. There was too much cross-cultural prejudice; these parties just won't work.

3. The party had been planned by the teacher and most of the students didn't know how to "enjoy" the party.

4. The students didn't like the teacher or American ways of having fun.

Some Answers

1. This choice is not a good one. True, the students may be very tired, but it is not likely that they are "partied out."

2. There might have been prejudice, but it could hardly account for the fact that so many did turn up for the party and even stayed.

3. This is a good choice. Apparently the students were not aware of the cultural rules regulating picnic attending and enjoyment in the United States. The Latin Americans went by their own time. The Japanese may have felt unwilling to commit themselves to such unfamiliar academic activity in a multicultural group. The Middle Easterners, usually enthusiastic party goers, may have been concerned about the preparation or content of the dishes served.

4. All too often we choose 4 and attribute student behavior to personal feelings of resentment or dislike.

What preparatory training should the teacher have provided?

Culture Capsules and Culture Clusters

Culture capsules, developed by Taylor and Sorenson (1961), are short explanations of minimal differences between two cultural groups. A capsule might explain a typical incident or event in a given culture. Students or trainees are not asked to choose culturally appropriate answers as they are with assimilators. In the case of the capsule, the student will be presented with culturally meaningful material and be expected to answer questions relating to that material. A capsule is presented in Example 14.3.

Sets of related culture capsules on a given subject are called clusters. The project on American education described in Appendix B represents such a cluster.

Example 14.3. Culture Capsules and Clusters.

Culture Cluster: American Traditional Food
Culture Capsule: The Hot Dog

Like any other cultural group, people in the United States celebrate certain holidays by serving traditional food. However, there are some kinds of food not associated with particular holidays but with types of events. Thus, it is the hot dog, not the hamburger, that might be called the great American sports snack. If an American never eats a hot dog anywhere else, he or she will certainly have one at a football, soccer, baseball game, or a picnic.

The hot dog, which is also called a frankfurter is made of smoked sausage (beef or beef and pork). It is composed of long (about four inches), reddish links. The name hot dog refers to the fact that it is served warm (not spicy) and possibly because it resembles the long, low German breed of dog, the dachshund. The name frankfurter refers to the German city of Frankfurt-am-Main, the source of the sausage.

Hot dogs are eaten on long oval-shaped buns, and liberally covered with mustard, ketchup, pickle sauce, and/or other such spicy sauces. They are usually served on a napkin or small paper dish. One devours them while shouting for the home team. There are chili dogs (Mexican style with chili sauce or filling), cheese dogs, and many other varieties of "dogs." However, it is the hot dog which has a special place in the American sports scene. Hamburgers are good at any time, but what is a baseball game without a hot dog?

Culture Cluster: hot dogs, hamburgers, turkey at Thanksgiving, pancakes on Sunday, and popcorn at the movies

Goal: recognition of expected or conventional behavior.

Objectives: Student will demonstrate an understanding of the cultural association of the hot dog with sports and outdoor events by answering the following questions.

1. What is a hot dog?

2. When is it usually eaten?

3. Why is it called a hot dog?

4. By what other name is it called?

5. How is the hot dog usually eaten?

Culture Discovery Techniques (See Area-Specific Training)

This is an approach that fosters the development of exploratory skills and the searching out of information about the target culture. Students may be assigned community research projects, taken on field trips with specific instructional goals, undertake surveys and polls, or be assigned other such activities. The basic approach used in this book was designed to provide you with practice in using a series of discovery techniques. The main value of this approach is the active involvement of the student in the learning episode.

Culture Quizzes

Such quizzes are types of testing or evaluation that call for trainees to supply culturally appropriate responses. This technique is particularly productive as a means of evaluating the effectiveness of culture assimilators, capsules, or clusters. It is well, however, to check out the answers to these questions with a panel of native culture bearers before presenting any definitive answers.

Culture Self-Awareness Techniques

These techniques are designed to bring to a conscious level personal assumptions, values, and attitudes affecting intercultural interaction. These may involve sensitivity exercises, self-assessment questionnaires, or problem solving. They are usually related to general human problems and designed to increase cross-cultural awareness and sensitivity.

This type of training may also focus on the development of personal self-discovery. Trainees may be asked to draw up profiles of personal attitudes and feelings, complete checklists of value orientations, or just practice listening to the opinions of others. Examples of such exercises may be found in Hoopes and Pusch (1979a: 104–204) and Pierre Casse (1981). The Cultural Hide and Seek Quiz in Chapter 10 of this book illustrates this training method.

Dialogues

Dialogues, as role play or situational exercises, have long been a part of ESL/EFL teaching strategies. In a multicultural context they provide excellent means to explain cultural patterns, reveal cultural meanings, and provide practice in their use. The dialogues might be directed toward instruction of some culturally sensitive materials, or merely be a dialogue contained in a language lesson in which cultural implications are hidden. The dialogues contained in Chapter 15 indicate the hidden cultural traps lurking in the most seemingly straightforward textbook content.

Dialogues call for the use of meaningful language. Student-produced shows or skits are an excellent means to test or evaluate the effects of cultural instruction. Practical experiential exercises are especially suited to the training of those who must adjust to the exigencies of life in a new culture—e.g., refugees, long-term sojourners, and immigrants. Many of the teaching materials developed for these groups are based on such practical experiential or situational episodes as asking for a job, going to the dentist, or getting a driver's license. The same strategies can be used for those not expecting to remain in the target culture, although the content should be adjusted to their needs.

Group Discussion

This strategy can be effective if the discussion is germane and the topic appropriate. Cross-cultural variations in group expectations, behavior, and norms are very great. Reaching consensus, or some sort of agreement, may be universally admired, but the ways in which this is effected are not.

Debates requiring participants to take a stand can produce practice in speaking but they may also set off World War III. A useful cross-cultural strategy is to assign students to a position to which they do *not* subscribe. If properly explained, students find this exercise exciting. The simulation of empathy for those who hold the opposing view is a useful device to promote intercultural understanding. This is a rewarding strategy, if handled with great care.

In addition, many students will find that "What if . . ." questions, often used to open up a discussion, are out of place in a classroom. Those unfamiliar with rhetorical forms and the argumentation format of Western cultures are often at a loss when asked to "fill the lifeboat" and decide who shall be saved in a nuclear war. A Middle Eastern Muslim student will most likely answer that it is all in the hands of Allah; a French student can be expected to leap eagerly into the argument; a Hispanic student may become emotional and agree with no one; a Chinese student will probably wish for more information; and those from Thailand, Vietnam, Japan, and points Far East will wonder what they are supposed to do.

Discuss, but be prepared for some cross-cultural sparks and intercultural miscommunication. But that, of course, is the way of culture learning.

Informant Interviewing

The use of the ethnographic technique of informant interviewing need not be restricted to anthropologists or to teachers who want to learn how to learn a culture; it is good for students as well. Furthermore, it is an excellent means of assuring contact with members of the native culture.

Language and Culture Connections

Making the language and culture connection should be a *sine qua non* in every language classroom. This strategy means that the teacher is always aware of cultural implications, ready to supply brief explanations or guidance, and cognizant of the cultural implications in the instructional content.

Making the language and culture connection is especially important in vocabulary development. It is concerned with the establishment of the connotative aspects of lexical items, with the uses of terms, and their evaluations in the native culture. The project concerning physical descriptors (Appendix B) is an example of such an approach. It may be duplicated with almost any other type of instructional material. Proverbs, sayings, superstitions, positive and negative evaluative statements, metaphors, humor, and sarcasm all involve language and all carry heavy cultural connotations or meanings.

Media Units

This technique involves the use of films, television programs, or other visual devices that provide information, generate questions, and develop cultural hypotheses. Television programs and commercials are particularly useful in demonstrating nonverbal communication, in analyzing intercultural variations and in providing culture-specific information. In fact, the students or trainees do not have to be silent audiences, but can participate either in actual televised role playing and analysis, or as discussants following the media presentation.

Problem-Solving Practice

Problem-solving practice is a means of involving students in the development of skills in presenting ideas, explaining positions, and arriving at solutions. Problems are universal, but methods of solving them are not. The use of critical incidents and culture assimilators (see above) is a type of problem-solving that focuses on culturally appropriate solutions. Many current student textbooks designed to elicit conversation are problem-oriented and students are encouraged to develop problem-solving skills. Yet the strategies and techniques encouraged are often those suitable to a Western context, and so may seem baffling, if not downright subversive, to students from other cultures.

Some student textbooks employ specialized problem-solving techniques. An example of such a textbook is *Language and Culture in Conflict: Problem-Posing in the ESL Classroom* by Wallerstein (1983). This textbook uses an approach developed by Paulo Freire for Brazilian slum dwellers. This method involves the discussion of problems students meet in daily life, and "encourages students to develop a *critical* view of their lives and the ways to *act* to enhance their self-esteem, and improve their lives" (Wallerstein 1983:3). Applied to the ESL adult education context, such an approach treats adults as adults and addresses real problems. Used successfully, solving problems and language learning may proceed apace.

Readings

This technique involves the use of background information from articles, novels, poems, newspapers, and other written sources which may give insight into culture-specific patterns. The selections may be explanatory, or simply reflect given patterns. Consider how much can be said about life in the United States simply by reading the daily newspaper comic strips or following the soap operas.

Simulation

You have experienced a simulation of the culture learning process in following the learning exercises recommended in this book. The culture rules exercise was a short simulation of some of the experiences a cross-cultural researcher might encounter in meeting a new and strange group. A simulation is a model of a physical or social situation;: it is a "game," but a game played with simplified rules and for specific purposes. The newspaper article shown in Example 14.4 reports the use of simulation to promote interracial understanding.

Example 14.4. Simulation

'Yooups' learned bitter discrimination lesson

ATLANTA (AP)—Seventy-five students who volunteered to be victims of discrimination knew what was going to happen, but still weren't prepared for what it felt like to be jeered and forced [to] use segregated restrooms, a teacher says.

The students at Sandy Springs Middle School were labeled "yooups" (YOu are one of the grOUP) for the day Tuesday in an effort to help them understand what it was like to be black in America before the civil rights movement. The experiment was part of the school's observance of the birthday of slain civil rights leader Martin Luther King Jr.

"The entire experiment was explained to them in advance by their homeroom teachers and they knew what was going to happen," said David Rector, who organized the experiment at the predominantly white school in suburban Atlanta. "But they weren't really ready for what happened. That's the whole point. It's something you have to live to understand."

The students—blacks, whites and Orientals—wore white armbands identifying them as yooups.

They were jeered by other students, forced to use the "yooups only" water fountain and restrooms, segregated during lunch and class and discriminated against by teachers who blamed them for the misconduct of other students.

The yooups also rode in the back of the bus on the way to school and entered the building through a specially marked "yooups only" entrance.

"This morning they thought it was going to be a fun activity," Rector said Tuesday after the experiment was over. "But there was a noticeable change as the day progressed.

"I could see the apprehension building in the yooups. As the day wore on, they began to ask questions about being physically and verbally abused," he said.

"It's terrible," Brant Petree said. "Everybody makes fun of you. It makes you feel bad, hurts your feelings."

"It was real hard work," said John Tyson. "Some of us aren't used to being told to sit in the back of the room, line up last, eat a different dessert, getting snapped at by the teachers."

By the end of the day, Rector said the yooups told him they had "learned a great deal about their fellow students and teachers. It was not a pleasant experience for many of them."

Source: Tampa Tribune, January, 1985

Professionally devised simulation exercises to encourage intercultural communication and cross-cultural awareness are available. Two of the most well-known are BaFá Bafá (G. Shirts, Simile II) and Aid to Minorians (L. R. Kohls, T. Edlich, M. Kiely, and B. Hoffman in Hoopes and Ventura 1979: 35–37).

There are risks and disadvantages in using simulation as a training tool. Most simulations take time and may lead to oversimplification and ungrounded generalizations on the part of the participants. On the other hand, a good simulation can be a powerful means of developing empathy. Example 14.4 is a case in point.

Situational Exercises

This method involves free-form skits in which the participants are presented with a situation and asked to devise scripts or conclude the skit. This is a very useful means of testing the effects of cultural training.

You, as classroom teachers, will find that you need to adapt instructional materials or even create your own. Cultural training, even more than language instruction, must be tailored to the audience. Do not be afraid to develop your own materials for your own students. Be prepared to make mistakes and take some risks.

14.3 A WORD ABOUT EVALUATION

Evaluating the effects of any training is difficult as any teacher knows. Questions of validity and reliability not to mention fairness and importance are seemingly almost unanswerable. When culture learning is added to the evaluation equation the odds of finding a "correct" solution are immeasurably lengthened. Bemoaning the difficulty of the task, however, does not serve much purpose. Evaluation must be done, so how can this best be accomplished?

What to Evaluate?

In considering types of testing and evaluation, it is important to distinguish between measuring student progress and the effectiveness of given cultural instruction. In truth, the first can only be evaluated by the learners themselves. The trainer does not serve as a judge or evaluator in the usual sense of these terms, but rather as a mediator or guide. Therefore, evaluative procedures should be in the form of feedback to the trainer for the purposes of adjustment and planning. This type of evaluation occurs during the process of training. The guided type of training, as discussed in this chapter, does lend itself to more traditional forms of evaluation, but with the full knowledge that testing culture learning is even more difficult than testing language learning.

Creativity in devising ways and means to test the results of cultural instruction calls for uses of all the senses—touch, sight, hearing and all the means by which human beings communicate. Renwick (1979:214) notes that, in general, there are five major categories of possible effects of a training program. They involve knowledge, perceptions, attitudes, skills, and patterns of behavior. In this book, each of these categories has been dealt with in their cross-cultural variations.

If we assume that the content has been determined, goals and objectives set, then what must be evaluated? Renwick suggests some points to be considered in choosing testing procedures and instruments. First, the methods must be compatible with the "values, preferences, and customary modes of response of the students" (219). This is most important. Male/female relationships, touching conventions, perception of "game playing" as a vehicle of learning, the value of competition—all play a part in many of the methods and techniques used in cultural training. Think twice before playing "Simon says" with those whose cultural taboo mandates that no one should be touched on the top of the head.

Renwick (219–220) comments:

> What is socially desirable for students from one culture is likely to be different for students from another. Attitudes toward candor, politeness, cautiousness and critiquing those in authority differ, as do attitudes toward expressing oneself or performing in front of others. The feelings of students about being rated by their peers (as well as by their teacher) are deeper for some students than for others, depending in part on the cultures from which they come. Anonymity is very important to some when they are expressing reactions and criticisms; others strongly want their names associated with their opinions.

Renwick also suggests the uses of a carefully selected variety of methods, an explanation of objectives of the training, and a clear delineation of the purposes of the evaluation.

Types of Measurement

Methods of evaluation include all those which might be used in testing the effects of any instruction, although culture learning lends itself to more informal methods than might be deemed suitable for other circumstances. Renwick (221–241) lists several types of evaluative measurements. These include:

1. Self-report: checklists about attitudes, rank ordering, scales to evaluate perceptions and attitudes; and training strategies such as critical incidents, case studies, discussion, and specific exercises to test given skills and competencies.
2. Enactment: demonstration of what has been learned—role play, simulation.
3. Production: This involves developing a concrete product, such as a report, finding information, or following a given set of procedures.

4. Observation by teacher or peer: systematic observation of demonstration of skills or behavior.

Seelye (1984), in a chapter titled "Testing Culture, or How Do You Know They Learned Something?" discusses (164–189) a number of testing formats. These include attitude tests, such as those which measure social distance; semantic differential ranges (or the distance between two descriptors), attitude statements about different groups, and personal attitude measurements.

Handbooks in the field of cross-cultural training and intercultural communication contain many examples of such tests. All the hazards of testing attitudes are doubled when testing culture learning as well. Such tests indicate what the test taker feels at the moment; they can seldom be regarded as valid, reliable, and sure-fire indicators of the effects of cultural instruction.

Seelye also discusses a series of criterion-referenced tests in which the teacher sets out the student competencies or skills to be developed. As can be noted in the examples of culture training projects reproduced in Appendix B, these criteria are spelled out in the planning process. Such tests should be confined to eliciting a demonstration of the competencies desired.

Pre-testing and post-testing may be useful in measuring competencies. Some strategies and exercises, such as culture assimilators, have built-in testing procedures. It is important that the information presented is correct and that test items are validated. Although the teacher may be well-informed about the target culture, it is wise to recall that no one culture bearer knows it all. Documented materials can provide validation for test items. (See Appendix C.)

A variety of formats can be used in culture tests. Many of the methods and techniques listed in this chapter form the bases for evaluation. For example, if a module has been presented concerning the recognition of different dialects of American English, the effects of the training can be measured by asking the students to identify different types of taped speech excerpts. In addition, role play and simulation lend themselves to evaluation as they take place.

14.4 PROCEED WITH CAUTION

As stated before, many of the strategies and techniques of cultural training are culture-bound and Western in perspective. So are evaluation procedures. Renwick (252) warns us:

Particular perspectives on learning and methods used by teachers and trainers usually develop within, and become increasingly reinforcing to, a single culture. . . . They are usually inappropriate, and can even be damaging, in multicultural classrooms. Teachers in multicultural education and trainers in intercultural programs therefore have a responsibility to explore new perspectives and create alternative teaching styles and methods. In the midst of their experiments, they must measure the effects of each. The results of their measurement can then become the basis for selecting those approaches which are most effective. Having more fully and confidently implemented these approaches, further evaluation becomes the basis for improving and refining them.

This is excellent advice for all teachers and a mandate for language teachers.

FOR STUDY AND DISCUSSION

1. Many methods and techniques of cultural training have been discussed in this chapter. Some are experiential in nature; others are designed to present culture-general or culture-specific information. What general training goals might be met by the use of the experiential types of exercises that would be more difficult to achieve with other types of training methods? Give some examples.

2. Kohls lists three divisions under which area-specific information may be organized: factual background, subjective culture, and integration problems faced by foreigners. Can you supply information on each of these categories on your target culture group? Give a brief report for the class concerning subjective culture (attitudes, values, beliefs), and integration problems that might be useful information to include in a training packet on your group.

3. What are some of the problems associated with the development and use of case studies? How might some of these problems be overcome?

4. If you were selecting a series of readings to illustrate American cultural values, what would you choose in order to present a Contrast American exercise for your target cultural group? List three readings.

5. Discuss the critical incidents shown in Example 14.1. What measures might be taken to alleviate the problems posed?

6. One of the sensitive issues in the world today has to do with the status of women. Attitudes, role expectations and values associated with the position of women vary cross-culturally. It is difficult, or even almost impossible, to avoid the issue in using modern language textbooks. If the issue is not met head-on, it is hinted at or comes up in student discussions.
   a) Should such issues be part of class discussions?
   b) How could such discussions be facilitated by the use of specific training methods, as, for example, a culture assimilator or critical incident?
   c) How can the assumptions concerning intercultural variations be uncovered? Should such controversial films as "The Death of A Princess" (1980ATV, Britain) or the writings of Phyllis Schlafly and Germaine Greer be used?

7. Several methods to evaluate the effectiveness of cultural training were suggested in this chapter. Which ones would you prefer to use? Why? Can you think of others?

8. What is meant by the statement that some of the methods and techniques used in cultural training are "culture-bound and Western in perspective"? In what ways might role play be "culture-bound"?

CULTURE LEARNING EXERCISE

A. Construct a culture assimilator concerning two situations likely to result in intercultural miscommunication. First, construct an assimilator appropriate for a student from your target culture studying or visiting in the United States. Then, construct one on another subject appropriate to a situation in which a teacher working in your target culture might become involved. Give the context and then offer four possible solutions; only one should be acceptable.

Some Suggested Topics

1. nonverbal communication between teacher and student
2. gift giving
3. use of personal space
4. asking directions
5. giving compliments

Additional suggestions can be found by consulting *American Cultural Encounters* by C. Ford and A. Silverman (1981).

B. Construct a cultural critical incident associated with your target culture. Include a description of the incident and a series of questions which might used to guide a discussion of the episode.

CULTURE TRAINING PROJECT

At the end of Chapter 12 you were asked to develop a plan for a culture training project. You are now asked to outline one unit in the module or component you planned. It is assumed that you would have planned several components. In this exercise you are asked to make more detailed plans for only one unit. This unit might be administered in one class period, or cover several days. In any case, your unit should be planned in sufficient detail for its implementation and evaluation. Use Form B, shown below, to complete your report.

CULTURE TRAINING PROJECT

FORM B

UNIT PLAN

I. Cultural Focus

II. Performance Objectives

III. Requirements

IV. Evaluation Bases

V. Resource Materials

VI. Conditions

FOR FURTHER READING

In addition to those books and articles already listed in Chapter 12 (Casse, Pusch, and others), the following are also recommended:

R. Brislin and P. Pedersen. 1976. *Cross-Cultural Orientation Programs.* This is a review of the major theoretical and practical concerns in the field of program planning as of 1976. While somewhat dated, it still offers insights into the processing, planning, and execution of orientation programs.

R. Brislin, S. Bochner and W. Lonner. 1975. *Cross-Cultural Perspectives on Learning.* This book should be of interest to second language teachers as it addresses problems of foreign students as issues in cross-cultural psychology.

J. Brown. 1979. "Case Study: An Exercise in Effective Communication." (13–32) is an interesting step-by-step implementation of an actual case study.

W. Davey (ed.). 1981. *Intercultural Theory and Practice: A Case Method Approach.* This book contains a series of case studies related to intercultural communication. The first essay, "Utilizing the Case Method in Intercultural Communication" (vii–x) by Robert Moran, discusses the history of the case study method and important questions that should be addressed in such studies in the intercultural context. Section V contains four case studies in education.

F. Fiedler, T. Mitchell, and H. Triandis. 1971. "The Culture Assimilator: An Approach to Cross-Cultural Training" (95–102). This article, along with the subsequent work of Triandis, describes the planning and production of culture assimilators.

P. Harris and R. Moran. 1979. Chapter 10, "Methods for Cross-Cultural Training" (147–162). This is a review of the development of cross-cultural training programs, especially those related to business.

D. Hoopes and M. Pusch. 1979. Chapter 6, "Teaching Strategies: The Methods and Techniques of Cross-Cultural Training" (104–204) contains descriptions and details of the application of various methods and techniques to develop cross-cultural awareness, including exercises to increase cultural self-awareness, clarify value orientations, and sensitize participants to the pitfalls of unexamined perceptions.

D. Hoopes and P. Ventura (eds.). 1979. *Intercultural Sourcebook: Cross-Cultural Training Methodologies.* This volume was part of the SIETAR (Society for Intercultural Education, Training, and Research) project funded by a combination of governmental and philanthropic organizations to review the state of SIETAR's domains of interest. It is just what it purports to be—a sourcebook for intercultural training. It contains discussions and examples of some of the methods and techniques touched upon in this chapter.

L. Kohls. 1984. *Survival Kit for Overseas Living.* This slim volume offers a mini-course in what every traveler should know. It is highly recommended.

G. Renwick. 1979. "Evaluation: Some Practical Guidelines" (205–255) is a thorough and practical review of various elements to be considered in the evaluation of the effects of cultural training programs. Questions as to who should do the evaluations, for what purpose, and how are discussed in detail as are various solutions to all of the above.

S. Savignon. 1983. Chapter 6, "Testing" (231–278). This chapter in the 1983 Savignon book discusses language testing in general and, in the final portion, the demands of testing for communicative competence. For those unfamiliar with language testing procedures, this chapter provides vital background information. The section dealing with communicative oral test items and profile reporting (summarizing levels of proficiency) should be of interest to those wishing to measure their students' communicative or cultural competence.

Chapter 15

Cross-Cultural Considerations in the Classroom

In a previous chapter we investigated the nature of culture learning and the various sociocultural factors influencing its processes. In this chapter the academic classroom as a culture learning context will be explored. Although our focus is on adult second language learning in North America as the target culture and the North American classroom as the general learning locus, the suggestions, comments, and proposals contained in this chapter can be accommodated to any language learning context.

If we review the general qualities identified as descriptive of a "good" language learning situation (Chapter 11), we must conclude that the average academic classroom anywhere is possibly one of the least promising locations imaginable for language learning and/or teaching. Consider the qualities of a "good" learning context and compare these with a familiar classroom. There are, of course, the standard requirements: opportunities for interaction, feelings of rapport between students and teacher, and a climate for learning, with opportunities to make mistakes as well as to give correct answers. These features, enhanced by the professional expertise and the desired personal qualities that distinguish the good teacher from the bad, and by adequate teaching materials, heighten the learning odds immeasurably. Each factor is subject to individual and cultural variations.

In this chapter we shall visit the language classroom again. This time we shall examine the various intrapersonal, interpersonal, systemic, and contextual factors at work in a multicultural classroom. Cross-cultural variations will be examined for the purpose of highlighting crucial differences and providing background for some lessons for the teacher.

15.1 LEARNING: CROSS-CULTURAL VARIATIONS

Learning, including cognition, thinking, perception, and information processing, has been defined as "the way a person abstracts information from the environment, remembers it, classifies it into concepts and categories, designs goals by using it in problem-solving, and creates new knowledge" (Mestenhauser 1981:116).

Gagné (1965) lists eight types of learning: signal, stimulus-response, chaining, verbal association, multiple discrimination, concept learning, principle learning, and problem solving. Each type of learning is related to second language learning; each type is served best by given methods and contexts. As Brown points out (1980:81), the first five types of learning are behavioristic in nature and well served by modification methods; the last three may be best approached by cognitive methods. In all types, the content "learned", as well as the strategies used to effect this learning, may show cross-cultural variation.

What are some of these differences? Isn't learning synonymous with living? Strategies related to cognitive processes, such as generalization, transfer, and simplification, are considered to be universal processes. Yet recent research in the fields of cross-cultural psychology and symbolic anthropology is bringing into question the nature, if not the reality, of such cognitive universals (Shweder and Bourne 1984).

Mestenhauser (1981:117) comments:

> Culture and sub-culture are the independent variables when learning is viewed cross-culturally. Important work is only now being done in this area, and some important conceptual and methodological difficulties are being encountered. . . . Many findings from studies in cross-cultural learning are incomplete. . . . Many of the experiments used by cross-culturally oriented scholars do not come from cross-cultural situations. Moreover, psychologists tend to use the term "culture" very broadly, applying it to distinctions based on social status, family socialization, class, or minority status.

Let us consider, then, some cross-cultural findings concerning learning, including cognitive styles and methods of argumentation.

Cognitive Styles

Just as learning strategies may show cross-cultural variation, so do cognitive styles. Cognitive style has been defined as "self-consistent and enduring individual differences in cognitive organization and functioning" (Ausubel 1968:170). The cognitive map of a learner includes "just about every imaginable sensory, communicative, cultural, affective, cognitive, and intellectual factor" (Brown 1980a:89). Several of these factors, as Brown suggests, are especially important in second language learning. In the following section we shall examine three types of cognitive style that carry particular force in intercultural contexts. They are: field-dependence/field-independence, reflectivity/impulsivity, and tolerance/intolerance of ambiguity.

Field-dependence/Field-independence. A field-dependent cognitive style is one in which the entire context or field is taken into consideration, field being defined as the "background" against which the cognitive operations take place. On the contrary, a field-independent style is marked by strategies to isolate given details or elements of the "field." Both strategies are used by given individuals, although apparently one style or the other will tend to be dominant.

There is a cultural connection between the type of style likely to occur under given circumstances. For example, field-independence appears to be more prevalent in highly industrialized, low-context, competitive societies, such as the United States, while field-dependence appears more frequently in societies characterized as traditional, high-context, authoritarian, and agrarian (Brown 1980a:91).

Whether one style is more helpful than the other in second language learning is still open to question. Field-dependent styles tend to be associated with feelings of empathy and personal group identification. Obviously, such behavior would be conducive to lowering the affective filter and increasing the social contacts so necessary in language learning and use. On the contrary, a field-independent style places a premium on analytical skills and the ability to deal with the demands of a cognitive or rule-oriented approach to language learning.

In his excellent discussion of the cognitive variations in language learning (90–98), Brown suggests that a field-independent style is better suited to the classroom context, and the field-dependent, to "natural" language learning in the "field." This may be true, but it is often the classroom teacher's fate to be faced with those whose cultural and social patterns have fostered the development of field-dependent styles. Happily, it has been established that a learner may switch styles, and probably does so, to fit the learning context. Thus, an individual can learn to use the most appropriate style in a given context. This being so, we as teachers should take care to be cognizant of individual and cultural differences in cognitive styles and to assist our students in the selection of the most productive mode in a given context. We certainly cannot assume that because our students are adults the field-independent cognitive style, which serves scientific endeavor so well, is understood, is used, or is even the most appropriate in all language learning contexts.

Reflectivity/Impulsivity. This learning style is a personality factor affecting the manner in which cognitive operations are carried out. It has to do with searching slowly for the answer or making a quick guess. Those who have tried to instruct students in the fine art of "guessing" at meaning and of skimming/scanning as desirable reading skills understand this factor. We know that there are cultural patterns that emphasize reflectivity and exact a heavy price for making mistakes. A case in point can be found among students from the Far East, especially Japan. To make a mistake is painful; to guess is to admit not having spent enough time in finding the correct answer. Being only partially "right," which may be acceptable to the impulsive learners and in other cultures, is often seen as totally "wrong" by those whose reflective learning styles are culturally sanctioned. Such styles are often accompanied by a relativistic approach to "truth" in which several choices or answers on True/False tests may represent "correct" answers.

In addition, silent periods of reflection before responding are observed in many cultures, particularly in the Far East. Such pauses are often interpreted incorrectly by teachers as an inability, or even a refusal, to respond. Lowered eyes and bowed heads, rather than silence, are more likely to be the nonverbal signals indicating no response is forthcoming.

Tolerance/Intolerance of Ambiguity. Tolerance of ambiguity has to do with a kind of open-mindedness about differences and contradictions. This might be, as Brown suggests, related to accepting the differences found in the target language (95). It also has to do with an approach to knowledge that does not mandate correct/incorrect, right/wrong, *yes/no* choices. In the North American cultural value schema, little premium is placed on the entertainment of contradictions. Tolerance of ambiguity, as a cognitive style, is ill-received in the scientifically oriented, competitive ambiance of the average classroom in the United States. On the contrary, particularly at higher levels of education, field-independence, impulsivity (often called creativity), and intolerance of ambiguity are generally rewarded. It behooves those concerned with the instruction of students who do not use these styles to make certain that these differences, and the expectations for behavior they imply, are understood.

The Power of Prior Learning

Another learning factor to be considered in the context of the multicultural language classroom is prior learning. Learning involves the incorporating of new information into old sets of beliefs and knowledge for the purpose of maintaining a consistent "world view" (Jervis 1976). This being true, then what the student has learned before is an important influence on the learning-yet-to-come.

Three factors appear to affect the ease with which new information is absorbed by a learner: New information is more likely to be absorbed: (a) the more ambiguous it is; (b) the more confident the person is that his world view is correct; and (c) the greater the commitment of that individual to his world view (Mestenhauser 1981:118).

While the role of the old in accepting the new is not entirely understood, what is clear is that we must not regard our students as without past experience in learning. This includes methods, styles, and strategies of learning, as well as personal experience. For example, young adult students from Lebanon studying in the United States in the mid-1980s have difficulty coping in a world without war; they have known nothing else. Their feelings of anxiety and close group identity are understandable, but these emotions do act as affective and effective learning barriers.

Another aspect of learning new information discussed by Mestenhauser (119–121) touches upon the need to make proper attributions (interpretations of behavior) and differentiation. Accurate assignment of new information is vital in the retrieval process. Differentiation, or classification for retrieval in appropriate memory units, involves synthesis of old and new information. As should be clear from previous discussions, there are cross-cultural variations in the assignment of terms, perceptions of reality, and classification. Language teachers must make sure that their students assign new information to the appropriate slot when dealing with the target culture. One way to effect this is to make clear the organizing principles and characteristics of native categories in presenting new information. Another way is to undertake "attributional" training for the purpose of assisting the learner in making appropriate distinctions (Triandis 1972, 1975).

Being Reasonable

Cross-cultural variations extend to methods of argumentation, and to the identification and presentation of evidence. Differences are also apparent in the manner in which the conclusions derived from the process of argumentation are presented. In an academic environment these differences are of major concern; in informal contact they often lead to charges of "inscrutability" or even deception. That the fault may lie in not only what is considered evidence, fact, and reality, but also in the manner in which these "truths" are presented, is often overlooked. Condon and Yousef (1975) devote several chapters to epistemological and rhetorical cross-cultural variations. As these authors state (213):

> We can say that what is "reasonable" is not fully separable from cultural assumptions. We need not go so far as to say that it is culture-bound. We cannot escape cultural influences by concentrating on perceptions of reality, nor by relying on logic. If nothing else, this recognition should caution us against criticizing statements from other societies which rely on different authorities, derive from different perceptions of the world, and follow a logic which is different from our own.

Several of these differences are discussed in the following portion of this chapter.

Just Give Me the Facts. Although data may be considered relatively culture-free, the conclusions to which they may lead often are not. Condon and Yousef suggest that the terms, *data* and *evidence* be considered separately, *evidence* being culturally colored. They explain that "what appears to us to be a *non-sequitur* in another society may actually be quite logical (consistent) given the assumptions of that culture" (216). For example, these authors cite the case of the dandruff on the collar of a U.S. ambassador to Japan. The dandruff was taken as evidence by some Japanese students that the ambassador's wife was not doing her job (1–2). Consider the conclusions an American might make about the sight of a foreign dignitary clapping for himself or herself. Clapping is a congratulatory gesture, but who is being congratulated?

Condon and Yousef also point out that the value orientations of a given culture are reflected in patterns of argumentation (218–222). They provide the example of the role of evidence. Physical evidence may be considered fundamental in some cultures but of little value in another. The emphasis in many societies, especially traditional ones, on the operations of chance, luck, and fate, as conditioning or qualifying influences in given events, stands in contrast to a dismissal of these influences as superstition in others.

Thus, dishing up the facts of the case and drawing logical conclusions is not a simple matter, cross-culturally speaking, and may not be as straightforward as many acculturated to the Western orientation may choose to believe.

Rhetorical Styles. There are culturally favored patterns of rhetorical style. For example, "three" seems to be a magic number in American descriptive rhetoric, according to Condon and Yousef (233). We like to measure out reality in sets of three: *Tom, Dick, and Harry; red, white, and blue.* We share this characteristic with other Westerners. Recall the battle cry of the French Revolution, *liberté, égalité, et fraternité.* Even the Romans called for a triumvirate.

Anyone who has shopped in Japan knows it is difficult to find sets of four as the number "four" is considered unlucky, possibly because the word for four, *shi,* in the Romanized form, also means "death."

On the other hand, choices come in pairs in American patterns: *fish or cut bait, sink or swim, put up or shut up.* Is the speaker influenced by these ethno-rhetorical (culture-specific) forms and patterns to any degree?

Condon and Yousef suggest a type of Whorfian rhetorical relativity hypothesis which states "that our culturally influenced rhetorical forms themselves help shape our world view, our thoughts, and our actions" (233). They point out (216):

> . . . across cultures, the "same evidence" can lead to quite different conclusions which are each logically consistent; this is possible because of different warrants directed toward different goals, and based on different values and assumptions of different cultures.

As we have found out in the discussion of the Sapir-Whorf hypothesis of language and culture, even though there may be force in these patterns, their power can be overcome; we can and do learn to think, view, and behave like others.

Thus, we, as teachers, must ask ourselves again and again whether or not our "corrections" relate to faults of logic or patterns of ethno-rhetoric. We must realize that sinking or swimming doesn't represent the full range of possibilities but only satisfies a culturally valued either/or approach to life's dilemmas. We must not forget that, although the rhythm of a descriptive series in triplicate satisfies a sense of completeness in English, it does not necessarily signal that all descriptive characteristics have been recognized.

Thus, patterns of reasoning and rhetoric (presentation of arguments for the purpose of eliciting a given response) are culturally influenced, reflecting ethnic history, values orientations, belief systems, and delineation of "fact."

Let Me Set You Straight. Cross-cultural differences may also be found in what Condon and Yousef refer to as *epistemic structures*. These authors define these structures as "the scaffoldings on which arguments are erected" (227). Such structures help determine both the order and content of argument; they are more akin to logic than argumentation. Condon and Yousef explain (229–230):

> The epistemic structure of an argument, then, is grounded in a culture's epistemology [theory of the nature and origin of knowledge]. Is truth found in specific facts or in abstract constructs? Is truth derivable from an essential dialectic of which all things are a part, or is a dialectic, any dialectical system, too rigid and antiquated a mold for the flux of reality? The student of intercultural communication is not so concerned with choosing the best epistemology as he is with recognizing that there are these differences, which are expressed in individual arguments as well as entire "bodies of knowledge."

In addition, even those who share Western-oriented approaches to logic, argumentation, and persuasion may not base their persuasions and arrive at their conclusions by the same paths of reason. Pribam (1949) identified four patterns of reasoning or analysis associated with Western thought: universalistic, hypothetical, intuitional, and dialectical. Condon and Yousef (1975:227–228) identify divergent patterns among those whose cultural and linguistic roots are Indo-European. Thus, a universalistic pattern of reasoning resting on the conviction that truth can be known by reasoning from fundamental concepts is widely used in France, around the Mediterranean, and in urban Latin America. On the other hand, Anglo-American thought tends to be hypothetical in nature, with an emphasis upon inductive not intuitional reasoning. Slavic Central European and German thought has been sometimes dialectical and often intuitional. It is not unusual to find reflections of these patterns in the lengthy introductions with which students from Western Europe and Latin America introduce their essays and in the convoluted and intricate syntax of the sculptured sentences gracing their discourse. They are only being "logical." Thus, even among those with whom we share much of our language and culture, logical discourse comes in many guises.

The author of this book still recalls sitting at a table in a small open air café in Baden Baden, Germany, in the late 1950s, listening to a brace of young French student intellectuals heatedly discuss *la littérature pure*. The mere mention of the term, three decades later, can still can send her husband and herself into gales of giggles at such an "absurd" Gallic search for *l'essence*. Little did they know that they themselves were simply exhibiting—and still are—rational ethnocentricity.

Table 15.1 contrasts Japanese and American patterns of thought and rhetoric along several dimensions. The Japanese pattern of thinking has been described as a point/dot/space orientation, as opposed to the Western linear route. The Japanese pattern is said to resemble the pattern of stepping stones in the courtyards of temples and shrines. Each point is autonomous and placed in relation to another, with gaps between, which the listener or reader must bridge. The Japanese mode of communication is tailored to a homogeneous, high-context culture in which much is understood.

TABLE 15.1 CULTURAL ASSUMPTIONS OF EAST AND WEST: JAPAN AND THE UNITED STATES

	Thought and Rhetorical Patterns	
	United States	**Japan**
1. Thought Patterns	analytical	synthetic (is-ness of things)
	absolutism	relativism
	facts, precision, specificity	stress on subjective ideas
	linear	point/dot/space
2. Rhetoric	confront, persuade, linear form of argument	harmony, consensus, circular form of argument
Organization	balance between general and supporting details	general or specific
	how or why	what
Proof	logical proof, facts	ambiguity, paraphrase
Style	explicit words (finally)	ambiguous words (perhaps, I think so)
Tone	low context (verbalize), speaker as agent of change	high context (silence, nonverbal), speaker as perceiver
	erabi (selective) choosing best answer	*awase* (adjustive) logic of gathering alternatives
Mode	dialogue—resolve differences digital—learned	*haragei*—art of the belly analogical—nonverbal important

Source: Roichi Okabe, "Cultural Assumptions of East and West: Japan and the United States," in W. B. Gudykunst (ed.). *Intercultural Communication Theory: Current Perspectives.* (Beverly Hills, CA: Sage, 1983), pp. 27–39.

Putting It in Writing. Cross-cultural variation may also be found in the way in which we bring reason to the written page. Robert Kaplan's article on cross-cultural variations in patterns of formal written discourse (1966) is well-known. He suggested that English patterns were linear while, among others, Semitic were marked by parallel constructions and Oriental by circular arrangements. Most composition teachers are all too familiar with the interminable "ands" of the Semitic pattern user and the seeming pointlessness of the Oriental writer.

But do these patterns have even more subtle effects than we imagine? Are they connected with the preference of students from Japan not to present a "clearly stated" main idea, but rather to coast to it obliquely. Are they related to the Japanese penchant to soften a strong assertion or conclusion with "This is my opinion"? Are they the source of the strongly worded, often repetitive and extravagant statements of Arabic speakers?

Are such compositional characteristics related to cultural habits, beliefs and values, and presentation of facts? The observations contained in Chapter 10 relating to values and assumptions would lead us to believe so. Some feel the Japanese patterns reflect the influence of Shintoist philosophy and cultural preconditioning.

Written rhetorical conventions also reflect the Japanese point/dot/space orientation, as shown in Table 15.1. Paragraph forms in Japanese tend to be organized by a *hosomi* form (slender), which dwells upon details only, or a *zundo* form (stumpy), which is limited to general statements. Neither of these forms is easily adapted to the standard American five-paragraph essay.

On the other hand, the forms and patterns of the Arabic language are reinforced by and reflected in the strong rhetorical patterns of assertion used by Arab speakers. Suleiman (1973:290–291) points to several types of grammatical methods of indicating assertion available in Arabic, including word endings, doubling of some consonants, and other rhetorical devices. Influenced by a strong religious belief in the messages of the *Quran*, the student using these patterns presents arguments apparently based solely on articles of personal faith and characterized by strong statements of assertion. Compositions fashioned in Arabic patterns, but judged by Western standards, often appear exaggerated and disorganized; by Arab standards they follow respected and effective linguistic and rhetorical traditions.

Now, as an exercise in contrastive rhetoric, read the following essay and comment upon the organization, evidence used, and conclusions. Is it logical? Convincing? Is the analogy appropriate? What questions would you pose concerning the warrants (proofs) used? What was the author's point?

> Even in a traditional country like Japan the movement of women's liberation is getting more and more popular in recent years. However, most of the men seldom think about it solemnly. They think the movement of women's liberation is like a car wash.

When we look at well-washed cars, our minds seem to be refreshed also, and we feel comfortable because we have done what we had to do. It doesn't matter to us whether our cars are dirty or not, if they still run well, but well-washed cars probably satisfy us because of their fitness.

To men, nothing is more dreamy and realistic than women; men can't live without women. The reverse is also the same. Men have works that make the world effective. Women have works that make the world attractive; the works of men and women are different naturally from each other. Most women who participate in the movement of women's liberation can't understand the difference of men and women.

The movement of women's liberation doesn't matter to men, but men understand it can inspire women's spirit and mean refreshed women. After the movement finishes, most of men who have such a kind of refreshed woman may be proud of themselves.

Lessons for the Teacher

What lessons about learning may the teacher learn from the above discussion of cross-cultural variations in cognitive styles and rhetoric?

First, both explaining and presenting new information in a manner consistent with cross-cultural variations are vital. We cannot assume that the same categories or evaluations are being used by students and by the teachers.

Second, don't hide cultural information. The connotations of terms are seldom explained in a dictionary. Bilingual dictionaries and direct translation may form traps for the culturally naïve. For example, consider how we use names and how much cultural information is concealed in name-calling.

Third, take into consideration the implications of cross-cultural differences in patterns of reasoning and rhetorical styles.

Now let us assess these lessons in terms of some genuine classroom dilemmas.

Lesson Number One: Explanation. The tabulation shown in Table 15.2 indicates the color associations that a group of foreign students studying English in the United States reported as generally shared in their countries or cultures. While the statements represent the perceptions of a small sample of students and cannot be taken as validated attributions, they indicate the range of meanings associated with the color spectrum.

What associations might be expected to be given by North Americans? By members of your target culture? Would any of you send white flowers to a newly married couple in China?

TABLE 15.2 COLORS AND MEANING—THE EYE OF THE BEHOLDER

Color	Japanese	Latin American	Saudi Arabian	Chinese	US
Red	Blood, sun, flag, excitement, some terror	excitement, happiness, festivals	blood, bride, royal	happiness, good things	
Yellow	foolishness, crazy people, unripe, pitiful	New Year's Eve	envy	———	
Green	beginning, growth	spring	life	good luck, wealth, adultery (green hat)	
Blue	sea, happiness, fishing jackets	feeling blue	happiness, sky	purity	
Violet	formal ceremony, "pitifully pretty"	mourning	———	———	
White	happiness (combined with red), sadness	happiness	purity	mourning	
Black	formality, sadness, grief	funerals	darkness, sadness, war, loneliness	mourning	
Gold	———	riches, prestige	———	happiness	

Lack of response (———) indicates that the students surveyed did not respond. It does not mean that the color indicated has no significance in the given culture.

Lesson Number Two: Don't Play Cultural Hide and Seek. Consider the following sets of adjectives: *slim, skinny, scrawny,* and *thin.* What do they have in common and how will they be used? Are some pejorative and others not? How has the meaning of *skinny* changed in the last few years? Those who are aware of North American values also know that being called "skinny" was formerly an insult, but to be called "skinny" today is the dream of every perspiring spa denizen.

We are encouraged, often subtly, by our lesson plans and texts to teach "culture." Do we really play fair? Consider, for example, the terms *well-built* and *heavy-set.* Are not heroes "well-built" and criminals "heavy-set"? Discrimination between these terms separates the native from the non-native communicator. If we are not to send out scores of naïve Pollyannas into the world, we must let our students in on these cultural secrets. One of the culture training projects contained in Appendix B addresses the use of personal physical descriptive terms as a combined composition and culture training project. It has proved very popular with students who clearly understand when they are being let in on some heretofore rather well-hidden but valuable cultural knowledge.

Lesson Number Three: Adjustment. Teaching advanced writing skills to any student is a formidable teaching task. Instructing non-native speakers in the fine art of writing in a "foreign" language is often traumatic to student and teacher alike. Some students feel that composition has little to do with communication and that speaking skills are primary. Others, such as those from the Middle East whose native learning practices include much repetition and oral recitation, consider writing skills of little or no practical use. Responses *viva voce* are the only valid ones. Those trained in the more florid styles of written rhetoric may regard composition instruction as an attempt to undermine the universal verities of argumentation and logic. Writing assignments are sometimes considered by these students as particularly painful forms of mental torture, unnecessarily inflicted and to be resisted at all cost.

Such is the dilemma. Are there any solutions? Adjusting to the various student proclivities and practices is one way to deal with rhetorical anarchy. For example, "brainstorming" and the setting down of ideas without regard to organization or rhetorical forms before writing a composition makes creative sense. However, care must be taken that organization of the concepts to be presented precedes the actual composing process. This can be done in many modes: recording, outlining, discussions.

Another effective method is to permit students to make recordings of their compositions. This done, corrections are made and the student then writes the composition in the appropriate format. The use of the oral channel satisfies the conversationalists and the reciters; it also serves to simplify the final products of the linguistically insecure, for oral discourse is not as grammatically threatening as written discourse. In any case, steps must be taken to assist the student in the shift from the rhetorical patterns of the native culture to those of the target culture. Commas, periods, and run-on sentences can be taken care of later.

Because argumentation and rhetoric play such important roles in human communication, attention must be given to variant ways of presenting truth, or the consequences may be severe indeed. Although we cannot settle the arguments about argument, we must clearly understand that the seemingly "illogical" or "unreasonable" characteristics of rhetoric our students bring to our classrooms are perfectly logical and reasonable in other contexts. We must recognize and accord validity to these other forms—the elaborated style beloved of Western Europeans and Latin Americans; the Middle Eastern method of stringing together seemingly unrelated facts in a series of parallel constructions; the oblique approach of the Far East that leaves so much to the imagination.

Finally, we must be open about the fact that, although academic insistence upon the "scientific" presentations of facts and evidence is culture-specific, these methods must be understood if academic work is to be undertaken in Western universities. Those whose sources of knowledge are tradition bound are not likely to understand the stigma of plagiarism and its academic consequences in the United States. Students who present term papers brimming with direct quotations but devoid of footnotes or quotation marks will be punished severely by teachers who are unaware of the acceptability of the form in some cultures. Such students are likely to be dismissed as mere "regurgitators" at best and thieves at worst by the culturally blind teacher.

15.2 THE CLASSROOM: MODES AND MANNERS

Let us now examine more closely some features of classrooms in general, language classrooms in particular, and very particularly multicultural language classrooms, to search out what modes and manners might be likely to create cultural learning barriers. Although the context of the American classroom is investigated in this chapter, some of the features discussed are endemic to any classroom; others are uniquely American. It is hoped that this discussion, even though culture-specific, will serve to alert the reader to potential intercultural classroom hazards.

Enhancing the Context

It has been observed that the classroom generally does not provide sufficient natural input to promote language acquisition but serves better the process of language learning (Krashen 1982). Attention to the incorporation of sociolinguistic variables and culturally relevant information should assure a deeper understanding of the "natural" input encountered outside the classroom. In such circumstances the classroom context then can become an "artificial" or protected community, dealing with language and social behavior. It can be the place to discuss such "taboo" subjects as suicide. It can be a haven in which errors, mistakes, and incomplete acquisition can be and are forgiven. It can be the place where the skills needed to make the most of natural input are acquired.

Let us consider several aspects of the typical second or foreign language classroom in the United States and some classroom behavior that may be either strange to or unnoticed by second language learners. What are expected behaviors and norms? What assumptions have been made about the role of the teacher? How can we include more intercultural learning activities in our daily routines? What can our students tell us about our classrooms? Is there such a state as "education shock"? If so, what is it and what should we do about it? What elements should be considered in devising the most productive contexts for our pedagogical efforts? What teacher competencies will contribute most to context enhancement? Often teachers carry their culturally biased beliefs and assumptions about classrooms into their own classrooms. Thus, as always, before we look at the context of the classroom, we must look at ourselves.

Great Expectations

There is no doubt that all teachers and students bring a set of expectations to the classroom. These expectations are rooted in personal experience and have been forged in the native culture of both students and teachers. Margaret LeCompte (1981) identified five rules characteristic of a typical U.S. classroom teacher's management style. As quoted by Seelye (1984:210), they are:

1. Do what the teacher says.
2. Live up to teacher expectations for proper behavior.
3. Stick to the schedule.
4. Keep busy.
5. Keep quiet and don't move too much.

We assume that most native schoolchildren internalize these rules of good conduct as they move through our educational system. They are rooted in common American values of the uses of time, the need for action, and a paradoxical command not to move while doing so. It is not surprising that the conflicting demands for classroom behavior prove hard to accept for many native students. They are often incomprehensible to the stranger.

In a multicultural classroom these expectations take on a crucial significance. They are usually tacitly assumed and taken as so fundamental as to need no explanation. That this is not justified in intercultural interaction is clear; that we should pay more attention to these unconscious assumptions is equally clear. Thus, the characteristics of the classroom, teacher behavior, and student behavior are major variables to be considered in enhancing the teaching context. Characteristics to be considered include class participation, uses of time, the teacher's role and status, and even discipline—in short, almost anything that goes on in a classroom.

Education Shock

Hoff, in a dissertation entitled "Classroom-Generated Barriers to Learning: International Students in American Higher Education" (1979) identified 89 classroom and classroom-generated elements characteristic of American classrooms and explored their significance for a small sample (40) of Chinese and Persian students studying in the California university system. These elements ranged from attitudes about quizzes to the use of first names.

In her study, she proposed the term "education shock" to describe a special form of culture shock afflicting foreign students studying in American educational establishments. For this study, Hoff (1979) defined education shock "as a state where a substantial portion of a learning situation is new to those experiencing the situation . . . a condition where components of a new learning situation are distressing to a substantial number of those experiencing them . . ." (130). She further defined education shock as "a clash of expectations" (134).

Education shock was identified in a variety of aspects. Some of the bases for distress or surprise were (105–117):

- Serious learning problems: long class hours, tardiness ignored or not punished, moving during lectures, students indicating they wished to speak out by speaking out, typed rather than handwritten reports, and no grades on papers.
- Moderated serious learning problems (those which were distressing only initially): eating, drinking, or smoking during lectures, reports or presentations with the professor offering comment from the audience, and field research assignments.

Many of the difficulties seen by students in this sample were only initially confusing and were later seen as learning enhancers. For example, the presentation of several conflicting theories by a professor was regarded as initially confusing, but later as valuable. Some clear positive values were the use of examples and analogies in lectures, use of handouts, and take-home exams.

Educational barriers (95–102), or new elements often making it "hard to learn," were identified as long class hours, brief writings, unsupervised testing, and several criteria for a final grade. Moderated barriers, those seen initially as barriers but later as enhancers, included small group activities, presentations of a variety of theories, and assignments to seek out information. Some "possible positive values" were moveable arm chairs, casual clothing, and personal contact.

Non-relevant items (for the sample) included the borrowing of notes or supplies, the presence of male and female students in the same classes, and the discouraging of classroom discussions of politics or religion.

Although the sample used in this study was small (40) and limited to only two groups, Chinese and Persian, studying in universities in Southern California and in their first year of study in the United States, the responses gathered are still of general interest as a means of exploring some of the perceptions of the educational system in the United States and the characteristics considered unique, disturbing, helpful, or irrelevant. Other groups might respond quite differently, of course. The responses gathered from this study are not as important as the characteristics listed and the questions asked.

In the Hoff study, 63% (56 items) of the 89 characteristics were new to 25% of the sample. Of these, 48% were seen as enhancing learning (129). Thus, teacher, ask yourself how many of these elements are present in your classroom, and how might they be at work as learning barriers, or enhancers, given the backgrounds of your students and your own pedagogical style and strengths.

Hoff reminds us that the American educational system is concerned with the transmission of content and personal development of the student, that is, informational and affective areas of learning. As such, its goals may not be appropriate for all types of foreign students learning English. According to this author (150):

> . . . the affective areas of learning—those processes which reflect the cultural realities of the American experience—are of minimal interest to many international students. That is, they want to know how, not why, American business is successful. . . . To put it very basically, table manners are not very important to a man or woman who has no food. American education would do well to acknowledge these goals.

Caveat Magister

What then is a teacher to do? Why not take the advice offered in this book and engage in some cultural exploration, in the company of our students?

A Japanese student, Mitsu Shimazu, writing in the *TESOL Newsletter* (April 1984) makes some concrete suggestions for dealing with Japanese students. She suggests several strategies for teachers to follow in dealing with these students in EFL/ESL classrooms. These include formalizing relationships, giving clear explanations, avoiding reprimanding or praising the group, keeping channels of communication open, and interpreting nonverbal communication, including *silence*. She concludes (19):

> Teachers dealing with Japanese students will find it helpful to be aware of the Japanese communicative styles and behaviors. . . . Japanese students' ways of doing things are often very different from teachers' expectations, and it is important not to jump to conclusions. By following some of the preceding suggestions, EFL/ESL teachers will be able to play an important role in helping their Japanese students achieve success.

And their students from Saudi Arabia and Lebanon and China and Brazil, but each in the context of their special communicative ways.

Student Expectations

In the previous section we listed some general problems which beset many students from foreign countries studying in the United States. Let us now consider some expectations they might bring to the second language classroom.

These expectations arise from cultural-specific patterns and orientations. For example, it can be expected that classroom behavior in Arab cultures will be strongly influenced by religious beliefs and tenets. Latin American patterns call for personal attention and warmth on the part of the teacher. Japanese patterns frequently reflect Japanese cultural styles that emphasize silent receipt of information, strong nonverbal communication patterns, and reluctance to enter into general discussions or to offer personal opinions.

Hints and culture-specific observations concerning these patterns abound in the suggested readings listed in this and other chapters of this book. How might these patterns be translated into classroom expectations? For instance, in dealing with students from India we must recognize the pervasiveness of their belief that "as all knowledge is probable and relative, the other person's point of view is as true as one's own" (Jain 1982:119). Among Puerto Ricans we must remember that there are such phenomena as *tertulias*—talking gatherings—and that to Latins silence, far from being golden, is often depressing. Nine Curt writes: "Apparently Latins need the presence of human noises to feel at ease; they need spaces filled with talk and human bodies" (33).

In the case of students from the Middle East, especially Saudi Arabia, the close association between organized education and Islamic principles is a given. Levine (1982:101–102) comments: "One outcome of this [Saudi] educational system is that the original thought is discouraged. . . . The Saudis' absolute belief in fate and in the wisdom of God's direction is diametrically opposed to the Western concepts of free will and self-determination." She points out that these characteristics pose difficulty when teachers try to engage these students in discussion and concludes (102–103):

> Asked by teachers, "What do you think?" or "What is your opinion?" a Saudi student may simply offer a rote response. This reaction is not indicative of an inability to articulate an original or creative thought, but rather reflects educational training that discourages independent thinking. Some Saudi students have reported that a teacher who elicits opinions in class or allows a student to challenge ideas is incompetent and therefore unqualified to teach.

As an exercise in structured observation, complete the following exercise. Consider the cross-cultural variations you have observed in your classrooms or experienced as a fellow learner. Use the grid provided in Figure 15.1 to investigate some of the conventional behaviors expected in university, secondary, or elementary schools in your target culture. Some categories for observation are listed to assist you. First, fill in details you would associate with the patterns in the United States at a given academic level. Then, compare and contrast these with those found in your target culture. Be careful! You may receive answers which apparently indicate few differences. However, careful questioning may help you uncover significant differences in norms, rules, or expectations. For example, the Japanese system of marking answers correct or incorrect includes the following: correct—O or X; incorrect—V. Can you imagine how confusing this might be for a Japanese student who receives all checkmarks from an uninitiated teacher? Again, as noted previously, listening body posture varies considerably cross-culturally. Observe, question, and learn. This exercise might be the most important one you complete. Remember that it is not what *is*, but what you *perceive* that is important in interpersonal and intercultural encounters.

Figure 15.1. Cultural Rules, Norms, and Expectations in the Classroom

Categories of Behavior	CULTURAL RULES	
	United States	Your Target Culture
1. Participation in Class		
2. Uses of Time		
3. Teacher Status/Role		
4. Listening Postures		
5. Attendance		
6. Classroom Conventions a) Grading Marking Bargaining b) Questioning c) Homework		
7. Discipline		
8. Taboos		

15.3 THE CHALLENGES OF THE COMMUNICATIVE COMPETENCE APPROACH REVISITED

The communicative competence approach calls for practice in the use of language. Classroom dialogues, all too frequently, are artificial, lacking in meaning, and even incomprehensible to the students who try to use them. "Input" may seem natural but the cultural connotations of the text are not part of that "input." The student may know what to say but not why or where to say it. Covert cultural meanings often pass unnoted.

Again, we may provide opportunities for our students to respond, but often the answers, while grammatically correct, would seldom be heard outside the classroom. For example, we must clarify the uses of register, dialect, formality/informality, and other sociolinguistic characteristics that mark human language use. The distinctions between written and spoken usage of language forms are as vital as any rule of grammar.

Consider the following dialogue. What does the reader need to know to "understand"?

Herbert gave Sarah a new coat. The girl said, "Bert, that coat has too many colors." Herbert replied, "Don't be silly, Sally. Give it to Joe. He likes such coats." Sarah sniffed, "Don't be funny."

How many people are involved in this story? Are Herbert and Bert the same person? What about Sarah and Sally? What's the joke? Who is Joe anyway? Some guidance might be needed concerning the use of nicknames: Sally for Sarah, Bert for Herbert, and Joe for Joseph. Unless the comma is noted, the student (at a beginning level and probably punctuation blind) might not understand that this episode involves only three people. Indeed, readers unfamiliar with Western naming patterns may have trouble separating the boys from the girls. Finally, if they are unfamiliar with Western culture and religion, they may not understand the seemingly illogical reference to Joseph and his coat of many colors.

Let us look at another episode contained in a student textbook (Alexander and Cornelius, Jr. 1978:17).

The telephone rang and I picked up the receiver.
"Hello," I said.
"Hello," said a voice. "This is Bill. Is Betty there?"
"I'm sorry," I said, "you have the wrong number."

A few seconds later the telephone rang again. Just as I suspected, it was Bill. "You've dialed the wrong number two times in a row," I explained.

Then the phone rang a third time. This made me angry. I spoke in a loud voice. "Hello, Bill. This is Betty."

For a moment there was complete silence. Then someone said, "What's the matter with you, Tom?"

It was my mother!

What if the names had been Masuhiro, Amigati, and Kumiko? Wouldn't the "joke" have been a little more difficult to understand? We can't be sure that all students will know that Bill and Tom are male and that Betty is female. There were no convenient personal pronouns to help the uninitiated.

The important "lesson" to be learned from the two excerpts is for the teacher. Cultural knowledge cannot be taken for granted. While some students would probably not be confused by the excerpt, we cannot *assume* that this is so. The teacher or guide must be ever alert for such seemingly small but sometimes treacherous cultural pitfalls. After all, wasn't there a song called "A Boy Named Sue" popular some fifteen or twenty years ago? Aren't there girls named Billie, but not Billy? The golden rule of the multicultural language classroom may be to assume little and explain much.

15.4 REWARDS FOR TEACHERS AND STUDENTS

The following entry from a student journal and the reply from the teacher should speak for themselves. They highlight the rewards for both teacher and student to be garnered in a joint venture in culture learning.

While I was reading a short story written by a Japanese author, I came across a scene in which a young man killed himself. Then, I noticed an interesting fact. In Japan, when a person jumps into a lake, river, or the sea to kill himself, he usually takes off his shoes. I wanted to know if the same thing happened in the U.S. or not, so I asked my boy friend about that. He said that he was not sure, but thought American people might not take off their shoes. He asked why I had asked about the story and said, "I think American people might not do such a thing." Japanese people's taking off shoes might have something to do with their habit that they take off their shoes before getting into houses. A person who kills himself with gas or poison does not take off his shoes even in Japan, and I feel there is a kind of similarity between jumping into a lake and getting into houses. . . . This is such an interesting subject that I really want to know if American or European people do the same thing or not.

The teacher, once having overcome her cultural reticence to discuss suicide, replied:

Your idea is very interesting. I am sure most Americans would not take off their shoes if they were going to kill themselves. I don't think the reasons would have anything to do with the custom of wearing shoes in the house in the United States. Americans are very practical. People would drown more quickly if they were heavy; thus, they would probably keep their shoes on to weigh themselves down and get the job over in a hurry. Do check this out with your other American and European friends.

Student and teacher alike had found a means to bring culture learning into the language classroom; they also demonstrated that culture learning isn't just for students.

FOR STUDY AND DISCUSSION

1. Identify the following terms:

   prior learning

   ethnorhetoric

   epistemic structures

2. Refer to the tabulation of colors and meanings shown in Table 15.2. What is the value of such information to a teacher in a multicultural classroom? How could this information be used to develop cross-cultural awareness?

3. Refer to the tabulation of classroom norms found in Figure 15.1. Comment on the implications of the Japanese system of marking correct and incorrect numbers. What confusion might this cause?

4. In the discussion concerning patterns of reasoning, it was noted that English speakers have a penchant for making assertions in triplicate. It was implied that three was regarded in some special manner. Can you think of other examples of the English pattern? What association with numbers can you uncover in your target culture?

5. If you were an ESL teacher of an advanced reading/composition class, how could the information in this chapter help you in teaching students from Japan? from Saudi Arabia? from Latin America? from your target culture?

6. Condon and Yousef comment that cultural variations in rhetorical style may not cause serious problems of misunderstanding, but rather might cause disputes about what questions are important (1975:229). How might this affect such activities as group discussions, debates, and problem-solving in a classroom in which several cultural groups were brought together? How would you deal with such problems?

7. Discuss ways in which the characteristics of field dependence/independence, reflectivity/impulsivity, and tolerance/intolerance of ambiguity would be related to the expectations of an American teacher? How would American teachers characterize the "good" student? The "bad" student? How do these characteristics relate to some of the cross-cultural variations in learning and cognitive styles described in this chapter?

8. Which of the elements of "education shock" listed in the Hoff study appear to be most amenable to adjustment? How could such adjustment be accomplished?

9. One of the two dialogues reprinted in this chapter focused on confusion in the use of personal names and their shortened forms. Can you list some names which might cause difficulty? How would you instruct your students in patterns of first name usage and forms in the United States? Are there metaphorical uses of names? Give some examples.

10. A statement was made in this chapter concerning the use of pejorative adjectives for personal description. Supply non-pejorative forms for: fat; old; swarthy; squat.

CULTURE LEARNING EXERCISE

Read the following dialogue. The names used in the original dialogue have been eliminated. What cultural clues are given which would help the reader who is familiar with American customs determine the gender of X and Y? Identify these clues. There are at least four.

Waiter: Would you care for a drink before lunch?

X: Y, do you want a drink?

Y: Just a Coke, thanks.

X: I'd like a bourbon on the rocks, please, and we'd like to order right away.

Waiter: Would you like an appetizer?

X: Yes, two dozen clams. Are the lobsters fresh?

Waiter: Oh yes. We have our own traps and the man just brought them in an hour ago.

X: Fine! Two boiled lobsters with French fries and salad.

Waiter: What kind of salad dressing do you want?

X: One French and one oil and vinegar.

Y: Oh, I can hardly move! I've never eaten so much in my whole life.

X: The food here is great, isn't it? Do you think you have any room left for dessert?

Y: Well, I guess I shouldn't, but I am dying for apple pie with ice cream.

X: I don't know where you put all that food, Y. It's amazing! You never seem to put on weight.

Waiter: Do you want coffee?

X: Please, and bring the check, too. We want to get to the marine museum before it closes.

(R. Scaun, C. Wilkes, L. Morelli, and H. Nadler in *American English Readings* II, 1971 American Language Institute, New York, 83–84). This excerpt has been edited and does not contain contextual clues provided in the original text. This liberty was taken in order to provide an exercise in "walking in the shoes" of some foreign language students who miss these clues.

CULTURE TRAINING PROJECT

In Chapter 12 you were asked to plan a culture training project (Form A), and in Chapter 14 you were asked to plan one of the modules to be used. In this exercise you are to complete a lesson plan, collect or create appropriate teaching materials, and administer this project to a student group. In Chapter 16 you will be asked to submit a brief report of the project and its results.

In completing this exercise, please use the following form. For an example of such projects, please see Appendix B.

CULTURE TRAINING PROJECT
FORM C
IMPLEMENTATION

I. Cultural Focus

II. Learning Activities

III. Resources

IV. Methods

V. Sequencing

FOR FURTHER READING

H. Brown. 1980a. Chapter 5, "Cognitive Variations in Language Learning" (80–99). This chapter contains a review of types, strategies, and styles of learning in general. It provides a good foundation for examining cross-cultural variations.

J. Condon and F. Yousef. 1975. Chapter 10, "Thinking About Thinking" (209–249). These authors build upon their discussions of value orientations in Chapters 4 and 5 of this book to structure a discussion of cross-cultural variations in argumentation and rhetoric. They contrast value orientations relative to evidence, warrants, and what they call "qualifiers," or cautionary terms. Of special interest to the language teacher is their discussion of rhetorical relativity and speech organization.

R. Kaplan. 1966. "Cultural Thought Patterns in Intercultural Education" (1–20). Kaplan's description of contrastive rhetorical patterns in five cultures should be on every language teacher's "must read" list. Kaplan made a major contribution to our field in alerting us to the existence of contrastive patterns and the need for all teachers to be aware of cross-cultural variations.

G. Lakoff and M. Johnson. 1980. *Metaphors We Live By* is a lively and fascinating discussion of the metaphorical concepts at work in contemporary English (American style) today. To these authors metaphors affect, or at least influence, attitudes and actions. This is a strong argument in favor of the cross-cultural realities posited by Whorf and those who have followed in his footsteps. The final chapters of the book deal with truth, the nature of objectivism and subjectivism, and what the authors call "The Experiential Alternative." Their conclusions are certainly controversial, but they do offer a fresh look at some very old Western assumptions about truth and reality.

D. Levine. 1982. "The Educational Backgrounds of Saudi Arabian and Algerian Students" (100–107). This is an interesting discussion of differences in educational backgrounds between Saudi Arabian and Algerian students. Written by a teacher and textbook author, this article reflects a pragmatic and knowledgeable approach to variations among groups that might be too easily subsumed under the term "Middle Easterners." While reference to areal distinctions in cultural groups has been used in this book, caution is urged in using such blanket terms. Often intracultural variations, individual and group, show a greater range than observed in cross-cultural groups.

E. Stewart. 1972. Part II, "Patterns of Thinking" (22–30). This chapter in Stewart's well-known volume, *American Cultural Patterns: A Cross-Cultural Perspective*, describes general patterns of American thinking that contrast with those of other cultures. He discusses differences in styles, uses of language, and explanation, pointing up areas of possible miscommunication.

Chapter 16

Mediation is the Message

This chapter will review some of the major issues in intercultural communication discussed in this book and their relationship to teacher preparation in second language programs. In addition, the teacher's role in multicultural and bilingual programs in educational institutions in the United States will be examined briefly. Finally, each of you will be asked to make a personal return visit to the classroom portrayed in Chapter 1 and to consider how you feel about the situation after having experienced culture shock, undergone some cultural training, and, it is hoped, acquired greater insight into the nature of culture learning, its pains and rewards.

16.1 REVIEW

In Chapter 1 we looked at the problems of teaching language in a multicultural classroom and found that whereas language and culture learning seem to go hand in hand, the efforts to meld cultural training with language instruction often appear to produce uneven progress—the number of cross-cultural drummers available being one of the hazards of such undertakings.

Some major issues in intercultural communication were presented in a brief questionnaire, designed to create more questions than answers. It is time to revisit this classroom and these questions again. Would you change your answers? Do you have more to say about the issues raised now than you did when you first read them? Each chapter should hold some part of the answers to these questions for you.

Chapter 2 examined the field of intercultural communication and the new perspectives offered. It traced the rise of the discipline and the major contributions from sister social sciences. You were urged to undertake a personal culture learning journey and, as your first assignment, were asked to examine current student textbooks to make yourselves more aware of the cultural information they contain.

Chapter 3 treated major questions and theoretical perspectives in the field of intercultural communication and presented several models for consideration.

Rohrlich's model was chosen as most useful for the pragmatic ethnographer (the reader) to use. Finally, you were asked to look in the mirror of culture and find yourselves.

Chapter 4 introduced an informal method of conducting cultural inquiry that incorporated the major tenets of anthropological investigation. Termed pragmatic ethnography, this approach directed the ethnographer along a path of cultural inquiry which simulated the processes of culture learning. The search of extant materials, the interviewing of native informants, and the preparation of ethnographic reports were the methods by which the learning processes were simulated.

By Chapter 5 we got down to the matter of definitions, examining several that relate to culture and communication. We noted the processes and components of communication and their implications in intercultural communication. We also experienced the trials of uncovering unfamiliar cultural patterns.

In Chapter 6 we addressed the problems that recur in the articulation of language and culture models. We examined the changing theories of language as expressed in the different schools of linguistic analysis. In moving from the structural/taxonomic analytical methods of early American linguistics, to those of the current schools, we found that each approach had some insight to offer us in unraveling the intricate relationship of language and culture. Each model of language espoused by a given school viewed language from a different perspective. Those who have regarded language as an analog of culture gave us the *-emic/-etic* distinction and reminded us of the powerful interconnections between linguistic and cultural patterns as well as methods of uncovering cultural meanings and categories.

Chapter 7 considered the relationships between language, thought, world view, and culture. The Sapir-Whorf hypothesis, in all its versions, was reviewed and was found to contain insights the pragmatic ethnographer and would-be intercultural communicator can ill afford to ignore. If the hypothesis has been found wanting, as it has in terms of research and theory formulation, it did and does warn us that perceptions differ and that the Sapir-Whorf hypothesis clothed in intercultural terms has a place in our efforts to understand those who neither speak nor behave as we do.

In Chapter 8 questions relating to cross-cultural research and its attendant problems were reviewed.

The roles of nonverbal behavior and nonverbal communication in all their rich cross-cultural guises were considered in Chapter 9. Because so much social meaning is carried on these channels, no language teacher should be unaware of their power, their uses, and their great diversity in form and meaning around the world.

In Chapter 10 cultural assumptions, world view, beliefs, norms, and rules in intercultural communication were discussed. Examples of cross-cultural variations in value orientations and of some general American assumptions and values as identified by writers in the field were provided. Exercises included in the chapter, as well as those in the discussion sections, were designed to demonstrate some of the practical, pedagogical rewards to be found in exploring cultural values in cross-cultural frames of reference.

Chapter 11 covered the subject of culture learning, not as a general process, but in terms of planning and evaluating culture learning and teaching in a multicultural classroom. Relationships of levels of language and culture learning to the degree of acculturation and cultural distance were examined and even experienced by *A Visit to the Land of THEM*. Sociocultural variables affecting second or foreign language learning were reviewed, as was the cultural critical period hypothesis concerning their interactive effects. Finally, typologies of clients (students) and the contexts in which language learning might take place were examined. In short, this chapter considered the myriad factors that impinge on language and culture learning processes.

Chapters 12 through 15 constituted not only a simulation of the culture learning process but also a practicum in putting the information, insights, and knowledge previously acquired to good use in the language classroom.

In Chapter 12 the processes of planning culture learning projects, either as part of the language skills curriculum, or as separate units within the curriculum, were discussed.

Chapter 13 was dedicated to cultural considerations in selecting, evaluating, and using student textbooks. A format for such evaluations was included.

In Chapter 14, the ways and means (methods, approaches, and techniques) of cultural training were reviewed and exemplified.

Chapter 15 brought us back to the language classroom. Characteristics of the American language classroom, the phenomenon of education shock, and areas of possible cross-cultural problems were reviewed.

As readers and active learners, you were asked to plan, implement, and critique a learning project. If you did not, then it is hoped that the examples given will provide you with the insights you might need when you find yourself in a real classroom with real students and think about asking, "How many of you come from families of more than five children?"

16.2 TEACHER TRAINING

As should be clear, forging the language and culture connection in the language classroom mandates special consideration of teacher training. That there is need for specialized training should be clear from the positions recommended in this book.

Changing Times

In the United States the teacher's role as a socializing agent is a natural result of the role assigned the school not only as an institution of academic learning but also as an agent of socialization. Saville-Troike (1978:1–2) writes:

Formal education (including the American educational system) is itself a cultural invention. In the United States, it is a system which serves primarily to prepare middle-class children to participate in their own culture. Students who come into the system from other cultures, including the lower social classes, have generally been considered "disadvantaged" or "deficient" to the degree that their own cultural experiences differ from the mainstream, middle-class "norms". . . . Our educational system cannot be blamed for attempting to teach the dominant American culture to all of its students, since such enculturation (or socialization) is the essential purpose of education in all cultures. We *can* blame our traditional educational system for inadequate provision or respect for students' culturally diverse backgrounds, however. . . .

In such contexts, teachers, then, are regarded as change agents or cultural guides. It is not surprising that in the United States the onus of cultural change and adjustment, which came as a result of the Civil Rights legislation of the mid-1960s, was placed on the schools. Because of this, it is also not surprising that teachers have been forced to reassess their roles. Whose culture were they to teach if there was to be an emphasis upon ethnic identity and cultural maintenance? Cultural pluralism seemed a more manageable concept in theory than in practice.

The Lau vs. Nichols decision, which set the stage for bilingual/bicultural programs in the nation's schools (Bilingual Education Act, 1968), and later the federal provisions for special programs brought culture learning into the classrooms, either in the form of special and remedial programs for the LEP (Limited English Proficient) students, as they are called today, or in the form of multicultural educational programs designed to foster cross-cultural tolerance and intercultural communication skills. The first focused on effecting change in the culturally different, and the second on tolerating these differences.

The concept of cultural pluralism replaced that of cultural eradication, at least in word if not spirit, and was founded on the provisions of the Civil Rights Act (1964), and other federal and state programs. In the United States, cultural pluralism came to mean a sort of legislated cultural relativism; multiculturalism in the school setting came to mean tolerance and understanding of subcultural variations by those of the mainstream culture. How successful these efforts have been remains to be seen.

The Implications of Cultural Pluralism

Programs of bilingual education in the United States were formed on the assumption that lack of English proficiency was a primary cause for academic failure on the part of the culturally different student; however, as Saville-Troike (1978) has pointed out, sociocultural factors, such as poverty, culture, language, mobility, and societal perceptions, play important roles in home/school "discontinuity" (vii).

Because of the heterogeneity of American culture in which diversity is the rule, no teacher can remain myopically monocultural or complacently bicultural. New perspectives, new roles, and new training programs are in order. Specialized personal, professional, and pedagogical skills are needed. Although the problems of the United States are particularly challenging, the solutions appropriate in this highly diverse culture might be also appropriate in cases of intracultural change in traditional societies. In the latter, the pressures of cultural change and diversity often are not found between the ethnically different, but between the young and the old, or among the socially different. Problems arise from different sources, but their solutions may be universally applicable.

16.3 NEW ROLES FOR TEACHERS

The nature of demands placed on the teacher vary according to the balance of the cultural load, as noted in Chapter 13. The typology of textbooks listed in that chapter is arranged according to the responsibilities of the teacher. Traditional textbooks call for little overt cultural instruction. The communicative textbooks demand knowledge of the nature of the target culture, but are less demanding than those of type III in which not only culture-specific but culture-general knowledge is necessary.

Our new syllabi, curricula, and textbooks have redefined teacher and learner roles. Learner-centered instruction, in the case of culture learning, means roles for teachers that may range from counselor to participant observer to resident pragmatic anthropologist to mediator to fellow learner. Taken together, these represent the range of skills expected of the modern language teacher. What is entailed in each of these roles?

As counselors, teachers must be aware of the stress of cultural change and the need to address the pains and problems of adjustment that both they themselves and their students face.

As participant observers, teachers should be aware of the various currents of cross-cultural differences and similarities that swirl around every classroom. They must be prepared to note these forces and take them into consideration as major classroom variables.

As pragmatic ethnographers, they must maintain a learning mode that enhances not only their own continuing search for understanding but also that of their students. Skills in culture learning and intercultural communication must be given equal status with the classic four: reading, writing, speaking, and listening. Such a commitment means that every lesson, every test, every textbook used, should be scrutinized for its cultural as well as linguistic purpose. Cultural instruction and learning projects should *not* be relegated to the passing of time on Friday afternoons or as "treats" for grammatically exhausted students. The ethnographic perspective ensures a continuing search for cross-cultural awareness and cultural meanings.

As mediators, teachers must put aside their own proclivities and attempt to stand in the shoes of others. Mediation does not mean imposing a sort of cross-cultural consensus, but rather fostering an ambiance in the classroom that encourages the development of empathy and, as some feel, a third culture in which cultural differences are recognized and respected.

16.4 IS CULTURAL MEDIATION THE MESSAGE?

What is cultural mediation? What does a cultural mediator do? What are the characteristics of a successful mediator?

The answers to these questions lie in the examination of types of culture learning contexts; the effects of culture contact and change upon personal and cultural identity; and the desired outcomes of cultural training beyond immediate goals and objectives.

Let us search for the answers in the works of Hall, Bochner, Adler, and others cited in the bibliography of this book, all of whom have addressed the problems lurking behind these questions.

Culture Learning Conditions

According to Bochner (1981a:3), the processes of second culture learning usually take place under three general conditions: by means of accident-of-birth dual enculturation, by extended sojourn(s) overseas, or by specific training as adults.

Culture learning, defined by Bochner and other social psychologists, "refers to changes in an individual during and after he has been immersed in an interface situation." Bochner (1981b:12) writes:

> Theoretically, four broad outcomes are possible: (1) A person may remain monocultural, by clinging to the culture of his origin and rejecting all alien influences. (2) An individual may reject his culture of origin and adopt a new culture. The result is still a monocultural person. (3) An individual can become bicultural, by retaining his culture of origin and also learning a second culture. (4) Finally, an individual may become multicultural, by retaining his culture of origin and also learning several other cultures.

Outcomes 3 and 4 are exactly those that would identify a successful outcome for a teacher training program. But the demands of mediation are such that simply being bicultural or even multicultural may not be enough. Bochner warns us (12) that ". . . knowing more than one culture is a necessary but not sufficient condition for cultural mediation."

Let us examine the concept of cultural mediation and characteristics of good mediators more closely in order to assess the implications of such roles for language teachers.

The Cultural Mediation Model

The model of cultural mediation was developed in the field of social and cross-cultural psychology through the work of Bochner and others (Bochner 1973, 1977, and 1981b; McLeod 1981). Their work has been identified with the effects of modernization and the diffusion of Western technology on indigenous cultures in the last half of the twentieth century. Problems of change have brought into question the goals of change and the role of the change agent. Discussions of the situation in the so-called Third World often focused upon the problems brought about by the onslaught of alien men and machines. In the United States the focus was upon the "problems" of the minority or ethnic groups.

Cultural Mediators

Cultural mediators serve as links between peoples of different cultures. According to Bochner (1981a:3), there are two types of cultural mediation, or bridging functions: translating and synthesizing. Translating merely involves the faithful representation of the cultural patterns of one group to another, while synthesizing calls for reconciliation of diverse patterns.

Translation expertise is often seen as the special role of the bicultural or multicultural person. Bochner defines a cultural mediator as "an individual who is multicultural, functions in a transnational role, has a transcultural reference group, obtains transcultural social support for his professional work, and has a social network spanning many cultures" (1981b:7). That few of us could hope to become cultural mediators with such credentials seems a foregone conclusion. However, some of the skills and perspectives of the cultural mediator, like those of the professional anthropologist, can serve the model of a modern, culturally sensitive language teacher very well. Indeed, McLeod (1981:40–41) sees true mediators as teachers because they take on a teaching role.

> The teacher [true mediator] may be a bicultural person, but does not necessarily have to be. But he must possess good communication skills, and, above all, an extensive and intensive knowledge and understanding of more than one culture, on both the cognitive and affective levels. He must use this knowledge to educate members of each culture about the other. . . . The actions of the true mediator should result in some mutual benefit to the two cultures involved.

Although biculturalism is helpful, it is not essential in the assumption of a mediation role. It involves more than translation, however. It is intimately linked with the social and cultural identity of its practitioners and with the concept of multicultural man.

16.5 MULTICULTURAL MAN IN A THIRD CULTURE

Hall, Adler, Bochner, and others who are concerned with the development of personality orientations that would serve their bearers well in the rapidly changing modern world have suggested that human beings must in some way transcend their cultures and become prepared psychologically to deal with flux and diversity. Multicultural man[1] is a new type of person with the ability to go beyond his native culture. Adler (1977:25-26) explains:

> Multicultural man is, at once, both old and new. He is very much the timeless "universal" person described again and again by philosophers through the ages. . . . What is universal about the multicultural person is his abiding commitment to essential similarities between people everywhere, while paradoxically maintaining an equally strong commitment to their differences. . . . What is new . . . is a fundamental change in the structure and process of his identity. His identity, far from being frozen in a social character, is more fluid and mobile, more susceptible to change and open to variation. The identity of multicultural man is based, not on a "belongingness" which implies either owning or being owned by culture, but on a style of self consciousness that is capable of negotiating ever new formations of reality. . . . He is neither totally *a part* of nor totally *apart from* his culture; he lives, instead, on the boundary.

That there will be danger in living in such a constant state of flux and change seems inevitable. Marginality and loss of cultural identity may be the prices to be paid, fees that may be very high indeed.

Marginality

Included in the possible outcomes of culture learning are several not always desirable results, such as alienation from the native culture and marginality. Marginality refers to a situation in which a person, for a variety of reasons (such as race or religion) remains on the outskirts of a social or cultural group. Marginal individuals or groups are isolated, and, in the words of John Lum, their actions "do not reflect well any one culture" (1982:385). Marginality is not necessarily always a negative factor. It plays a part in all cultural change; it is part of the lives of children whose parents remain monocultural while they become bicultural. Richard Rodriguez' poignant book *Hunger of Memory* recounts the pains of cultural transition and the agonies of the loss of cultural identity. In anthropology, the marginal person has often been seen as the one most likely to accept change and to be willing to deal with the foreigner (e.g., the anthropologist) who comes along and asks such seemingly stupid questions.

That marginality and mediation are lonely states is also beautifully expressed in an often-quoted passage from the autobiography of Nehru (1941:353):

I have become a queer mixture of the East and the West, out of place everywhere, at home nowhere. Perhaps my thoughts and approach to life are more akin to what is called Western than Eastern, but India clings to me, as she does to all her children, in innumerable ways; and behind me lie, somewhere in the subconscious, racial memories of a hundred, or whatever the number may be, generations of Brahmans. I cannot get rid of either that past inheritance or my recent acquisitions. They are both part of me, and, though they help me in both the East and the West, they also create in me a feeling of spiritual loneliness not only in public activities but in life itself. I am a stranger and alien in the West. I cannot be of it. But in my own country also, sometimes, I have an exile's feeling.

Lum concludes that "marginal people who fall may be rootless or alienated; those who rise may be synthesizers" (386). They may become marginal in all cultures, belonging wholly to none and without cultural identity. On the other hand, they may cross cultural boundaries and leap cultural chasms.

Cultural Identity

Cultural identity involves the interplay of culture and personality. As Adler (1977:27) comments:

> Cultural identity is the symbol of one's essential experience of oneself as it incorporates the world view, value system, attitudes, and beliefs of a group with whom such elements are shared. . . . The center, or core, of cultural identity is an image of the self and the culture intertwined in the individual's total conception of reality. . . . This boundary of cultural identity plays a large part in determining the individual's ability to relate to other cultural systems.

Loss, or the altering of cultural identity, then, plays an important role in cross-cultural contact. Although these changes can be devasting, they need not be so.

Multiculturalism Revisited

Multiculturally oriented persons appear to operate with what might be called a third-culture perspective, which develops as intercultural contact takes place. This "third culture" takes the form of "patterns generic to the intersections of societies." It is associated with "behavior patterns created, shared, and learned by men of different societies who are in the process of relating their societies, or sections thereof, to each other." (Useem, Useem, and Donoghue 1963:169). Gudykunst, Wiseman, and Hammer (1977:424) find such a perspective is characterized by an openness to change, empathy, the ability to perceive differences and similarities accurately, the ability to describe rather than evaluate unfamiliar behavior, astute observation of personal behavior and that of others, lowered ethnocentricity, and the ability to establish meaningful relationships with "strangers." It is a frame of reference for evaluating foreign contexts.

As Klineberg points out, however, the structure of each binational third culture depends on the original societies involved. He warns that the concept of a third culture may not be an unmixed blessing in the context of mediation (1981:132).

> Could perhaps a greater contribution be made by those who retain their own cultural identity, even though they may borrow those aspects of the new culture which they find palatable? Do not an understanding of and respect for another culture make mediation possible without belonging to a third culture? This important problem I shall have to leave to future investigation.

And so shall we. Yet, we must endorse a position which encourages mediation as a means both to deliver our messages and to develop a classroom ambiance marked by empathy and respect for cultural differences. Does this quotation not speak to the skills most teachers should possess?

16.6 TEACHER TRAINING IN A MULTICULTURAL WORLD

Although teachers may not wish to become or be able to acquire the skills to be cultural mediators, they can prepare themselves to ply their profession in our multicultural world of today.

In Chapter 1 several assumptions concerning professional training for second language teachers were questioned. They included assumptions concerning the effects of overseas experience in developing cultural sensitivity, the need to recognize the language learner's rights in undertaking cultural instruction, the assumption that the teacher would be skilled in presenting all facets of a given culture as a type of supertranslator, and the hope that a "friendly" classroom atmosphere would assure culture learning.

More is needed. Teachers must develop special competencies as cross-cultural guides and intercultural communicators. Such competencies include personal commitments to the development of expertise in the processes of culture learning, understanding and knowledge of the cultural patterns of those they teach, and understanding of their own cultural givens.

Other desired competencies include pedagogical skills in the transmission of this understanding and knowledge, with all due concern for the many personal, social, cultural, and educational factors affecting language and culture learning processes. Also needed are the professional skills to facilitate a continuing search for new knowledge and deeper understanding of the major modes of intercultural communication, training procedures, cross-cultural research, and cultural discovery methods.

16.7 BEYOND CULTURE

Culture has been seen by anthropologists as the human system of evolutionary adaptation. Mankind has evolved or changed by means of what Hall calls (1977) "extensions"—language, institutions, tools—which speed up evolutionary change. The slow processes of natural selection have been bypassed; by means of extensions, human beings may create their own environment (26). This is what Hall meant when he said "Culture is man's medium; there is not one aspect of human life that is not touched and altered by culture" (16). Culture, then, is seen as mankind's primary adaptive mechanism; extensions are its primary processes.

Problems arise, according to Hall, when the models of reality formed by human extensions are taken for reality. This brings on "extension transference," or an "E.T." syndrome, in Hall's terms. Human beings have extended their powers and capabilities, but in doing so have become trapped in their models of the universe, alienated from their natural selves (4).

Hall suggested human beings can recognize the symptoms of the E.T. syndrome and go beyond their own cultures, or even the concept of culture, and communicate on a more natural plane. Extensions must not be seen as distinct and separate from the user. He writes (37):

> After a time, the extended system accretes to itself a past and a history as well as a body of knowledge and skills that can be learned. Such systems can be studied and appreciated as entities in themselves. Culture is the prime example.

Even though we cannot shed all our cultural blinders, throw off all our cherished models of the universe, and become one with the world, we can constantly remind ourselves that, as Hall warns (220):

> Culturally based paradigms place obstacles in the path to understanding because culture equips each of us with built-in blinders, hidden and unstated assumptions that control our thoughts and block the unraveling of cultural processes. Yet, man without culture is not man. One cannot interpret any aspect of culture apart from, and without the cooperation of, the members of a given culture.

16.8 OF KOALA BEARS AND EUCALYPTUS LEAVES

Let us return to a final consideration of the question of which is more important in intercultural communication: human differences or human similarities. Because mankind has traveled so far along the path of change by the use of culture and by human extensions, it is difficult to transcend culture. Not even Hall was able to tell us just how to get ourselves out of the "dilemma of the cultural bind." He points out (222):

> One cannot normally transcend one's culture without first exposing its major hidden axioms and unstated assumptions. . . . Because cultures are wholes . . . and are highly contexted as well, it is hard to describe them from the outside. . . . One has to know how the whole system is put together. . . . This brings us to a remarkable position; namely, that it is not possible to adequately describe a culture solely from the inside or from the outside without reference to the other. Bicultural people and culture-contact situations enhance the opportunity for comparison.

In addition, it must be considered that diversity may be mankind's best hope. Bochner concludes (1981b:9) that, "on a limited scale, *Homo sapiens's* intraspecies variability in cultural adaptations mirrors the biologically based interspecies heterogeneity of the rest of nature."

Thus, we should remember the koala bear. It has a more profound message than that so familiar to us from airline advertisements. The koala bear is an arboreal marsupial that lives in Australia and feeds almost exclusively on eucalyptus bark and leaves. What this engaging, although reputedly anti-social, little animal probably doesn't know is that it is clearly on the road to extinction. Maybe someone should explain the "Law of Evolutionary Potential," enunciated by Sahlins and Service (1960), which states that the more specialized and adapted a form is in a given evolutionary stage, the smaller is its potential for passing to the next stage. Should something happen to the eucalyptus trees. . . .

Although there are many who do not accept the tenets of evolutionary theory in terms of human history, it does appear obvious that there is strength in diversity in terms of human extensions. There is yet a final lesson to be learned. The encouragement of third-cultural perspectives and the development of behavior patterns created, shared, and learned in cross-cultural interactions appear more desirable than the choosing up of sides. Until the perfect solutions to human problems have been devised, we must agree with Bochner (1981b:9):

> And just as nature does not put all of its evolutionary eggs in the one basket, it would be very foolish for the human species to stake its future on one single course, or even a limited number of alternatives.

Hall urges us to take on a difficult task. He proposes (1977:222):

> The task is far from simple, yet understanding ourselves and the world we have created—and which in turn creates us—is perhaps the single most important task facing mankind today.

We know. And the joy and the reward are in the doing!

FOR STUDY AND DISCUSSION

1. Identify these terms:

   multiculturalism

   mediation

   cultural mediators

   marginality

2. What did Hall mean when he suggested that mankind should go "beyond culture"?

3. The question of teacher preparation was raised in Chapter 1 and again in this chapter. In what ways does the injection of cultural learning/teaching in the classroom call for the revision of teacher training?

4. If you were choosing a staff for an English language program for your target group, which teacher competencies would you require? Would you mandate any special training for this staff? Can you list five background articles or books you would recommend to be used for staff training?

5. It is suggested in this chapter that the goals of teacher training programs should lead to the development of the role of the teacher as a mediator. Are such goals feasible? desirable? dangerous? What does it take, according to Bochner, to be a cultural mediator?

6. What was the "message" of the koala bear story?

7. The term "multicultural man" has been used in this chapter to describe personalities who seem to possess the ability to transcend their native cultures. Adler describes "multicultural man" as a person "neither totally *a part* of nor totally *apart from* his culture; he lives, instead, on the boundary (1977:26)." How does that concept differ from the marginal man described by Lum?

CULTURE TRAINING PROJECT

Evaluation

Write a brief report concerning the administration of the Culture Training Project. Include observations concerning your experience as well as those of your students. Try to answer the following questions in your report.

1. Was the training effective?

2. What would you change about your training program?

3. What parts of the program were most successful? In your opinion, what factors were at work in this success?

4. What parts of the program were not successful? In your opinion, what factors were at work in this failure?

5. What did you learn from this experience?

FOR FURTHER READING

P. Adler. 1977. "Beyond Cultural Identity: Reflections upon Cultural and Multicultural Man" (24–41) is a discussion of the nature of multiculturalism and cultural identity. Adler furnishes four case histories of multicultural persons. These studies make clear the stresses, tensions, and strengths that multiculturalism may bring, as well as its place in intercultural communication.

G. Baker. 1983. *Planning and Organizing for Multicultural Instruction* is a practical approach to adding a multicultural perspective to the classroom. The focus of this book is on primary and secondary educational contexts, but its suggestions would obtain for higher levels of instruction. If cultural pluralism is to be an accepted and welcome fact of American life, then this author sees multicultural education as one way to deal effectively with diversity.

S. Bochner. 1977. "The Mediating Man and Cultural Diversity" (23–37). This is an article written by Bochner on the subject of the "mediating" personality as an outcome of cross-cultural contact. The relationship of mediation and education is treated in Bochner's 1973 book, *The Mediating Man: Cultural Interchange and Transnational Education.*

S. Bochner. 1981a. *The Mediating Person: Bridges Between Cultures.* This is a book of readings relative to the concept of the mediating person and the process of mediation as a bridging function. Bochner's article, "The Social Psychology of Cultural Mediation" (6–36) and McLeod's article, "The Mediating Person and Cultural Identity" (37–52) are of particular interest.

C. Castaneda. 1972. *Journey to Ixtlan.* The mystical anthropologist, Carlos Castaneda, was chosen by Adler as an example of a multicultural personality. (See above.) This work describes Castaneda's experiences in altered realities under the tutelage of a Yaqui Indian medicine man and with the aid of drugs. Perhaps more marginal than multicultural, Castaneda is a fascinating example of a man who has gone far beyond his native (Brazilian) culture.

J. Lum. 1982. "Marginality and Multiculturalism: Another Look at Bilingual/Bicultural Education" (384–388). Lum examines the question of marginality and multiculturalism and has a few words of warning concerning the expectations of bilingual/bicultural program directors.

M. Pusch, H. Seelye, and J. Wasilewski. 1979. Chapter 5, "Training for Multicultural Education Competencies" (85–103). This chapter, which is one of three on the subject of multicultural education in the Pusch volume, concerns the development of skills needed for teachers working in multicultural programs. Also included in this volume are articles by Seelye and Wasilewski—Chapter 3, "Historical Development of Multicultural Education" (39–61), and Chapter 4, "Curriculum in Multicultural Education" (62–84). All of these are recommended reading for those interested in the subject of multicultural education in the United States.

M. Saville-Troike. 1978. *A Guide to Culture in the Classroom.* This small volume, published by the National Clearinghouse for Bilingual Education, focuses on the problems of children of minority cultures in American schools. The chapters concerning teacher training, cultural competencies for bilingual education, and use of cultural information in instruction, curriculum, and evaluation are particularly germane to the subjects discussed in this chapter.

H. Trueba and C. Barnett-Mizrahi (eds.). 1979. *Bilingual Multicultural Education and the Professional. From Theory to Practice.* This reader contains an excellent collection of articles concerning the state of bilingual education at the end of the 1970s. The section on culture and bilingual education should not be missed. Of particular interest are the articles by Saville-Troike, "Culture, Language, and Education" (139–148) and "Profiles of Bilingual Children" (164–174).

NOTE

Many readers will feel that the use of the term *multicultural man* implies a sexual bias that is both outmoded and unconscionable. It is understood that the term *man* implies *mankind* as it does in much of the literature cited in this book. Adler himself took note of the implications of the term. Although we do not agree with his conclusion that "it is virtually impossible to express certain concepts in language that is sexually neutral" (1977:24), we applaud his disclaimer of bias and accept his assurance that the term *multicultural man* refers both to men and women. We urge our readers to be equally indulgent on this point.

Appendixes

Appendix A

Procedures

When engaging in anthropological, sociological, or educational research using human subjects, the researcher is obliged, for professional and personal ethical concerns, to proceed with caution and fairness. As you know, the university places restrictions upon the use of human subjects for research. Considerations of privacy and ethical use of personal information must and shall be of primary importance in all our discussions, research, and conclusions.

We may be observing real people in real organizations. We must avoid injury to any persons concerned. We shall not only observe all university-wide regulations but will also impose our own. This means that:

1. No students will be identified by name or implications in class discussion except in the most general terms and in such manner as to avoid any invasion of individual privacy;

2. Classroom materials (student work, comments, etc.) will not be used in any report without the written permission of the student or informant concerned;

3. Any person providing information relative to any research undertaken for this class will be made aware of the purpose of the investigation and will grant written permission to use the information.

A suggested permission form is reproduced below.

I grant permission to _____ to use quotations from or refer to excerpts from class work or interviews. It is understood that this permission is granted for the sole use of these materials in research in the development of teaching aids and texts and will not involve the identification of any personal data beyond age, sex, and native country/language.

Permission granted _____ Date _____

Appendix B

Cultural Training Component Project

Cultural Training Project 1
General Plan

I. Cultural Focus:
   American education module
   organization
   philosophy and major influences
   key terms
   problems

   (approximately four hours over five class periods; integrated with general instruction)

II. Target Group: students in an academic program who will attend an American university or college.

III. General Goals: to acquaint the students with basic information pertaining to the organization, philosophy, and terms related to American education.

IV. Instructional Goals:

   Goal A—cultural connotations of words and phrases (academic jargon).

   Goal B—evaluating statements—students should be able to make generalizations concerning the academic environment in the United States.

   Goal C—sense, or functionality, of culturally conditioned behavior.

   Goal D—research items of interest concerning American education.

V. Theoretical Support: Both by personal observation and through text comment (Seelye 1984: 48–59; Krashen 1982; and Brown 1980a: 250) the developer of this teaching module has become convinced that, while the classroom may not be the ideal place for second culture learning,

1) cultural content will and should be part of the general lesson plan of any language classroom; 2) learning a second culture is part of learning a second language; and 3) the input provided in the language classroom should be as useful as possible for both language learning and language acquisition.

Source: Seelye, H. Ned. 1984 *Teaching Culture.* Lincolnwood, Ill: National Textbook Company. Brown, H. Douglas. 1980 *Principles of Language Learning & Teaching.* Englewood Cliffs, N.J.: Prentice Hall. Krashen. S.D. 1982 *Principles and Practice in Second Language Acquisition.* Oxford: Pergamon.

FORM B1

Lesson Plans

Unit One: Introduction—educational system in the United States
  I. Cultural Focus: advanced reading/composition class in an academic setting. Overview of American educational system and establishing of points for comparison and contrast with native system of students.
 II. Performance Objectives:
     To "explain" the educational system of the United States, establishing some points for comparison and contrast, including financing, access, organization, and general features.
III. Requirements:
     Students will read materials concerning the organization and philosophy of American education.
     Students will discuss these materials and others furnished by instructor.
     Students will write essays comparing and contrasting the educational systems of their countries with that of the United States.
 IV. Evaluation Bases:
     Students will focus upon the similarities and differences in the systems, particularly in relation to philosophy, as preparation for further independent investigation of the educational system.
     Essay will be graded for compositional skills, but not for cultural content *per se.*
  V. Resource Materials: instructor lecture; written materials; class discussion.
 VI. Conditions: in class 15 minutes, and follow-up discussion; essay as homework and part of general instruction.

FORM B2

Unit Two: Philosophy and Major Influences
  I. Cultural Focus:
     Continued examination of the American educational system from historical point of view. Goals B and D.

II. Performance Objectives:
   Students will investigate given figures in American education for the purpose of uncovering basic cultural themes that have affected American education.
III. Requirements:
   Students will be asked to find biographical material concerning persons of importance in the history of American education and to determine their importance and contributions.
   Students must perform independent library work and present oral reports on the persons assigned to them.
IV. Evaluation Bases:
   Oral reports will be graded on investigative expertise, oral skills, and cultural content.
 V. Resource Materials:
   Library and guidance of instructor.
VI. Conditions: One class period for library work; one class period for oral reports.
   A subsequent written report will also be presented.

FORM B3

Unit Three: Key terms
  I. Cultural Focus:
   American higher education; major trends and organization. Goal A
 II. Performance Objectives:
   Students, with the assistance of the instructor, will explore major terms used in academia and compare these to the native system. Students will also investigate some facet of the university system independently.
III. Requirements:
   Students will identify a list of key terms used in university-related matters. Students will be provided key questions, which they must answer by seeking information at appropriate university sources.
IV. Evaluation Bases:
   Oral reports (pair work if needed); ability to uncover relevant information and share it.
   These reports should be clear enough that all students can answer five simple questions concerning university matters.
 V. Resource Materials:
   University
VI. Conditions: One class period for research; thirty minutes for oral reports.

FORM B4

Unit Four: Problems and Life Styles
  I. Cultural Focus:
  Life on present-day American university campuses; conditions; problems.
  Goal C.
  II. Performance Objectives:
  Students will be encouraged to ask questions, investigate areas that they do
  not understand, and expand knowledge of the cultural life of the university.
  III. Requirements:
  Students will identify general characteristics of current university life.
  Students will choose appropriate responses to simulated problems and/or
  conditions.
  Students will be able to contrast culturally appropriate behavior in the
  United States and in their cultures.
  IV. Evaluation Bases:
  Small group work with critical incidents and other cultural training
  materials relating to American university life.
  Sharing of personal experiences and possible solutions. Short quiz
  reviewing culturally appropriate student behavior.
  V. Resource Materials:
  American university students; handouts of critical incidents.
  VI. Conditions: One class period.

FORM C

Implementation
Lesson Plan

  I. Cultural Focus. Unit Two
  II. Learning Activities
  Present topic, general discussion; contrastive points; research.
  III. Resources (handouts, materials)
  Copied chapters on American education reviewed; American educators*
  IV. Methods (discussion research)
  Reading research and discussion.
  V. Sequencing
      Discussion
      Reading
      Discussion
      Report
      Reading/Composition
      Library Report

*American Educators

Listed below you will find the names of persons whose actions or ideas have had a great influence on education in the United States. Answer the questions below as they relate to the person you have been assigned. Locate the necessary information in the library.

Write out a report answering these questions. Do not use a note or outline form. You will be asked to give a brief report in class about this person.

List of Persons:—John Dewey, Thomas Jefferson, Andrew Carnegie, Booker T. Washington, B. F. Skinner, Helen Keller, Horace Mann, Benjamin Franklin, Benjamin Spock, Maria Montessori, Eli Yale

Questions:

1. Who was this person (brief biographical sketch with an emphasis upon educational influence)?

2. How did this person affect or change educational policies or theories in the United States?

3. In what manner is this influence felt today in modern education in the United States?

FORM A

Cultural Training Project 2
General Plan

I. Cultural Focus:
American Euphemisms Module
Introduction and definition (including principles for understanding euphemisms)
Positive and negative euphemisms
Sensitive areas:

death	economic condition
body parts	sex and reproduction
occupation	body configuration
excretion	anti-social behavior
age	others

II. Target Group: high-intermediate level college bound students in an academic ESL program

III. General Goals: to familiarize students with subjects that are sensitive in American culture and the corresponding language used to broach, cushion, or avoid such subjects.

IV. Instructional Goals:
   Goal A—Cultural connotations of words and phrases (euphemisms)
   Goal B—conventional behavior—students should indicate an understanding
      of the role convention plays in what subjects are considered
      appropriate or inappropriate in American culture and how
      sensitive topics may be approached.
   Goal C—research sensitive topics by interviewing members of target
      culture
 V. Theoretical Support: Rawson (1979) states that euphemisms have very
   serious reasons for being in that they conceal things people fear the most,
   they cover up the facts of life, and they are used by individuals and
   institutions who wish to present the best possible image of themselves to
   the world. Both as a practical matter and as a means of gaining further
   cultural insight, a study of euphemisms seems valuable for ESL students.

Source: Seelye, H. Ned. 1984 *Teaching Culture*, Lincolnwood, Ill: National Textbook Company. Rawson, Hugh, 1979 *A Dictionary of Euphemisms and Other Doubletalk*, New York: Crown

FORM B1

Lesson Plans

Unit One: Introduction—What are euphemisms? Some principles for
understanding them.
   I. Cultural Focus: introduction of the concept of euphemisms with a
      discussion of how and why they're used. Goal A.
      Group: a high-intermediate structure class of varied cultural/linguistic
      origins.
  II. Performance Objectives: to define euphemisms, give some examples of how
      they are created and explain their functions.
 III. Requirements:
      1. Students will listen to a short introductory lecture (given by instructor)
         on euphemisms and principles for understanding them.
      2. Students will take notes, in preparation for the remainder of the module.
      3. Class will discuss material presented and ask questions, if any.
      4. Students will be assigned the task of thinking of two euphemisms from
         their native language and sharing these with the class on the following
         day. They should briefly explain the meaning of each euphemism, how
         it is used and which principle it follows.
  IV. Evaluation Bases:
      1. Students will display their understanding of the concept of euphemism
         by explaining two from their own language and giving the principle by
         which it is formed.

2. Students will not be graded, but will be acknowledged for satisfactory/ unsatisfactory completion of the task.
V. Resource Materials: instructor lecture, guide sheet for note-taking, instructor available for consultation.
VI. Conditions: Discussion and questions, 20 minutes in class; assignment as homework.

FORM B2

Unit Two: Sensitive Areas—An examination of some specific sensitive subject areas in which euphemisms are employed.
  I. Cultural Focus: discussion of specific subject areas and the euphemisms used for softening the impact of such topics. Specific examples of euphemisms and discovery of the meaning of others via interviews with native informants. Goals A, C.
     Group: a high-intermediate structure class of varied cultural/linguistic origins.
 II. Performance Objectives: to give some specific examples of euphemisms that fall into different sensitive topic areas and to motivate students to discover the meaning and usage of some others.
III. Requirements:
     1. Students' reports on their native language euphemisms will be used as a springboard for discussion of sensitive topic areas in their cultures and the similarities to and differences from American culture. Instructor will offer specific examples of American euphemisms and their uses.
     2. Instructor will divide students into groups of two or three and ascertain with which euphemisms they are unfamiliar. Each group will be assigned one or more euphemisms to research by interviewing native speakers.
     3. On the following day, each group will perform a short dialogue, which they will have written, illustrating the usage of the assigned euphemism. The class will then try to guess the meaning of the euphemisms from the context of dialogue.
IV. Evaluation Bases:
     1. Students will display their understanding of the assigned euphemisms by writing and performing dialogues using them, and by guessing the meaning of the euphemisms in the dialogues performed by others.
     2. Students will be graded with a plus (+), check (✔), or minus (−), according to how well the assignment is completed.
 V. Resource Materials: instructor lecture, notes, native informants, instructor available for consultation.
VI. Conditions: discussion of assignment from previous day and further discussion of American euphemisms, 30 minutes in class; next-day presentation of dialogues and discussion, 20 minutes in class.

FORM C1

Implementation
Lesson Plan 1

I. Cultural Focus—Introduction to Euphemisms.
II. Learning Activities
    a. Students will listen to a lecture defining euphemisms and giving principles for understanding them. They will take notes on the guide sheet provided (see attached).
    b. Class will discuss material presented and ask questions, if any.
    c. Assignment will be given: Pick two (2) euphemisms from your native language. Be able to explain their meaning and how they are used, to the class. (You may use notes.) Also, tell which of the six principles they follow.
III. Resource—see guide sheet below.
IV. Methods—lecture, examples.
V. Sequencing—Lecture
                 Discussion
                 Assignment

American Euphemisms

I. What are euphemisms?
II. Why do people use them?
III. Why should we study them?
IV. Types: Positive and Negative
    A. Positive
    B. Negative
V. Principles for creating and understanding euphemisms:
    A. Foreign languages sound better
    B. Bad words are better when abbreviated
    C. Abstractions are okay
    D. Indirect is better than direct
    E. Understatement reduces risk
    F. Longer is better

FORM C2

Lesson Plan 2

I. Cultural Focus—Sensitive topic areas and their corresponding euphemisms.
II. Learning Activities
    a. Students will report on their native language euphemisms. Discussion of similarities and differences in relation to American euphemisms.

Instructor will give specific examples of American euphemisms and their uses.

b. Instructor will assign one or two euphemisms to each group of two or three students. They are to interview native speakers to find the meaning and usage of the assigned euphemisms. The other students will try to guess the meaning of the euphemisms.

c. The following day, students will perform dialogues they have written to illustrate the usage of the assigned euphemisms. The other students will try to guess the meaning of the euphemisms.

III. Resource—list of possible euphemism assignments.

IV. Methods—contrastive analysis, informant interviewing, dialogues.

V. Sequencing—Reports and comparison and contrast discussion.

Explanation of assignment.

Dialogue performance (following day).

Evaluation and Feedback

The module was presented over a period of three days. The first day, which included a lecture on euphemisms, went well, with the students able to get the idea of euphemisms and able to ask intelligent questions. The guide sheet seemed to make them more at ease taking notes from a lecture, but it took somewhat longer than anticipated to deliver the lecture and explain the concepts satisfactorily.

The second day the students brought two euphemisms each from their own languages, explained to the class their usage and how they are formed. This required them to integrate some of the principles given in the lecture. This was quite successful in that: 1) the students showed they understood what a euphemism is, 2) their presentations were quite interesting and informative and engaged the interest of everyone in the class, and 3) the students were motivated (excited) by being able to explain an aspect of their language and culture.

On the third and final day the students performed dialogues which incorporated a euphemism that they had been assigned to research by talking to native speakers. The results were good, although some students complained that many of the native speakers they asked said they didn't know the meaning of the euphemism. This was positive, however, in that the students were often forced to explain "euphemism" to the native informants before they could get the desired information. The euphemisms assigned for research were given with no other context and no clues. They were: *tushie, feeling mellow, keister* and *take the last count.* The students said they enjoyed the module and felt they had learned about an important part of the language.

I think the lesson could have been improved by allowing more time for the initial lecture, as well as giving the assigned euphemisms in sentences that would help the native informant figure out how it was being used without giving away the meaning to the students. Also, I think that the last lesson could have been nicely rounded out by giving an exercise with some previously unseen euphemisms in context and letting the students guess at their meanings. As it was, the last lesson ended with a discussion of the students' experiences with their native informants and in their giving feedback about the lesson. They seemed to genuinely enjoy it, as did I.

FORM A

Culture Training Project 3
General Plan

I. Cultural Focus: The Acculturation Process   (integrated with general instruction over the last week as part of review of R/C skills taught)
   1. Identifying Lebanese cultural patterns
   2. Identifying American cultural patterns
   3. Describing the acculturation process
II. Target Group: Students in a homogeneous class of Lebanese Level I reading and composition in an EAP program. These students plan to attend an American university to receive professional training, and then return to the Middle East.
III. General Goals: To acquaint students with the process of acculturation and cross-cultural awareness in order to prepare them for effective personal adjustment to the stresses of intercultural experiences. (Pusch)
IV. Instructional Goals:
   1. To open avenues of learning and growth which inter- and multi-cultural experience makes accessible.
   2. To increase tolerance and acceptance of different values, attitudes, and behavior. (Pusch)
   3. To indicate an understanding of the role convention plays in shaping behavior by demonstrating how people act in common mundane situations in the target culture. (Seelye)
V. Theoretical Support: The concept of guided cultural discovery in the silent mode through carefully constructed reading and writing activities has been suggested in an effort to assist the learner in coping with difficult periods of change and to provide a basis for continued culture learning. "These general objectives include assisting the student to 1) become less ethnocentric by bringing his or her own cultural givens and patterns to a conscious level, 2) understand the target givens and patterns, 3) assess the cultural chasm which lies between, and 4) build a personal bridge across the chasm" (Damen 1983,57).

Both Foust (1981) and Pusch (1979) have proposed that teaching about the acculturative process can prepare the learner to adjust to its various stages. Brown (1980) relates the importance of acculturation to second language learning with the "cultural critical hypothesis." He emphasizes the interrelationship between culture shock, culture learning, and language learning.

References

Brown, H. Douglas. 1980. *Principles and practice of Language Learning and Teaching.* Englewood Cliffs, N.J.: Prentice-Hall.

Damen, Louise. 1983. "Reading, Writing, and Culture shock." *Cross Currents,* Vol. X, 2,51–70.

Foust, S. *et al.* 1981. "Dynamics of Cross-cultural Adjustment: From Pre-arrival to Re-entry." *Learning Across Cultures.* Althen, G., ed. Washington, D.C.: NAFSA.

Hanvey, Robert. 1979. "Cross-cultural Awareness." In *Toward Internationalism,* Smith and Luce, eds. Rowley Mass. Newbury House Publishers.

Pusch, M.D. 1979. *Multicultural Education: A Cross-Cultural Training Approach.* Chicago: Intercultural Press.

Seelye, H. Ned. 1984. *Teaching Culture.* Lincolnwood, Ill.: National Textbook Company.

FORM B1

Lesson Plans

Unit I—Identifying Lebanese cultural patterns

  I. Cultural Focus—Dinner in the Lebanese home
 II. Performance Objectives:
    1. Provide a writing sample about dinner (time, setting, food, order of eating, prayer, etc.) in the Japanese home. (Students will write about the Lebanese dinner.)
III. Requirements:
    1. The teacher will:
       a. Discuss and explain new vocabulary.
       b. Explain topic organization
    2. The students will:
       a. Read the selection and ask questions to ensure comprehension.
       b. Using the selection as a model, write a similar composition describing a typical dinner in their home in Lebanon (including time, setting, food, order of eating, service, prayer, etc.).
       c. Discuss the features of the Lebanese dinner in class.

IV. Evaluation Bases: The students will meet 100% of the terminal behavior.
V. Resource materials: Handouts of the reading selection, map of the world, pictures of dinner in the Japanese home.
VI. Conditions:

> Classroom setting with chalkboard, students read material and discuss meaning of selection in class. Writing done as homework and reviewed in class the following day.

FORM B2

Unit II—Identifying American Cultural Patterns

I. Cultural Focus: Dinner in the American home
II. Performance Objectives:
  1. Provide a reading selection describing dinner in the American middle-class home. Include information about time, setting, food, order of eating, prayer, etc. OR
  2. Provide a reading selection describing dinner in an American restaurant.
  3. Students write about their dinner at Fontana Hall cafeteria (include serving time, food, seating, etc.) or at a local Tampa restaurant.
III. Requirements:
  1. The teacher will:
    a. Discuss and explain new vocabulary.
    b. Answer questions about reasons for American eating habits and customs.
    c. Provide reading comprehension (M/C) questions to accompany the reading selection.
  2. The students will:
    a. Read the selections.
    b. Ask questions to ensure understanding.
    c. Write following the model describing their experiences at Fontana Hall cafeteria or at a Tampa restaurant.
    d. Discuss the features of eating dinner at Fontana or at an American restaurant.
IV. Evaluation Bases:

> The students will perform 100% of the terminal behavior.

V. Resource materials:

> Sample menus from Fontana Hall, area restaurants, and McDonald's. Handouts with reading selections for each student.

VI. Conditions:

> Classroom setting with chalkboard. Students read material in class and discuss vocabulary and reading comprehension exercises. Writing will be done as homework and reviewed in class the following day.

FORM B3

Unit III—The Acculturation Process

I. Cultural Focus:
Overview of the acculturation process
II. Performance objectives:
1. Provide an example (reading selection) of an individual's experience with the acculturation process in the context of a review.
2. Review test-taking skills in the U.S. in preparation for the course final exam.
III. Requirements:
1. The teacher will:
   a. Assist students in defining vocabulary.
   b. Assist students in review of skills in reading/comprehension and composition.
      (1) vocabulary
      (2) finding the main idea
      (3) answering T/F questions
      (4) use of articles/connectors
      (5) capitalization and punctuation
2. The students will:
   a. Read the prepared selection.
   b. Identify the main idea of the passage.
   c. Answer T/F questions based on the content of the passage.
   d. Sequence ideas in a paragraph.
   e. Briefly discuss the acculturative experience of the main character.
   f. Briefly compare experiences they have had in the U.S. with that of the main character.
IV. Evaluation Bases:
Students will demonstrate five out of the six required behaviors.
V. Resource materials: handouts for each student, map of the world, photographs of life in Nepal.
VI. Conditions: classroom setting with chalkboard, read material and go over meaning together. Do exercises individually with students and discuss answers aloud.

Form C

Implementation
Lesson Plan

I. Cultural Focus: Unit III

II. Learning Activities
   Reading
   Vocabulary Development
   Review
   Discussion
III. Resources: See materials below
IV. Discussion; practice
V. Sequencing:
   Reading
   Discussion
   Exercises
   Discussion

Bill's Life in Nepal

Bill had grown up and lived all his life in the United States. One day he decided that he might like to live and work in a foreign country. He got a job working in Nepal, a small mountainous country north of India. He quickly packed his bags, went to the airport, and flew to Katmandu, the capital city of Nepal. Then he traveled by bus to a small village.

When he arrived there, he was nervous and surprised by what he saw. Many things were different. The people looked and smelled different. Their clothes were different. The women walked behind the men and did not touch them. The men walked in front, hand in hand. This seemed unusual to Bill.

He was hungry, so he found a restaurant. Because he did not speak Nepali, the native language, it was difficult to order. He pointed to the food he wanted. He expected the waiter to bring him a knife and fork to eat with, but he did not. Bill looked around and found that the Nepalese were eating with their hands. The food looked and smelled strange to Bill. It was typical Nepalese food, hot and spicy.

The village itself was small. Bill looked and looked, but he could not find a movie theater. There were no electric lights. In fact, people used torches to light the routes, which really weren't streets at all, but narrow walking paths.

Bill walked around the village. Many people looked at him and stared. At first, he felt famous and enjoyed the people's interest in him. The new food and people seemed interesting. He liked the new sights and sounds. He was excited about living in this new country.

After about a month, he started noticing how difficult it was to communicate with the Nepalese. He began feeling uncomfortable and missed the United States, his family, and his friends. He missed American food and customs. If only he could find a hamburger to eat! He began to seek out the company of people from his own country. He felt comfortable with them and together they talked and made fun of the strange customs and habits of the local people.

During the next several months, he and his friends began to learn more Nepali. They started visiting with Nepalese at work and in the village. They noticed that the Nepalese were very warm and friendly people. Their culture was interesting, too, and not as strange as it had first seemed. Actually, thought Bill, they are really very like people at home! Bill started to enjoy the Nepalese food. He visited the homes of his new Nepalese friends and began to speak Nepali.

At the same time, Bill noticed that he felt separated from his native country, and those feelings made him uncomfortable. On the other hand, he didn't feel completely at ease in Nepal, and this also made him uncomfortable.

After having worked in Nepal for two years, Bill began to feel almost completely at home. He could speak Nepali fairly well and simple things, such as ordering in restaurants, talking on the telephone, asking directions, and carrying on friendly conversations with the local people, were no longer problems.

He enjoyed his new friends and his new life in Nepal. He was happy and pleased that he could live comfortably in a new, exciting, and different country.

A. *Choose* the best answer for the following question. Circle the correct answer.

The main idea of this passage is:

1. Bill felt uncomfortable in Nepal.
2. Bill was always happy in Nepal.
3. Bill's ideas about Nepal changed while living there.
4. Bill learned about Nepal.

B. Write True (T) or False (F) in the blank provided.

_____ 1. Bill could speak Nepali before he came to Nepal.

_____ 2. Two years after he came to Nepal, Bill stopped missing his family.

_____ 3. When Bill first came to Nepal, he was lonely.

_____ 4. It took only six months for Bill to adjust to life in Nepal.

_____ 5. At first, Bill wanted to eat American food.

_____ 6. Bill had lived most of his life outside the United States.

_____ 7. Bill studied in Nepal for two years.

_____ 8. Bill was used to eating food with his hands.

_____ 9. After the first month, Bill began to feel more uncomfortable in Nepal.

_____ 10. Life in Nepal was similar to life in the United States.

C. The sentences below are not in correct order. Put them in an order that shows the connection between the ideas. Write the number 1 in front of the sentence that you think should be first, number 2 in front of the sentence that you think should be second, and so on.

_____ In conclusion, culture shock may be a common feeling people experience when they move from one culture to another.

_____ Then, they begin to notice differences between themselves and the local people.

_____ First, they are surprised and entertained by all the different things they observe.

_____ They seek out people from their own country and with them they may make fun of the local people and their strange customs and habits.

_____ These differences cause them to feel uncomfortable.

_____ When people move from one culture to another, they often experience culture shock.

_____ Finally, they begin to feel comfortable with their new language and started to enjoy being with the local people.

DISCUSSION QUESTIONS

1. How did Bill feel when he first came to Nepal?
2. Why did Bill want to be with people from his own country?
3. When did Bill start to feel comfortable in his new country?
4. Do you think Bill's experience in Nepal is a common experience for many people who travel abroad? Why or why not?
5. Have you experienced any problems similar to Bill's since coming to the United States?

REVIEW

A. Fill in the blanks with one of the words listed below.

because	but	then
before	after	while
and	because of	so

1. Bill ate strange food _____ living in Nepal.
2. Bill lived in Nepal _____ he didn't learn Nepali until he had been there for a few months.
3. Bill and his friends talked _____ joked about the local people.
4. Bill felt uncomfortable _____ he didn't speak Nepali very well.
5. Bill worked in Nepal for two years _____ he returned home.

6. _____ going to Nepal, Bill didn't know very much about Nepalese customs.

7. Bill didn't know how to eat with his hands, _____ he had to learn.

8. _____ Bill learned to speak the language, he felt more comfortable.

9. Bill enjoyed living in Nepal _____ the interesting people and customs.

B. Capitalization and Punctuation.

Rewrite the following sentences using correct punctuation, capitalization, and forms of the pronouns.

1. yes bill went to nepal to work

---

2. did bill fly from new york to katmandu

---

3. bill returned home for christmas on december 24 1982

---

4. bills brother tom took him to sears to buy new clothes

---

5. bill was happy to be back in the usa

Cultural Training Project 4

FORM A

General Plan

  I. Cultural Focus: (approximately two hours over two
     Physical descriptors class periods; integrated with general
     Description instruction)
     Use of Description
  II. Target Group: Students in mid-level writing or conversation class.
  III. General Goals: To acquaint the students with the use of culturally loaded descriptors of the physical attributes.
  IV. Instructional Goals: Goal A.—cultural connotations of words and phrases
  V. Theoretical Support: The use of terms in physical description may carry positive, negative, or ambivalent evaluations. For example, both "slim" and "scrawny" are used to indicate someone who is thin. Yet, "slim" has positive implication, while "scrawny" is generally considered in the North American context to be pejorative. Social evaluations in language use form much of the conceptual basis for current sociolinguistic research today. To

be unaware of these cultural choices is to get only half the message and to miss most of the fun. Our students should be let in on this secret.

Sources: Seelye, H. Ned. *Teaching Culture.* 1984. Lincolnwood, Ill.: National Textbook Company.
Chaika, E. 1982. *Language: The Social Mirror.* Rowley, Mass.: Newbury House.
Labov, W. 1966. *The Social Stratification of English in New York City.* Washington, D.C.: Center for Applied Linguistics.
Damen, L. 1984. "Overcoming the Pollyanna Syndrome." *Cross Currents.* XI, Spring 1984, 59–63.

FORM B

Lesson Plan

Unit One: Description and Use of Descriptors (in U.S.)

I. Cultural Focus: Practice in the use of physical descriptors with an emphasis upon the cultural connotations of the uses of certain forms.
II. Performance Objectives:
Students, with the assistance of the instructor, will explore major descriptors and their cultural meanings. Descriptors will be presented illustrating positive, negative, or ambivalent evaluation.
III. Requirements:
Students will identify general connotations of descriptors presented. Students will be encouraged to compare and contrast these with terms in their native languages.
IV. Evaluation Bases:
Students will write an in-class assignment using terms presented. Students will be assigned an essay to be completed as homework. This essay will also demonstrate use of the descriptive forms presented.
V. Resource Materials:
Teacher prepared
VI. Conditions:
One class period of two hours; one homework assignment.

FORM C

Implementation
Lesson Plan

I. Cultural Focus—Unit One—culturally loaded descriptors
II. Learning Activities
1. Students will be presented with a list of adjectives used to describe human beings. These adjectives are marked as negative, positive, or ambivalent

2. Demonstration by the teacher of the features: Students will be encouraged to contribute other words or uncover other attributes.
3. Students will be asked to write a brief report to the police (see attached sheet) to report a friend who is missing. This report must be grammatically correct and give a close physical description of the friend. One class period (report finished for homework).
4. Essay describing a person using at least five of the adjectives supplied.

III. Resource: See list below
IV. Methods: Demonstration by teacher
V. Sequencing
   Demonstration
   Practice

DESCRIBING PEOPLE

Descriptive Terms: Human—Positive, Negative, or Ambivalent

	Terms	Positive	Negative	Ambivalent
Height	feet/inches			+ −
	tall	+		
	gigantic		−	
	small, short			
	male		−	
	female	+		
	midget		−	
	squat		−	
	average			+ −
Weight	pounds			+ −
	slender, thin, slim	+		
	plump, chubby			+ −
	skinny, scrawny		−	
	flabby		−	
Age	years			+
	child, childlike	+		
	youth, youthful	+		
	young	+		
	mature	+		
	kid (informal)			+ −
	juvenile delinquent		−	
	childish		−	
	old		−	
	elderly		−	
	senior citizen		−	

Descriptive Terms: Human—Positive, Negative, or Ambivalent (*continued*)

	Terms	Positive	Negative	Ambivalent
Body Form	*Men*			
	well-built, athletic	+		
	muscular, brawny	+		
	heavy set		−	
	Women			
	well-built, buxom	+		
	slight	+		
	matronly		−	
	motherly	+		
	big-boned		−	
Eyes	color (blue, brown, hazel, green)			
	red-eyed		−	
	cross-eyed		−	
	bright	+		
	bleary		−	
	squint-eyed		−	
	penetrating, intense, soulful	+		
Hair	curly, long, short	+		
	straight	+		
	kinky, matted, uncombed		−	
	bald			+ −
	Color			
	Brown, auburn, black, silver, blond	+		
	gray		−	
Voice	soft, soothing	+		
	strong	+		
	high, squeaky, harsh		−	
Complexion	fair, dark, olive	+		
	swarthy		−	
	pasty		−	
	rosy	+		
	sickly		−	
Face Shape	heart-shaped	+		
	oval	+		
	horse-faced		−	
	lantern-jawed		−	
	flat		−	
Nose	*Female*			
	snub, turned-up	+		
	aquiline	+		
	bulbous		−	
	hooked		−	
	straight	+		

Descriptive Terms: Human—Positive, Negative, or Ambivalent (*continued*)

	Terms	Positive	Negative	Ambivalent
Hands	*Female*			
	slender	+		
	white	+		
	clawlike		−	
	Men			
	strong	+		
	square	+		
	clumsy		−	

Overall Appearance or Impression

Positive	Negative
commanding	nondescript
scholarly	moronic
intelligent	stupid
impressive	unimpressive
well-groomed	sloppy, drab

DESCRIBING A PERSON

Write an essay of five paragraphs or longer describing a person. Be sure to include a thesis sentence that makes clear how you feel about that person. You should also have an introductory and a concluding paragraph. Your developmental or body paragraphs might be:

1. A description of the general physical characteristics and overall appearance;

2. A description of any unique features or facial features;

3. A description of the personality characteristics of the person.

The essay might be entitled:

    The Most Important Person in My Life
    The Ugliest Man Alive
    The Most Beautiful Girl in the World
    My Favorite Movie Star

Police Report

A friend of yours has disappeared and you have been requested to write a report to the police to help them find your friend. This report should tell the police when and under what circumstances your friend disappeared, what your friend looks like, and any explanation you might have for this disappearance. It may be that your friend has amnesia or, perhaps, has been involved in some questionable activity. Please help the police and your friend by giving as much information as possible. Of course, the police will insist upon having a report that is grammatically correct and very clear.

Acknowledgments:

The author wishes to thank M. Lindsey (Culture Training Project 2) and S. Kahn and W. Davis (Culture Training Project 3) for their contributions.

Appendix C

Additional Resources

One of the most distinctive features of the field of intercultural communication is its eclecticism. This is both a boon and a bane, as has been pointed out repeatedly in this book. On the one hand, a variety of resources, theoretical and practical, can be drawn from many fields and sources. On the other hand, the list of possible resource materials is very nearly endless. If additional listing of area-specific and culture-general information sources were to be added to this book, yet another volume would be needed to do justice to the undertaking. In addition, such lists and addresses quickly become outdated or even unavailable.

One way in which the quest for information and guidance can be assisted is in pointing out conduits to these materials. These channels are the professional journals of the organizations of the major disciplines contributing to the field of intercultural communication. In these journals and through these organizations bibliographies, reference lists, and suggestions can be located. Listed below are some suggestions for those who would pursue their interest in intercultural communication, language teaching and learning, and cross-cultural understanding. These are only a few of the many sources available and, of course, are in addition to culture-specific materials contained in guides and area handbooks.

Journals

Perusal of journals from various parts of the world is an excellent means to tap into useful information and gain a wider perspective of the field of intercultural communication. Some journals to consider are:

- *Bulletin of Latin American Research.* Published by the Society for Latin American Studies, this journal contains contributions from disciplines in the field of social sciences and humanities.

- *Cross Currents:* This journal is published by the Language Institute of Japan for the purpose of the exchange of ideas in the areas of communication, language skills acquisition and cross-cultural training and learning.

- *International Journal of Intercultural Relations.* Published by SIETAR (Society for Intercultural Education, Training, and Research), the journal contains articles on theory, practice, and research in inter- and intragroup relations.
- *JALT Journal:* This semi-annual journal is published by the Japan Association of Language Teachers and features articles relevant to language teaching/learning in Japan and Asia.
- *Journal of Cross-Cultural Psychology.* This periodical features articles on cross-cultural psychology.
- *The Modern Language Journal:* Published by the National Federation of Modern Language Teachers, this journal contains articles related to foreign language and pedagogical research.
- *TESOL Quarterly:* This is the official publication of TESOL (Teachers of English to Speakers of Other Languages), the professional organization for those concerned with teaching English as a second or foreign language and of standard English as a second dialect.

General Sources

Some general sources of information include the materials published by the Brigham Young University David M. Kennedy Center for International Studies. This organization has available directories, reference lists, and other bibliographic guides. Of particular importance is the list of resources contained in pages A-65 through A-106 in *Intercultural Ready Reference*, 1981.

In addition, as noted previously, the Brigham Young Center has published a series of short publications (culturgrams) concerning more than ninety countries and cultures, ranging from Australia to Wales. Their *Communication Learning Aid* series (*Bridges to Understanding*) are self-instructional publications discussing aspects of life in given cultures.

The publications of the Intercultural Press, Inc., available through SIETAR, are also tailor-made for orientation, guidance, and grounding in the field of intercultural communication.

Also extremely useful are materials to be found in the *Language Teaching and Linguistics Abstracts* published quarterly and the ERIC Clearinghouse abstracts and reports.

Harris and Moran in *Managing Cultural Differences* (1979) in Appendix D, "Resources for Intercultural Effectiveness," supply a lengthy list of organizations, periodicals, learning aids, and articles on the subject of cross-cultural education and management.

The above recommended sources of information, in conjunction with the articles and books listed in the Bibliography of this book and in the suggested readings, point the way to a wealth of resource material for the interculturally minded. Happy hunting!

Glossary

Acculturation individual learning process related to adjustment to non-native cultural patterns; second culture learning; adjustment to new cultural patterns. (See *enculturation.*) (1) (8) (11)

Administered (artificial) community protected or intermediate community or group established for purposes of acculturation, or socialization; as used in this book, a culturally sensitive and protected learning context. (1)

Affective variables related to feelings and emotions; attitudinal, motivational, and personality factors affecting second language acquisition. (11)

Analogical expression term used to describe nonverbal behavior exhibiting a correspondence between the behavior and intended message; opposed to digital expression which does not. (9)

Approach A set of assumptions concerning a given phenomenon; a philosophy or point of view. (12)

Argumentation process of determining and providing proofs. (15)

Assimilation complete acculturation or embracing of the characteristics and behaviors of a new culture group. (11)

Associative group analysis a research method designed to define cultural frames of reference; used in conjunction with the development of semantographs. (8)

Attributional training training designed to develop skills in the recognition of culturally assigned meanings and culturally correct interpretation. (12)

Back translation translation from one language to another and a reverse translation for the purpose of establishing the accuracy of the translation. (8)

Behavioreme a unit of behavior, verbal or nonverbal, or events assigned meaning, form, and distribution in a given culture. See *-emic.* (6)

Belief system series of convictions in the truth or actuality of a given phenomenon or circumstance. (10)

Biculturalism development of expertise in communication with a member or members of a culture group not native to the individual involved; the demonstration of culturally appropriate behavior in two cultures. (11)

Bilingual education an educational program in which two languages are used in instruction. (16)

Bilingualism fluency in two languages by individuals or groups. (11)

Body language   general term pertaining to human body movements assigned communicative force. (See *kinesics*.) (9)

Code   a system or set of signals used in communication. (9)

Cognitive style   individual manner of mental organization and functioning. (15)

Communicative competence   functional language proficiency; negotiation of meaning in interaction between two or more persons on any communicative channel. It involves knowing what to say, when to say it, how, and to whom in any given speech community. (6) (11)

Competence/performance   what a native speaker/hearer knows about the structure of his or her native language or culture (competence); manifestation of that knowledge (performance). (6) (11)

Componential analysis   search for the elements or components of meaning associated with cultural symbols (Spradley 1979:174); analyses of components or units of native meanings. (6)

Context   social, cultural, and personal elements or variables, internal and external, acting upon the communicative process. (3) (5)

Contrastive analysis   systematic comparison of structural features of linguistic or cultural systems. (4) (6)

Cross-cultural awareness   understanding of similarities and differences in cultural patterns of other than native culture. (8) (11)

Cultural critical approach   a perspective or position concerning intercultural communication training emphasizing critical cross-cultural differences. (12)

Cultural dialog approach   perspective or position emphasizing cross-cultural similarities and the development of intercultural communicative skills. (12)

Cultural distance   dimension measuring the dissimilarity or proximity of given cultural groups. (See *social distance* and *perceived social distance*.) (11)

Cultural emphases   areas of critical interest in a given culture, often marked in linguistic categories. (7)

Cultural hypotheses   guesses as to appropriate behaviors, attributions, or expectations in a given culture. (4)

Cultural identity   personal identification of the individual with given social or cultural groups. (8) (16)

Cultural load   emotional, affective, and often culture-specific power associated with types of content, methods, and perspectives in given textual material. (13)

Cultural meaning   cultural-specific meanings; relationship between a symbol and its referent as expressed in a given culture. (4)

Cultural mediation   process of creating "bridges" of understanding between persons of different cultures. (16)

Cultural patterns   structured and repeated assumptions, principles, values, beliefs, and courses of action relative to human social interaction; culture-general in their occurrence, but culture-specific in content. (8)

Cultural pluralism supportive position relative to cultural variation. (16)

Cultural postulates underlying philosophical bases for cultural belief and value systems and orientations to the world, others, and self. (4) (8)

Cultural relativity a nonevaluative approach to the observation of cultural patterns and cultural diversity; avoidance of measurement by standards or criteria alien to the culture in question. (See *linguistic relativity*.) (4) (11)

Cultural themes central organizing principles, postulates, or positions, declared or implied, and usually controlling behavior or stimulating activity in a given culture (Opler 1945). (4) (8)

Culture learned and shared human patterns or models for living; day-to-day living patterns. These patterns and models pervade all aspects of human social interaction. Culture is mankind's primary adaptive mechanism. (2) (5)

Culture learning process of the development of intercultural communicative skills and cross-cultural awareness; understanding the ways of another; changes in individual social and cultural behavior. (See *enculturation* and *acculturation*.) (1) (8) (11)

Culture shock feelings of disorientation often experienced in instances of contact with unfamiliar cultural patterns or with cultural change. (11)

Curriculum a guide to the selection and organization of a course or program of study. It may also refer to the complete educational program of a given institution. (British: syllabus). (13)

Digital expression (See *analogical expression.*)

Display rules terms used in reference to the rules or sequences associated with the displaying or manifesting of nonverbal behaviors. (9)

EFL English as a Foreign Language; term used to designate English instruction given in a non-English speaking environment. (See *ESL.*) (1)

Elaborated code extensive use of verbal and nonverbal means of communication. (See *restricted code.*) (5)

-emic/-etic terms used to describe cultural phenomena or behavior based upon distinctions made in linguistics between phonemic and phonetic. *-emic* units are considered parts of a given cultural system; *-etic* units are classifications or analytical units not necessarily defined in culture-specific terms. (4) (6)

Empathy the skill or ability to transcend one's own personal cultural patterns, beliefs, and values in order to understand the thoughts, feelings, motives, and patterns of another not sharing those patterns. (11) (16)

Enculturation processes of socialization within primary culture; culture learning in native culture. (1) (8)

Epistemic structures structural framework for argumentation; related to order of argument, logical proof, and a general system of knowledge. (15)

Error analysis systematic description and study of learner deviations from patterns of a given linguistic system. (4) (6)

ESL   English as a Second Language; term used to designate English instruction in an English-speaking environment. (See *EFL*.) (1)

Ethnocentrism   belief in the inherent validity and rightness of one's own cultural values, ways, and beliefs. (1) (11)

Ethnography   a method of describing and collecting information concerning a culture or features of a cultural group. (4) (6)

Ethnorhetoric   patterns of rhetoric or persuasion identified with a given culture. (15)

Ethnoscience   analytical approach to culture-specific phenomena, emphasizing the study of folk classifications and categories. (See *ethnosemantics* and *New Ethnography*.) (5) (6)

Ethnosemantics   subclassification of ethnoscience devoted to the uncovering of cultural systems of meaning. (6)

Field-dependence/field-independence   method describing individual perceptual discrimination of elements of a context. (15)

Frame of reference   criteria by which distinctions are made, categories recognized, and meanings assigned within a given cultural or linguistic system. (4)

Grounded theory approach   a set of analytical methods and perspectives developed for the purpose of discovering analytical categories and the development of theory from data. (3)

Historical particularism   approach to anthropological study emphasizing the history and unique aspects of a given culture; associated with a Boasian approach to anthropological field work. (5)

Holism   theoretical principle that cultural elements should be viewed as parts of an integrated system. (5)

Informants   native culture bearers supplying information and explanation about their native cultures. (2) (4)

Instrumental motivation   an orientation to learning or study marked by concern for the practical use to which that learning might be applied. (11)

Integrative motivation   an orientation to learning or study marked by concern for acceptance as a member of a given group; reflects an openness to the target group. (11)

Intercultural communication   acts of communication by individuals identified with groups who exhibit intergroup variation in their shared but individually expressed social and cultural patterns. (1) (2)

Interlanguage system   language learner's transitional competence in a target language system; an approximation of the knowledge of adult native speakers of the target language; an intermediate linguistic system. (11)

Intracultural communication   acts of communication between individuals sharing given cultural characteristics within a culture; communication between subcultural groups. (2)

Kineme   unit of body behavior carrying meaning in a given culture. (9)

Kinesics   the scientific description of body motion and the study of the communicative aspects of various movements and postures. (9)

L 1   native or first language (1)

L 2 (See *second language.*) (2)

Language acquisition   term used to describe mastery of a linguistic system. (1)

Language learning   internalization of elements of a linguistic system, including both verbal and nonverbal elements. (1)

Lingua franca   a language used as a communicative vehicle among speakers of different languages, as, for instance, Swahili in Africa. (1)

Linguistic determinism   theoretical position positing a causal relationship between language forms and cultural forms with language being afforded primacy. (See *linguistic relativity*.) (7)

Linguistic relativity   a) theoretical position positing a strong but not necessarily causal relationship between linguistic and cultural forms; b) theoretical position avoiding measurement of linguistic forms by standards outside that linguistic system. (See *linguistic determinism* and *cultural relativity*.) (7)

Marginality   term used to describe persons or cultural elements not accorded full acceptance in a given society or culture. (16)

Meaning/form/distribution   terms used to describe a functional unit within a linguistic or cultural system; refers to slot, filler and the correlation of all slots and all possible fillers. (See *-emic*.) (4) (6)

Method   means of presenting and evaluating teaching materials. (14)

Multiculturalism   a situation in which different cultural and subcultural groups are placed in proximity; an approach to cultural diversity designed to emphasize cultural tolerance and *rapprochement*. (16)

New ethnography   analytical and descriptive methods used to uncover culture-specific categories and systems of meanings. (6)

Nonverbal communication   human behavior and/or orientation carrying communicative force generally on other than the oral channel and via the verbal code. (9)

Notional-functional syllabus   an organization of language content by semantic and functional categories. (12)

Paralanguage   pertaining to vocal signals or features outside the conventional linguistic codes, including such features as voice set, voice qualities, and vocalizations. (9)

Perceived social distance   social distance from the point of view of the beholder. (11)

Perception   process by which human beings evaluate, store, and assimilate sensory data. Perceptual patterns are shared by members of interacting groups so that they tend to "see" events or elements in a similar manner (Singer 1982). (7)

Phoneme   a minimal speech sound signalling meaningful differences in a given linguistic system; evidence in minimal pairs such as /tin/ and /pin/ in English. (4)

Phonemics   scientific study of elements of sound in a given linguistic system signalling meaningful differences. (4)

Phonetics   scientific study of sounds and their articulation as used in human language. (4)

Pragmatic ethnography term used in this book to refer to the informal employment of selected anthropological field methods in culture learning; simulation of natural processes of culture learning; systematic compilation of descriptive materials in reference to a particular cultural group through the use of informants and the investigating of contrasting frames of reference for the purposes of developing valid cross-cultural hypotheses and ultimately more effective intercultural communication skills. (4)

Pragmatics study of the interface between formal elements of a language and external context; the science of language use. (6)

Primary message systems term used by Edward Hall to indicate types of human communicative activities, including, but by no means limited to, language. (5)

Proxemics the study of the human use of space in its cultural context. (9)

Psychocultural variables characteristics internal to a communicator that affect the process of communication. (3)

Restricted code form of communication making broad use of implicit cues in the environment. (See *elaborated code*.) (5)

Rhetoric presentation of arguments for the purpose of eliciting a given response; selection and manner of presentation of proofs. (15)

Second language (L2) a language learned after the basics of a first or primary language have been acquired; foreign language; "target" language. The term "second" is used to indicate "additional" rather than as a numerical reference. (1)

Second language acquisition the achieving of some degree of mastery of a non-native language system. (1)

Semantic differential technique method of analysis designed to measure cross-cultural variations in affective meaning. (8)

Semantics pertaining to systems of meaning in language. (6)

Semantograph contrastive series of meaning components identified by cultural groups and displayed in graph form. (8)

Setting environment or surroundings of the communicative act; external context. (5)

Simulation a simplified version of a real-life situation. (14)

SLA second language acquisition or the development of competence in a language other than the native language of the learner. (1) (11)

Social distance dissimilarity or proximity of the patterns of interacting cultural groups as measured in terms of social processes and structural features affecting communicative patterns. (See *cultural distance* and *perceived social distance*.) (11)

Sociocultural variables variables affecting human interaction including social categories such as age, sex, or social class and cultural variations as, for example, in cognitive styles, value and belief systems, or other cultural patterns. (3) (11)

Sociolinguistic competence (See *communicative competence*.)

Sociolinguistics study of language in its social context. (6)

Sojourner a temporary resident; often students or professional personnel. (11)

SPEAKING   mnemonic device suggested by Hymes to identify significant elements affecting given speech acts. (6)

Speech act   a functional unit of speech that derives its meaning from interpretive rules in a given speech community. (6)

Stereotyping   process whereby certain characteristics are assigned to and evaluations made about members of a cultural group without regard to individual variation; blind categorization; overgeneralization. (11)

Strategy   an attack plan; a *modus operandi*; a technique or method used to solve a problem. (15)

Subjective culture   the patterns of values, beliefs, and assumptions associated with a given cultural group and used by that group in perceiving and interpreting their shared subjective reality; "aspects of culture manifested in the commonalities of perceptual–cognitive patterns in individuals within a given cultural group" (Gudykunst and Kim 1984:119). (3)

Subjective reality   the personal interpretation of the world by a given individual; subjective reality is colored and constrained by the subjective cultural context in which that individual interacts. (3)

Syllabus   a schedule of teaching units (daily or weekly). British: statement of content of a course; an ordering of that content. (13)

Target language   the language being taught or learned. (11)

Technique   a device, strategy, or plan used to accomplish a given goal. (13)

TESOL   Teachers of English to Speakers of Other Languages.

Third culture perspective   a point of view that emphasizes suppression of native perspectives in interpreting the actions of persons from other cultures. (See *empathy*.) (3) (16)

TOEFL   Test of English as a Foreign Language; a standardized test designed to measure a student's English proficiency; often used as a basis for admission to colleges and universities in the United States.

Transcultural variables   research variables measurable on an equivalent basis cross-culturally. (3) (8)

Value orientations   positions, attitudes, or principles *vis à vis* general human situations and relationships, such as the family, interpersonal relationships, knowledge, and nature. (10)

Value systems   interrelationships of evaluative attitudes concerning family, interpersonal relations, and other human conditions associated with a given cultural group or individual. (10)

World view   series of beliefs, assumptions, and values associated with basic philosophical positions of a given cultural group; culture-specific response to the universe. (7) (10)

Bibliography

Abe, H. and R. Wiseman. 1983. "A cross-cultural confirmation of the dimensions of inter-cultural effectiveness." *International Journal of Intercultural Relations* 7 (1):53–67.

Abraham, P. and D. Mackey. 1982. *Contact USA: an ESL reading and vocabulary textbook.* Englewood Cliffs, N.J.: Prentice-Hall.

Abrams, S. and D. Rein with D. Byrd. 1982. *Spectrum I workbook: a communicative course in English.* New York: Regents Publishing Company.

Acton, W. 1979. Perception of lexical connotation: professed attitude and socio-cultural distance in second language learning. Unpublished doctoral dissertation. University of Michigan.

Adelman, M. and W. Lustig. 1981. "Intercultural communication problems as perceived by Saudi Arabian and American managers." *International Journal of Intercultural Relations* 5 (4):365–381.

Adler, P. 1975. "The transitional experience: an alternative view of culture shock." *Journal of Humanistic Psychology* 15 (4):13–23.

———. 1977. "Beyond cultural identity: reflections upon cultural and multicultural man." In R. Brislin (ed.), Vol. II.

Albert, E. 1968. "Value systems." *International encyclopedia of the social sciences.* New York: Crowell, Collier, and Macmillan Inc., 287–291.

Albert, R. and H. Triandis. 1979. "Cross-cultural training: a theoretical framework and some observations." In H. Trueba and C. Barnett-Mizrahi (eds.).

———. 1985. "Intercultural education for multicultural societies: critical issues." *International Journal of Intercultural Relations* 9 (3):319–337.

Alexander, L. and E. Cornelius, Jr. 1978. *Comp: exercises in comprehension and composition.* New York: Longman.

Althen, G. (ed.). 1981. *Learning across cultures: intercultural communication and international educational exchange.* Washington, D.C.: National Association for Foreign Student Affairs.

The American Heritage Dictionary of the English language. 1969. W. Morris (ed.). New York: American Heritage Publishing Company, Inc. and Houghton Mifflin.

Angrosino, M. 1976. "Anthropology and the aged: a preliminary community study. "*The Gerontologist* 16 (2):174–180.

Ardener. E. 1983. "Social anthropology, language, and reality." In Roy Harris (ed.).

Argyle, M. 1975. *Bodily communication.* London: Methuen; New York: International Universities Press.

————. 1979. "New developments in the analysis of social skills." In Wolfgang (ed.).

Asante, M., E. Newmark, and C. Blake (eds.). 1979a. *Handbook of intercultural communication.* Beverly Hills, Ca.: Sage Publications.

————. 1979b. "The field of intercultural communication". In M. Asante, E. Newmark, and C. Blake (eds.).

Asante, M. and E. Vora. 1983. "Toward multiple philosophical approaches." In W. Gudykunst and Y. Kim (eds.).

Asia in American textbooks. 1976. New York: The Asia Society.

Ausubel, D. 1964. "Adults versus children in second language learning: psychological considerations." *Modern Language Journal* 48:420–424.

————. 1968. *Educational psychology: a cognitive view.* New York: Holt, Rinehart, and Winston.

Bachman, L. and A. Palmer, 1982. "The construct validation of some components of communicative proficiency." *TESOL Quarterly* 16 (4):449–465.

Baker, G. 1983. *Planning and organizing for multicultural instruction.* Reading, Mass.: Addison-Wesley.

Barna, L. 1982. "Stumbling blocks in intercultural communication." In L. Samovar and R. Porter (eds.).

Barnak, P. 1979. "Critical incidents exercise." In D. Hoopes and P. Ventura (eds.).

Barnlund, D. 1975. *Public and private self in Japan and the United States: communicative styles of two cultures.* Tokyo: Simul Press.

Barzini, L. 1964. *The Italians.* New York: Atheneum.

Baudoin, E., E. Bober, M. Clarke, B. Dobson, and S. Silberstein (eds.). 1977. *Reader's choice: a reading skills textbook for students of English as a second language.* Ann Arbor, Mich.: The University of Michigan Press.

Baxter, J. 1983. "English for intercultural competence: an approach to intercultural communication training." In D. Landis and R. Brislin (eds.). *Handbook of intercultural training: issues in training methodology.* Vol. 11. New York: Pergamon Press.

Benedict, R. 1932. "Configurations of culture in North America." *American Anthropologist* 34:1–27.

————. 1934. *Patterns of culture.* Boston: Houghton Mifflin.

————. 1946. *The chrysanthemum and the sword: patterns of Japanese culture.* Boston: Houghton Mifflin.

Bennett, J. 1977. "Transition shock: putting culture shock in perspective." In N. Jain (ed.).

Berlin, B. and P. Kay. 1969. *Basic color terms.* Berkeley, Calif.: University of California Press.

Berns, M. 1983: "Functional approaches to language and language teaching: another look." In S. Savignon and M. Berns (eds.).

Bernstein B. 1966. "Elaborated and restricted codes: their social origins and some consequences." In A. Smith (ed.). Reprinted from J. Gumperz and D. Hymes (eds.). "The ethnography of communication." *American Anthropologist* 66(2), 1964.

_____ . 1972. "A sociolinguistic approach to socialization; with some reference to educability." In J. Gumperz and D. Hymes (eds.).

Berreman, G. 1966. "Anemic and emetic analyses in social anthropology." *American Anthropologist* 68,2(1):346–354.

Berry J. 1969. "On cross-cultural comparability." *International Journal of Psychology* 4:119–128.

Berry, J. and W. Lonner. 1975. *Applied cross-cultural psychology.* Amsterdam: Swets and Zeitlinger.

Binford, L. 1968. "Post-pleistocene adaptations." In L. Binford and S. Binford (eds.) *New perspectives in archaeology.* Chicago: Aldine.

Birdwhistell, R. 1970. *Kinesics and context: essays on body motion communication.* Philadelphia: University of Pennsylvania Press.

_____ . 1972. "Kinesics and communication." In V. Clark *et al.* (eds.)

Blackman, B. 1983. "Toward a grounded theory." In W. Gudykunst (ed.).

Bloom, B. (ed.). 1956. *Taxonomy of educational objectives. Handbook 1: cognitive domain.* New York: David McKay.

Bloomfield, L. 1933. *Language.* New York: Holt, Rinehart, and Winston.

Boas, F. 1911. "Introduction." *Handbook of American Indian languages.* 1–83. Bureau of American Ethnology Bulletin 40. Smithsonian Institution. Washington, D.C.: Government Printing Office.

Bochner, S. 1972. "Problems in culture learning." In S. Bochner and P. Wicks (eds.). *Overseas students in Australia.* Sydney: New South Wales University Press.

_____ . 1973. *The mediating man: cultural interchange and transnational education.* Honolulu: East-West Center, University of Hawaii.

_____ . 1977. *The mediating man and cultural diversity.* In R. Brislin (ed.).

_____ . (ed.). 1981a. *The mediating person: bridges between cultures.* Boston: G.K. Hall.

_____ . 1981b. "The social psychology of cultural mediation." In S. Bochner (ed.).

_____ . (ed.). 1982. *Cultures in contact: studies in cross-cultural interaction.* New York: Pergamon Press.

Bochner, S., A. Lin, and B. McLeod. 1980. "Anticipated role conflict of returning overseas students." *Journal of Social Psychology* 110:265–272.

Breen, M. and C. Candlin. 1980. "The essentials of a communicative curriculum in language teaching." *Applied Linguistics* 1 (2):89–112.

Brislin R. 1977. *Cultural learning: concepts, applications, and research.* Honolulu: East-West Center, University of Hawaii.

_____ . 1981. *Cross-cultural encounters: face-to-face interaction.* Oxford: Pergamon Press.

Brislin, R., S. Bochner, and W. Lonner (eds.). 1975. *Cross-cultural perspectives on learning.* New York: John Wiley (Sage).

Brislin, R., W. Lonner, and R. Thorndike. 1973. *Cross-cultural research methods.* New York: John Wiley and Sons.

Brislin, R. and P. Pedersen. 1976. *Cross-cultural orientation programs.* New York: Wiley/Halstead Press.

Brown. H. 1973. "Affective variables in second language acquisition." *Language Learning.* 23:231–244.

———. 1980a. *Principles of language learning and teaching.* Englewood Cliffs, N.J.: Prentice–Hall.

———. 1980b. "The optimal distance model of second language acquisition." *TESOL Quarterly* 14 (2):157–164.

Brown, J. 1979. "Case study: an exercise in effective communication." *Cross Currents* VI (1):13–32.

Brown, R. 1976. "In memorial tribute to Eric Lenneberg." *Cognition* 4:125–153.

Brumfit, C. and K. Johnson (eds.). 1979. *The communicative approach to language teaching.* Oxford: Oxford University Press.

Bruneau, T. 1982. "The time dimension in intercultural communication." In L. Samovar and R. Porter (eds.). Reprinted from *Communication: A Journal of the Communication Association of the Pacific* 3 (August 1979):169–181.

Burling, R. 1970. *Man's many voices: language in its cultural context.* New York: Holt, Rinehart, and Winston.

———. 1982. *Sounding right.* Rowley, Mass.: Newbury House.

Canale, M. and M. Swain. 1980. "Theoretical bases of communicative approaches to second language teaching and testing." *Applied Linguistics* 1 (1):1–47.

Candlin, C. 1980. "Preface." In C. James, iii–v.

Carroll, J. 1956. "Introduction." *Language, thought, and reality: selected writings of Benjamin Lee Whorf.* New York: Wiley.

———. 1964. *Language and thought.* Englewood Cliffs, N.J.: Prentice-Hall.

———. 1973. "Linguistic relativity and language learning." In J. Allen and S. Corder (eds.). *Readings for applied linguistics: language and language learning.* London/Oxford: Oxford University Press.

Casmir, F. (ed.). 1978. *Intercultural and international communication.* Washington, D.C.: University Press of America, Inc.

Casse, P. 1981. *Training for the cross-cultural mind.* Washington, D.C.: SIETAR.

Casson, R. 1981. *Language, culture, and cognition: anthropological perspectives.* New York: Macmillan.

Castaneda, C. 1972. *Journey to Ixtlan.* New York: Simon and Schuster.

Cathcart, D. and R. Cathcart. 1982. "Japanese social experience and concept of groups." In L. Samovar and R. Porter (eds.).

Chomsky, N. 1965. *Aspects of the theory of syntax.* Cambridge, Mass.: MIT Press.

_____ . 1966. "Linguistic theory." In R. Mead (ed.). *Language teaching: broader contexts.* Northeast Conference Working Committee Report on the Teaching of Foreign Languages. New York: Modern Language Association Materials Center.

Church, A. 1982. "Sojourner adjustment." *Psychological Bulletin* 91 (3): 540–572.

Clark, V., P. Eschholz, and A. Rosa (eds.). 1972. *Language: introductory readings.* New York: St. Martin's Press.

Clarke, M. 1976. "Second language acquisition as a clash of consciousness." *Language Learning* 26 (2):377–390.

Clifton, J. 1968. *Introduction to cultural anthropology.* Boston: Houghton Mifflin.

Coffey, M. 1983. *Fitting in: a functional/notional text for learners of English.* Englewood Cliffs, N.J.: Prentice-Hall.

Cole, M. and S. Scribner. 1974. *Culture and thought: a psychological introduction.* New York: John Wiley and Sons.

Collis, H. 1981. *Colloquial English: how to shoot the breeze and knock 'em for a loop while having a ball.* New York: Regents Publishing Company.

Condon, E. 1982. "Cross-cultural interferences affecting teacher-pupil communication in American schools." In L. Samovar and R. Porter (eds.). Reprinted from *International and intercultural communication annual III,* December 1976.

Condon, J. 1974. *Semantics and communication.* Second Ed. New York: Macmillan.

_____ . 1984. *With respect to the Japanese: a guide for Americans.* Yarmouth, Me.: Intercultural Press.

Condon, J. and F. Yousef. 1975. *An introduction to intercultural communication.* Indianapolis: Bobbs-Merrill Educational Publishing.

Conklin, H. 1955. "Hanunóo color categories." *Southwestern Journal of Anthropology* 11:339-344.

Corder, S. 1981. *Error analysis and interlanguage.* Oxford: Oxford University Press.

Cowles, H. 1976. "Textual materials evaluation: a comprehensive checklist." *Foreign Language Annals* 9:300–303.

Damen, L. 1983. "Reading, writing, and culture shock." *Cross Currents.* X(2):51–70.

_____ . 1984. "The ABCs of advanced composition: a cross-cultural approach." In C. Cargill-Power (ed.). *Aspects of TESOL: an anthology, grammar and composition.* College Park, Md.: Warwick Press.

Daoud, A. and M. Celce-Murcia. 1979. "Selecting and evaluating a textbook." In M. Celce-Murcia and L. McIntosh (eds.). *Teaching English as a second or foreign language.* Rowley, Mass.: Newbury House.

Darwin, C. 1872. *The expression of the emotions in man and animals.* London: John Murray.

Davey, W. (ed.). 1979. *Intercultural theory and practice: perspectives on education, training, and research.* Washington, D.C.: SIETAR.

_____(ed.). 1981. *Intercultural theory and practice: a case method approach.* Washington, D.C.: SIETAR.

DeCamp, D. 1963. "Review. *Jamaica talk: three hundred years of the English language in Jamaica* by F. Cassidy." *Language* 39:536–544.

Dodd, C. 1977. *Perspectives on cross-cultural communication.* Dubuque, Iowa: Kendall/Hunt Publishing Company.

Doi, T. 1973a. *Anatomy of dependence* (translated by John Bester) Tokyo: Keykyusha (1975).

————. 1973b. "The Japanese patterns of communication and the concept of *amae*." The Quarterly Journal of Speech. 1973. Vol. 59(2): 180–185.

DuBois, C. 1944. *The people of Alor: a social-psychological study of an East-Indian island.* Minneapolis: University of Minnesota Press.

Dulay, H. and M. Burt. 1972. "Goofing: an indicator of children's second language learning strategies: *Language Learning* 22 (2):235–252.

————. 1974a. "You can't learn without goofing." In J. Richards (ed.).

————. 1974b. "Errors and strategies in child second language acquisition." *TESOL Quarterly* 8 (2):129–136.

Dunnett. S. (ed.), F. Dubin, and A. Lezberg. 1981. "English language teaching from an intercultural perspective." In G. Althen (ed.).

Durbin, M. 1972. "Linguistic models in anthropology." In B. Siegel (ed.), A. Beals and S. Tyler (assoc. eds.). *Annual review of anthropology.* Palo Alto, Calif.: Annual Reviews Inc.

Ebersole, F. 1979. *Language and perception: essays in the philosophy of language.* Washington, D.C.: University Press of America.

Ekman, P. 1975. "The universal smile: face muscles talk every language." *Psychology Today* 9 (4):35–39.

Ekman, P. and W. Friesen. 1971. "Constants across cultures in the face and emotion." *Journal of Personality and Social Psychology* 17:124–129.

Ekman, P., E. Sorensen, and W. Friesen. 1969. "Pan-cultural elements in facial displays of emotion." *Science* 164:86–88.

Fast, J. 1970. *Body language.* New York: M. Evans Co.

Fiedler, F., T. Mitchell and H. Triandis. 1971. "The culture assimilator: an approach to cross-cultural training." *Journal of Applied Psychology* 55:95–102.

Fieg, J. 1976. *The Thai way: a study in cultural values.* Washington, D.C.: Meridian House International.

Finocchiaro, M. and C. Brumfit. 1983. *The functional-notional approach: from theory to practice.* New York: Oxford University Press.

Firth, J. 1964. "On sociological linguistics." In D. Hymes (ed.). 1964a. Extracted from J. Firth "The technique of semantics." *Transactions of the philological society.* (London: 1935).

————. 1964. *Tongues of men/speech.* London: Oxford University Press. Reprint of works first published in 1937 and 1930 respectively.

Fishman. J. 1973. "The Whorfian hypothesis." In J. Allen and S. Corder (eds.). *Readings for applied linguistics, language and language learning.* London: Oxford University Press.

———. 1982. "Whorfianism of the third kind: ethnolinguistic diversity as a worldwide societal asset (the Whorfian hypothesis: varieties of validation, confirmation, and disconfirmation II)." *Language in Society* II, August 1982:1–14.

Fishman, J. *et al.* 1966. *Language loyalty in the United States.* The Hague: Mouton.

Flint, A. (ed.). 1979. *Insights: a contemporary reader.* Rowley, Mass.: Newbury House.

Foley, B. and H. Pomann. 1981. *Lifelines: coping skills in English.* New York: Regents Publishing Company.

Ford, C. and A. Silverman. 1981. *American cultural encounters.* San Francisco: Alemany Press.

Foust, S., J. Fieg, J. Koester, L. Sarbaugh, and L. Wendinger. 1981. "Dynamics of cross-cultural adjustment from pre-arrival to re-entry." In G. Althen (ed.).

Frake, C. 1961. "The diagnosis of disease among the Subanun of Mindanao." *American Anthropologist* 63:113–132.

———. 1962. "The ethnographic study of cognitive systems. Comment by H. Conklin." In T. Gladwin and W. Sturtevant (eds.). *Anthropology and human behavior.* Washington, D.C.: Anthropological Society of Washington.

———. 1981. "Plying frames can be dangerous: some reflections on methodology in cognitive anthropology." In R. Casson (ed.). Reprinted from *Quarterly Newsletter of the Institute for Comparative Human Development* Vol. 1 (3): 1–7. New York: Rockefeller University.

Frank, L. 1957. "Cultural patterning of tactile experiences." *Genetic Psychology Monographs* 56:209–225.

Freeman, D. 1982. *Speaking of survival.* New York: Oxford University Press.

Freire, P. 1970. *Pedagogy of the oppressed.* New York: The Seabury Press.

Fromkin, V. and R. Rodman. 1978. *An introduction to language.* 2nd edition. New York: Holt, Rinehart, and Winston.

Gagné, R. 1965. *The conditions of learning.* New York: Holt, Rinehart, and Winston.

Galloway, C. 1976. *The silent language of the classroom.* Bloomington, Indiana: Phi Delta Kappa Fastback Series.

———. 1979. "Teaching and nonverbal behavior." In A. Wolfgang (ed.).

Gardner, R. and W. Lambert. 1972. *Attitudes and motivation in second language learning.* Rowley, Mass.: Newbury House.

Gaston, J. 1984. *Cultural awareness teaching techniques.* Resource Handbook 4. Brattleboro, Vt.: Pro Lingua Associates.

Geertz, C. 1966. "Person, time, and conduct in Bali: an essay in cultural analysis." *Yale SE Asia Studies, Cul. Rep. Ser. # 14.* Detroit: Cellar Book Shop.

———. 1972. "Deep play: notes on the Balinese cockfight." *Daedalus* 101:1–37.

———. 1973. *The interpretation of culture: selected essays.* New York: Basic Books.

Gingras, R. (ed.). 1978. *Second-language acquisition and foreign language teaching.* Washington, D.C.: Center for Applied Linguistics.

Glaser, B. 1978. *Theoretical sensitivity.* Mill Valley, Calif.: Sociology Press.

Glaser B. and A. Strauss. 1967. *The discovery of grounded theory: strategies for qualitative research.* Chicago: Aldine.

Goffman, E. 1959. *The presentation of self in everyday life.* Garden City, N.Y.: Doubleday/Anchor.

Goodenough, W. 1956. "Componential analysis and the study of meaning." *Language* 32:195–216.

—————. 1964. "Cultural anthropology and linguistics." In D. Hymes (ed.). Reprinted from P. Garvin (ed.). *Report of the seventh annual round table meeting on linguistics and language study.* 1957. Washington, D.C.: Georgetown University Press.

—————. 1965. "Yankee kinship terminology: a problem in componential analysis." *American Anthropologist* 67(5), Part 2:259–287.

—————. 1971. *Culture, language, and society.* Addison-Wesley Module in Anthropology. No. 7. Reading, Mass.: Addison-Wesley.

Gorden, R. 1974. *Living in Latin America: a case study in cross-cultural communication.* Skokie, Ill.: National Textbook Company.

Gorer, G. 1943. "Themes in Japanese culture." *Transactions of the New York Academy of Sciences.* Series II, Vol. 5: 106–124.

Gorer, G. and J. Rickman. 1949. *The people of great Russia.* London: Cresset.

Goytisolo, J. 'Captives of our Classics.' *The New York Times Book Review.* May 26, 1985:1.

Green, J. 1968. *A gesture inventory for the teaching of Spanish.* Skokie, Ill.: Rand McNally.

Greenfield, P. 1973. "Culture and cognitive growth." In J. Bruner (A. Gil, ed.) *The relevance of education.* New York: W.W. Norton and Company, Ltd.

Greenwood, D. and W. Stini. 1977. *Nature, culture, and human history. A bio-cultural introduction to anthropology.* New York: Harper and Row.

Gregg, J. 1981. *Communication and culture: a reading-writing text.* New York: D. Van Nostrand.

Griffin, S. and J. Dennis. 1979. *Reflections: an intermediate reader.* Rowley, Mass.: Newbury House.

Grove, C. 1981. "Book review." *International Journal of Intercultural Relations* 5 (4):407–410.

Gudykunst, W. 1977. "Intercultural contact and attitude change: a review of the literature and suggestions for further research." In N. Jain (ed.). Vol. IV.

Gudykunst, W. (ed.). 1983a. *Intercultural communication theory: current perspectives.* Beverly Hills, Calif.: Sage Publications.

—————. 1983b. "Theorizing in intercultural communication: an introduction." In W. Gudykunst (ed.).

Gudykunst, W. and Y. Kim. 1984. *Communicating with strangers: an approach to intercultural communication.* Reading, Mass.: Addison-Wesley.

Gudykunst, W., R. Wiseman, and M. Hammer. 1977. "Determinants of the sojourner's attitudinal satisfaction: a path model." In B. Ruben (ed.). *Communication Yearbook 1* New Brunswick, N.J.: Transaction Books.

Guiora, A., R. Brannon, and C. Dull. 1972. "Empathy and second language learning." *Language Learning* 22:111–130.

Gullahorn, J.T. and J.E. Gullahorn. 1963. "An extension of the U curve hypothesis." *Journal of Social Issues* 19 (3):33–47.

Gumpert, G. and R. Cathcart. 1982. "Media stereotyping: images of the foreigner." In L. Samovar and R. Porter (eds.).

Gumperz, J. and D. Hymes (eds.). 1972. *Directions in sociolinguistics: the ethnography of communication.* New York: Holt, Rinehart, and Winston.

Hall, E. 1959. *The silent language.* New York: Doubleday/Fawcett.

_____. 1963. "A system for the notation of proxemic behavior." *American Anthropologist.* 65 (5):1003–1026.

_____. 1969. *The hidden dimension.* Garden City: Anchor Books/Doubleday.

_____ (ed.). 1974. *Handbook for proxemic research.* Washington, D.C.: Society for the Anthropology of Visual Communication.

_____. 1977. *Beyond culture.* Garden City, N.Y.: Anchor Press/Doubleday.

Halliday, M. 1970. "Language structure and language function." In J. Lyons (ed.). *New horizons in linguistics.* Harmondsworth, England: Penguin.

_____. 1973. *Explorations in the functions of language.* London: Edward Arnold.

_____. 1978. *Language as a social semiotic: the social interpretation of language and meaning.* London: Edward Arnold.

Hamnett, M. and D. Porter. 1983. "Problems and prospects in western approaches to cross-national social science research." In D. Landis and R. Brislin (eds.). *Handbook of intercultural training: issues in theory and design.* Vol. 1. New York: Pergamon Press.

Hanvey, R. 1979. "Cross-cultural awareness." In E. Smith and L. Luce (eds.). Reprinted from R. Hanvey. 1976. *An attainable global perspective.* New York: Center for Global Perspectives.

Hardman, M. (ed.). 1981. *The Aymara language in its social and cultural context.* Gainesville, Fla.: University Press of Florida.

Harms, L. 1973. *Intercultural communication.* New York: Harper and Row.

Harris, M. 1968. *The rise of anthropological theory.* New York: T.Y. Crowell.

Harris, P. and R. Moran. 1979. *Managing cultural differences.* Houston: Gulf Publishing Company.

Harris, R. (ed.). 1983. *Approaches to language.* London: Pergamon Press.

Harrison, P. 1983. *Behaving Brazilian: a comparison of Brazilian and North American social behavior.* Rowley, Mass.: Newbury House.

Harrison, Randall. 1972. "Other ways of packaging information." In V. Clark *et al.* Reprinted from *Communication Spectrum.* 1968. Lawrence, Kansas: International Communication Association: 121–136.

Harrison, Randall and M. Knapp. 1972. "Toward an understanding of nonverbal communication systems." *The Journal of Communication* 22 (4):339–352.

Harrison, Roger and R. Hopkins. 1967. "The design of cross-cultural training: an alternative to the university model." *Journal of Applied Behavioral Science* 3:4 431–460.

Haugen, E. 1977. "Linguistic relativity myths and methods." In W. McCormack and S. Wurm (eds.).

Hawkes, T. 1977. *Structuralism and semiotics.* Berkeley, Calif.: University of California Press.

Herder, J. 1803. *Outlines of a philosophy of the history of man.* Translated by T. Churchill. London: Luke Hansard.

Herskovits, M. 1948. *Man and his works.* New York: Alfred A. Knopf.

―――― . 1964. *Cultural dynamics.* New York: Alfred A. Knopf.

Hickerson, N. 1980. *Linguistic anthropology.* New York: Holt, Rinehart, and Winston.

Hiebert, P. and E. Winans. 1976. *Cultural anthropology.* Philadelphia: J.B. Lippincott Co.

Hockett, C. 1960. "The origin of speech." *Scientific American* 203 (3):89–96.

Hoff, B. 1979. Classroom-generated barriers to learning: international students in American higher education. Unpublished dissertation, School of Human Behavior, U.S. International University, San Diego, California.

Hoijer, H. (ed.). 1954. *Language in culture: conference on the interrelation of language and other aspects of culture.* Chicago: University of Chicago Press.

―――― . 1968. "The Sapir-Whorf hypothesis." In M. Fried (ed.). *Readings in anthropology,* 2nd ed. New York: T.Y. Crowell Co.

Holmes, H. and S. Guild. 1979. "Critical incidents: making value judgments and reaching consensus." In Hoopes and Ventura (eds.).

Hoopes, D. (ed.). 1971–1973. *Readings in intercultural communication.* Vols. 1–3. Pittsburgh: Regional Council for International Education, University of Pittsburgh.

―――― . 1979a. "Intercultural communication concepts and the psychology of intercultural experience." In M. Pusch (ed.).

―――― . 1979b. "Introduction: notes on the evolution of cross-cultural training." In D. Hoopes and P. Ventura (eds.).

――――(ed). 1984. *Global guide to international education.* New York: Facts on File Publications.

Hoopes, D., P. Pedersen, and G. Renwick (eds). 1977, 1978. *Overview of intercultural education, training, and research.* Vols. I–III. Pittsburgh: SIETAR.

Hoopes, D. and M. Pusch. 1979a. "Definition of terms." In M. Pusch (ed.).

―――― . 1979b. "Teaching strategies: the methods and techniques of cross-cultural training." In M. Pusch (ed.).

Hoopes, D. and P. Ventura (eds.). 1979. *Intercultural sourcebook: cross-cultural training methodologies.* Chicago: Intercultural Press.

Hudson, R. 1980. *Sociolinguistics.* Cambridge: Cambridge University Press.

Hui, C. 1982. "Locus of control: a review of cross-cultural research." *International Journal of Intercultural Relations* 6(3): 301–323.

Hymes, D. 1962. "The ethnography of speaking." In T. Gladwin and W. Sturtevant (eds.). *Anthropology and human behavior.* Washington D.C., Anthropological Society of Washington.

———. 1964a. *Language in culture and society: a reader in linguistics and anthropology.* New York: Harper and Row.

———. 1964b. "Introduction." in J. Gumperz and D. Hymes (eds.). "The ethnography of communication." *American Anthropology* 66(6). Part II: 1–34.

———. 1971. "Competence and performance in linguistic theory." In R. Huxley and E. Ingram (eds.). *Language acquisition: models and methods.* London: Academic Press.

———. 1972a. "Introduction." In C. Cazden, V. John, and D. Hymes (eds.). *Functions of language in the classroom.* New York: Teacher's College Press.

———. 1972b. "Models of the interaction of language and social life." In J. Gumperz and D. Hymes (eds.).

———. 1974. *Foundations in sociolinguistics: an ethnographic approach.* Philadelphia: University of Pennsylvania.

Hymes, D. and W. Bittle (eds.). 1967. *Studies in southwestern ethnolinguistics.* The Hague: Mouton.

Jain, N. (ed.). 1977–1979. *International and intercultural communication annual.* Vols. IV–VI. Falls Church, Va.: Speech Communication Association.

———. 1982. "Some basic cultural patterns of India." In L. Samovar and R. Porter (eds.).

Jakobson, R. and M. Halle. 1956. *Fundamentals of language.* The Hague: Mouton.

James, C. 1980. *Contrastive analysis.* Harlow, Essex: Longman.

Jaramillo, M. 1973. "Cultural differences in the ESOL classroom." *TESOL Quarterly* 7 (1):51–60.

Jensen, J. 1970. *Perspectives on oral communication.* Boston: Holbrook Press, Inc.

Jervis, R. 1976. *Perception and misperception in international politics.* Princeton, N.J.: Princeton University Press.

Johnson, J. 1979. *Living language: USA culture capsules for ESL students.* Rowley, Mass.: Newbury House.

Joiner, E. 1974. "Evaluating the cultural content of foreign-language texts." *Modern Language Journal* 58:242–244.

Jones, S. 1979. "Integrating -*etic* and -*emic* approaches in the study of intercultural communication. In M. Asante *et al.*

Joos, M. 1967. *The five clocks: a linguistic excursion in the five styles of English usage.* New York: Harcourt, Brace, and World.

Kachru, B. 1976. "Models of English for the third world: white man's linguistic burden or language pragmatics?" *TESOL Quarterly* 10:221–239.

Kaplan, R. 1966. "Cultural thought patterns in intercultural education." *Language Learning* 16 (1–2):1–20.

Keesing, R. 1974. "Theories of culture." *Annual review of anthropology.* B. Siegel, A. Beals, and S. Tyler (eds.). Vol. 3. Annual Review: Palo Alto, Calif.

———. 1981. *Cultural anthropology: a contemporary perspective*. 2nd ed. New York: Holt, Rinehart and Winston.

Kim, Y. 1982. "Communication and acculturation." In L. Samovar and R. Porter (eds.).

Kipling, R. 1970. "We and they." *The collected works of Rudyard Kipling*. Vol 27. New York: AMS Press.

Kleinjans, E. 1972a. *Cross-cultural linguistic communication. Paper No. 12*. Paper at Japan Association of College English Teachers' Annual Conference, Hachioji, August 1971.

———. 1972b. *On culture learning: paper no. 13*. Japan Association of College English Teachers' Annual Conference, Hachioji.

Klineberg, O. 1981. "The role of international university exchanges." In S. Bochner (ed.), 1981a.

Kluckhohn, C. 1944. *Mirror for man*. New York: McGraw-Hill.

Kluckhohn, F. and F. Strodtbeck. 1961. *Variations in value orientations*. Evanston, Ill.: Row, Peterson, and Company.

Knapp, M. 1972. *Nonverbal communication in human interaction*. New York: Holt, Rinehart and Winston.

Knepler, H. and M. Knepler. 1983. *Crossing cultures: readings for composition*. New York: Macmillan Publishing Company.

Knowles, M. 1970. *The modern practice of adult education: andragogy to pedagogy*. New York: Association Press.

Kohls, R. 1979. "Conceptual model for area studies." In D. Hoopes and P. Ventura.

———. 1981. *Developing intercultural awareness*. Washington, D.C.: SIETAR.

———. 1984. 2nd ed. *Survival kit for overseas living*. Yarmouth, Me.: Intercultural Press, Inc.

Kraemer, A. 1973. *Development of a cultural self-awareness approach to instruction in intercultural communication*. Alexandria, Va.: Human Relations Resources Research Organization.

Kraft, C. 1978. "Worldview in intercultural communication." In F. Casmir (ed.).

Krashen, S. 1976. "Formal and informal linguistic environments in language learning and language acquisition." *TESOL Quarterly* 10:157–168.

———. 1978. "The monitor model for second-language acquisition." In R. Gingras (ed.).

———. 1982. *Principles and practice in second language acquisition*. Oxford: Pergamon Press.

Krasnick, H. 1985. "Intercultural competence in ESL for adults." *JALT Journal* 7 (1):15–41.

Kroeber, A. and C. Kluckhohn. 1952. "Culture: a critical review of concepts and definitions." *Papers of the Peabody Museum of American Archaeology and Ethnography*. Harvard University. Vol. 47. New York: Random House.

Kuhn, T. 1962 *The structure of scientific revolutions*. Chicago: University of Chicago Press.

Kuntz, L. 1982. *The new arrival: ESL stories for ESL students* Book 1. Haywood, Calif.: The Alemany Press.

Kushner, G. 1973. *Immigrants from India to Israel: planned change in an administered community.* Tucson, Ariz.: University of Arizona Press.

La Barre, W. 1945. "Some observations on character structure in the Orient: The Japanese." *Psychiatry* 8:319–342.

Labov, W. 1966. *The social stratification of English in New York City.* Washington, D.C.: Center for Applied Linguistics.

———. 1972. *Sociolinguistic patterns.* Philadelphia: University of Pennsylvania Press.

Lado, R. 1957. *Linguistics across cultures: applied linguistics for language teachers.* Ann Arbor: The University of Michigan Press.

Lakoff, G. and M. Johnson, 1980. *Metaphors we live by.* Chicago: The University of Chicago Press.

Lambert, W. 1967. "A social psychology of bilingualism." *The Journal of Social Issues* 23:91–109.

———. 1975. "Culture and language as factors in learning and education." In A. Wolfgang (ed.). *Education of immigrant students: issues and answers.* Symposium Series 5. Toronto: Ontario Institute for Studies in Education.

Lanier, A. 1978. *Living in the USA.* Chicago: Intercultural Press.

Larson, D. and W. Smalley. 1972. *Becoming bilingual: a guide to language learning.* South Pasadena, Calif.: William Carey Library.

Latin America. 1977. Provo, Utah: Brigham Young Center for International and Area Studies.

Leathers, D. 1976. *Nonverbal communication systems.* Boston: Allyn and Bacon.

Lee, D. 1950. "Lineal and nonlineal codifications of reality." *Psychosomatic Medicine* 12:89–97.

———. 1959. *Freedom and culture.* Englewood Cliffs, N.J.: Prentice-Hall.

Lee, E. 1980. *The American in Saudi Arabia.* Chicago: Intercultural Press.

Le Guin, U. 1985. "She unnames them." *The New Yorker,* January 21, 1985, 27.

Lenneberg, E. 1953. "Cognition in ethnolinguistics." *Language* 29:463–471.

———. 1967. *Biological foundations of language.* New York: John Wiley and Sons.

Lévi-Strauss, C., 1963. *Structural anthropology.* New York: Basic Books.

———. 1964. "Structural analysis in linguistics and in anthropology." In D. Hymes (ed.).

Levine, D. 1982. "The educational backgrounds of Saudi Arabian and Algerian students." In L. Samovar and R. Porter (eds.).

Levine, D. and M. Adelman. 1982. *Beyond language: intercultural communication for English as a second language.* Englewood Cliffs, N.J.: Prentice-Hall.

LeVine, R. and D. Campbell. 1972. *Ethnocentrism: theories of conflict, ethnic attitudes, and group behavior.* New York: Wiley.

Levine, R. and E. Wolff, 1985. "Social time: the heartbeat of culture." *Psychology Today,* March, 1985, 28–30,32,35.

Lewis, R., S. Weir, and M. Vincent. 1977. *Reading for adults.* London: Longman.

Live, A. and S. Sankowsky. 1980. *American mosiac: intermediate-advanced reader.* Englewood Cliffs, N.J.: Prentice-Hall.

Lounsbury, F. 1964. "A formal account of Crow- and Omaha-type kinship terminologies." In W. Goodenough (ed.) *Explorations in cultural anthropology.* New York: McGraw-Hill.

Lugton, R. 1978. *American topics: a reading vocabulary text for speakers of English as a second language.* Englewood Cliffs, N.J.: Prentice-Hall.

Lum, J. 1982. "Marginality and multiculturalism: another look at bilingual/bicultural education." In L. Samovar and R. Porter (eds.). Reprinted from Culture Learning Institute Report. 1977. Vol 5(1). Honolulu: East-West Center.

Lysgaard, S. 1955. "Adjustment in a foreign society: Norwegian Fulbright grantees visiting the United States." *International Social Science Bulletin* 7:45–51.

Malinowski, B. 1922. *Argonauts of the Western Pacific.* London: Routledge.

———— . 1923. "The problem of meaning in primitive languages." In C. Ogden and I. Richards (eds.) *The meaning of meaning.* London: Kegan Paul.

———— . 1927. *Sex and repression in savage society.* London: Routledge and Kegan Paul.

———— . 1937. "The dilemma of contemporary linguistics." *Nature* 140:172–173.

Manners, R. and D. Kaplan (eds.). 1968. *Theory in anthropology: a source book.* New York: Aldine-Atherton.

Maslow, A. 1954. *Motivation and personality.* New York: Harper and Row.

McCormack, W. and S. Wurm (eds.). 1977. *Language and thought: anthropological issues.* The Hague: Mouton.

McLeod, B. 1976. "The relevance of anthropology to language teaching." *TESOL Quarterly* 10 (2):211–220.

———— . 1981. "The mediating person and cultural identity." In S. Bochner (ed.).

McMichael, C. and W. Orr. 1983. "A guide to gestures in the ESL classroom." Workshop. TESOL '83, March 15–20, 1983. (Intensive English Language Program, North Texas State University, Denton, Texas.)

Mead, M. 1928. *Coming of age in Samoa.* New York: Morrow.

———— . 1942. *And keep your powder dry: an anthropologist looks at America.* New York: W. Morrow.

———— . 1954. "The swaddling hypothesis: its reception." *American Anthropologist* 56:395–409.

Mehrabian, A. 1972. *Nonverbal communication.* Chicago/New York: Aldine, Atherton.

Mehrabian, A. and S. Ferris. 1967. "Inference of attitudes from nonverbal communication in two channels." *Journal of Consulting Psychology* 31 (3):248–252.

Mehrabian, A. and M. Wiener. 1967. "Decoding of inconsistent messages." *Journal of Personality and Social Psychology.* 6:109–114.

Mestenhauser, J. 1981. "Selected learning concepts and theories." In G. Althen (ed.).

Metzger, D. and G. Williams. 1963. "A formal ethnographic analysis of Tenejapa Ladino weddings." *American Anthropologist* 65:1076–1101.

_____ . 1966. "Some procedures and results in the study of native categories: Tzeltal 'firewood.' " *American Anthropologist* 68:389–407.

Miller, P. 1981. "Silent messages." *Childhood Education* 58 (1):20–24.

Miner, H. 1956. "Body ritual among the Nacirema." *American Anthropologist* June 1956 58(3):503–507.

Miracle, Jr., A. and J. Yapita Moya. 1981. "Time and space in Aymara." In M. Hardman (ed.).

Moran, R. 1981. "Utilizing the case method in intercultural communication." In W. Davey (ed.).

Morris, C. 1939. "Foundations of the theory of signs." *International Encyclopedia of Unified Science,* Vol 1(2), Chicago.

_____ . 1946. *Signs, language, and behavior.* New York: Prentice Hall.

Morris, D., P. Collett, P. Marsh, and M. O'Shaughnessy. 1980. *Gestures, their origins, and distribution.* New York: Stein and Day.

Morsbach, H. 1982. "Aspects of nonverbal communication in Japan. In L. Samovar and R. Porter (eds.) Reprinted from *Journal of Nervous and Mental Diseases.* 1973 157 (4):262–277.

Motta, J. and K. Riley. 1983. *Impact: adult reading skills development.* Book 3. Reading, Mass: Addison-Wesley.

Munby, J. 1978. *Communicative syllabus design.* Cambridge: Cambridge University Press.

Nehru, J. 1941. *Toward freedom: the autobiography of Jawaharlal Nehru.* New York: The John Day Company.

Neustadt, B. 1981. *Speaking of the USA: a reader for discussion.* New York: Harper and Row.

Nine Curt, C. 1976. *Non-verbal communication in Puerto Rico.* Cambridge, Mass.: National Assessment and Dissemination Center for Bilingual/Bicultural Education.

Nishida, H. 1985. "Japanese intercultural communication competence and cross-cultural adjustment." *International Journal of Intercultural Relations* 9 (3):247–269.

Nomura, N. and D. Barnlund. 1983. "Patterns of interpersonal criticism in Japan and the United States." *International Journal of Intercultural Relations* 7 (1):1–18.

Nostrand, H. 1966. "Describing and teaching the sociocultural context of a foreign language and literature." In A. Valdman (ed.) *Trends in language teaching.* New York: McGraw Hill.

_____ . 1978. "The 'emergent model' (structured inventory of a sociocultural system) applied to contemporary France." *Contemporary French Civilization II* (ii, winter):277–294.

Oberg, K. 1979. *Culture shock and the problem of adjustment to new cultural environments.* In E. Smith and L. Luce (eds.) Originally published 1958, Washington, D.C.: Department of State, Foreign Service Institute.

Okabe, R. 1983. "Cultural assumptions of East and West: Japan and the United States." In W. Gudykunst (ed.).

Okada, B. and N. Okada. 1973. *Dos and don'ts for the Japanese businessman abroad.* New York: Regents Publishing Company.

Oller, J. 1971. "Difficulty and predictability." *Working papers in linguistics* (Hawaii) 3:79–98.

Oller, J., L. Baca, and F. Vigil. 1977. "Attitudes and attained proficiency in ESL: a sociolinguistic study of Mexican Americans in the Southwest." *TESOL Quarterly* 11 (2):173–183.

Oller, J., A. Hudson, and P. Liu. 1977. "Attitudes and attained proficiency in ESL: a sociolinguistic study of native speakers of Chinese in the United States." *Language Learning* 27:1–27.

Oller, J. and S. Ziahosseiny. 1970. "The contrastive analysis hypothesis and spelling errors." *Language Learning* 20:183–189.

Olsson, M. 1985. "Meeting styles for intercultural groups." *Occasional papers in intercultural learning.* No. 7. New York: AFS International/Intercultural Programs, Inc.

Opler, M. 1945. "Themes as dynamic forces in culture." *The American Journal of Sociology* 51:198–206.

Osgood, C. 1964. "Semantic differential technique in the comparative study of cultures." *American Anthropologist* (66):171–200.

Osgood, C., W. May, and M. Miron. 1975. *Cross-cultural universals of affective meaning.* Urbana, Ill.: University of Illinois Press.

Osgood, C., G. Suci, and P. Tannenbaum. 1957. *The measurement of meaning.* Urbana, Ill.: University of Illinois Press.

Patai, R. 1983. *The Arab mind.* Rev. ed. New York: Scribner.

Paulston, C. 1974. "Linguistic and communicative competence." *TESOL Quarterly* 8 (4):347–362.

――――. 1978. "Biculturalism: some reflections and speculations." *TESOL Quarterly* 12 (4):369–380.

Pedersen, P., W. Lonner, and J. Draguns (eds.). 1976. *Counseling across cultures.* Honolulu: The University Press of Hawaii.

Pelto, P. 1970. *Anthropological research: the structure of inquiry.* New York: Harper and Row.

Pennycook, A. 1985. "Actions speak louder than words: paralanguage, communication, and education." *TESOL Quarterly* 19 (2):259–282.

Pifer, G. and N. Mutoh. 1977. *Points of view.* Rowley, Mass.: Newbury House.

Pike, K. L. 1954. *Language in relation to a unified theory of the structure of human behavior.* Vol. 1. Glendale, CA: Summer Institute of Linguistics. Second rev. ed. 1967. *Language in relation to a unified theory of human behavior.* The Hague: Mouton.

――――. 1964. "Towards a theory of the structure of human behavior." In D. Hymes (ed.). Reprinted from *Estudios antropólogicos publicados en homenaje al Doctor Manual Gamio.* Mexico, D.F.: Sociedad Mexicana de Antropología, 1956:659–671.

――――. 1966. "Etic and emic standpoints for the description of behavior." In A. Smith (ed.).

Porter, R. and L. Samovar. 1982. "Approaching intercultural communication." In L. Samovar and R. Porter (eds.).

Pribram, K. 1949. *Conflicting patterns of thought.* Washington, D.C.: Public Affairs Press.

Price-Williams, D. 1975. *Explorations in cross-cultural psychology.* San Francisco: Chandler and Sharp.

———. 1982. "Cross-cultural studies" in L. Samovar and R. Porter (eds.). Reprinted from B. Foss (ed.) *New horizons in psychology.* 1966. Baltimore: Penguin Books.

Prosser, M. 1973. *Intercommunication among nations and peoples.* New York: Harper and Row.

———. 1978. *The cultural dialogue: an introduction to intercultural communication.* Boston: Houghton Mifflin.

Pusch, M. (ed.) 1979. *Multicultural education: a cross-cultural training approach.* Chicago: Intercultural Press.

Pusch M., A. Patico, G. Renwick, and C. Saltzman. 1981. "Cross-cultural training." In G. Althen (ed.).

Pusch, M., H. Seelye, and J. Wasilewski. 1979. "Training for multicultural education competencies." In M. Pusch (ed.).

Renwick, G. 1979. "Evaluation: some practical guidelines." In M. Pusch (ed.).

Rich, A. and D. Ogawa. 1982. "Intercultural and interracial communication: an analytical approach." In L. Samovar and R. Porter (eds.).

Richards, J. 1971. "A non-contrastive approach to error analysis." *English Language Teaching* 25:204–219.

———. (ed). 1974. *Error analysis: perspectives on second language acquisition.* London: Longman.

Ritchie, W. 1967. "Some implications of generative grammar for the construction of courses in English as a foreign language." *Language Learning* 17 (3-4):111–131.

Rodriguez, R. 1981. *Hunger of memory; the education of Richard Rodriguez. An autobiography.* Boston: David R. Godine.

Rogers, C. 1951. *Client-centered therapy: its current practice, implications, and theory.* Boston: Houghton Mifflin.

Rohrlich, P. 1983. "Toward a unified conception of intercultural communication: an integrated systems approach." *International Journal of Intercultural Relations* 7(2):191–209.

Ross, R. 1979. "The case study method." In D. Hoopes and P. Ventura (eds.).

Ruben, B. 1975. "Intrapersonal, interpersonal, and mass communication process in individual and multiperson systems." In B. Ruben and Y. Kim (eds.). *General systems theory and human communication.* Rochelle Park, N.J.: Hayden.

Ruffner, T. 1982. *Americana articles: an intermediate ESL reader.* Berkeley, Calif.: T. Ruffner.

Sakamoto, N. and R. Naotsuka. 1982. *Polite fictions: why Japanese and Americans seem rude to each other.* Tokyo: Kinseido.

Samovar, L. 1979. "Intercultural communication research: some myths, some questions." In W. Davey (ed.).

Samovar, L. and R. Porter (eds.). 1982. *Intercultural communication: a reader.* 3rd ed. Belmont, Calif.: Wadsworth.

Samovar, L., R. Porter, and N. Jain. 1981. *Understanding intercultural communication.* Belmont, Calif.: Wadsworth.

Sapir, E. 1921. *Language: an introduction to the study of speech.* New York: Harcourt, Brace and World.

_____. 1929. "The status of linguistics as a science." *Language* 5:207–214.

_____. 1931. "Conceptual categories in primitive languages." *Science* 74:578.

_____. 1964. *Culture, language, and personality: selected essays.* Edited by David G. Mandelbaum. Berkeley and Los Angeles, Calif.: University of California Press.

Sarbaugh, L. 1979. *Intercultural communication.* Rochelle Park, N.J.: Hayden Book Co., Inc.

Saussure, F. de. 1915. *Course in General Linguistics (Cours de linguistique générale).* Edited by C. Bally, A. Sechehaye and A. Riedlinger. Translated by W. Baskin. 1959. New York: McGraw-Hill.

Savignon, S. 1983. *Communicative competence: theory and classroom practice. Texts and contexts in second language learning.* Reading, Mass.: Addison-Wesley.

Savignon, S. and M. Berns (eds.). 1984. *Initiatives in communicative language teaching: a book of readings.* Reading, Mass.: Addison-Wesley.

Saville-Troike, M. 1978. *A guide to culture in the classroom.* Rosslyn, Va.: National Clearinghouse for Bilingual Education.

_____. 1982. *The ethnography of communication: an introduction.* Baltimore: University Park Press.

Scaun, R., C. Wilkes, L. Morelli, and H. Nadler. 1971. *American English Readings II.* New York: American Language Institute, New York University.

Schachter, J. 1981. "The hand signal system." *TESOL Quarterly* 15(2):125–138.

Scherer, K. and P. Ekman (eds.). 1982. *Handbook of methods in nonverbal behavior research.* Cambridge: Cambridge University Press/Paris: *Editions de la Maison des Sciences de l'Homme.*

Schneider, D. 1968. *American kinship: a cultural account.* Englewood Cliffs, N.J.: Prentice-Hall.

_____. 1972. "What is kinship all about?" In P. Reining (ed.) *Kinship studies in the Morgan centennial year.* Washington, D.C.: Anthropological Society of Washington.

Schumann, J. 1974. "The implications of interlanguage, pidginization and creolization for the study of adult language acquisition." *TESOL Quarterly* 8 (2):145–152.

_____. 1975. "Affective factors and the problem of age in second language acquisition." *Language Learning* 25:209–236.

_____. 1976a. "Second language acquisition: the pidginization hypothesis." *Language Learning* 26:391–408.

_____. 1976b. "Social distance as a factor in second language acquisition." *Language Learning* 26 (1):135–143.

_____. 1978. "The acculturation model for second-language acquisition." In R. Gingras (ed.).

Schuon, F. 1976. *Understanding Islam.* London: Unwin Paperbacks.

Scovel, T. 1969. "Foreign accents, language acquisition, and cerebral dominance." *Language Learning* 19 (3 and 4):245–254.

Searle, J. 1969. *Speech acts: an essay in the philosophy of language.* Cambridge, England: Cambridge University Press.

Sechrest, L, T. Fay, and S. Zaidi. 1972. "Problems of translation in cross-cultural research." *Journal of Cross-Cultural Psychology, Vol. 3(1),* 41–56.

Seelye, H. 1984. *Teaching culture: strategies for intercultural communication.* Lincolnwood, Ill.: National Textbook Company.

Seelye, H. and J. Wasilewski, 1979a. "Historical development of multicultural education." In M. Pusch (ed.).

———. 1979b. "Toward a taxonomy of coping strategies used in multicultural settings." Paper presented at SIETAR, Mexico City, March 1979.

Selinker, L. 1971. "A brief reappraisal of contrastive linguistics." *Working papers in linguistics.* Pacific Conference on Contrastive Linguistics and Language Universals. Hawaii 3.4:1–10.

———. 1972. "Interlanguage." *International Review of Applied Linguistics* Vol. 10 (3):201–231.

Service, E. 1960. "The law of evolutionary potential." *The Bobbs-Merrill reprint series in the social sciences, A-206.* Reprinted from M. Sahlins and E. Service (eds.). *Evolution and culture.* Ann Arbor: University of Michigan Press.

Shimazu, M. 1984. "Japanese students in EFL/ESL classrooms." *TESOL Newsletter* April 1984:19.

Shirts, R. 1977. *BaFá BaFá: a cross-cultural simulation.* Del Mar, Calif.: Simile II.

Shweder, R. and E. Bourne. 1984. "Does the concept of the person vary cross-culturally?" In R. Shweder and R. LeVine (eds.).

Shweder, R. and R. LeVine (eds.). 1984. *Culture theory: essays on mind, self, and emotion.* Cambridge: Cambridge University Press.

Silverman, S. 1966. "An ethnographic approach to social stratification: prestige in a central Italian community." *American Anthropologist* 68 (4):899–921.

Singer, M. 1982. "Culture: a perceptual approach." In L. Samovar and R. Porter (eds.). Reprinted from D. Hoopes (ed.) *Readings in intercultural communication* Vol. 1, 1971.

Sitaram, K. and R. Cogdell (eds.) 1976. *Foundations of intercultural communication.* Columbus, Ohio: Charles E. Merrill Publishing Co.

Skinner, B. 1957. *Verbal behavior.* New York: Appleton-Century-Crofts.

Smalley, W. 1963. "Culture shock, language shock, and the shock of self-discovery." *Practical Anthropology* 10:49–56.

Smart, R. 1983. *Using a western learning model in Asia: a case study.* Occasional papers in Intercultural Learning. AFS International/Intercultural Programs Inc.

Smith, A. (ed.). 1966. *Communication and culture: readings in the codes of human interaction.* New York: Holt, Rinehart, and Winston.

Smith, E. and L. Luce (eds.). 1979. *Toward internationalism: readings in cross-cultural communication.* Rowley, Mass.: Newbury House.

Smith, H. 1979. "Nonverbal communication in teaching." *Review of Educational Research* 49 (4):631–672.

Sonka, A. 1981. *Skillful reading.* Englewood Cliffs, N.J. Prentice-Hall.

Spradley, J. 1979. *The ethnographic interview.* New York: Holt, Rinehart, and Winston.

Stern, H. 1983. *Fundamental concepts of language teaching.* London: Oxford University Press.

Stewart, E. 1972. *American cultural patterns: a cross-cultural perspective.* Chicago: Intercultural Press.

————. 1977. "The survival stage of intercultural communication." In N. Jain (ed.). *International and intercultural communication annual. Vol. IV.* Falls Church, Va.: Speech Communication Association.

————. 1978. "Outline of intercultural communication." In F. Casmir (ed.).

————. 1979. "Research in intercultural communication. In Davey (ed.).

Sturtevant, W. 1964. "Studies in ethnoscience." *American Anthropologist* Special Publication 66 (2):99–131.

Suleiman, M. 1973. "The Arabs and the West: communication gap." In M. Prosser (ed.).

Sumner, W. 1940. *Folkways.* Boston: Ginn.

Szalay, L. 1981. "Intercultural communication—a process model." *International Journal of Intercultural Relations* 5:133–146.

Szalay, L. and G. Fisher. 1979. "Communication overseas." In E. Smith and L. Luce (eds.).

Taft, R. 1981. "The role and personality of the mediator." In S. Bochner (ed.).

Taylor, H.D. and J. Sorenson. 1961. "Culture capsules." *Modern Language Journal* 45:350–354.

Taylor, H. M. 1974. "Japanese kinesics." *Journal of the Association of Teachers of Japanese* 9:65–75.

————. 1976. "Nonverbal communication and cross cultural communication problems." In B. Robinett (ed.). *1976–1977 papers in ESL.* Washington, D.C.: National Association for Foreign Student Affairs.

————. (ed.). 1979. *English and Japanese in contrast.* New York: Regents Publishing Company.

————. 1980. "Beyond words: nonverbal communication in EFL." In K. Croft (ed.) *Readings on English as a second language.* Cambridge, Mass.: Winthrop Publishers.

Tiersky, E. and M. Tiersky. 1975. *The USA* (Vol IV). New York: Regents Publishing Company.

Trager, G. 1964. "Paralanguage: a first approximation." In D. Hymes (ed.). Reprinted from *Studies in Linguistics* (1958) 13:1–12.

Triandis, H. 1975. "Culture training, cognitive complexity, and interpersonal attitudes." In R. Brislin, S. Bochner, and W. Lonner (eds.).

_____ (ed.). 1980. *Handbook of cross-cultural psychology.* Vols. I–VI. Boston: Allyn and Bacon.

_____ . 1984. "A theoretical framework for the more efficient construction of culture assimilators." *International Journal of Intercultural Relations* 8(3):301–330.

Triandis, H., V. Vassiliou, Y. Tanaka, and A. Shanmugam (eds.). 1972. *The analysis of subjective culture.* New York: John Wiley and Sons.

Trifonovitch. G. 1980. "Culture learning/culture teaching." In K. Croft. *Readings on English as a second language* Cambridge, Mass.: Winthrop Publishers.

Trubetzkoy, N. 1969. *Principles of phonology.* Berkeley, Calif.: University of California Press.

Trueba, H. and C. Barnett-Mizrahi (eds.). 1979. *Bilingual multicultural education and the professional: from theory to practice.* Rowley, Mass.: Newbury House.

Trueba, H., G. Guthrie, and K. Hu-Pei Au (eds.). 1981. *Culture and the bilingual classroom: studies in classroom ethnography.* Rowley, Mass.: Newbury.

Trueba, H. and P. Wright. 1980/1981. "On ethnographic studies and multicultural education." *NABE Journal,* Vol. V.(2) Winter 1980-81, 29–56.

Tylor, E. 1871. *Primitive culture: researches into the development of mythology, philosophy, religion, language, art, and custom.* London: John Murray.

Useem, J., R. Useem, and J. Donoghue. 1963. "Men in the middle of the third culture: the roles of American and non-Western people in cross-cultural administration." *Human Organization* 22:169–179.

Wallerstein, N. 1983. *Language and culture in conflict: problem-posing in the ESL classroom.* Reading, Mass: Addison-Wesley.

Warren, D. and P. Adler. 1977. "An experiential approach to instruction in intercultural communication." *Communication Education* 26 (2):128–134.

Watzlawick P., J. Beavin, and D. Jackson. 1967. *Pragmatics of human communication.* New York: Norton.

Weeks, W., P. Pedersen, and R. Brislin (eds.). 1982. *A manual of structured experiences for cross-cultural learning.* Chicago: Intercultural Press.

Weingrod, A. 1962. "Administered communities: some characteristics of new immigrant villages in Israel." *Economic Development and Cultural Change* 11 (1):69–84.

_____ . 1966. *Reluctant pioneers: village development in Israel.* Ithaca: Cornell University Press.

Welte, C. 1977. "Interrelationships of individual, cultural, and pan-human values." In W. McCormack and S. Wurm (eds.).

Whorf, B. 1956. *Language, thought, and reality: selected writings of Benjamin Lee Whorf.* J. Carroll (ed.). Cambridge, Mass.: MIT Press, John Wiley.

Widdowson, H. 1978. *Teaching language as communication.* Oxford: Oxford University Press.

_____ . 1979. *Explorations in applied linguistics.* Oxford/New York: Oxford University Press.

Wilkins, D. 1976. *Notional syllabuses.* London: Oxford University Press.

Wilson, A. 1985. "Returned exchange students: becoming mediating persons." *International Journal of Intercultural Relations* 9 (3):285–304.

Wolfgang, A. (ed.). 1979a. *Nonverbal behavior: applications and cultural implications* New York: Academic Press.

————. 1979b. "The teacher and nonverbal behavior in the multicultural classroom." In A. Wolfgang (ed.).

Wolfson, N. 1981. "Compliments in cross-cultural perspective." *TESOL Quarterly* 15 (2):117–124.

Wurzel, J. (ed.). 1981a. *Toward a multicultural perspective: readings in cross-cultural awareness.* Lexington, Mass.: Ginn.

Wurzel, J. and M. Claffey. 1981b. "Toward cultural conflict reduction: a conceptual framework for curriculum development in multicultural education." In J. Wurzel (ed.).

Yoshida, Y., N. Kurantani, and S. Okunishi (eds.). 1976. *Japanese for beginners.* Tokyo: Gakken Company Ltd.

Your/their new life in the United States. 1981. Washington, D.C.: Center for Applied Linguistics.

Yousef, F. 1982. "North Americans in the Middle East: aspects of the roles of friendliness, religion, and women in cross-cultural relations." In L. Samovar and R. Porter (eds.).

Index

Index